# A HISTORY OF
# FARM BUILDINGS
## IN ENGLAND AND WALES

# A HISTORY OF
# FARM BUILDINGS
## IN ENGLAND AND WALES

Nigel Harvey
MA ARICS

**DAVID & CHARLES**
Newton Abbot    London    North Pomfret (Vt)

*Dedicated with affection and respect*
*to the memory of*
*J. K. W. SLATER*
*Head of the Farm Buildings Unit*
*of the Agricultural Research Council*
*1957–65*

**British Library Cataloguing in Publication Data**

Harvey, Nigel
  A history of farm buildings in England
  and Wales.—2nd ed.
  1. Farm buildings—England—History
  I. Title
  631.2′0942      S787.G7

  ISBN 0 7153 8383 3

First published 1970, new edition 1984

© Text: Nigel Harvey 1970, 1984

Photoset by Northern Phototypesetting Co., Bolton
and printed in Great Britain
by Butler & Tanner Ltd., London and Frome
for David & Charles (Publishers) Limited
Brunel House  Newton Abbot  Devon

Published in the United States of America
by David & Charles Inc
North Pomfret  Vermont 05053  USA

# CONTENTS

ornamentations – graffiti dates – carbon dating –
dendrochronology

# FOREWORD

by A. N. DUCKHAM, CBE, MA, FIBiol
*Emeritus Professor of Agriculture, University of Reading*

Farm buildings account for about 60 per cent of the total of over £600 million of long-term capital invested in British agriculture in the last decade. Such buildings provide shelter for our livestock and protection for farmers and workers, for farm machinery, and for stores of grain, feedingstuffs, hay and silage. But while their main function may still be protective, the introduction of grain-drying and handling machinery, of parlour milking, and of feed-conveying systems and the like are giving increasing scope for factory-style production-line methods. The evolution of farm buildings from simple protection against weather, wild animals and thieves to the processing units which are emerging today is the subject of Mr Harvey's book. He traces the development of farm buildings through some 1,500 years. In doing so, he shows us the effects on the farmstead, the cowshed, the piggery and the old barn, both of changing husbandry techniques and of the increasing 'industrialisation' and mechanisation of agriculture.

But interest in farm buildings is not confined to the farmer, the farm worker and the rural landowner. Those concerned with rural amenities, town and country planning, and animal welfare also have points of view which may conflict with the needs of those who live on or by the land.

Mr Harvey's book should prove helpful to both farming and non-farming interests. It is an important and very readable contribution to a rapidly growing, and visible, sector of agricultural investment. History helps us to comprehend the past, understand the present and map the future. This book admirably performs this function. It should be useful not only to farmers, landlords and historians but also to those concerned with rural amenities and with the interactions between food production and the rest of the community.

# INTRODUCTION TO
# THE SECOND EDITION

Farm buildings are among the most conspicuous objects in the agricultural landscape. They are also among the most important and the most interesting. They are important because they are the central storage depots and processing shops of the farms they serve, and on their efficiency depends much of the farming system. They are interesting because they record with peculiar clarity many of the technical and economic changes which have come to the farming industry in recent centuries. And it is by understanding the reasons for their present importance that we can best appreciate their value as guides to the farming past.

It is in the buildings of the farmstead that livestock are housed and fed, dairy cows are milked and manure accumulates for periodical removal. It is here that litter and bulky fodders are stored, concentrate fodder milled and mixed, and seeds and fertilisers, tractors and implements housed. Into the farmstead come animals, machines, crops, fodders and litter from the fields and varied materials from the economic world beyond the farm gate. Out of it go manure and machinery to the fields, milk, crops and livestock to market. The farmstead is the operational centre of the farm, where the farmer spends as much time as in his fields. The demands of the farm on it are considerable, continuous and varied; and each individual building in it was designed to meet a particular selection of these demands.

It is, therefore, convenient to think of farm buildings as tools, each with its own particular jobs to do. But it is more accurate to think of them as means of enabling jobs to be done, for it is the processes they house which determine their form. Only in terms of the needs they serve are they comprehensible, since they are planned for and around highly specific jobs and routines, and few considerations other than agricultural efficiency are allowed to influence their design. These needs may be poorly interpreted or poorly fulfilled, but traditionally the degree of their success in meeting them is the sole criterion by which the farmer judges his buildings. There cannot be many branches of architecture in which form follows function as closely and as uncompromisingly as in the design of farm buildings.

9

In principle, therefore, the farmstead is a group of highly specific and inter-related industrial buildings designed to meet a wide and exacting range of demands, and there are few aspects of the farming system which do not directly or indirectly affect it. Hence, ideally, it should be possible to deduce from the buildings on a farm the needs they serve, and from those needs to form a detailed picture of the type of enterprise, the methods used and the scale of operations of the holding.

In general terms, this is true. A walk around a farmstead will give the informed observer a fair idea of the size and type of the farm on which it stands. But in practice, of course, an exact equilibrium between ends and means is seldom achieved and can never be maintained. For every farmstead is the product of history as well as technology, and agricultural needs change more rapidly than buildings. General remodelling is expensive and the farmer has normally contented himself with piecemeal adaptations and improvements which preserve much of the old pattern of the farmstead and many of the buildings which compose it. In particular, the depression which began in the latter part of the nineteenth century and lasted until the Second World War ended the orderly process of farmstead development and left a lifetime's arrears of modernisation which the present age is still redeeming. Many, possibly most, farmers have inherited more buildings than they have erected and, though medieval and Tudor buildings may be individual rarities, Hanoverian and Victorian work still provides a substantial proportion of the farmer's building stock.

The economic disadvantages of such a mass of obsolete equipment are obvious. But the farmer's embarrassment is the historian's opportunity, for these old buildings are a unique and valuable source of historical knowledge and understanding. In particular, they preserve fossil-fashion the imprint of the technologies for which they were originally designed; in general, they record in various ways generations of change in the life and work of the countryside and in the economy of which it forms a part. They are 'structural documents' which, as features of the landscape, as tools of the farming trade, as buildings, and as the products of particular social systems, tell their varied stories from remote times to the present day of reclamation, settlement and enclosure; of farms and farming methods, of building materials and techniques, of craftsman and designer, peasant and yeoman, churchman and secular lord, squire and farmer, engineer and manufacturer. Few other industries can show so continuous and comprehensive a series of such 'documents' to illustrate their past.

Nor are these documents very difficult to read. If you lean on a gate and look across the fields, you will sometimes glimpse behind the combine-harvester or the grazing cows the ghosts of the men who created the farming landscape – the farmers of the horse age, the Victorian deep-drainage gangs, the enclosure commissioners with their attendant hedgers and ditchers, the ploughmen following their horned teams up the long acres of the open-fields, and behind them all the shadowy outlines of the tall trees and the tangled undergrowth and the little groups of men in shapeless suits of hodden-grey who went out with axe and fire and mattock, generation after generation, to win farmland from the primeval wilderness. In so doing, however, you will be relying mainly on your memory of the written word and your constructive imagination, for the land itself will give you little more than hints and suggestions. But if you look at the farmstead with the same eyes, you will not need to summon ghosts from the printed page. You will find the buildings telling their own story, freely and in considerable detail.

Thus the design of the barn reminds us that it was once the workshop of the flailers, who threshed the corn on which England depended for her daily bread. The derelict chimney in the north range recalls the coming of steam power to the farm, the yards the need for housing the increased head of stock which fed on the new crops of the Agricultural Revolution, the cowhouse the new type of enterprise made possible by the railways and necessary by the overseas competition which overwhelmed so much of the traditional system. The different materials and types of construction used in the buildings of different ages tell us much about the development of building methods and show with the clarity of a geological exposure the drastic changes wrought by the goods and services of the Industrial Revolution. The conversion of old buildings to new purposes illustrates the ways in which the farmer has striven to adapt his systems and equipment to changing needs, while the monastic barns and the massive home farms of Hanoverian or Victorian magnates record the wealth and power of the medieval churchmen and of the landed gentry who succeeded them. And all around, soils and slopes, streams and springs, suggest the reasons why the forgotten founder of the farm, perhaps a Saxon or medieval pioneer, perhaps a Tudor or Stuart farmer reclaiming forest or fen, perhaps a Hanoverian landowner planning his new enclosed holding, chose this particular spot to build a homestead for himself and his descendants. There is a great deal of general as well as agricultural history in the farmstead.

Nevertheless, recognition of the historical importance of farm buildings is a very recent development. Essentially, it forms part of the remarkable expansion of agrarian history of the past generation, since farm buildings are neither fully comprehensible nor fully informative without a proper understanding of their agricultural function and background. But it involves a number of other disciplines and interests, among them those of the archaeologist, the industrial archaeologist, the architect, the landscape historian and the conservationist. The achievement in the past few years of this varied alliance has been considerable.

Thus, in 1959 Trow-Smith, in his *History of British Livestock Husbandry, 1700–1900*, noted sadly that no detailed history of farm buildings had been written and that 'the most adequate of the brief introductions' to the subject then available was a booklet of a few dozen pages. In 1969, the first substantial area survey of farm buildings in their agricultural context was published. By 1979, the subject had accumulated a number of general and research publications and a number of exhibits in the farm museums whose increase was such a feature of this period, and had also inspired its first specialised conference, its first specialised exhibition and its first comprehensive proposal for a system of structural recording. Today there is a growing body of information on the number and types of old buildings still in existence, the possibility of seeing documented examples in museums, and a widespread realisation of their historical value. Indeed, the subject is now a recognised theme in rural and architectural history.

The aim of the second edition of this book is the same as that of the first. It seeks to summarise the information at present available on library shelves and thus limits itself to collecting and collating published evidence. But the amount of material which has appeared since the publication of the first edition makes necessary a change in treatment. In 1970 it was possible to present a narrative history of the subject, supported by specific references to most of the major items of information in the relevant sources. Today this is no longer possible. There is far too much material, including a mass of dimensional and design detail too substantial and too complicated for effective summary. Consequently, this edition is in some measure two books within one set of covers. The first is the narrative history, supported as before by specific references. The second consists of further selected references to the topics under discussion, to provide a running sourcebook or guide to the material which cannot be included in the narrative text. The first, the author hopes, will meet the needs of the general reader, the second the needs of those who wish to study the subject in further detail. His main hope, however, remains that of the first edition: that this book tells its story in a way which increases the reader's understanding of our agricultural past and, in particular, enables him to learn more about it for himself from the farmsteads he sees when he walks or drives in the countryside.

# 1 PROLOGUE: TO AD1000

## In the Beginning

Men have farmed the soil of Britain for many, many centuries and from the very beginning have left enduring traces of the pits they dug and the buildings they erected to serve their farming needs. There is, indeed, a growing mass of archaeological evidence on the homesteads of the early peoples from Neolithic to Roman times. But over much of the country the continuous history of farming, and therefore of farm buildings, starts with the Saxons who began their occupation of the lowlands of England in the fifth and sixth centuries AD.

In the five hundred years of their dominance, these newcomers established over much of the south, the east and the midlands a pattern of settlement that endured to Hanoverian times. To a large extent, therefore, the history of farm buildings in England is the history of the development of the farmsteads founded by these early settlers and their descendants. But not entirely. In the colder, wetter, uplands of the north and west, as well as in Wales, different systems of farming continued, producing different types of farmstead in a different type of agricultural landscape.

We know very little about the farmsteads of these dark centuries and not one farm building of the period has survived above ground. But by the collation of various evidences, by deduction and conjecture, it is possible to form a general impression of the manner in which our ancestors planned and built their farmsteads in the Saxon period.

## Saxon Settlement in the Lowlands

The full story of the Saxon settlement is lost beyond recall. But it is clear that they continued the ancient task of their predecessors of reclaiming fields from forest and scrub, and probable that they consciously sought the better soils for the establishment of their farms.[1] It is clear, too, that their primary concern was a reliable supply of fresh water. So they chose sites near springs or streams, taking advantage of whatever protection local topography offered, and there they built their hamlets and reclaimed their fields.[2]

Their general pattern of settlement, traces of which are still preserved in many of our villages – sometimes even in towns where builders have continued the old street plans or laid roads along the lines of ancient field-edges – was determined largely by the demands of their farming system. For the Saxons of the south and east were corn growers, whose lives depended on their crops of wheat and oats, barley and rye. The fields for such crops could be reclaimed from the waste by individual effort. The crops themselves could be sown, harvested and threshed by individual men. But the preparation of the seedbed entailed ploughing, which depended on animal power, and few individual settlers could muster so considerable a unit as a plough team. Only by combination could the newcomers raise the resources to secure their food supply. So they established themselves in their forest clearings not as individual families but as small communities housed in little groups of steadings huddled together for mutual comfort and support round a central green where stock could graze in safety.

Around their villages they established some form of what is generically called 'the open-field system'. The origins of this system are uncertain, but in its thousand years of history it was found in a wide variety of types and stages of development over large areas of the lowlands. Today it survives in only one parish in this country, Laxton in Nottinghamshire. Nevertheless, some understanding of it is essential to any appreciation of farmstead history.[3]

In necessarily over-simplified terms, the open-field system, as exemplified at Laxton, comprised three large arable fields bounded by hedges, walls or fences and divided, but not by any barrier, into a number of small strips. Each of these strips was cultivated by an individual farmer who might farm any number of these small 'fields' in different parts of the three fields of physically undivided ploughland which gave the system its name. The cropping of these three fields was determined by communal law and custom. Typically, it followed a rotation of a winter sown corn crop, spring sown crops, mostly corn but perhaps including beans or peas, and a fallow which allowed the land to recuperate and farmers to control weeds by cultivation and grazing. Detailed regulations allowed farmers to turn their livestock into the open-fields when they were not carrying a crop where they grazed on stubbles and weeds and on the grass of any land too steep or wet for ploughing which the fields contained. In addition, each farmer was allocated a share of the meadowland and grazing rights on the village green and other commons, which were often of considerable extent.

There were, of course, endless variations of the system, with different numbers of fields and different sequences of cropping as well as considerable changes in particular systems in the course of their long history. But essentially, the open-field farm consisted of a number of scattered strips in the open-fields and rights of hay-cutting in the communal meadows and of grazing livestock on the arable land when the crops had been harvested and on the communal pastures. And the farmer lived in the village. There were no buildings in the open-fields or on the communal grazings. He went out to his work from his home every day and he housed his livestock and stored his crops near his home.

The needs of the open-field corn crops called into existence the primary building of the farmstead: the barn. The harvested corn required protection from the elements if it was to be safe, and threshing before it could yield the grain on which the farmer's life depended. Hence arose the primitive barn, a shelter in which the precious harvest could be stored and gradually and laboriously threshed by flail on a hard floor in the winter days when little other farm work was possible. But man does not live by bread alone, and the Saxon farmer depended on his livestock for meat and manure, milk, leather and wool as well as power. The strictness and detail with which grazing rights on the open-fields and on common land were defined from the earliest times for which records are available bears striking witness to the importance of livestock in the Saxon economy.

At this stage, however, the demands of his animals on the farmstead were small. The horse had not yet become a farm animal. Sheep required, at most, a yard where they could be better protected against wolves and thieves and where, incidentally, their manure could usefully be accumulated. Pigs could support themselves for much of the year on the beechmast, acorns, grubs and carrion which the woodlands around the village provided. Indeed, they were still pastoral rather than agricultural animals, and the horse which the swineherd needed to collect his half-wild flock recalled a time in human history before the coming of the plough. This left only cattle, which grazed in the open in the summer months but required some sort of shelter in the winter. Yet the number of cattle requiring such shelter was small, for the size of the herds that any community could support was rigidly and inescapably limited by the amount of winter fodder available.

For at this time and for centuries to come the farmer knew only one way of conserving the surplus of summer-grown forage to feed his ruminants in the winter months when nothing grew. He made grass into hay; and the supply of hay made by men working by hand in an exceptionally unreliable climate was limited. Yet the amount of hay available controlled the number of cattle which could be kept through the winter; the number of cattle which survived the winter determined the amount of power and manure available for the ploughlands; and the power and manure available for the ploughlands controlled the future supply of corn on which the community depended. Here, then, was one of the limiting factors to food production which endured until the days of the Agricultural Revolution. The individual thoughts of the Saxon farmers have perished, but it is significant that the emblem of their patron saint, the forgotten Walstan of Bawburgh, was not a plough but a hayrake.

We do not know the form in which the Saxon farmer met his simple needs of protection for his corn and hay, provision of a threshing floor and shelter for a limited number of cattle. The protection for his harvested crops may have been no more than thatch on a stack, the threshing floor and shelter for the cattle a part of his home. But the combination of cover for corn crop and threshing floor, which developed into the barn, and shelter for cattle, which developed into the yard, illustrates the basic characteristics as well as the basic structural needs of the mixed-farming system which is so fundamental a part of our agricultural history. One served the farmer as corn grower, the other served him as stockman. Yet both were interdependent. The processes of the barn provided the yard with straw for litter; the processes of the yard provided the fields with manure and so contributed to the contents of the barn.

Here was the beginning of a tradition which lasted almost down to our own times. In the centuries to come, we shall see many changes in the buildings of the farm, but from the days of the Saxons to the days of Queen Victoria, the alliance of grain building and cattle building dominated the lowland farmstead just as the alliance of corn and horn which created and maintained it dominated the farming system. The barn is now obsolete, but to this day the yard of concrete and asbestos-cement sheeting depends on the barn's successors for its straw and so takes its place in a technical line of descent which stretches back unbroken to the primitive cattle shelters of the early Saxons.

### Farming and Farmsteads in the Uplands

The pioneering Saxons, however, occupied only the lowlands. In the more mountainous and wetter areas of the north and west, the Celtic peoples continued an older and more pastoral system of farming based not on compact villages but on dispersed farmsteads standing sometimes in isolation, sometimes in small groups, a pattern which was followed by many of the Saxon and Norse colonists who later settled there. Here the climate was harsher, the winters longer than in the milder lowlands and cattle needed more protection for more months in the year. Possibly, therefore, the upland farmer used the longhouse which sheltered his family and his cattle under one roof and thus provided protection, warmth and convenience in a manner

16

which secured its survival down to our own century. But existing evidence allows little more than conjecture.

Certain upland farms may, however, preserve a structural tradition from times far beyond the written record. For the design and corbelled stonework construction of some sixty circular, conical 'pigsties' which survive in Wales[4] and occasional potato cellars in the Yorkshire Dales[5] suggest a connection with the ancient beehive huts of Wales, Scotland and Ireland. None of these curious structures can be dated and nothing is known about their history, but the farmer may have continued to use this simple and traditional method of construction for housing his stock and crops long after he and his family had sought more comfortable accommodation.

## Transhumance

Open-field villages and scattered pastoral farms alike assumed a settled agriculture. But in suitable areas farmers from early times practised 'transhumance', increasing their supply of fodder by the seasonal grazing of cattle away from the main homesteads on pastures served by secondary homesteads or temporary shelters. In upland areas in this period, they may have migrated with their cattle to summer grazings higher up the mountainside. In some lowland areas, they certainly exploited the lush summer growth of fens and marshes — Somerset derives its name from the 'summer dwellers' who occupied islands in the wetlands during the good grazing months and retired to their villages when winter and the floods came.[6] The pastoral migrations of this early period have left few traces, but, as we shall see, many such temporary settlements of a later age eventually became the sites of permanent farmsteads.

## Building Materials

We do not know what types of farmstead the farmers of this period built. But we do know, from deduction supported by such evidence as is available, what materials they used. Like their successors for so many centuries, they used such materials as were available locally. Their homesteads, like their tools, their power, their clothes and their food, were the products of a self-sufficient community which required only salt and iron from outside sources. Thus, from the start, farm buildings illustrate the characteristics of the rural economy of which they form part.

Existing evidence tells us very little about the farm buildings of these centuries. But it tells us a good deal about the environment in which the men who built them lived and worked and about the necessities and the resources, the constraints and the opportunities which it offered or imposed. In so doing, it sets the scene for the future story of farm buildings in this century.

## NOTES

1. 'The incoming Saxons had a good eye for country. They always found the best soils . . . If we are told that there were fifteen farms on a particular manor in 1066 and there are twentyfive farms there today, we can usually discover most of the original farms by asking local farmers which are the best farms in the parish. We may be sure then that we have discovered most, if not all, of those of Saxon foundation or older' (Hoskins, W. G. 'Farmhouses and History', *History Today*, vol 10, no 5, May 1960, p. 336). Elsewhere Hoskins' notes that the first Saxon villages in Leicestershire were built on the islands of sand and gravel which were drier than the surrounding clays. (*The Midland Peasant*, 1957, p. 3). Hall, D. *Medieval Fields*, 1982, shows that the early Saxons settled on light soils, which were easy to work (pp 45–6).

2. For the effects of watersupplies on Saxon and later farm settlement, see Grigson, G. *An English Farmhouse*, 1948, pp 14–15; Hoskins, W. G. and Finberg, H. P. R. *Devonshire Studies*, 1952, p 80; Hoskins, W. G. 'Farmhouses and History', *History Today*, vol 10, no 5, May 1960, p 336; Havinden, M. A. *Estate Villages*, 1966, pp 23, 25; Hoskins, W. G. *History from the Farm*, 1970, pp 29, 35, 37, 76; Harris, H. *Industrial Archaeology of the Peak District*, 1971, p 139; Jennings, P. *The Living Village*, 1972, pp 293–4; Hoskins, W. G. *One man's England*, 1978, p 129.

3. The origins of this system are obscure. For discussions of current views see Baker, A. R. H. and Butlin, R. A. *Studies of Field Systems in the British Isles*, 1973, pp 622–44, 655–6; Taylor, C. *Fields in the English landscape*, 1975, pp 68–77; Rowley, T. (ed.) *Origins of Open-Field Agriculture*, 1981; Hall, D. *Medieval Fields*, 1982, pp 43–55, which includes evidence that the open-field system was not introduced by the first Saxon settlers but developed later (p 45–6, 53). For a general account of the system as it developed see Ault, W. O. *Open Field Farming in Mediaeval England*, 1972. For Laxton see Chambers, J. D. *Laxton, the last Open Field Village*, 1964; Orwin, C. S. *The Open Fields*, 1967; 'The Open Field Village of Laxton', special number of the *East Midland Geographer*, December 1980.

4. Peate, I. C. *The Welsh House*, 1944, pp 42–5; Naish, R. B. 'A traditional Welsh pigsty in Berrow village', *Proceedings of the Somersetshire Archaeological and Natural History Society*, vol 107, 1962, pp 108–9 for an example in Somerset; Wiliam, E. 'Circular corbelled pigsties in Wales', *Vernacular Buildings*, no 6, Scottish Vernacular Buildings Working Group Newsletter, 1980, pp 1–5. Incidentally, Davies, W. *General View of the Agriculture and Domestic Economy of South Wales*, vol 1, 1814, p 155 commented that farmers were 'not as comfortably lodged in many places' as the pigs they housed in these conical structures.

5. Walton, J. *Homesteads of the Yorkshire Dales*, 1979, p 41.

6. Quayle, T. 'Our first dairy farmers', *The Milk Producer*, vol 4, no 2, February 1957, p 7; Hoskins, W. G. *The Westward Expansion of Wessex*, 1960, p 6. The placename Somerton preserves the memory of one such summer settlement (Havinden, M. *The Somerset Landscape*, 1981, p 33).

# 2 THE LONG, SLOW CENTURIES: AD1000–1500

### Agricultural expansion

After the Saxons came the Normans, after the Normans, the Angevins and the Plantagenets, the Lancastrians and the Yorkists, until the better part of a thousand years separated the farmer from his forgotten ancestors who had served or conquered the Roman Empire. Throughout this long period, the needs of a growing population compelled a steady increase in the area of farmland and the number of farms. Sometimes this agricultural expansion was achieved by communal action, by the foundation of settlements by king, abbot or baron, or by a group of migrant peasants. Sometimes it was the result of the efforts of individual pioneers who added new strips from the surrounding scrubland to their open-field holdings or hewed their pattern of hamlets and single farms from the wilderness. Patiently and doggedly, generation by generation, the reclamation continued until, by the end of the Middle Ages, the greater part of the country was effectively settled. The triumph of the farmer over his wild environment was symbolised by the destruction of one of his ancient enemies. According to tradition, the last wolf in England was killed in the last years of this period. The plough and the pastured animal were conquering the primeval waste, and many modern farms date from this long period of expansion.[1] A number of farms are known from the written record to have existed at some specific year in some remote century, but the remains of their structural history lie buried and sealed beneath the buildings we see today.

This general colonisation included a slow but constant advance by the Saxons and their Anglo-Norman successors into the Celtic lands of the west and the creation of new, mixed patterns of settlement.[2] But this did not overthrow the ancient distinction between the agricultural economies of hill and plain. Throughout this period, the open-field system, with its little groups of farmsteads in the midst of arable fields and communal grazings, reigned in much of the lowlands, the pastoral system with its dispersed homesteads in the uplands.[3]

Neither was there any drastic technical development. Villages, hamlets and scattered settlements were larger and more numerous,

19

but those who inhabited them won and worked their land in much the same way as their ancestors. In particular, they could neither avoid nor overcome the shortage of winter fodder which continued to set rigid limits to the number of cattle their farms could carry and therefore to the production of food. They fed more people by cultivating more land, but systems and methods of farming changed little.

Thus, Benedict, son of Edric Siward, who established his farm at Cholwich Town on the south-west slopes of Dartmoor in the early thirteenth century, settled as an individual, not as a member of a migratory band. But otherwise he behaved much as his forefathers had done centuries before him. He chose a site with a reliable supply of water – the spring still flows in the farmyard – and shelter in the lee of a ridge from the bitter winds which swept down from the heights above him. He then reclaimed his fields from the surrounding wilderness, using the stones he cleared from them to build his farmstead and the banks of the lane which still leads to it, and farmed his new land with implements and stock little different from those used in the days of the Saxon settlement.[4]

## Peasant and Magnate

Nevertheless, Benedict was many generations away from primitive tribalism and it is significant that he chose to establish his farming home in these unprepossessing uplands, since by his time the growing population had occupied most of the better and more easily won land. Transhumance continued, but the area of seasonal grazing, based on the summering-houses called *shielings* in the north of England and *hafotai*, the plural of *hafod*, in Wales, shrank as land-hunger forced the line of permanent settlement higher up the hillsides.[5] It is also significant that we know Benedict's name, which is preserved in the charter that granted him the land. For he lived in the literate, stable, hierarchic community of medieval Christendom, of the feudal system, which over the centuries had made possible concentrations of power and wealth and therefore forms of agricultural exploitation unknown in earlier ages. The temporal and spiritual lords of the land, with their huge estates and their minor bureaucracies of seneschals, clerks and accountants to administer them, now lived in a different economic world from that of the peasantry. So, increasingly, did the rising class of the lesser landowners, the ancestors of the later squires.

And this difference dominates the sources of farmstead history. The landlords left behind them a mass of estate documents which include a certain amount of varied information on the steadings with which they equipped their farms. Thus, the first surviving contract for a farm building dates from 1473.[6] Again, between 1421 and 1423 New College, Oxford, built on its Adderbury estate a barn, a kiln, a piggery or pig-shelter, and a sheep-shelter. The barn still survives. So do the financial accounts for the work which show, for example, that William Mason received a total of £20 5s 4d for 'making the walls of the barn with seven buttresses', John Gilkes £26 for carpentry and John Badby £6 for roofing the building with stone slates.[7] The peasantry, even the prosperous peasantry, left no such records of their buildings.

### Peasant Farmsteads

In recent years, however, archaeological research has begun to recover something of their story. In particular, it seems clear that by the later Middle Ages the longhouse was a common form of building in the uplands and was also known in the lowlands[8] (see Figs 1, 2 and Plate 2). On other lowland farms, however, the house and the service buildings stood separate round a yard to form courtyard steadings similar in basic design to those of later times.[9] The difference between the two types of steading was probably reduced by the need of longhouse farmers for outbuildings. They sheltered their cattle under the same roof as their families, but they may have housed other livestock in separate buildings or stored their corn in small barns. On some farms the longhouse may have been the only building; on others, it may have been the main building of the farmstead.

In the lowlands, it is possible that the dual-purpose longhouses served the poorer peasantry, while their more substantial brethren lived more comfortably in houses standing apart from the service buildings. It is also inherently possible that the use of the longhouse

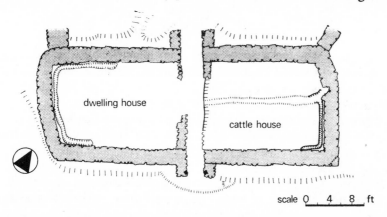

dwelling house

cattle house

scale 0   4   8  ft

1   Plan of the simplest form of longhouse. This example, which dates from the thirteenth century, was excavated in Devonshire (Based on *Mediaeval Archaeology*, vol 6–7, 1962–3, p343) (*Mrs E. M. Minter*)

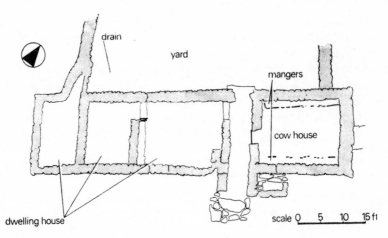

2   Plan of longhouse shown on page 33 (Based on *Cornish Archaeology*, vol 5, 1966, p44)
(*Mrs E. M. Minter*)

decreased as standards of living improved: an interesting excavation
in Wiltshire has traced the development of a twelfth-century longhouse steading into a thirteenth-century steading consisting of
one longhouse converted into a farmhouse, another converted into a
cattlehouse and a new barn[10] (see Fig 3). These generalisations,
however, are no more than hypotheses based on a limited number of
excavations and scanty documentary references, all inevitably telling
a purely local story. Evidence, particularly archaeological evidence,
on the buildings which served the mass of the population for so many
centuries grows year by year. But it will be some time before we have
any general history of the development of farmsteads in this period.

## Manorial Farmsteads

Most of the surviving evidences for this period concern the buildings
of the magnates and are sufficient to show the needs of substantial
farmers and the manner in which they met them in their steadings of
farmhouse and farm buildings standing round a yard.

The main crop on many of these farms was corn. Consequently, the
main building was the barn – preferably two barns, one for the wheat
which was sold off the farm, one for the spring corn which was fed on
it. The standardised pattern of this type of building was determined by
the storage and processing needs of the grain harvest. Its two ends
housed sheaves of straw while the central area, where the waggons
entered, provided the hard floor on which in the winter months the
corn was threshed by flail and winnowed by being tossed with a
wooden shovel into the draught of air created by opening the two

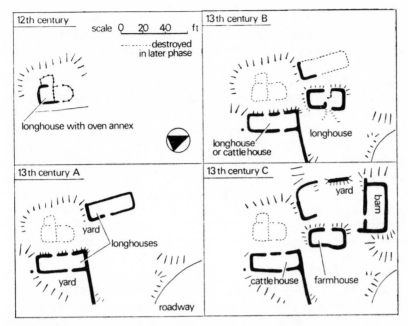

3   The development of a medieval farmstead site in Wiltshire (Based on *Mediaeval Archaeology*, vol 10, 1966, p215) (*Mr J. W. G. Musty*)

doors on opposite sides of the threshing floor. The first detailed reference to such a barn comes from the records of an ecclesiastical estate in Essex in the twelfth century and describes a building 49ft 6in (14.85m) long, 35ft 6in (10.65m) wide and 24ft 6in (7.35m) to the ridge with lean-tos at both ends.[11] Barns of such a size must have been the largest secular buildings in the villages they served and they and their successors continued to dominate the landscape almost down to our own age.[12]

The threshed corn was probably stored in the barn or in a separate granary. The importance of the safe storage of the grain on which the farmer depended for future sowing as well as for food and profit is illustrated by the precautions taken to secure such buildings: the commonest reason for the purchase of locks in medieval records was for barn or granary.[13] But the farmer's vigilance was not limited to his grainstore. The first surviving farm building contract, agreed between Thomas Peyton, lord of the manor of Water Hall in Suffolk, and John Whyghte, carpenter of Sible Hedingham in Essex, on 17 October 1473, for an oak-framed stable and cattleshed, specified pillars in windows 'so thykke set that a child cannot go inne between the same pelers' to defeat the young pupils of medieval Fagins.[14]

The various livestock houses and yards probably stood in the shelter

23

of the barn. Cattle were the most important type of stock here, though by the later Middle Ages the horse had begun its career as an agricultural animal. Fattening and rearing beasts were presumably housed in sheds or yards, but draught animals and dairy cows required some form of tie-up stable for ease of yoking or milking. Pigs were still largely woodland animals and a thirteenth-century treatise warned landowners against keeping pigs on manors where there was no woodland.[15] Nevertheless, they were beginning to spend more time in the farmyard, for the ancient forests, which the Domesday Book commissioners had assessed in terms of the pigs they could support, were now shrinking. In Saxon times, it was common for pigs to graze in the forest for the last four months of the year. By the fourteenth century, a period of six to eight weeks was more usual.[16] It is probably significant that the records of a Middlesex manor at the end of this period contain references to 'hog-cotes' as well as to pigs wintered in Enfield Chase.[17]

No specialised livestock buildings of this period remain above ground, though certain existing Sussex barns with upper floors over part of their length, some of which date from the later Middle Ages, were probably general-purpose buildings housing cattle on part of the ground floor with hay and straw stored on the floor above them.[18] Apart from these examples, all the evidence on livestock housing is documentary or archaeological. In the twelfth century, for instance,

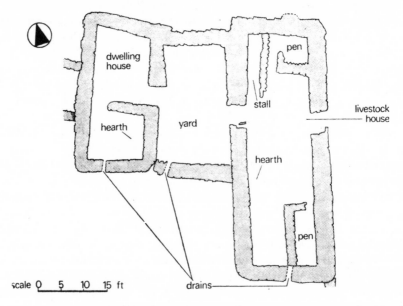

4   Plan of thirteenth-century steading built on Dartmoor by the monks of Buckfast (Based on *Mediaeval Archaeology*, vol 2, 1958, p146) (*Lady Aileen Fox*)

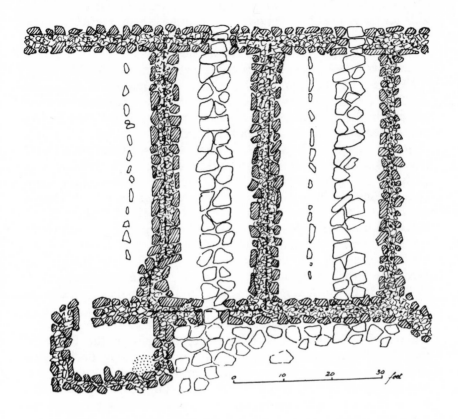

5  Plan and conjectural restoration of Cistercian sheep unit on Malham Moor, Yorkshire, to which there are various documentary references between 1290 and the Dissolution of the Monasteries (From Raistrick, A. and Holmes, P. F. 'The Archaeology of Malham Moor', *Field Studies*, vol I no 4, 1964, p23) (*Field Studies Council*)

manorial records refer to an oxhouse 33ft (10m) long and 12ft (3.5m) wide on the estate of the canons of St Paul's Cathedral at Kensworth in Hertfordshire, and in the fourteenth century to a cattle shed on the Templars' farm at Rothley in Leicestershire which held twenty-four oxen, eleven cows, nine bullocks, four calves and a bull.[19]

Excavation has also provided a case study of a more pastoral type of steading which was built on Dartmoor by the monks of Buckfast Abbey in the middle of the thirteenth century and apparently abandoned after the Black Death a hundred years later. Sited in a sheltered spot near a spring, this consisted of a two-roomed house joined by a walled yard to a general-purpose livestock building. The walls were of granite boulders taken from the remains of a nearby Bronze Age settlement – an interesting example of the use of secondhand materials in farm buildings. The roofs were of thatch on timber frames, and the doors were secured against the moorland winter by iron fastenings, traces of which were found by the archaeologists. A lay brother probably slept in the house, the herdsman either in the house or, at calving or lambing time, in the stockbuilding, which contained a hearth. Together they looked after the monastery's livestock grazing on the bleak uplands and brought them into shelter when hard weather threatened[20] (see Fig 4).

Similarly, the huge Cistercian sheep ranches in the Pennines provided winter shelter for at least some of their flocks. The sheephouse of Bolton Abbey on Malham Moor, which was repaired with a thousand boards in 1290 at a cost that included 23p for drinks for the men who carted the timber, comprised housing for a shepherd, a shelter, possibly with a slatted floor, for fifty or sixty ewes, and a yard[21] (see Fig 5). In the lowlands, too, the value of protecting the flock from the worst of the winter weather was recognised by the thirteenth century, and Walter of Henley's recommendation that sheep should be housed in bad weather 'between Martinmass and Easter'[22] was followed for at least some of these months on the better-managed estates. Evidence for this is provided by the thatched 'bercaries' of stone and timber, with their hayracks and mangers, on Wiltshire farms, the sheephouse 100ft (30m) long and 14ft (4m) wide built at Appledore by the monks of Battle Abbey in 1352, another 39ft (12m) long, 12ft (3.5m) wide and 22ft (6.5m) high, presumably to allow for the storage of hay over the stock, and a smaller lambhouse at Kensworth.[23]

In addition, a less predictable type of housing served the flocks of the Middle Ages. In this period the sheep, not the cow, was the primary dairy animal, since most cows probably gave little more milk than their calves required.[24] So on large enterprises the shearing sheds with boarded floors for the storage of fleeces were matched by dairies

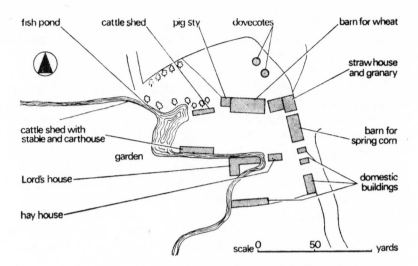

fish pond  cattle shed  pig sty  dovecotes  barn for wheat

straw house and granary

cattle shed with stable and carthouse

garden

barn for spring corn

Lord's house

domestic buildings

hay house

scale 0 ___ 50 ___ yards

6  Conjectural plan of the steading of a large farm in Oxfordshire in the early fourteenth century (Based on *A Mediaeval Oxfordshire Village, Cuxham, 1240–1400* by D. P. A. Harvey, 1965, p33) (*Oxford University Press*)

equipped with strainers, settling pans, presses and churns for making ewes' milk into butter and cheese.[25] The Cistercian sheephouse on Malham Moor, for example, included a dairy, and sent butter and cheese to Bolton Priory. All these have now gone, but in Northumberland occasional 'buchts', the remains of small rectangular enclosures where sheep were collected for milking, preserve the memory of the sheep as a dairy animal.[26]

### Corn-drying Kilns

Corn-drying kilns have been found on various sites of this period, on manorial and on peasant holdings, mostly in the uplands but sometimes in the lowlands. They are difficult to date, but it is possible that they were originally common in the wet hill areas and were used more widely elsewhere when the climate deteriorated in the fourteenth and fifteenth centuries. In general, they consisted of an oven with a long flue leading to a stokehole, and they were probably used to dry beans, peas, flax and hay as well as corn. In areas where the corn was cut at too high a moisture content for either threshing or storage, they may have dried the corn twice, first in the sheaf, after which it was threshed, then as grain in preparation for storage.[27]

### Buildings for Lowland Farm and Upland Ranch

The value of surviving evidence on the farm buildings of this period is usually much reduced by lack of information on the particular farming system of which they formed part. By the fortunate chance, however, the records preserve fairly detailed accounts of two groups of buildings serving substantial but sharply contrasted enterprises.

The first was the steading of the 'home farm' of an estate at Cuxham in South Oxfordshire owned by Merton College. This was a large farm which in the early fourteenth century grew nearly 300 acres of corn and carried a dozen plough oxen and four plough horses, a dairy herd and a pig herd. The documentary references confirm the agricultural deductions. The buildings, which were grouped round a yard, included two barns – one for wheat, one for oats and barley – a granary, cattlesheds, a stable and a carthouse, a hayhouse and a strawhouse, as well as a henhouse and dovecotes. There was also a pigsty, for there were no woodlands on this estate, although it seems that many of the pigs spent some of their time foraging in the woods of nearby Ibstone (see Fig 6).[28]

The second was a series of cattlesheds, each 80ft (24m) long, built for a specialised agricultural venture very different from this mixed farm in prosperous and well-settled Oxfordshire. In the same period, the Earl of Lincoln undertook the conversion of a huge area of wild Lancashire moorland into a cattle ranch for the production of cows and working oxen. Here he built sheds for his 'vaccaries', each for seven-five to eighty beasts, half of them breeding cows with their appropriate bull, the rest heifers or young steers. It was an ambitious project which at one time comprised nearly thirty vaccaries. But the physical and economic difficulties were too great and eventually the moors and the buildings on them were abandoned to the wolves which from time to time had taken a toll of these premature upland herds.[29] No traces now remain of either of these two sets of farm buildings.

### 'Tithe' Barn and Dovecote

Indeed, few traces now remain of any of the farm buildings of this period and, predictably, most of those that do survive were the work of the great lords of Church and State. They include the large corn barns that are among the glories, and the medieval dovecotes which are among the delights, of the modern countryside.[30] But these survived because they were exceptional and they do not tell us much about the normal medieval farmstead.

Many of the huge and gracious barns of this period are commonly, though not always accurately, called 'tithe barns'. This term is rightly applied to barns built on ecclesiastical estates to store tithes or other dues paid in corn, but it is often casually applied to any medieval barn. But it is probable that many ecclesiastical barns housed produce other than tithes while some, like those on secular estates, fulfilled the functions of the conventional farm barn in which the harvests of the surrounding fields were threshed and stored. Others were primarily the central storage depots of huge agricultural estates, housing the harvests of scattered farms run by bailiffs as well as any local dues which were paid in kind. The line of massive flint barns between the Sussex Downs and the sea still testifies to the size of the 'federated grain factories' which the churchmen farmed as owner-occupiers. Battle Abbey was one of the more advanced of these huge farming corporations; in 1982 the author watched the successor of the Abbey's farm manager at Alciston unload his combine-harvested grain into the barn where, as surviving records show, his predecessor exactly six centuries earlier had stored the harvest of 130 acres of cornland from which he had secured yields markedly above those of neighbouring manors.[31]

More subtly, the room over the porch at the monastic barn at Bredon in Worcestershire, which served as office and living quarters for the monk or bailiff in charge of the farm, illustrated the managerial resources of the organisations which planned and operated the farming empires of which these huge buildings formed part. The descendants of the 'tithe barn' include the merchant's warehouse as well as the farmer's grainstore.[32]

Such barns proclaimed the wealth and authority of the medieval Church. At the end of this period, however, a barn similar in general size and type foreshadowed the shape of things to come. Hales Hall barn in Norfolk, the largest barn in a county of large barns, was built at the end of the fifteenth century by a layman, James Hobart, Attorney General to Henry VII. Such men lived between two worlds, as his barn duly records. On the one hand, it recalled the past: the ventilation slits in its walls which appear purely agricultural from the outside appear from the inside as wider, arched openings similar to the loop-holes in the defensive wall which one side of the barn continues. Hobart's background was the prolonged lawlessness of the Wars of the Roses and his barn formed part of the defensive system of his homestead. On the other hand, its size and splendour announced the emergence of a new class of politicians and officials who would rise to power in the service of the Tudor State, in time replacing the monks and the warring barons as landowners and establishing a new tradition of landownership.[33]

So the barn illustrated developments and changes in political power. The dovecote illustrated continuing feudal privilege, for from Norman times the right to keep pigeons was a doubly valuable monopoly of the lord of the manor. On the one hand, it produced a supply of fresh meat and eggs to alleviate the monotonous winter

diet of salted beef from cattle slaughtered in the autum to save winter
fodder, and also added rich residues to his dunghill. On the other, it
provided these benefits partly at the cost of his neighbours, whose
crops helped to fatten his birds. It was, in effect, a crude but effective
method of levying taxation in kind on the locality and its yields were
substantial. In the fourteenth century, almost every manor of the
Berkeley estates had one or two pigeonhouses, and from one house
alone Thomas, Lord Berkeley, received over 2,000 birds a year, from
each of two other houses 1,000 a year.[34]

The massive stone dove-towers of the early Normans, which
substantially symbolised this privilege, were later replaced by lighter,
more ornamental buildings. But the general design altered little, and
they remained roofed walls thick enough to contain rows of nesting
holes which could be reached by ladder or from a wooden frame
revolving round a central stanchion (see Plate 6). From these cotes
fluttered hundreds of birds – a flock commonly contained five or six
hundred birds – whose ceaseless depredations are remembered in the
old agricultural proverb of the four grains sown in a row:

> One for the pigeon, one for the crow,
> One to rot and one to grow.

The order is significant. Medieval dovecotes please the modern eye,
but it is salutary to remember that a thousand pigeons will eat some 4
tonnes of grain in a month.[35]

## Stone and Clay, Timber and Thatch

Partly by example and partly by contrast, the 'tithe' barns and
dovecotes which survive from this period provide indirect evidence on
the farm buildings of their time. In general, they have survived because
they were built of stone, local stone – it is no accident that so many of
the barns are concentrated in the areas of good building stone within a
radius of some 75 miles of Bristol.[36] They thus reflect the dependence
of rural builders on local materials. For in this period, as for centuries
later, farmers built their farmsteads with materials won from the local
farmlands – timber and the willow and hazel rods which were used for
wattle-and-daub walling from the woods, straw from the fields, reeds
from the marshlands, heather from the moors for thatching, clay from
village pits. They used whatever local nature happened to provide,
including such materials as could be salvaged from old buildings.
Even churchmen used old ecclesiastical buildings as quarries: the
pigeonhouse on the Benedictine manor of Frocester, built at some
unknown date before 1515, includes material from a Norman
church.[37]

The general failure of their farm buildings to survive shows that few were built in such an enduring but intractable material as stone. Wealthy landlords like the twelfth-century Cistercians of Warden Abbey in Bedfordshire, who brought stone from a quarry 30 miles distant to build their steading at Bradfield, might do so.[38] So might farmers like Benedict, son of Siward, to whom desolate Dartmoor offered little else,[39] or the builder of the Wiltshire longhouse who used sarsen stone from the slopes around his new home.[40] But this was exceptional. Most farmers only used stone for such limited purposes as wall footings and depended for walls and roofing on the more perishable materials their fields and woods provided. A late medieval peasant on his lonely farm in the Chiltern woodlands was prepared to haul limestone several miles for his dwarf walls, but the walls he mounted on them were wattle-and-daub.[41]

Their buildings have now returned to the soil from whence they came. But various references in the written record over the centuries illustrate the use of local resources. The Earl of Norfolk, for instance, built the walls of his farm buildings with local clay, framed their roofs with local timber and thatched them with local straw, though he chose the longer-lasting reed-thatch for his hall.[42] The Earl of Lincoln used timber and thatch for his upland cattle shelters,[43] the churchmen of Carlisle used the bones of sheep as pegs for the stone roofing of their 'tithe barn',[44] the farmers of the Sussex Weald walled their barns with wattle-and-daub,[45] the peasants of the Isle of Axholme cut turves for walling as well as for fuel,[46] and the preference of the medieval thatchers of Wigston in Leicestershire for reeds from a certain pool earned the slope on which it stood the name of Thatchers Hill.[47] Similarly, the detailed descriptions of the building of two barns, an oxhouse, a sheephouse and a dairy in the thirteenth and fourteenth centuries list felling timber, gathering withies for wattling, making daub walls, carting straw for thatching and stones for foundations and collecting moss for waterproofing a tiled roof.[48] These tiles were probably local products,[49] and only the iron for nails and hinges came from an economy beyond the boundaries of the estate.

Such surviving documentary evidence, however, is rare and little is known about the methods of construction used. Presumably the smaller buildings were merely walls or uprights with a thatched roof on a crude timber frame. The barns and larger livestock houses on the farms of the more substantial peasantry probably used the familiar 'cruck' system of long, heavy timbers cut from naturally curving trees, roughly squared, split in two and set opposite each other in the earth or on a stone base to make the arches which formed the framework of the building[50] (see Plate 3). It has been suggested that the common spacing of approximately 16ft (4.8m) between crucks found in various types of building in and after the Middle Ages originated in cattle sheds, since a bay of this width holds two pairs of oxen conveniently.[51] The belief is reasonable and, if true, implies the common use of this type of construction in the medieval farmstead.

Crucks offered a simple and effective method of providing a framework for walls and roofing with such materials as were locally available, but they set rigid limits to the height and width of buildings. The bigger manorial buildings, therefore, continued the aristocratic tradition of the Saxon nobleman's hall, using the more sophisticated and expensive post-and-truss or 'framed' construction, in which upright posts supported roof members to form aisled structures (see Plate 4). This system was used for barns from the eleventh century onwards; the earliest known example, at Paul's Hall, Belchamp St Paul's, Essex, retains, despite much rebuilding, an earth-shored post which may be pre-Norman. The developments in carpentry techniques which the builders of framed barns evolved down the generations provide valuable clues to the dates of many such buildings and supplement the growing body of evidence provided by dendrochronology and carbon dating.[52]

Aisled barns were found mainly in the south-east, though they were also known in Yorkshire. In the poorer and more pastoral north and west cruck construction was normal.[53] Despite the increasing volume of archaeological and documentary evidence, this is one of the few generalisations we can at present make on any class of medieval farm building. The next age is the first to have left us sufficient evidence to make possible informed and general conclusions on the various types of building used by the farmer and the manner in which he combined them to form his steading.

## NOTES

1. The present siting of farmsteads often preserves some of the story of the manner of early settlement. See Peters, J. E. C. *The Development of Farm Buildings in Western Lowland Staffordshire up to 1880*, 1969, pp 16–28; Harvey, N. *The Industrial Archaeology of Farming in England and Wales*, 1980, pp 17–41, 44, 62; Caffyn, L. A. *A Study of Farm Buildings in Selected Parishes of East Sussex*, unpublished MA thesis, Manchester University, 1981, pp 36–7; Wiliam, E. *Traditional Farm Buildings in North-East Wales, 1550–1900*, 1982, pp 30–2.
2. In the Westcountry compact villages and their open-fields existed side by side with dispersed farms and hamlets. In Devon, it seems, the Saxon villages were founded first and individual pioneers later created their farms around them, whereas in Cornwall the Saxon villages were imposed upon the Celtic pattern of scattered steadings (Beresford, M. W. 'Dispersed and group settlement in mediaeval Cornwall', *Agricultural History Review*, vol 12, pt 1, 1964, p 13). Similarly, in south Wales open-field villages in the coastal lowlands and main valleys, where English influence was strongest, contrasted with the scattered homesteads of the pastoral uplands (Davies, M. 'Rhossili open field and related South Wales field patterns', *Agricultural History Review*, vol 4, pt 2, 1956, pp 86–7).
3. A number of isolated farms were, however, established even in predominantly open-field areas, particularly in the later Middle Ages (Hoskins, W. G. 'Anatomy of the English countryside', *Listener*, 25 April 1954, p 773; Cunliffe, B. 'Saxon and mediaeval settlement in the region of Chalton, Hampshire', *Mediaeval Archaeology*, vol 16, 1972, pp 1–12; Roberts,

Plate 1    Laxton in Nottinghamshire, the last Open Field village in England. As in Saxon times, all the farmsteads stand in the village. Part of the West Field can be seen in the background (*Farmers Weekly*)

Plate 2    A medieval longhouse, probably thirteenth century, excavated in Devon. The section of the building nearest the camera is the cowhouse. The flat vertical stones near the wall formed mangers. Holes were bored in them to allow tethering. A plan is shown on page 22 (*Woolf-Greenham Collection*)

Plate 3　A cruck barn in Herefordshire (*Mr R. Winstone*)

B. K. *Rural Settlement in Britain*, 1977, p 167).

4. Hoskins, W. G. and Finberg, H. P. R. *Devonshire Studies*, 1952, pp 78–81. The history of the Wyanscroft family, who about 1200 received a grant of 15 acres in the Forest of Arden from an Earl of Warwick anxious to encourage the colonisation of this area, and by 1250 farmed a compact holding of 45–50 acres equipped with a cattleshed and sheepfold, provide another instance of this same general process (Robert, B. K. 'Mediaeval colonisation in the Forest of Arden', *Agricultural History Review*, vol 16, pt 2, 1968, p 107). So do the account rolls of the Bishop of Winchester in the 1250s, which give details of the equipment of newly reclaimed land in Wiltshire and Berkshire with buildings, in the first case a barn, an oxhouse and a sheephouse, in the second a dairy (Titow, J. Z. *English Rural Society, 1200–1350*, 1969, pp 198–202).

5. For example, Houndtor on Dartmoor began, possibly as early as the seventh or eighth century, as three shielings of turf houses. It later became a permanent settlement with a courtyard farmstead, four longhouses, four small houses and three corn-drying barns. It was abandoned in the fourteenth century, probably because of climatic deterioration. Incidentally, the Houndtor farmers used an ancient stone circle as a cattlepen (Beresford, G. 'Three deserted mediaeval farmsteads on Dartmoor', *Mediaeval Archaeology*, vol 23, 1979, pp 104, 110–12). For a northern example, see Richardson, C. G. B. 'Kings Stables, an early shieling on Black Lyne Common, Bewcastle', *Transactions of the Cumberland and Westmorland Antiquarian and Archaeological Society*, vol 79, 1979, pp 19–27. See also Peate, I. C. *The Welsh House*, 1944, pp 142–7; Royal Commission on Historical Monuments, *Shielings and Bastles*, 1970; Davies, E. 'Hendre and hafod in Merioneth', *Journal of the Merioneth History and Record Society*, vol 7, 1973, pp 13–27; Davies, E. 'Hendre and hafod in Denbighshire', *Transactions of the Denbighshire Historical Society*, vol 26, 1977, pp 49–72.

6. Dymond, D. 'A fifteenth century building contract from Suffolk', *Vernacular Architecture*, vol 9, 1978, pp 10–11. The contract, dated 17 October 1473, was between Thomas Peyton, lord of the manor of Wixoe, and John Wyghte, carpenter of Sible Hedingham, and concerned a combined stable and cattleshed.

7. Hobson, T. F. 'Adderbury Rectoria', *Oxfordshire Record Society*, vol 8, 1926, pp 75–6.

8. 'There is no evidence that there was widespread distribution of the longhouse [in England] till the later thirteenth or fourteenth centuries' (Beresford, G. 'Three deserted mediaeval settlements on Dartmoor', *Mediaeval Archaeology*, vol 23, 1979, pp 124–5). Beresford suggests that their use in pastoral areas may have been encouraged by a combination of an increase in the number of cattle owned by the peasantry and climatic deterioration in this period which caused the winter housing of previously outwintered stock in order to reduce the poaching of pasture. No longhouses were recorded in arable [and dry] East Anglia where cattle were outwintered until the fourteenth century and then inwintered in yards (p 127). See also Beresford, M. and Hurst, J. G. *Deserted Mediaeval Villages*, 1971, pp 104–15. Local references to medieval longhouses include Field, R. K. 'Worcestershire peasant dwellings, household goods and farm equipment in the later Middle Ages', *Mediaeval Archaeology*, vol 9, 1965, pp 114–15, 119–21; Hurst, D. G. and Hurst, J. G. 'Excavations at the mediaeval village of Wythemail, Northamptonshire', *Mediaeval Archaeology*, vol 13, 1969, pp 167–203; Taylor, C. *Dorset*, 1970, p 108; Rowley, T. *The Shropshire Landscape*, 1972, pp 115–16; Hoskins, W. G. *The English Landscape*, 1973, p 30 (Dartmoor); Wiliam, E. 'Traditional farm buildings in Wales' *Amgueddfa*, no 15, Winter 1973, p 14 (English abstract of Welsh text); Brandon, P. *The Sussex Landscape*, 1974, p 141; Steane, J. *The Northamptonshire Landscape*, 1974, p 166; Hurst, J. 'Villagers who kept moving house', *Observer Magazine*, 25 May 1975, pp 22–3 (Yorkshire); Mercer, E. *English Vernacular Houses*, 1975, pp 34–6; Allison, K. J. *The East Riding of Yorkshire Landscape*, 1976, p 94; Devon County Council, *Devon's Traditional Buildings*, 1978, pp 7–10, which refers to thirteenth-century longhouses that 'already showed a plan form that was to be used for some five centuries'; 'Devon, Meldon Quarry', *Mediaeval Archaeology*, vol 21, 1978, p 256; *Mediaeval Archaeology*, vol 22, 1978, p 182 (Devon); Trow-Smith, R. *Farming Through the Ages in Pictures*, 1978, p 27 (Bedfordshire); Beresford, G. 'Three deserted mediaeval settlements on Dartmoor', *Mediaeval Archaeology*, vol 23, 1979, pp 98–128, which refers on p 125 to a Cornish longhouse dated c950; Beresford, M. W. and Hurst, J. G. 'Wharram Percy, a case-study in microtopography', in Sawyer, P. H. ed, *English Mediaeval Settlement*, 1979, pp 61, 64; Walton, J. *Homesteads of the Yorkshire Dales*, 1979, pp 24–7; Weller, J. *History of the Farmstead*, 1982, pp 43–6. Havinden, M. *The Somerset Landscape*, 1981, p 90, quotes a tenth-century charter reference to 'a cattleshed with house attached'. Hoskins, W. G. 'Farmhouses and history', *History Today*, vol 10, no 5, May 1960, p 339, refers to a fifteenth-century building on Dartmoor with two storeys, the ground floor for cattle, the first floor for the farmer and his family, ie a version of the longhouse principle in which the distinction between accommodation for livestock and humans was vertical, not horizontal.

9. Beresford, M. and Hurst, J. G. *Deserted Mediaeval Villages*, 1971, pp 104–15. From

the thirteenth century onwards, courtyard farmsteads were found in many areas (p 107). Local references to medieval farmsteads of this general type include *Mediaeval Archaeology*, vol 15, 1971, pp 171–2 (Lincolnshire crofts with yards); Wiliam, E. 'Traditional farm buildings in Wales', *Amgueddfa*, no 15, Winter 1973, p 14 (English abstract of Welsh text) which refers to 'a house with a single farm building facing it across the yard' as 'one common form of farmstead'; Steane, J. *The Northamptonshire Landscape*, 1974, p 167, which refers to frequent rebuilding at Faxton 'with a tendency . . . to change from temporary structures to permanent stonebuilt sheds fixed in relation to the farmhouse and enclosing roughly rectangular courtyards'; *Mediaeval Archaeology*, vol 18, 1974, pp. 216–7, vol 20, 1976, pp 198–9 and vol 21, 1977, p 256 (Hertfordshire, farmhouse with two barns surrounding a cobbled yard with another, separate barn and a dovecote); Hurst, J. 'Villagers who kept on moving house', *Observer Magazine*, 25 May 1975, p 22 (Yorkshire); Archaeology report, *The Times*, 10 December 1976, p 18 (Milton Keynes, small courtyard farmstead); *Mediaeval Archaeology*, vol 21, 1977, pp 255–6 (Buckinghamshire, house, barn and other building forming three sides of cobbled yard); Beresford, M. W. and Hurst, J. G. 'Wharram Percy, a case-study in microtopography', in Sawyer, P. H. ed, *English Mediaeval Settlement*, 1979, pp 64–6 (manorial farmstead round yard – elsewhere in Yorkshire peasants were building courtyard farmsteads by the thirteenth century).

10. 'Bratton, Wiltshire', *Mediaeval Archaeology*, vol 10, 1966, pp 214–15.

11. Horn, W. and Born, E. *The Barns of the Abbey of Beaulieu and its Granges of Great Coxwell and Beaulieu St Leonards*, 1965, pp 11, 13, 17. This barn stood on the estates of the Dean and Chapter of St Paul's which in this period owned thirteen manors, the number of barns on each manor varying between three and five. 'Thirteen of these barns are so well described [in the estate records] that they can be reconstructed on the drawing board' (Horn, W. 'On the origins of the mediaeval bay system', *Journal of the Society of Architectural Historians*, vol 17, 1958, pp 11–12).

12. The total number of barns was considerable. It is estimated that the Cistercians built between 2,000 and 3,000 of which only 2 survive (Heyworth, P. L. 'A lost Cistercian barn', *Oxoniensa*, vol 36, 1971, pp 52–4). See also note 32.

13. Rogers, T. *Agriculture and Prices in England*, vol 1, 1866, p 513 and vol 4, 1882, pp 460–5. A granary built on a Hertfordshire farm in the early fifteenth century has recently been restored and erected by the Cambridge Preservation Society at Wandlebury on the Gog Magog hills near Cambridge. In its present form it includes Tudor reconstruction. In its original form it probably stood on staddle stones and was thatched with straw (Clark, W. 'A granary regained', *Farmers Weekly*, 19 March 1982, pp 114–15) (see plate 5). For a granary which from constructional evidence appears to date from the Middle Ages see Snoxell, T. 'Brenley Farm', *Traditional Kent Buildings*, vol 3, 1983, p 34, published by Kent County Council.

14. Dymond, A. 'A fifteenth century building contract for Suffolk', *Vernacular Architecture*, vol 9, 1978, p 10.

15. *Seneschausie*, in Lamont, E. ed, *Walter of Henley's Husbandry*, 1890, pp 113–15.

16. Davidson, H. R. *The Production and Marketing of Pigs*, 1966, p 230.

17. Edmonton Manor records for 1479–80 refer to 'hog-cotes' built by Sir Thomas Lovell (Jones, I. K. 'Mediaeval Enfield', *Enfield Archaeological Society News*, September 1977, p 5). The manor was wintering some four hundred pigs in Enfield Chase at the time, so presumably these 'cotes' housed the pigs for the remainder of the year.

18. Martin, D. and Martin, B. 'Floors in barns', *Historic Buildings in Eastern Sussex*, vol 1, no 2, 1978, pp 25–9.

19. Trow-Smith, R. *A History of British Livestock Husbandry to 1700*, 1957, p 113.

20. Fox, A. 'A monastic homestead on Dean Moor, S. Devon', *Mediaeval Archaeology*, vol 2, 1958, pp 140–57.

21. Raistrick, A. and Holmes, P. F. 'The archaeology of Malham Moor' *Field Studies*, vol 1, no 4, 1962, pp 20–3 (reprint pagination), reports the excavation of this sheephouse. Nearby an Iron Age site was adapted by monastic shepherds to make a sheepfold (p 14). Bolton Abbey had another sheephouse at Appletreewick (p 20). Fountains Abbey had a sheephouse at Coniston and possibly another at Malham Moor (Raistrick, A. *Monks and Shepherds in the Yorkshire Dales*, 1976, p 12). For a recently excavated example of a similar outpost of a Cistercian sheep enterprise see BBC *Origins* programme, 4 October 1981 and *Farmers Weekly*, 20 August 1982, pp 102–3 (Sheffield University, Department of Archaeology dig, Minninglow Hill, Derbyshire).

22. Lamont, E. ed, *Walter of Henley's Husbandry*, 1890, p 31.

23. Trow-Smith, R. *A History of British Livestock Husbandry to 1700*, 1957, pp 113–14. The accounts of Crowland Abbey's manor at Wellingborough, Northamptonshire, refer in 1291 to the purchase of three cartloads of brushwood for bedding the ewes and for thatching the sheepfold (Steane, J. *The Northamptonshire Landscape*, 1974, p 123). For sheepcotes on the estates of Abingdon Abbey see Bond, C. J. 'The reconstruction of the

mediaeval landscape', *Landscape History*, vol 1, 1979, p 63.

24. Trow-Smith, R. *Life from the Land*, 1967, p 59.

25. Trow-Smith, R. *A History of British Livestock Husbandry to 1700*, 1957, p 114.

26. Jobey, G. 'A note on sow kilns', *Journal of the University of Newcastle upon Tyne Agricultural Society*, 1966, p 38.

27. Beresford, G. 'The mediaeval manor of Penhallen in Cornwall', *Mediaeval Archaeology*, vol 18, 1974, p 111; Beresford, G. 'Three deserted mediaeval settlements on Dartmoor', *Mediaeval Archaeology*, vol 23, 1979, pp 140–2, Their date was unknown but estimated at between 1250 and 1350. See also Jope, E. M. and Threlfall, R. I. 'Excavation of a mediaeval settlement at Beere, North Tawton, Devon', *Mediaeval Archaeology*, vol 2, 1958, pp 112–25; Dudley, D. and Minter, E. M. 'The mediaeval village at Garrow Tor, Bodmin Moor, Cornwall', *Mediaeval Archaeology*, vol 6–7, 1962–3, pp 273–94; Beresford, M. and Hurst, J. G. *Deserted Mediaeval Villages*, 1971, p 115; Steane, J. *The Northamptonshire Landscape*, 1974, pp 166–8; 'Wharram Percy', *Mediaeval Archaeology*, vol 23, 1979, pp 272–3; Brunskill, R. W. *Traditional Farm Buildings of Britain*, 1982, pp 94–5.

28. Harvey, D. P. A. *A Mediaeval Oxfordshire Village, Cuxham, 1240–1400*, 1965, pp 32–9. The steading of a similar type of farm in Norfolk with 200 acres of corn as it was in the later years of the thirteenth century is described in Davenport, F. G. *The Economic Development of a Norfolk Manor*, 1906, pp 21, 27, 33–5. This consisted of a barn and a granary, a cattleshed, a hayshed and three stables, a dairy and poultry housing. Pigs are mentioned, but there was no piggery. Presumably they foraged as best they could according to the season, either in the yards on household and farm waste or in the local woods. The home farm of the manor of Wellingborough, owned by Crowland Abbey, included a barn, a stable, a cowshed, a granary and two dovecotes (Steane, J. *The Northamptonshire Landscape*, 1974, p 122).

29. Trow-Smith, R. *A History of British Livestock Husbandry to 1700*, 1957, pp 107–8.

30. Most sources are concerned with such buildings as individual structures. Bond, C. J. 'The reconstruction of the mediaeval landscape', *Landscape History*, vol 1, 1979, pp 58–75, describes the estates of Abingdon Abbey and shows, so far as the limited evidence allows, barns, dovecotes and sheepcotes in the context of the agricultural empire of which they formed part. See also Price, E. G. 'Survivals of the mediaeval monastic estate of Frocester', *Transactions of the Bristol and Gloucestershire Archaeological Society*, vol 98, 1980), pp 73–88.

31. Brandon, F. *The Landscape of Sussex*, 1974, p 120. See also Brandon, F. 'Demesne arable farming in coastal Sussex', *Agricultural History Review*, vol 19, pt 2, 1971, pp 113–34. For the 'grain factories' see p 113; for the Alciston figures pp 127, 131.

32. It is more convenient to amalgamate references to all barns rather than attempt to distinguish between 'tithe barns' and other barns. References to individual 'tithe barns' abound in architectural and topographical works, though the hope of J. D. U. Ward ('Tithe barns of the south-west', *Agriculture*, vol 65, July 1958, pp 195–8) that these barns might be 'surveyed, measured and listed comprehensively by trained scholars' (p 198) has not been fulfilled. Sources include Sheldon, L. 'Devon barns', *Report and Transactions of the Devonshire Association*, vol 64, 1932, pp 389–95; Horn, W. 'The great tithe barn of Cholsey, Berkshire', *Journal of the Society of Architectural Historians*, vol 22, 1963, pp 13–23; Wood-Jones, R. B. *Traditional Domestic Architecture of the Banbury area*, 1963, notably pp 15–17 for the Enstone barn and its datestone placed there in 1382 by the Abbot of Winchcombe at the request of Robert Mason, the bailiff of the manor; Peters, J. E. C. 'The tithe barn, Arreton, Isle of Wight', *Transactions of the Ancient Monuments Society*, NS vol 12, 1964, pp 60–9; Horn, W. and Born, E. *The Barns of Beaulieu and its Granges at Great Coxwell and Beaulieu St Leonards*, 1965; Horn, W. and Charles, F. W. B. 'The cruckbuilt barn of Middle Littleton in Worcestershire', *Journal of the Society of Architectural Historians*, vol 25, 1966, pp 229–39; Hewett, C. A. 'The barns of Cressing Temple, Essex, and their significance in the history of English carpentry', *Journal of the Society of Architectural Historians*, vol 26, 1967, pp 48–70; Rigold, S. E. 'Some major Kentish timber barns', *Archaeologia Cantiana*, vol 81, 1967, pp 1–30; Rigold, S. E. 'The Cherhill barn', *Wiltshire Archaeological and Natural History Magazine*, vol 63, 1968, pp 58–65; for a group of barns built by the Abbot of St Albans in the last years of the fourteenth century see Weaver, O. J. 'A mediaeval aisled barn at St Julian's Farm, St Albans', *Hertfordshire Archaeology*, vol 2, 1970, pp 110–12; Castle, S. A. 'The aisled barn at Parsonage Farm, Abbots Langley', *Hertfordshire Archaeology*, vol 3, 1973, pp 131–4; Castle, S. A. 'The mediaeval aisled barns at Kingsbury Manor Farm, St Albans, and Croxley Hall Farm', *Hertfordshire Archaeology*, vol 3, 1973, pp 134–8; Gibson, A. V. B. 'The mediaeval aisled barn at Parkbury Farm, Radlett', *Hertfordshire Archaeology*, vol 4, 1974–6, pp 158–63; Weaver, J. O. 'A note on the history of Parkbury', *Hertfordshire Archaeology*, vol 4, 1974–6, pp 163–4; Roberts, J. H. 'Five mediaeval barns in Hertfordshire', *Hertfordshire Archaeology*, vol 7, 1979, pp 159–80; Heyworth, P. L. 'A lost Cistercian barn', *Oxoniensia*, vol 36, 1971, pp 52–4; Davey, C. R. 'The Carlisle tithe barn',

*Transactions of the Cumberland and Westmorland Antiquarian and Archaeological Society*, vol 72, 1972, pp 74–84; Scarfe, N. *The Suffolk Landscape*, 1972, p 172, for a barn at Kelsale where roundels on the brickwork show the rampant lions of the Mowbrays and of the Bigods before them; Charles, F. W. B. and Horn, W. 'The cruck-built barn at Leigh Court, Worcestershire', *Journal of the Society of Agricultural Historians*, vol 32, 1973, pp 5–29, which includes carbon dating of the barn to the fourteenth century and a modern drawing of the method of erection of a cruck barn; Hewett, C. A. *Abbot's Hall Barn*, published by the Museum of East Anglian Life, 1975; Parker, R. *The Common Stream*, 1975, p 107, for Mortimer's barn at Foxton in Cambridgeshire, which was six centuries old when it was pulled down but preserved the name of a family whose male line ended in Plantagenet times; Brown, F. E. 'Aisled timber barns in Kent', *Vernacular Architecture*, vol 7, 1976, pp 36–40, which shows that the medieval barns in this area founded a structural tradition which continued to the eighteenth and nineteenth centuries; Reynolds, J. *The Hampshire Barn*, unpublished thesis, Architectural Association, 1978, pp 14–20; Bailey, J. *Timberframed Buildings*, Bedfordshire, Buckinghamshire and Cambridgeshire Historic Buildings Research Group, 1979, pp 26–9; Bond, C. J. 'The reconstruction of the mediaeval landscape', *Landscape History*, vol 1, 1979, pp 64–8 for barns of Abingdon Abbey; Ryder, P. F. *Timber-framed Buildings in South Yorkshire*, South Yorkshire County Council Archaeological Monograph no 1, 1979, including cruck and aisled barns; Essex County Council, *The Essex Countryside, Historic Barns*, 1980; Hewett, C. A. *English Historic Carpentry*, 1980, which gives the development of the timber structure of barns; Price, E. G. 'Survivals of the monastic estate of Frocester', *Transactions of the Bristol and Gloucestershire Archaeological Society*, vol 98, 1980, pp 73–88; Havinden, M. *The Somerset Landscape*, 1981, plates 34, 36; Peters, J. E. C. *Discovering Traditional Farm Buildings*, 1981, pp 10–24; Brunskill, R. W. *Traditional Farm Buildings of Britain*, 1982, pp 32–48. See also notes 11, 12.

33. 'Hales Hall Barn', *Food from the Land Card B21*, published by Norfolk Heritage.
34. Curtler, W. H. R. *A Short History of English Agriculture*, 1909, pp 48–9.
35. See Cooke, A. D. *A Book of Dovecotes*, 1920; Smith, D. *Pigeoncotes and Dove Houses of Essex*, 1931; Mansfield, W. S. *The Farmer's Friend*, 1947, pp 25–6; Brunskill, R. W. *Traditional Farm Buildings of Britain*, 1982, pp 80–6; 'Shooting and Conservation', *Farmers Weekly Supplement*, 29 April 1983, p 14, for figures of corn consumption. For dovecotes on the estates of Abingdon Abbey see Bond, C. J. 'The reconstruction of the mediaeval landscape', *Landscape History*, vol 1, 1979, p 65. There are many references to dovecotes in general and local publications, but no comprehensive study of these buildings and the part which the domesticated pigeon played in agricultural history has so far appeared.
36. Ward, J. D. U. 'Tithe barns of the south-west', *Agriculture*, vol 65, July 1958, p 195.
37. Price, E. G. 'Survivals of the monastic estate of Frocester', *Transactions of the Bristol and Gloucestershire Archaeological Society*, vol 98, 1980, p 78. The materials used in the construction of five large barns built by the Abbot of St Albans at the end of the fourteenth century included local stone or clunch, local timber, wattle-and-daub cladding, clay tiles, probably from local clay burnt in local kilns, which were secured by oak pegs, Roman bricks from Verulamium and timbers from old buildings (Roberts, J. H, 'Five mediaeval barns in Hertfordshire', *Hertfordshire Archaeology*, vol 7, 1979, pp 163–4, 1969). For the reuse of old timbers in a late medieval barn see Hewett, C. A. *Abbot's Hall Barn*, published by the Museum of East Anglian Life, 1975, p 6. See p 26 and note 21.
38. Trow-Smith, R. *Life from the Land*, 1967, p 79.
39. See p 20. It has been suggested that certain granite buildings, apparently of longhouse type, on the fringes of Dartmoor may date from the original colonisation of the moor in the thirteenth century (Barley, M. W. *The English Farmhouse and Cottage*, 1961, p 11).
40. 'Wiltshire, Fyfield Down, Wroughton Copse', *Mediaeval Archaeology*, vol 5, 1961, p 330.
41. Chambers, R. A. 'A deserted mediaeval farmstead at Sadler's Wood, Lewknor', *Oxoniensia*, vol 38, 1973, p 166.
42. Davenport, F. G. *The Economic Development of a Norfolk Manor*, 1906, pp 21, 32.
43. Trow-Smith, R. *A History of British Livestock Husbandry to 1700*, 1957, p 108.
44. Ward, J. D. U. 'A glance at tithe barns', *Esso Farmer*, vol 14, Spring 1962, pp 20–1. Some of these pegs were still *in situ* at that time.
45. Martin, D. and Martin, B. 'Wall framing in barns', *Historic Buildings in Eastern Sussex*, vol 1, no 1, 1977, p 12.
46. Barley, M. W. *English Farmhouses and Cottages*, 1961, p 36.
47. Hoskins, W. G. *The Midland Peasant*, 1957, p 191.
48. Titow, J. Z. *English Rural Society, 1200–1350*, 1969, pp 198–204. The use of moss to waterproof roofing continued in Wales certainly into the late eighteenth century and probably into the nineteenth (Wiliam, E. *Traditional Farm Buildings in North-East Wales, Wales, 1550–1900*, 1982, p 96).
49. For other examples of the use of tiles on farm buildings, all dating from the late

thirteenth or fourteenth century, see Harvey, D. P. A. *A Mediaeval Oxfordshire Village, Cuxham, 1240–1400*, 1965, p 37; Lloyd, E. 'The farm accounts of the manor of Hendon, 1316–1416', Transactions of London and Middlesex Archaeological Society, vol 21, 1962–7, p 159, which refers to the roofing of three monastic barns with tiles over thatch; Packe, A. H. and Broadbent, 'Hitcham Old Barn', *Records of Buckinghamshire*, vol 18, 1969, which refers on p 316 to evidence that 'it was possible for farm buildings to be tiled as early as 1372'; Chambers, R. A. 'A deserted mediaeval farmstead at Sadler's Wood, Lewknor', *Oxoniensia*, vol 38, 1973, p 166. See also note 37.

50. Charles, F. W. B. *Mediaeval Cruck Building and its Derivatives*, 1967; Brunskill, R. W. *Traditional Farm Buildings of Britain*, 1982, pp 123–6.

51. Addy, S. O. *The Evolution of the English House*, 1933, pp 85–8.

52. Hewett, C. A. *English Historic Carpentry*, 1980, including references to the Belchamp St Paul's barn on pp 23–4, 37 and 43, where the carbon dating of the post is put at 1026 (931–1121). Essex County Council, *The Essex Countryside, Historic Barns*, 1980, illustrates the development of aisled barn construction from the eleventh to the fifteenth century, pp 7–13, gives cases of carbon dating on p 3 and refers to the Belchamp St Paul's barn on p 7 and to the architectural detailing of such barns on pp 17–22. See Appendix p 262 for dating of pre-industrial farm buildings. A pleasing detail in timber construction can be seen at the Battle Abbey barn at Alciston, Sussex. The timber uprights stand on timber bases. These bases are laid with the grain of the timber parallel to the floor to decrease the uptake of moisture.

53. Rigold, S. E. 'The distribution of aisled timber barns', *Vernacular Architecture*, vol 2, 1971, pp 20–4; Clarke, D. *Vernacular Architecture*, vol 3, 1972, p 20.

# 3 THE END OF AN AGE: 1500–1750

## New Sources of Information

We are accustomed to regard this period as the time in which our own age was formed. When it began, England was a medieval country. The Renaissance, the Reformation and the rise of the national state were still in the future. By the time it ended, we were in the familiar world of parliamentary government, transatlantic trade, the stock exchange, newspapers and coffee shops.

Politically and intellectually, this may well be true. Agriculturally, it is false, for the scope and scale of these prodigious changes were not reflected in the farmlands. There was certainly considerable expansion of the cultivated area during this period. There was also, less precedently, considerable technical development in its last hundred years, notably the use of new forage crops and a consequent increase in the livestock population. But there was no dramatic rural revolution. The improved agricultural system which Defoe saw from horseback in the days of George I was a recognisable version of that which the Royal Society strove to survey in the days of Charles II, which was in turn a recognisable version of that which Tusser described in the days of Elizabeth.

These names, however, remind us that we have now reached the age of the printed word and general literacy, and from Tudor times onwards our sources of information on the history of farming, and therefore on the history of farm buildings, increase with each succeeding period. There was as yet no specialist literature on farm buildings, but the incidental references to them grew proportionately with the increasing number of general and agricultural books, of legal records and estate papers. Towards the end of this period, for example, we find the first detailed descriptions of a cowhouse with manger and tie, its stalls 'a yoak wide', its floor hard and sloping to carry away the liquids[1]; and the first references to the appreciation by landowners of the importance of good buildings for attracting or keeping good tenants.[2]

Furthermore, this is the first age to leave us a significant number of examples of its ordinary farm buildings.[3] For most of the period, admittedly, such survivals are no more than a chance collection of the most substantial and durable buildings of their particular time, and they probably include a historically disproportionate number of barns. But from the later sixteenth century onwards, as the generations pass, an increasing number of contemporary farm buildings survive as sources of historical knowledge.[4]

## More Food for More People

These new sources of information tell an old agricultural story. But they tell it in more urgent form. For the population was growing more rapidly than in the Middle Ages: there were probably under 3 million people in England and Wales in 1500, 4 million in 1600 and some $5\frac{1}{2}$ million in 1700. Further, more and more of these newcomers were living in towns. Both absolutely and proportionately there were many more mouths for the farmer to feed. By the end of the seventeenth century, for instance, London housed over half a million people, and the demands of this huge market brought butter from Suffolk, cheese from Cheshire, cider from Devon and cattle for meat from Wales and Scotland. Yet for many years the ancient tradition of increasing food production by adding to the agricultural area rather than improving agricultural methods continued to meet the needs of the time. Generation by generation, new farmland was reclaimed from the ancient forests, from the hills, from marshes, fens and sea coasts. Significantly, many medieval deerparks and hunting forests were converted to ploughland and pasture as the growing demand for food made corn, beef and mutton more valuable than sport, venison and timber. Old Park Farm near Axminster, for instance, began as 'a barn or hayhouse' recorded in 1574 as 'newly scyted' in parkland formerly belonging to Newenham Abbey.[5] Most of this new farmland was won with increasing difficulty and expense, as by this time the more promising areas were already under cultivation. But until the days of the Stuarts it was sufficient to maintain the necessary increase in the nation's food supply. Only in the later years of this period was there enough technical improvement to make any substantial contribution to the rise in agricultural production.

## New Farmland, New Farms and New Farm Buildings

Sometimes the new land was added to existing farms. In Oxfordshire a barn built about 1720 to serve ploughland won from rough hill grazings still stands as a memorial to this process.[6] The cornstore which John Lyson of North Cotes in Lincolnshire built in the early seventeenth century, and the two new barns and the beasthouse with which Nicholas Sampson in the manor of Sheffield doubled his accommodation in the same period, may reflect similar expansion.[7] So may the barn which still survives at Arreton on the Isle of Wight, which was rebuilt and enlarged in the sixteenth century and enlarged again in the seventeenth century.[8] More generally, the fine timber barns built by the yeomen of Essex and Kent in the sixteenth and seventeenth centuries, and the equally impressive combined barn-and-cowhouses which their Pennine cousins built of stone in the seventeenth century, illustrate the prosperity and confidence of an age of expansion.[9]

Sometimes the new land was formed into new farms, such as the holdings reclaimed from the forest land around Tonbridge in the later sixteenth and early seventeenth centuries, which included two keepers' cottages converted to farmsteads, [10] and William Zellacke's lonelier creation of Moorhays Farm, near Cruwys Morchard in mid-Devon. In 1653 he secured a ninety-nine-year lease of 'all that parcell of waste grounde and lande lyinge in near or by the highwaye adjoining the moore commonly called South Moore', for a yearly rent of 6 shillings and one capon, provided that he built a house on it. He also built farm buildings and by 1694 the new farm was worth 10 shillings a year and a fine at entry of £150.[11] But such 'parcells of waste grounde' were becoming scarce and many of the new farms were won from land already used for seasonal or extensive grazing rather than from uncultivated wilderness.

Thus, in the 1670s, 2,245 acres of White Coombs uplands in Cheshire were rented to a group of eleven graziers. By 1750 this area was divided into three farms, each with its own farmstead.[12] Probably, too, the buildings for inwintering cattle found in some Yorkshire dales and in Wales in this period were evidence of more intensive upland husbandry.[13] More particularly, the same pressures were now beginning to end the ancient practice of transhumance. In Northumberland, frontier conditions favoured its survival until the Union of the Crowns in 1603. But in the next century and a half the seasonal grazings where Camden had seen the lowland farmers 'lying out and summering with their cattle in little cottages they called sheals or shealings' were gradually replaced by pastoral farming and the 'sheals or shealings' either abandoned or converted into homesteads.[14] In more settled Wales the same change came early and by the end of the seventeenth century the traditional system only survived in a few limited districts.[15]

The advance of settled farming into the lonely uplands is typified by the substantial steading of Middle House Farm built in the late sixteenth or early seventeenth century on Malham Moor, which was formerly one of the ranches of the Cistercian sheep empire. It stands on the site of a monastic shepherd's lodge but its name suggests continuity with an even older settlement, the 'mootlow' or meeting place of the scattered sheep farmers whose Viking ancestors had colonised these high pastures in later Saxon times. The buildings of this courtyard farmstead include a pigeonhouse, evidence of the cultivation of corn in an area which was once, and is now again, entirely pastoral.[16]

The incentives which caused the continuing reclamation of the waste and the development of the uplands also caused changes in the settled lowlands. In particular, various local forms of enclosure consolidated a number of scattered open-field holdings into more convenient individually managed farms.[17] Such changes meant an increase in the number of farmsteads standing apart or remote from villages on land where ploughmen had once cultivated their intermingled strips or cattle grazed on communal pastures. In the Durham parish of Shadforth, for instance, ten farmsteads were built in the seventeenth century to serve new farms created by an enclosure agreement of 1634; in a Midland area in 1500 isolated farmsteads formed 14 per cent of the total, in 1600 25 per cent, in 1700 39 per cent.[18] Greater changes lay ahead, but the siting of such new farmsteads in this period illustrates an early stage in one of the major processes which later shaped so much of the modern agricultural landscape.

## The End of the Lowland Longhouse

New farm buildings and new farmsteads, however, did not mean any radical break with the past. The old dependence of site on natural water supplies, the old principles of planning and the old methods of construction continued, and it is typical of the times that the most striking change was in regional tradition.

In this period the lowland farmer abandoned the longhouse. After early Tudor times, separation of the domestic and industrial buildings of the farm was the rule except in hill areas.[19] The scale of this change is difficult to estimate, for present evidence on the incidence of different types of steading is scanty. Its causes, too, are uncertain, though presumably the contemporary rise in the standard of living and comfort was mainly responsible. But its importance in farmstead development is decisive. In the lowlands, from this time onwards, the house of the farmer stands apart from the buildings of the farm.

This change, of course, was not immediate. Cheshire farmers, for example, continued to house their cattle under the same roofs as themselves well into the seventeenth century.[20] And, of course, there was an inevitable interim period. In the early seventeenth century, the 'backhouse' of East Anglian farms had become a combination of

43

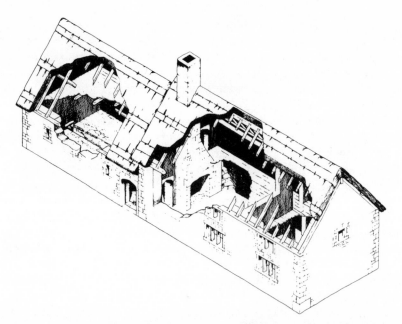

7    A Devon longhouse of the type built between the middle of the sixteenth and the middle of the seventeenth century, showing the separation of farmhouse and cowhouse (Mercer, E. *English Vernacular Houses*, 1975, p40) (*Royal Commission on Historical Monuments, England*)

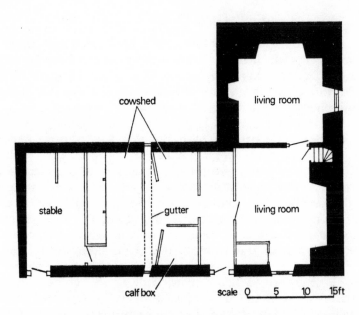

cowshed

living room

stable

gutter

living room

calf box

scale  0    5    10    15ft

8    Plan of the Welsh longhouse shown on page 103 (*The National Museum of Wales, Welsh Folk Museum*)

kitchen, milkroom and buttery, whereas in more conservative Yorkshire in the same period the lower end of the house was a general storeroom which had not yet acquired any regular domestic function. The cattle had left it too recently for the possibility of their return some hard winter to be forgotten.[21] These, however, were passing anachronisms. The contrast which Harrison drew in 1577 between the one-roof steadings of 'some of the north parts of our countrie' and the functionally divided buildings elsewhere was prophetic, and the longhouse shown in a 1585 engraving of the unlikely village of Bermondsey belonged to a dying tradition.[22] A modern historian's surprise at finding in a conventional farming area of Devon the 'unusual arrangement' of dwelling house and farm buildings under one roof dating from this period bears witness to the completeness of the change.[23] By Elizabethan times, it seems, the longhouse was no longer being built in the lowlands.

## The Longhouse in the Uplands

The extent to which the new lowland pattern of farmstead spread into the uplands of the north and west is uncertain.[24] It is, however, clear that the longhouse continued as a common type of farmstead, particularly in Devon and in Wales.[25] But in the hills, too, the new influences were spreading and, as the years passed, the division between the farmhouse and cowhouse became more pronounced. The creation of lobbies and finally internal walls between the two sections of the building and the provision of separate doors for men and animals reflected the farmer's desire for higher standards of comfort and cleanliness. In surviving examples on Dartmoor and in Cumberland of longhouses built in the latter half of this period, there is no direct communication between the two parts of the building.[26] The age of the primitive longhouse was nearing its end. But the improved longhouse in which there was no internal access between dwelling house and cattlehouse still had many years of life ahead of it. (See Figs 7, 8 and Plate 9.)

## The Successors of the Longhouse

So did the general principle of housing different types of activity under one roof. This principle took a variety of forms. In the north, for example, from the later seventeenth century, laithe barns housed cattle, hay and threshing floors and, with the addition of dwellings attached to them but separated by doorless partitions, became laithe houses;[27] in the Lake District from the early eighteenth century two-storey bank barns built into slopes provided storage for hay, corn and

45

straw above and housing for cattle below, with entrances at each level.[28] More comprehensively, the tradition continued in the linear farmstead (see page 48).

A curious localised version of the all-in-one farmstead was the 'bastle' of the northern border counties, a two-storey, thick-walled 'vertical longhouse' which housed cattle on the ground floor and the farmer and his family on the first floor. But here the purpose was military, not agricultural. The bastle provided a farmer with a combined home and livestock shelter that could be defended against raiders. They mostly date from the late sixteenth to the early seventeenth century and ceased to be built after the Union of the Crowns in 1603 established peace in this traditionally lawless zone. The custom of living over livestock, however, continued long after cattle raiders had passed into history and the tradition endured into the twentieth century.[29]

### Developments in the Farmstead

Technically, this period saw no drastic or widespread improvements in methods of husbandry or systems of farming. Economically, patterns of regional specialisation were developing to meet new commercial opportunities, but the days of the specialist farm were still far in the future. There was, therefore, little change in the demands of the farm on the farmstead and developments were few and simple.

Horses, for instance, were now replacing oxen as work beasts, but this only meant an increase in stabling, for there were horses on many farms by this time, and the old ox-stalls could be used for other cattle. Indeed, draught oxen have left few traces in the farmstead, though certain Welsh buildings of this period preserve the wide doors made necessary by the spread of the horns of the local breed.[30] Neither did changing systems of pig management cause major changes in the farmstead. Many pigs were still ranched in the woodlands, as shown by the seventeenth century contrast between the large pig population of well-wooded Hampshire and the small number of pigs kept in poorly wooded south Wiltshire.[31] But the old areas of forest were shrinking fast and pigs were now spending more time in sties or yards, where they fattened on the waste products of the fields, the butter or cheese dairy and the farmhouse[32] (see Plate 7). In the later sixteenth century, for example, Tusser assumed from his experience in East Anglia, where woodlands were few, that pigs would be housed in the farmstead, though not very elaborately. The winter accommodation he suggested was either a 'hovel' under the logs and bundles of brushwood stacked for winter fuel or shelter under the carts in the cartshed.[33] Such crude housing was easily incorporated into the traditional type of farmstead.

Typically, the only conspicuous innovation in building design in this period on the general farm represented no more than a new form of answer to the ancient problem of storing and feeding winter fodder in climatically difficult areas. This was the appearance in the West-country of the 'linhay' or 'linney', a two-storey building with an open front, created by the addition of a hayloft to a traditional cattleshed, and of a similar but fully enclosed building in the north of England.[34]

Indeed, there were no fundamental changes in this period in the inherited alliance of barn, beasthouse and yard. In arable areas, of course, there was greater emphasis on the corn barn[35] and the increasingly common granary. On smaller farms grain had custo-marily been stored in a room in the farmhouse, where it was dry and safe from thieves. But, as corn production increased, harvests outgrew attics or 'corn chambers' and the grainstore moved from farmhouse to farm buildings. In some areas the domestic connection was continued by attaching the granary to the house and preserving domestic architectural features.[36] More often, however, grain was stored either in lofts over such buildings as cartsheds, where it would not be contaminated by foul air from livestock, or in free-standing granaries, usually single-storey, sometimes double-storey, mounted on brick piers or staddlestones to protect it from rats and mice.[37] In the pastoral areas, the emphasis was on livestock buildings, though there were few changes except in number and scale. But it remained a matter of local emphasis. The need for a considerable degree of self-sufficiency ensured the continuation of mixed farming and with it the types of building required to serve it.

A catalogue of chance descriptions of farmsteads in different parts of the country in the seventeenth century shows the pervading similarity of the mixed farming pattern; in East Anglia, a barn, a carthouse and a stable;[38] in Devon, a barn, a cowhouse and 'a new stable and a corn-chamber which I have built;[39] in Leicestershire, a barn, a stable and hovels;[40] in Herefordshire 'a large new frame of buildings', including two barns, a large beasthouse, a swinehouse, a sheepcote and a pigeonhouse;[41] in upland Yorkshire, a stable, a barn and a cowshed;[42] and on an estate in lowland Yorkshire a group ranging from Richard Wilson's collection of a three-bay cornbarn, a two-bay haybarn, a four-bay beasthouse, a two-bay carthouse and a piggery to Simon Heathcot's single hovel for livestock and 'cornebarn made of poules, very badd'.[43] Simi. 'y, an analysis of the surveys of three Sussex estates, two in the sixteenth century and one in the seventeenth, showed that thirty-six farms mustered between them thirty-three barns, some of which probably followed the local practice of housing livestock as well as corn, four hay-shelters, nine stables, six cattle-shelters and one unspecified 'outhouse', all familiar types of building, with, in addition, three oasthouses, an innovation discussed later in this chapter (see p 49).[44] The only other obvious novelty in the records of this period was an increase in the number of references to cartsheds, which presumably reflected the growing importance of farm transport in an increasingly commercialised rural economy. As early as the seventeenth century the two sheds on Henry Best's Yorkshire farm housed seven carts, whose repair and maintenance under cover was a standard winter chore: 'our folkes were (this year) employed about this business on Powder Treason day'.[45]

These were not, of course, the only buildings on the farm. The practice of housing sheep in the winter was on the decline and by the end of the period survived only in hill areas,[46] but pigeons still needed housing. In Tudor times the depredations of the manorial flocks were among the grievances which led to Ket's Rising in 1549,[47] but in the early seventeenth century this feudal monopoly was apparently abandoned and pigeoncotes appeared on formerly unprivileged farms. The number of pigeoncotes in this period was considerable, some 26,000 according to a contemporary estimate,[48] and the flocks made a minor but appreciable contribution to farm income. The accounts of Robert Loder, who farmed in Berkshire in the time of Charles I, show that they earned him from £5 to £10 a year of his total farm income of some £400, as well as supplying him with manure.[49] Some flocks, indeed, made a contribution to non-farm income, for they were owned by people without farmland and lived on the crops of their agricultural neighbours – a peculiarly profitable type of intensive livestock production.[50]

### Farmstead Layout

There is little general or systematic information on the arrangement of these varied buildings into steadings. The 'linear farmstead' with a yard in front was known both in the lowlands and the uplands, and a Midland survey found that farmsteads 'in which the agricultural buildings stood in a straight line (were) the earliest surviving classifiable type of farm layout'. The oldest of such farmsteads identified in this study dated from the beginning of the sixteenth century, the oldest of the next type to appear, the L-shaped steading which gave better protection to the yard, in the later years of the century.[51] In Wales, a single range of buildings or two parallel ranges seem to have been the earliest type of layout.[52] But scattered evidences suggest that the type of steading which was to dominate the next age, the 'courtyard farmstead' in which the buildings stand on three or four sides of a central yard, was already becoming more frequent.[53]

## Processing Buildings

In this period, too, signs of general economic change were already visible in the farmstead. All dairy farmers had long been accustomed to processing milk into butter and cheese for sale off the farm – evil communications do more than corrupt good manners, they also render impossible the general transport and sale of such a perishable commodity as liquid milk. Such processing was the traditional responsibility of the farmer's wife and daughters, whose workshops were rooms in the farmhouse. Now, however, farmers began to process other products for market.

Some began to sell cider commercially. At first, cider, made by laborious manual methods, was exported from Cornwall to Plymouth. Then the invention in the mid-seventeenth century of the horse-driven circular mill made possible a more ambitious trade, from Devon and Herefordshire to London.[54] Others learnt from the Continent the novel art of hop-growing and with it, necessarily, of hop-drying.

At first, in Tudor times, they used malt kilns or improvised drying rooms. But by the middle of the seventeenth century Kent hop-growers had adopted the Flemish type of specialised rectangular oasthouse with a loading room, a kiln room and a cooling room. The kiln room housed a furnace fuelled originally by wood, later by charcoal, which served a slatted drying floor above it. The upward draught was sometimes improved by a system of cone-shaped flues of lath-and-plaster or brick, and the smoke escaped to the open air through cowls in the ridge. Later, however, technical need and economic change combined to produce a new type of oasthouse. The story is complicated and obscure, but it appears that Kent hop-growers, experimenting with designs in which the smoke did not pass through the hops with risk to their flavour, and seeking to replace charcoal by coal (a more efficient but also more contaminating fuel then becoming available), evolved the cockle kiln. In these oasts, flues from enclosed iron stoves, locally called cockles, circled the inner walls of the oast and discharged smoke through a chimney, thus keeping it away from the hops. By 1750 cockle kilns were recognised as 'exceeding all others for the sweetest and most regular manner of drying hops'. The next age brought further improvements and cockle kilns joined the earlier oasts, indistinguishable from barns except for the cowls or other outlets at their ridges, as reminders that the familiar type of oasthouse which we now regard as 'traditional' is only one stage in a long story of development.[55]

Cider mills and oasthouses were confined to limited areas, but both provided early examples of the effects of agricultural change on the equipment and buildings of the farmstead. They also illustrated the growing commercialism of farming, as did a new form of an old technique. The ancient practice of drying corn on farm kilns continued in areas of high rainfall.[56] An agreeably domestic version of such kilns were the drying-chambers near chimneys found in some West-country farmhouses, probably for drying small quantities of corn too wet for threshing to provide seed for autumn sowing.[57] But this period also saw the first reference to grain drying as a means of securing safe storage to secure good prices. The story is told by the inventor of the drill, Jethro Tull, one of whose Oxfordshire neighbours in the early eighteenth century used to dry grain on a malt kiln to rid it of the 'superfluous moisture which caused the corruption and made it liable to be eaten by the weevil', and then store it until the market was favourable. The practice was sound, the rewards considerable. 'From a small substance he began with, he left behind him about forty thousand pounds, the greatest part whereof was acquired by his drying method.' But he was a lone pioneer, probably because few could match his personal skill in judging the degree of drying necessary. The principle he so successfully exploited did not become general practice till the days of the combine-harvester.[58]

## The First Town Dairies

Meanwhile, equally prophetic types of intensive production were establishing themselves in London streets. These were the 'town dairies' which made their appearance in the seventeenth century, when the city began to outgrow its local milk supply. Their origin is obscure. Some probably developed from farms whose fields were replaced by spreading suburbs, but their connection with traditional farming was purely contractual. For here was 'factory farming' at its most literal, divorced from farmland but dependent on it for its animal machines, which were bought newly calved, milked through their lactation and then fattened for sale, and for the hay and straw which fuelled them. The cowsheds in forgotten courts and alleys which housed the herds of men like Mr Harrard who milked 'three hundred or sometimes four hundred' cows in Hoxton in the 1690s had little in common with the steadings of conventional farms.[59] But they were the ancestors of a line of development with a long and important future.

## Building Materials and Methods

The new age brought little change in the construction of farm buildings. The ancient tradition of local sufficiency was as yet unchallenged, and throughout this period 'Devon cob and thatch, Dartmoor granite, Dorset plaster and thatch, Cotswold limestone,

Plate 4    A late medieval aisled barn in Middlesex (*Farmers Weekly*)

Plate 5    This granary was built in the early fifteenth century, about the time of Agincourt. It was originally thatched and stood on staddlestones. In Tudor times, it was tiled and placed on brick piers. After long abandonment, it was reconstructed by the Cambridge Preservation Society, using as far as possible the methods and materials of the Middle Ages, and now stands at Wandlebury, on the Gog Magog Hills near Cambridge (see page 36) (*Cambridge Preservation Society and Mr Graham Black*)

Plate 6 Internal view of a medieval dovecote in Somerset, showing the revolving ladder from which the nests could be reached (see page 30) (*Farmers Weekly*)

chalkland flints, Sussex weather-boarding and tiles, Midland brick and mud-and-stud, Northamptonshire iron stone, northern slate and millstone grit',[60] the primitive 'bundle thatching'[61] and the heather used for thatching in the north of England and in Wales,[62] continued to proclaim the farmer's dependence on local materials just as his methods of building continued to proclaim his dependence on local skills.[63] For example, in Stuart times, Henry Best's large barn, capable of holding six loaded waggons, was framed in timber, clad in wattle-and-daub and floored in rammed clay 'which we used to digge and lode for our barne from John Bonwicke's hill'[64] while the walls of another Yorkshire steading were built of stones from a nearby river.[65] More generally, the reference in the accounts of a contemporary landowner to a loan of a horse to a tenant who was repairing his house and barn 'to tread clay and sledge it to the house' and the frugal satisfaction with which he recorded that the barn was thatched with 'sainfoin straw, except a good horseload of rushes' typify the practice and principles of the time.[66]

Old buildings, too, continued to provide a variety of materials, particularly when the Reformation made available so many convenient 'structural quarries'. In the north, for example, the hewn blocks of Furness Abbey, sometimes with elaborate decorations, appeared in farmsteads in the Dalton area; in Hampshire the only good building stone was the limestone which monks had imported from the Isle of Wight or Normandy; and a barn dated 1632 at Toddington in Gloucestershire includes a twelfth-century window frame, presumably from some abandoned or rebuilt church.[67] Less ecclesiastically, a seventeenth-century Westmorland landowner cannibalised a ruinous old hall for a new barn, and a Lincolnshire landowner in the same period dismantled a house 'as carefully as may be to prevent the breaking of any wood or tenures' to re-erect it as a barn.[68] It has, indeed, been suggested that the reused timbers in the farm buildings of this and later times, traditionally believed to come from dismantled ships, were more probably taken from demolished houses.[69]

There is no specific evidence that farm buildings shared in the 'Great Rebuilding' which so improved domestic standards in the countryside in the earlier years of this period, though farms may have benefitted from the relegation of old housing to agricultural purposes.[70] But it is probable that farm buildings shared in the general tendency towards more spacious design and more lasting materials. The process of improvement began, predictably, in the wealthier and more advanced areas.

Thus, in the early part of this period, the ancient regional distinction between the cruck barns of the west and the more sophisticated and spacious post-and-truss barns of the east continued, but the latter were gaining ground.[71] In Elizabethan times, for example, they were beginning to supersede their obsolescent rivals in the east Midlands,[72] whereas in north-east Wales cruck barns appear to have been built until the early eighteenth century.[73] A comparison in Somerset of medieval cruck barns and the aisled barns which replaced them suggests the reason for the change. The latter were more spacious, the largest dating from the sixteenth and seventeenth centuries when agricultural development was making more covered space necessary.[74] Again, in the prosperous south-east of England the use of brick in farmsteads increased from the later sixteenth century,[75] in less advanced north-east Wales from the later seventeenth century.[76] The general process of change is illustrated in the conclusions of a study of farm buildings in Monmouthshire, now Gwent, where the period 1550–1650 saw the erection of three classes of building – a mass of framed timber buildings, a few cruck timber buildings of the old tradition and a few stone-walled buildings of the more durable tradition to come.[77]

This period therefore saw a slow and general improvement in building materials and in methods of construction as the national standard of living steadily rose.[78] But the pace of agricultural development was not sufficient to create any general need for new designs and new types of construction. When, for example, the eighteenth-century farmers of Radnorshire, now in Powys, found that cattle paid better than corn, they simply converted part of their barn space to cowsheds.[79] It was significant that the spate of improving agricultural literature which was such a feature of the later years of the period made so few references to farmstead problems. In 1731, for instance, the only specific reference to farm buildings in a 300-page book on the management of farms and estates was the suggestion that they should be roofed with slates or tiles instead of straw, partly to reduce the risk of fire, partly to prevent the loss of the manurial value of the straw.[80] For the writer, like his predecessors and contemporaries, assumed as a matter of course that a combination of commonsense and local tradition would enable any landowner or farmer to equip his land with satisfactory buildings.

The accounts of Sir Daniel Fleming of Rydal Hall in Westmorland provide an interesting commentary on this assumption. He was a competent and energetic landowner, whose construction of three barns and various other farm buildings between 1659 and 1688 can be followed in detail in his records. On 6 March 1688, for instance, he gave 4s to his workmen at Coniston when he and his son 'went thither to sett out ye new great barn'. On 20 March the foundation was laid, on 10 July he sent 10s for ale 'at ye raising of ye great barn' when the roof timbers were hoisted on to completed walls. This barn still stands, a lasting memorial to a man whose careful planning allowed a delay in felling oaks for building timber until the bark was ready for peeling for sale to the tanners.[81]

In this period, therefore, most farmers built as their ancestors had built before them. In the design and construction of farm buildings, as in other branches of agricultural technology, local resources continued to meet local needs.

## NOTES

1. 'A. S. Gent', 1697, quoted in Fussell, G. E. *The English Dairy Farmer*, 1966, p 137.

2. Holderness, B. A. 'Farm buildings; investment and depreciation, 1750–1870', paper given at December 1982 meeting of the British Agricultural History Society referring to landlords' actions in periods of low prices between 1670 and 1740 with special reference to Felbrigg estate, Norfolk.

3. Apart from barns, 'practically all ancillary [timber] buildings [on farms], such as byres, granaries, cartsheds and the like, are post-mediaeval and few date from before 1600 or thereabouts' (Mason, R. T. *Framed Buildings of England*, 1973, p 118). The same generalisation probably also applies to stone buildings, 'Apart from the great mediaeval barns, few timberframed farm buildings date from before the sixteenth century, few stone or brick farm buildings from before the mid-seventeenth century' (Brunskill, R. W. *Illustrated Handbook of Vernacular Architecture*, 1978, p 132). Peters, J. E. C. *The Development of Farm Buildings in Western Lowland Staffordshire up to 1880*, 1969, pp 67, 111, 133, 188, 196, 202, found some fifteenth- and sixteenth-century barns but few other buildings dating from before 1600. Sweetland, P. *Barns of Bredon Hill*, unpublished thesis, Birmingham School of Architecture, 1979, Table B, identified no buildings dating from before 1600. Caffyn, L. *A Study of Farm Buildings in Selected Parishes of East Sussex*, unpublished MA thesis, Manchester University, 1981, pp 51, 54, found only one building, a fourteenth-century barn, dating from before the sixteenth century; 5 barns were sixteenth century, 4 late sixteenth or early seventeenth, 9 seventeenth, 11 eighteenth and the remaining 19 late eighteenth or nineteenth century. Wiliam, E. *Traditional Farm Buildings in North-east Wales, 1550–1900*, 1982, pp 26–8, found that 2 per cent of dated buildings were sixteenth century, 10 per cent seventeenth century and 19 per cent eighteenth century, half of the latter being pre1750. The earliest dated barn was built in 1612, though some undated barns were probably late sixteenth century.

4. For references to methods used for dating pre-industrial farm buildings for which no documentary evidence is available see Appendix, p 262.

5. Fox, H. S. A. 'Field systems of east and south Devon', *Report and Transactions of the Devonshire Association*, vol 104, 1974, p 117.

6. Jones, E. L. 'The bird pests of British agriculture in recent centuries', *Agricultural History Review*, vol 20, 1972, p 114.

7. Barley, M. W. *The English Farmhouse and Cottage*, 1961, pp 90, 118–19. For case studies of improvements see Tyson, B. 'Rydal Park Farm. The reconstruction of a farm building in Westmorland in the seventeenth century', *Transactions of the Cumberland and Westmorland Antiquarian and Archaeological Society*, vol 79, 1979, pp 86–97, and Tyson, B. 'Rydal Hall Farm. The development of a Westmorland farmstead before 1700', *Transactions of the Cumberland and Westmorland Antiquarian and Archaeological Society*, vol 80, 1980, pp 113–36.

8. Peters, J. E. C. 'The tithe barn, Arreton, Isle of Wight', *Transactions of the Ancient Monuments Society*, NS vol 12, 1964, pp 60–79. For another case of barn enlargement see Kent County Council Education Committee, *Traditional Kent Buildings*, no 2, 1981, pp 11–14. For the replacement of a medieval by a seventeenth-century barn at Milton Keynes see *Postmediaeval Archaeology*, vol 7, 1973, p 109.

9. Mason, R. T. *Framed Buildings of the Weald*, 1969, p 24; Harding, J. M. *Four Centuries of Charlwood Houses*, published by the Charlwood Society, 1976, pp 92–3; Essex County Council, *The Essex Countryside. Historic Barns*, 1979, pp 14–15; Walton, J. 'South Pennine barn buildings', *Architectural Review*, vol 90, October 1941, pp 122–4. Other examples are the manorial barns at Gunthwaite Hall, c1550 (Ryder, P. F. *Mediaeval Buildings of Yorkshire*, 1982, p 146), at Westenhanger Castle which probably dates from the sixteenth century (Gorman, M., Tinner, J., Vanhinsbergh, S. and Weedon, N, 'Westenhanger

# The End of an Age: 1500–1750

Castle Barns', *Traditional Kent Buildings*, no 3, 1983, pp 17–23), at Home Farm, Vaynol, Gwynedd, *c*1605 (Rickards, A. R. 'Vaynol', *Journal of the Land Agents Society*, vol 60, 1961, p 155), and the two barns built at some time before 1725 on Cogges Manor Farm, Oxfordshire, now an agricultural museum.

10. Chalklin, C. W. 'The rural economy of a Kentish wealden parish, 1650–1750', *Agricultural History Review*, vol 10, 1962, p 30. For the creation of farms with farmsteads based on the lodges of former forest officials in Braydon Forest in Wiltshire in the early seventeenth century see Grigson, G. 'The ghost of a forest', *Country Life*, 24 January 1957, pp 138–40, and Huxley, E. *Gallipot Eyes*, 1976, pp 135, 145.

11. Hoskins, W. G. and Finberg, H. P. R. *Devonshire Studies*, 1952, p 329.

12. In 1960 one of these preserved what appeared to be its original cowhouse, a low building with stone divisions between the cows (Davies, C. S. *The Agricultural History of Cheshire, 1750–1850*, 1960, p 8).

13. Hartley, M. and Ingilby, J. *Askrigg*, 1953, p 246, refer to these as 'outhouses', single-storey buildings for cattle fed from a nearby haystack, which were later replaced by the familiar and more substantial two-storey field barn. Brooks, S. D. *The History of Grassington*, 1979, p 27, however, refers to 'meadows [which] often had barns with hay stored above and cattle housed below in winter and quite often a farm man and his family living in cramped quarters at one end' (ie the later type of field barn with the addition of living quarters) on the evidence of a 1603 survey. See also Smith, P. *Houses of the Welsh Countryside*, 1975, p 145.

14. Butlin, R. A. 'Northumberland field systems', *Agricultural History Review*, vol 12, 1964, p 116 for Camden. See also Royal Commission on Historical Monuments, *Shielings and Bastles*, 1970; Harbottle, B. and Newman, T. G. 'Excavations and survey on the Starsley Burn, North Tynedale', *Archaeologia Aeliana*, 5 ser, vol 1, 1973, pp 146–7; Fowler, P. *Farms in England*, 1983, plate 12. Roberts, B. K. *Rural Settlement in Britain*, 1977, pp 182–3 gives a map of shielings in an area of County Durham in the late fourteenth century. By 1596 the whole area was farmed and a number of farmsteads stood on shieling sites.

15. Thirsk, J. ed, *The Agrarian History of England and Wales*, vol 4, 1967, pp 117, 149; Beresford, M. and Hurst, J. G. *Deserted Mediaeval Villages*, 1971, pp 254–60; Allen, D. 'Excavations at Hafod y Nant Criofalen, Brenig Valley, Clwyd', *Postmediaeval Archaeology*, vol 13, 1979, pp 47–57. See also Peate, I. C. *The Welsh House*, 1944, pp 142–7. Wiliam, E. *Traditional Farm Buildings in North-East Wales, 1550–1900*, 1982, dates the end of transhumance in this area as the seventeenth century or later (p 266), but notes that a group of summering houses was established in the Brenig valley as late as the sixteenth century (p 8).

16. Raistrick, A. *Malham and Malham Moor*, 1976, pp 95–101.

17. Harvey, N. *The Industrial Archaeology of Farming in England and Wales*, 1980, pp 46–7.

18. Clack, P. A. G. 'Post-mediaeval farms in Shadforth', *Transactions of the Architectural and Archaeological Society of Durham and Northumberland*, NS vol 5, 1980, pp 97–105; Peters, J. E. C. *The Development of Farm Buildings in Western Lowland Staffordshire up to 1880*, 1969, pp 17, 20–5. For upland examples of this process see Jarrett, M. G. and Wrathmell, S. 'Sixteenth and seventeenth century farmsteads; West Whelpington, Northumberland', *Agricultural History Review*, vol 25, 1977, pp 110–11; Wrathmell, S. 'Village depopulation in the seventeenth and eighteenth centuries', *Postmediaeval Archaeology*, vol 14, 1980, p 120. For lowland examples see Emery, F. *The Oxfordshire Landscape*, 1974, p 113; Reed, M. *The Buckinghamshire Landscape*, 1979, p 197; Sweetland, P. *Barns of Bredon Hill*, unpublished thesis, Birmingham School of Architecture, 1979, pp 9–10. It has been suggested that in arable areas such change was facilitated by a decline in the size of plough teams from Tudor times, presumably due to better feeding or improved stock, which reduced the need for neighbourly co-operation (Peters, J. E. C. *The Development of Farm Buildings in Western Lowland Staffordshire up to 1880*, 1969, p 21. See also Eyre, S. R. 'The curving ploughstrip and its historical implications', *Agricultural History Review*, vol 3, 1955, pp 93–4).

19. Hurst, J. G. *Agricultural History Review*, vol 9, 1961, p 129; Alcock, N. W. 'Houses in an east Devon parish', *Report and Transactions of the Devonshire Association*, vol 94, 1962, p 226; Taylor, C. *Dorset*, 1970, pp 146–7; Beresford, M. and Hurst, J. G. *Deserted Mediaeval Villages*, 1971, p 11; Mercer, E. *English Vernacular Houses*, 1975, pp 34–49; Devon County Council, *Devon's Traditional Buildings*, 1978, pp 7–8; Homes, I. 'The agricultural use of the Herefordshire house and its outbuildings', *Vernacular Architecture*, vol 9, 1978, p 12. In an area of Sussex containing a number of sixteenth- and seventeenth-century farmhouses, only one farmhouse out of sixty-three is attached to farm buildings (Caffyn, L. *A Study of Farm Buildings in Selected Parishes of East Sussex*, unpublished MA thesis, Manchester University, 1981, p 37).

20. Barley, M. W. *The English Farmhouse and Cottage*, 1961, p 119.

21. Barley, M. W. *The English Farmhouse and Cottage*, 1961, p 120.

22. Addy, S. O. *The Evolution of the English House*, 1933, p 95 for Harrison; Cook, O. *English Cottages and Farmhouses*, 1982, p 16 for Bermondsey. See also Mercer, *English Vernacular Houses*, 1975, pp 36–41.

23. Hoskins, W. G. and Finberg, H. P. R. *Devonshire Studies*, 1952, p 144.

24. In farmsteads in High Furness rebuilt between 1650 and 1710 the house usually stood apart from the farm buildings (Millward, R. *Lancashire*, 1955, p 43). For a medieval moorland longhouse settlement in which the longhouses became dwellings and separate farm buildings were built around them to form small farmsteads see Alcock, N. W., Child, P. and Laithwaite, M. 'Sanders, Lettaford. A Devon longhouse', *Devon Archaeological Society Proceedings*, vol 30, 1972, pp 227–33 (see Plate 10); Devon County Council, *Traditional Devon Buildings*, 1978, p 25. In Breconshire the first farmhouse built separately from the farm buildings dates from the seventeenth century (Jones, S. R. 'The houses of Breconshire', *Brycheiniog*, vol 11, 1965, p 86).

25. Peate, I. C. *The Welsh House*, 1944, p 59; Brunskill, R. W. 'The development of the small house in the Eden Valley', *Transactions of the Cumberland and Westmorland Antiquarian and Archaeological Society*, vol 53, 1953, p 177; National Museum of Wales, Welsh Folk Museum, *Farmhouses and Cottages in Wales*, 1972, plates 16–19; Jones, S. R. 'The houses of Breconshire', *Brycheiniog*, vol 9, 1963, pp 5–34; vol 11, 1965, pp 50–89; vol 13, 1968, pp 54–65; vol 16, 1972, pp 15–16; Alcock, N. W. 'Devonshire farmhouses. Some Dartmoor houses', *Report and Transactions of the Devonshire Association*, vol 101, 1969, pp 83–106; Jones, S. R. 'Devonshire farmhouses. Moorland and non-moorland longhouses', *Report and Transactions of the Devonshire Association*, vol 103, 1971, pp 35–71; Wiliam, E. 'Traditional buildings in Wales', *Amgueddfa*, no 15, Winter 1973, p 14 (English abstract of Welsh text); Chapman, V. 'North country farms of the moorland fringe', *Beamish One. The First Report of the North of England Open Air Museum Joint Committee*, Spring 1978, pp 53–6; Darley, G. *The National Trust Book of the Farm*, 1981, pp 57–9.

26. Barley, M. W. *The English Farmhouse and Cottage*, 1961, pp 109–10, 236–7; Spooner, G. M. ed, *Worth's Dartmoor*, 1967, pp 407–14; Alcock, N. W., Child, P. and Laithwaite, M. 'Sanders, Lettaford. A Devon longhouse', *Devon Archaeological Society Proceedings*, vol 30, 1972, pp 227–33; Hartley, M. and Ingilby, J. *Life in the Moorlands of North-East Yorkshire*, 1972, pp 1–2; Hayes, R. H. and Rutter, J. G. 'Cruckframed buildings in Ryedale and Eskdale', *Scarborough and District Archaeological Research Report no 8*, 1972; Brunskill, R. W. *The Vernacular Architecture of the Lake Counties*, 1974, pp 78–9; Jarrett, M. G. and Wrathmell, S. 'Sixteenth and seventeenth century farmsteads; West Whelpington, Northumberland', *Agricultural History Review*, vol 25, 1977, pp 108–19; Devon County Council, *Devon's Traditional Buildings*, 1978, pp 7–11; Homes, I. 'The agricultural use of the Herefordshire house and its outbuildings', *Vernacular Architecture*, vol 9, 1978, p 12; Walton, J. *Homesteads of the Yorkshire Dales*, 1979, pp 24–7. See also Weller, J. *History of the Farmstead*, 1982, pp 43–6. The division between living quarters for the farmer and his family and accommodation for livestock is found in certain two-storey Cumberland steadings of this period. These were built into the hillside and provided ground-floor housing for cattle and a first-floor home for the family (Walton, J. 'Upland houses', *Antiquity*, vol 30, 1956, pp 144–5). See also note 25 above.

27. Walton, J. 'South Pennine barns', *Architectural Review*, vol 90, October 1941, pp 122–4; Walton, J. *Homesteads of the Yorkshire Dales*, 1979, pp 37–40; Higgs, J. *The Land*, 1964, photo 92; Stell, C. 'Pennine houses. An introduction', *Folklife*, vol 3, 1965, pp 20–1; Hartley, M. and Ingilby, J. *Life and Tradition in the Yorkshire Dales*, 1968, p 13, photo 16; Hoskins, W. G. *History from the Farm*, 1970, pp 41–5, 87; Raistrick, A. *West Riding of Yorkshire*, 1970, pp 92, 96; Raistrick, A. *Old Yorkshire Dales*, 1971, p 69, which quotes from accounts of Richard Wigglesworth of Coniston for building a laithe barn in 1689; Brunskill, R. W. *Vernacular Architecture of the Lake Counties*, 1974, p 81; Rollinson, W. *Life and Tradition in the Lake District*, 1974, p 31; Mercer, E. *English Vernacular Houses*, 1975, pp 45–6; Countryside Commission, *A Study of the Hartsop Valley*, 1976, pp 22–3; Raistrick, A. *Malham and Malham Moor*, 1976, pp 81–2; Arts Council, *Traditional Farm Buildings*, 1978, p 27; Davies, N. W. I. *Barns and Barn Conversion in Cumbria*, unpublished BSc thesis, Brunel University, 1979, pp 30–3; Tyson, B. 'Low Park barn, Rydal. The reconstruction of a farm building in Westmorland in the seventeenth century', *Transactions of the Cumberland and Westmorland Antiquarian and Archaeological Society*, vol 79, 1979, pp 92–4; Darley, G. *The National Trust Book of the Farm*, 1981, pp 54–5, 58–9, 216; Brunskill, R. W. *Traditional Farm Buildings of Britain*, 1982, pp 107–8; Cook, O. *English Farmhouses and Cottages*, 1982, pp 88–90; Weller, J. *History of the Farmstead*, 1982, pp 43–6. Brunskill, R. W. 'The development of the small house in the Eden Valley', *Transactions of the Cumberland and Westmorland Antiquarian and Archaeological Society*, vol 53, 1953, pp 160–89, includes descriptions of the farmsteads of the 'statesmen', the small farmers of the area. These consisted of a house, byre, barn and loft under one roof. Examples date from 1670 to 1769 but the concentration was between 1680 and 1710, the period which saw 'the zenith and decline

of the statesman class' (p 173). House-and-byre farmsteads were common in Wales at the end of this period (Smith, P. *Houses of the Welsh Countryside*, 1975, pp 144–5, plates 46–9).

28. Walton, J. 'Upland houses', *Antiquity*, vol 30, 1956, pp 143–4; Brunskill, R. W. *The Vernacular Architecture of the Lake Counties*, 1974, pp 82–7, which gives 1735 as the first datable example of such a barn, though there may be earlier examples; Rollinson, W. *Life and Tradition in the Lake District*, 1974, p 31; Messenger, P. 'Lowther farmstead plans: a preliminary survey'. *Transactions of the Cumberland and Westmorland Antiquarian and Archaeological Association*, vol 75, 1975, pp 341–3; Davies, N. W. I. *Barns and Barn Conversions in Cumbria*, unpublished BSc thesis, Brunel University, 1979, pp 10–13 and 126 for the well-known Town End Farm barn at Troutbeck; Brunskill, R. W. *Traditional Farm Buildings of Britain*, 1982, pp 112–15. For a similar type of building in Wales in this period see Wiliam, E. *Traditional Farm Buildings in North-East Wales, 1550–1900*, 1982, pp 121–3.

29. Royal Commission on Historical Monuments, *Shielings and Bastles*, 1970, pp 61–95; Atkinson, F. *Life and Traditions in Northumberland and Durham*, 1977, pp 55–7; Brunskill, R. W. *Traditional Farm Buildings of Britain*, 1982, pp 108–9. See p 256.

30. Raglan, Lord and Fox, Sir Cyril, *Monmouthshire Houses*, pt 2, 1953, p 81 for doors. A section of a longhouse later used for draught oxen can be seen at Castle Farm Folk Museum, Marshfield, Avon. For oxhouses and stabling in this period see Peters, J. E. C. *The Development of Farm Buildings in Western Lowland Staffordshire up to 1880*, 1969, pp 110–14; Brunskill, R. W. *Vernacular Architecture of the Lake Counties*, 1974, p 78; Caffyn, L. *A Study of Farm Buildings in Selected Parishes of East Sussex*, unpublished MA thesis, Manchester University, 1981, pp 67–72; Wiliam, E. *Traditional Farm Buildings in North-East Wales*, 1982, pp 160–64.

31. Trow-Smith, R. *A History of British Livestock Husbandry to 1700*, 1957, pp 185–6.

32. Seebohm, M. F. *The Evolution of the English Farm*, 1952, pp 207, 237.

33. Tusser, T. *His Points of Good Husbandry*, Hartley, D. ed, 1931, pp 76, 141. In Devon little shelter was provided for pigs until the eighteenth century. A 1678 document refers to 'a pigges roof by the entry' (Devon County Council, *Devon's Traditional Buildings*, 1978, p 20).

34. Alcock, N. W. 'Devonshire linhays; a vernacular tradition', *Report and Transactions of the Devonshire Association*, vol 95, 1963, pp 117–30; Thirsk, J. ed., *The Agrarian History of England and Wales*, vol 4, 1967, p 750; Devon County Council, *Devon's Traditional Buildings*, 1978, pp 18–19.

35. For corn barns see Rigold, S. E. 'Some major Kentish timber barns', *Archaeologia Cantiana*, vol 81, 1967, pp 1–30; Peters, J. E. C. *The Development of Farm Buildings in Western Lowland Staffordshire to 1880*, 1969, pp 67–81; Brooksby, H. 'The houses of Radnorshire, farm buildings', *Transactions of the Radnorshire Society*, vol 43, 1973, pp 64–77; Harding, J. M. *Four Centuries of Charlwood Houses*, published by the Charlwood Society, 1976, pp 91–5; Harris, R. *Discovering Timber-framed Buildings*, 1978, pp 8–9, 58, 67–9; Reynolds, J. *The Hampshire Barn*, unpublished thesis, Architectural Association, 1978; Bailey, J. *Timberframed Buildings*, Bedfordshire, Buckinghamshire and Cambridgeshire Historic Buildings Research Group, 1979, pp 26–9; Martin, D. and Martin, B. 'Ancillary farm buildings' and 'Agriculture', *Historic Buildings in Eastern Sussex*, vol 1, nos 3 and 4, 1979, pp 59–60, 64–5 and pp 97–8 respectively; Sweetland, P. *Barns of Bredon Hill*, unpublished thesis, Birmingham School of Architecture, 1979; Caffyn, L. *A Study of Farm Buildings in Selected Parishes of East Sussex*, unpublished MA thesis, Manchester University, 1981, pp 50–65; Brunskill, R. W. *Traditional Farm Buildings of Britain*, 1982, pp 36–48; Wiliam, E. *Traditional Farm Buildings in North-East Wales, 1550–1900*, 1982, pp 102–49.

36. Brunskill, R. W. *The Vernacular Architecture of the Lake Counties*, 1974, p 80; Homes, I. 'The agricultural use of the Herefordshire house and its outbuildings', *Vernacular Architecture*, vol 9, 1978, p 14.

37. For grain storage and granaries see Alcock, N. W. 'Devonshire farmhouses. Some Dartmoor houses', *Report and Transactions of the Devonshire Association*, vol 101, 1969, p 99; Peters, J. E. C. *The Development of Farm Buildings in Western Lowland Staffordshire up to 1880*, 1969, pp 195–8; Smith, P. *Houses of the Welsh Countryside*, 1975, p 147; Dowland, C. J. 'Staddlestones at work', *Countryman*, Autumn 1976, pp 118–19; Harding, J. M. *Four Centuries of Charlwood Houses*, published by the Charlwood Society, 1976, pp 94–5; Weald and Downland Open Air Museum, *Guide*, 1976, pp 18, 21, *Guide*, 1982, pp 22–3 for 1731 granary now in the museum; Harris, R. *Discovering Timber-framed Buildings*, 1978, p 59; Reynolds, J. *The Hampshire Barn*, unpublished thesis, Architectural Association, 1978, p 4; Martin, D. and Martin, B. 'Ancillary farm buildings' and 'Agriculture', *Historic Buildings in Eastern Sussex*, vol 1, nos 3 and 4, 1979, pp 59–60 and pp 97–9 respectively; Nicholson, P. 'Wiltshire buildings; barns, granaries and staddlestones', *Wiltshire Folklife*, vol 2, no 3, Spring 1979, pp 49–55; Caffyn, L. *A Study of Farm Buildings in Selected Parishes of East Sussex*, unpublished MA thesis, Manchester University, 1981, pp 72–6, which dates the

earliest surviving granary as sixteenth century; Powell, G. H., 'Granaries on staddlestones in the Isle of Wight', *Proceedings of the Isle of Wight Archaeological Society*, vol 7, no 4, 1981, pp 259–63; Brunskill, R. W. *Traditional Farm Buildings of Britain*, 1982, pp 87–94; Wiliam, E. *Traditional Farm Buildings in North-East Wales, 1550–1900*, 1982, pp 239–45. For a granary over a cartshed, *c*1600, see Darley, G. *The National Trust Book of the Farm*, 1981, pp 80–1. Worlidge, J. *Systema Agriculturae*, 1687 (4th ed), p 217, recommended the use of staddles to protect 'binns or hutches for corn'. Farmers also used biological controls: some eighteenth-century barns, stylistically similar to a Cotswold barn that can be dated to the 1720s, include owl holes. The dated barn had a cat hole in the door; by the mid-eighteenth century cats were regarded as lucky, whereas previously they had often been feared as 'familiars' of witches. The last witch was burnt in Britain in 1722, in the same decade as the barn was built. Jones, E. L. 'The bird pests of British agriculture in recent centuries', *Agricultural History Review*, vol 20, 1972, pp 114–15).

38. Barley, M. W. *The English Farmhouse and Cottage*, 1961, p 202.
39. Barley, M. W. *The English Farmhouse and Cottage*, 1961, p 274.
40. Hoskins, W. G. *The Midland Peasant*, 1957, p 148.
41. Thirsk, J. ed, *The Agrarian History of England and Wales*, vol 4, 1967, p 106.
42. 'Reynard made a meadow', *Farmers Weekly*, 13 December 1968, p 81.
43. Addy, S. O. *The Evolution of the English House*, 1933, pp 236–9.
44. Martin, D. and Martin, B. 'Ancillary farm buildings', *Historic Buildings in Eastern Sussex*, vol 1, no 3, 1979, pp 59–69. For the cattle housing in such barns see Martin, D. and Martin, B. 'Floors in barns', *Historic Buildings in Eastern Sussex*, vol 1, no 2, 1978, pp 25–9; Caffyn, L. *A Study of Farm Buildings in Selected Parishes of East Sussex*, unpublished MA thesis, Manchester University, 1981, p 53.
45. Best, H. *Rural Economy of Yorkshire in 1641*, Surtees Society, 1857, p 137. A little earlier, Gervase Markham had recommended sheds to protect carts from 'three enemies', sun, wind and rain (quoted in Darley, G. *The National Trust Book of the Farm*, 1981, p 83) and before him Tusser had referred to 'a shed ready dight' for tumbrils and carts (Tusser, T. *His Points of Good Husbandry*, Hartley, D. ed, 1931, p 141). Practice, however, lagged behind precept. In 1663 the wealthy landowner Sir Nicholas Lechmere added a carthouse to the big barn he had built on his home farm in 1658 (Lees-Milne, J. 'Severn End, Worcestershire', *Country Life*, 24 July 1975, p 196), but an analysis of farm inventories in East Anglia dated between 1630 and 1760 found very few references to cartsheds or implement sheds (Holderness, B. A. 'Farm buildings: investment and depreciation, 1750–1870', paper given at the British Agricultural History Society Winter Conference, 1982). An analysis of 89 early eighteenth-century farming inventories in East Sussex found only four specific references to shelters for carts or implements. This, however, was apparently an improvement on previous practice; no earlier reference to such buildings was found in even the most detailed records (Martin, D. and Martin, B., 'Ancillary farm buildings', *Historic Buildings in Eastern Sussex*, vol 1, no 3, 1979, p 67). The first reference to a cartshed found in a Midland study was in 1706, but by 1760 eleven out of nineteen farms on one estate had cartsheds (Peters, J. E. C. *The Development of Farm Buildings in Western Lowland Staffordshire up to 1880*, 1969, p 187).
46. For sheep housing see Trow-Smith, R. *A History of British Livestock Husbandry to 1700*, 1957, p 245; Garnier, R. M. *History of the English Landed Interest (Modern Period)*, 1893, p 271; Thirsk, J. ed, *The Agrarian History of England and Wales*, vol 4, 1967, pp 187, 190. Kerridge, K. *The Agricultural Revolution*, 1967, refers to 'cotting' in this period (pp 52, 67, 147, 149, 240, 312–13, 321), but it is not clear if 'cotting' means folding or housing. Garnier, quoting Camden but giving no specific reference, implies that 'cotting' was a form of housing; Wright, T. *The English Dialect Dictionary*, 1898, defines 'sheepcote' as a 'sheepfold'. A wealthy Bedfordshire landowner who died in 1545 left his son advice on running his estate as a home farm, including recommendations for a flock of four hundred sheep with 'large and great cotts' (National Trust, *Willington Dovecote and Stable*, 1976). Young ewes were inwintered in the Lake District in hogg-houses (Brunskill, R. W. *Vernacular Architecture of the Lake Counties*, 1974, p 80). Whitaker, J. M. 'Factory farming', *The Times*, 23 July 1969, p 9, suggests that some of these date from the early eighteenth century.
47. Thirsk, J. ed, *The Agrarian History of England and Wales*, vol 4, 1967, p 224.
48. Briggs, M. S. *The English Farmhouse*, 1953, p 56.
49. Fussell, G. E. ed, *Robert Loder's Farm Accounts, 1610–1620*, 1936, table IV.
50. Garnier, R. M. *History of the English Landed Interest (Earliest Times to the Eighteenth Century)*, 1892, p 338. For dovecotes see *Country Life*, 23 February 1972, p 692; 13 July 1972, p 92; 2 November 1972, p 1139; Pridham, J. C. *Dove and Pigeoncotes in Worcester*, published by Hereford and Worcester County Council, 1974; Firmin, J. 'Old monuments strictly for the birds', *Farmers Weekly*, 8 August 1975, pp 82–3; *Country Life*, 24 July 1975, pp 196–7; National Trust, *Willington Dovecote and Stable*, 1976; Durham County Library Local History Publications, *Rural Durham*, 1977, pp 64–70; Devon County

Council, *Devon's Traditional Buildings*, 1978, p 20; Stainburn, I. R. *A Survey of Dovecotes in the Old County of Herefordshire*, published by Hereford and Worcester County Council, 1979; National Trust and Avoncroft Museum of Buildings, *Dovecotes*, 1980; 'Pigeons for food', *Food from the Land* card B29 published by Norfolk Heritage, 1980; Brunskill, R. W. *Traditional Farm Buildings of Britain*, 1982, pp 80–6; Wiliam, E, *Traditional Farm Buildings in North-East Wales, 1550–1900*, 1982, pp 250–4; Fowler, P. *Farms in England*, 1983, plates 91–5. A pigeonhouse at Garsington Manor, Oxfordshire, is ascribed to the seventeenth century, but may be earlier. It stands in the garden described in Aldous Huxley's *Crome Yellow* which parodied rather than disguised the Bloomsbury guests of Lady Ottoline Morrell (Venison, T. 'Enigma in an Italian manner', *Country Life*, 18 March 1982, p 692). For the use in the early seventeenth century of the soil of dovecotes as a source of saltpetre for the remarkably inappropriate manufacture of gunpowder see Sheldrick, A. W. 'The dovehouses of Hertfordshire and the saltpetre industry', *Hertfordshire Countryside*, vol 24, May 1970, pp 28–9. A pleasing and highly individual development of the pigeonhouse produced *c*1700 a three-storey building which ingeniously used changes in ground level to provide housing for pigs on the bottom floor, hens on the floor above them and pigeons on the top floor (Kent County Council Education Committee, *Traditional Buildings in Kent*, no 1, 1980, pp 9–11).

51. Peters, J. E. C. *The Development of Farm Buildings in Western Lowland Staffordshire up to 1880*, 1969, pp 49, 51. See also Davies, D. C. G. *Historic Farmstead and Farmhouse Types of the Shropshire Region*, unpublished MA thesis, Manchester University, 1952, pp 89, 91, 105; Hoskins, W. G. *History from the Farm*, 1970, p 87; Newton, R. *The Northumberland Landscape*, 1972, p 139 for linear Whiteley Shield Farm, probably seventeenth century; Hartley, M. and Ingilby, J. *Life and Tradition in the Yorkshire Dales*, 1968, p 16 for 1635 linear example; Brunskill, R. W. *The Vernacular Architecture of the Lake Counties*, 1974, pp 79–81, which includes L-pattern examples; Messenger, P. 'Lowther farmstead plans: a preliminary survey', *Transactions of the Cumberland and Westmorland Antiquarian and Archaeological Association*, vol 75, 1975, pp 330, 335, 338 which includes L-pattern examples; Clack, P. A. G. 'Post-mediaeval farms in Shadforth', *Transactions of the Architectural and Archaeological Society of Durham and Northumberland*, NS vol 5, 1980, pp 97–105 for linear farmsteads; Fowler, P. *Farms in England*, 1983, plate 11 for linear farmstead. See also Weller, J. *History of the Farmstead*, 1982, pp 54–61.

52. Smith, P. *Houses of the Welsh Countryside*, 1975, p 147; Wiliam, E. *Traditional Farm Buildings in North-East Wales, 1550–1900*, 1982, p 39.

53. Hoskins, W. G. 'Some old Devon bartons', *Country Life*, 22 September 1950, p 913–14; Whitlock, R. *A Short History of Farming*, 1965, pp 197–8; Essex County Council, Essex Record Office Publication 46, *The Face of Essex*, 1967, plate 12; Beresford, M. and Hurst, J. G. *Deserted Mediaeval Villages*, 1971, p 112; Fox, L. *Mary Arden's House*, 1972, pp 2–3; McRae, S. G. and Burnham, C. P. *The Rural Landscape of Kent*, 1973, p 192. Wiliam, E. 'Farm buildings in the Vale of Clwyd, 1550–1800', *Folklife*, vol 18, 1973, p 43, describes an early and substantial example of a 'courtyard' farmstead, Bachegraig, Tremeirchen, Flintshire (modern Clwyd), built by Sir Richard Clough, a wealthy merchant, in 1567; Smith, P. *Houses of the Welsh Countryside*, 1975, p 147; Weller, J. *History of the Farmstead*, 1982, pp 47–54. A seventeenth-century example of a courtyard farmstead survives at Harnage Grange, Shropshire (Institute of Industrial Archaeology, 'Recording the farmstead' conference, October 1983).

54. Sheldon, L. 'Devon barns', *Report and Transactions of the Devonshire Association*, vol 64, 1932, p 391; Thirsk, J. ed, *The Agrarian History of England and Wales*, vol 4, 1967, p 75; Thacker, D. M. D. 'Country cider', *Folklife*, vol 6, 1968, pp 108–9; Devon County Council, *Devon's Traditional Buildings*, 1978, p 22; Quinion, M. B. *A Drink in its Time*, 1979, published by the Museum of Cider, pp 6–7; Peters, J. E. C. *Discovering Traditional Farm Buildings*, 1981, pp 54–5.

55. For hop-drying buildings see Parker, H. H. *The Hop Industry*, 1934, pp 13, 27, 30, 76–7 with 1750 quotation on p 30; Burgess, A. H. 'Hopdrying', *Agriculture*, vol 46, 1939, pp 524–5; Gaut, R. C. *A History of Worcestershire Agriculture*, 1939, p 170; Locke, P. E. 'Landscape with oasts', *House of Whitbread*, vol 19, no 1, Spring 1959, pp 17–20, including reference to a surviving 'barn' type of oast; Burgess, A. H. *Hops*, 1964, pp 3–6; McRae, S. G. and Burnham, C. P. *The Rural Landscape of Kent*, 1973, p 193; Cronk, A. 'Oasts in Kent and east Sussex', *Archaeologia Cantiana*, vol 94, 1978, pp 99–110; Homes, I. 'The agricultural use of the Herefordshire house and its outbuildings', *Vernacular Architecture*, vol 9, 1978, pp 12–13; Martin, D. and Martin, B. 'Ancillary farm buildings', *Historic Buildings in Eastern Sussex*, vol 1, no 3, 1979, pp 61–3; Darley, G. *The National Trust Book of the Farm*, 1982, p 184. For two surviving oasthouses of this period see Caffyn, L. *A Study of Farm Buildings in Selected Parishes of East Sussex*, unpublished MA thesis, Manchester University, 1981, pp 79–81.

56. Barley, M. W. *The English Farmhouse and Cottage*, 1961, p 59; Royal Commission on

Historical Monuments, *Shielings and Bastles*, 1970, pp 44–7, 52–3; Brunskill, R. W. *Vernacular Architecture of the Lake Counties*, 1974, p 80; Rollinson, W. *Life and Tradition in the Lake District*, 1974, p 31; Brunskill, R. W. *Illustrated Handbook of Vernacular Architecture*, 1978, p 163; Brunskill, R. W. *Traditional Farm Buildings of Britain*, 1982, pp 93–5; Weller, J. *History of the Farmstead*, 1982, p 146; Wiliam, E. 'A guide to old farm buildings', *The Re-use of Redundant Farm Buildings*, published by the Welsh Office Agriculture Department, 1982, p 24; Fowler, P. *Farms in England*, 1983, plate 66.

57. Williams, E. H. D. 'Corn drying kilns', *Proceedings of the Somerset Archaeological and Natural History Society*, vol 116, 1972, pp 101–3; Williams, E. H. D. 'Curing chambers and domestic drying kilns', *Proceedings of the Somerset Archaeological and Natural History Society*, vol 120, 1976, pp 57–61.

58. Tull, J. *Horse-hoeing Husbandry*, Cobbett, W. ed, 1824, pp 215–16.

59. Trow-Smith, R. *A History of British Livestock Husbandry to 1700*, 1957, p 197; Stout, A. 'Three centuries of London cow-keeping', *Farmers Weekly*, 18 August 1978, pp v–xiii.

60. Mingay, G. F. *English Landed Society in the Eighteenth Century*, 1963, pp 233–4. For descriptions of materials in particular areas as an introduction to the agricultural use made of them see Peters, J. E. C. *The Development of Farm Buildings in Western Lowland Staffordshire up to 1880*, 1969, pp 1–5; Ebbage, S. *Barnes and Granaries*, 1977, pp 21–42, (Norfolk); Devon County Council, *Devon's Traditional Buildings*, 1978, pp 1–6; Reynolds, J. *The Hampshire Barn*, unpublished thesis, Architectural Association, 1978, pp 6–10; Sweetland, P. *Barns of Bredon Hill*, unpublished thesis, Birmingham School of Architecture, 1979, pp 34–9; Caffyn, L. *A Study of Farm Buildings in Selected Parishes of East Sussex*, unpublished MA thesis, Manchester University, 1981, pp 83–90, 95; Wiliam, E. *Traditional Farm Buildings in North-East Wales, 1550–1900*, 1982, pp 61–101. For a Cornish farmstead, probably Elizabethan, built 'from top to bottom' of local slate see Hoskins, W. G. *One Man's England*, 1982, p 52.

61. Bundles of faggots tied with withies were laid on rough cross-beams and thatched, thus making any carpentered roof structure unnecessary (Smedley, N. *Life and Tradition in Suffolk and North-East Essex*, 1976, p 20; Peters, J. E. C. 'The solid thatch roof', *Vernacular Architecture*, vol 8, 1977, p 825; Council of British Archaeology, Group 9, *Newsletter 10*, 1980, p 95; *Newsletter 12*, 1982, pp 107–8; Steane, J. M. ed, *Cogges, a Museum of Farming in the Oxfordshire Countryside*, published by the Oxfordshire County Council Department of Museum Services, 1978, pp 22–3.)

62. Hartley, M. and Ingilby, J. *Life and Tradition in the Yorkshire Dales*, 1968, pp 107–10. See also Newton, R. *The Northumberland Landscape*, 1972, p 138; Allen, D. 'Excavations at Hafod y Nant Criafolen, Brenig Vallen, Clwyd', *Postmediaeval Archaeology*, vol 13, 1979, plate 1; Walton, J. *Homesteads of the Yorkshire Dales*, 1979, pp 17, 53. The withy ring for tethering cows (Hartley, M. and Ingilby, J. *Life and Tradition in the Yorkshire Dales*, 1968, p 30), also illustrates the use of local materials for the fitting of farm buildings.

63. For an example of Roman numerals cut on barn timbers for the guidance of the erectors of 'prefabricated' timbers brought ready-cut to the site see Hughes, W. 'Jo moves into a barn', *Farmers Weekly*, 8 August, 1978, p 89. Such numerals can be seen on the crucks of the former longhouse at Castle Farm Folk Museum, Marshfield, Avon.

64. Best, H. *Rural Economy in Yorkshire in 1641*, Surtees Society, 1857, pp 47, 107. Similarly, the Stryt Lydan barn in the Welsh Folk Museum, which dates partly from *c*1550, and partly from *c*1600, was built of timber framing, roofed with wheat thatch and clad with panels of riven oak wattling. Cholstrey barn in the Avoncroft Museum of Buildings, which probably dates from the sixteenth century was built of timber framing, split oak pales woven between staves, and stone from a local quarry for the plinth wall (*Cholstrey Barn*, published by the Avoncroft Museum of Buildings, 1980).

65. 'Reynard made a meadow', *Farmers Weekly*, 13 December 1968, p 81.

66. Barley, M. W. *The English Farmhouse and Cottage*, 1961, p 209. For case studies of the use of local materials see Tyson, B. 'Rydal Park Farm. The reconstruction of a farm building in Westmorland in the seventeenth century', *Transactions of the Cumberland and Westmorland Antiquarian and Archaeological Society*, vol 79, 1979, pp 86–97, and Tyson, B. 'Rydal Hall Farm. The development of a Westmorland farmstead before 1700', *Transactions of the Cumberland and Westmorland Antiquarian and Archaeological Society*, vol 80, 1980, pp 113–16. Agreeably, the materials used included 'a great cheesecake', ale and five pounds of of tobacco for a celebration 'for all ye bearers' on the day 'ye corne barn was raised', 28 June 1670 (p 116).

67. Millward, R. *Lancashire*, 1955, p 43 for Furness Abbey; Reynolds, J. *The Hampshire Barn*, unpublished thesis, Architectural Association, 1978, pp 6, 20; and Hampshire County Council Planning Department, *Saving Old Farm Buildings*, 1982, p 3; *Country Life*, 25 June 1970, p 1262 for Toddington barn. It has been suggested that moulded timber trusses in a

Dorset barn believed to have been built about 1545 came from nearby Milton Abbey at the Dissolution of the Monasteries (Oswald, A. 'The story of three Dorset houses', *Country Life*, 26 July 1962, pp 201–2). For other examples of the use of ecclesiastical materials see *Country Life*, 15 April 1971, p 887; Brill, E. *Life and Tradition in the Cotswolds*, 1973, p 29; Wiliam, E. 'Farm buildings in the Vale of Clwyd, 1550–1880', *Folklife*, vol 2, 1973, p 45; Cronk, A. 'Oasts in Kent and Sussex', *Archaeologia Cantiana*, vol 94, 1978, p 107; Cook, O. *English Cottages and Farmhouses*, 1982, p 72; Fowler, P. *Farms in England*, 1983, plate 63. The Bishop's Palace at Charing in Kent is now a barn, and the buildings of Castle Farm Folk Museum, Marshfield, Avon, include reused stones probably from a nearby chapel which was listed in a survey of 1584 but has now disappeared. Over two hundred years after the Reformation Loudon noted that the conversion of monastic buildings to agricultural purposes, 'though very uncommon in Britain, is yet frequent on the Continent' and regretted that such 'large buildings, erected at enormous expense' should not be converted to useful purposes when no longer required by their original occupants (Loudon, J. C. *An Encyclopaedia of Cottage, Farm and Village Architecture*, 1836, p 567). Historically, his regret was misplaced: English farmers were well aware of the possibilities of abandoned church buildings long before he wrote, though they generally used them as quarries to be exploited rather than as buildings to be adapted.

68. Tyson, B. 'Low Park Barn, Rydal. The reconstruction of a farm building in Westmorland in the seventeenth century', *Transactions of the Cumberland and Westmorland Antiquarian and Archaeological Association*, vol 79, 1979, p 90; Barley, M. W. *The English Farmhouse and Cottage*, 1961, p 209 for Lincolnshire example. The date of 1685 on a Sussex barn 'may refer either to the date when built or possibly to a reconstruction with timber from another building' (Armstrong, J. R. 'Sullington Great Barn', *Parish Magazine of Storrington, Sullington and Thakenham*, June 1981, p 18). See also Smith, P. *Houses of the Welsh Countryside*, 1975, plate 17; Raistrick, A. *Malham and Malham Moor*, 1976, p 14; Price, E. G. 'Survivals of the monastic estate of Frocester', *Bristol and Gloucestershire Archaeological Society Transactions*, vol 98, 1980, p 72. The roof of a stable at Castle Farm Folk Museum, Marshfield, Avon, probably built in the eighteenth century, includes reused cruck timbers from a building which has now disappeared. For the reuse of old timbers in a seventeenth-century cowhouse see Fowler, P. *Farms in England*, 1983, plate 76.

69. Walton, J. 'The timberwork of English farm buildings', *Country Life*, 19 June 1942, p 1181; Charles, F. W. B. *Mediaeval Cruck Building and its Derivatives*, 1967, p vii, dismisses the belief in ships' timbers in barns as a myth, possibly recalling the time when rivers and streams were used for floating timber down from upland forests. However, the use of timbers from old ships on farms near harbours or rivers seems not improbable in an age of shrinking forests and growing demands for wood, and Defoe refers to farm buildings in the Yarmouth and Cromer area made of 'old planks, beams . . . the wrecks of ships and ruins of mariners' and merchants' fortunes' (quoted by Darley, G. *The National Trust Book of the Farm*, 1981, p 160). Only one well-documented example, however, is known. This is the famous seventeenth-century barn at Old Jordans in Buckinghamshire (personal communications from the Librarians of the Forestry Commission, the Forest Products Research Laboratory, the Timber Research and Development Association and the National Maritime Museum). This barn is certainly built of ships' timbers though, sadly, it is equally certain that they are not, as has been claimed, the timbers of the *Mayflower* (Harris, R. *The Finding of the Mayflower*, 1920; Horrocks, J. W. 'The Mayflower', *Mariner's Mirror*, vol 8, 1922, pp 2–9, 81–8, 140–7, 236–43, 354–62). An Oxfordshire pigeonhouse ascribed to the seventeenth century uses 'salt-hardened timbers form ships of an earlier period' (Venison, T. 'Enigma in an Italian manner', *Country Life*, 18 March 1982, p 692.) Raistrick, A. *Malham and Malham Moor*, 1976, p 14, mentions but does not quote 'records and proofs' that old ships' timbers were used in the Dales.

70. In the seventeenth century the Martindales, a yeoman family in Lancashire, built a new house for themselves but temporarily moved back to the old house and used the new one as a barn 'to furnish more stowage for corn'. They finally built a new stone house, continued to use the second house as a barn and demolished the original house (Campbell, M. *The English Yeoman*, 1960, pp 228–9). Certain semi-agricultural buildings mentioned in a Wiltshire survey in 1631–2 were possibly medieval houses partly converted to cowhouses or stables (Hoskins, W. G. *The Midland Peasant*, 1957, pp 287–8). The conversion of some old cottages to barns was noted in a Yorkshire survey of 1603 (Brooks, S. D. *A History of Grassington*, 1979, p 29). A longhouse at Castle Farm Folk Museum, Marshfield, Avon, was converted to an oxhouse and stable some time after the middle of the sixteenth century. The dates of conversion of one medieval hall house to the 'Old Barn' at Wheeler Street, near Headcorn, Kent, and another in Oxfordshire to a barn (Morrey, M. T. and Smith, J. T. 'The Great Barn, Lewknor. The architectural evidence', *Oxoniensia*, vol 38, 1973, pp 338–45) are not known. For a late medieval house which ceased to be inhabited in the seventeeth century and was later converted first into a stable or cowhouse and later into an oasthouse and

is still used for farm storage see Burchess, M. and Crawley, K. 'The Hall House at Romden', *Traditional Kent Buildings*, no 3, 1983, pp 4–10, published by Kent County Council. See also Brooksby, H. 'Houses of Radnorshire – farm buildings', *Transactions of the Radnorshire Society*, vol 43, 1973, p. 75; Cook, O. *English Cottages and Farmhouses*, 1982, p 72; Fowler, P. *Farms in England*, 1983, plate 81. A section of a longhouse later used for draught oxen can be seen at Castle Farm Folk Museum, Marshfield, Avon.

71. Thirsk, J. ed, *The Agrarian History of England and Wales*, vol 4, 1967, p 723. 'With some overlapping of the cruck tradition [the aisled barn] was the standard farm building in the Pennines before 1750' (Clarke, D. W. 'Pennine aisled barns', *Vernacular Architecture*, vol 4, 1973, pp 25–6). Crucks continued to be used in Devon in barn construction 'until at least the end of the seventeenth century' (Devon County Council, *Devon's Traditional Buildings*, 1978, p 18). Cholstrey barn in the Avoncroft Museum of Buildings, Worcestershire, which probably dates from the sixteenth century, was a late example of this type of construction in the area. *Cholstrey Barn*, 1980, published by the Museum includes other local examples of cruck barns. In Hampshire, the last known cruck barn was built in the late sixteenth century; in Oxfordshire all true crucks date from before 1550; in Yorkshire most cruck barns date from the sixteenth or early seventeenth centuries (Reynolds, J. *The Hampshire Barn*, unpublished thesis, Architectural Association, 1978, p 21; Wood-Taylor, B. *Traditional Domestic Architecture of the Banbury Region*, 1963, p 228; Ryder, P. F. *Mediaeval Buildings of Yorkshire*, 1982, p 148). In the west of Radnorshire (part of modern Powys) crucks may have been used in barn construction until the early eighteenth century, though in the east they had by that time 'long been superseded' by framed construction (Brooksby, H. 'The houses of Radnorshire – farm buildings', *Transactions of the Radnorshire Society*, vol 43, 1973, p 65).

72. Hoskins, W. G. *The Midland Peasant*, 1957, p 284.

73. Wiliam, E. *Traditional Farm Buildings in North-East Wales, 1550–1900*, 1982, p 156.

74. Williams, E. H. D. and Gilson, R. D. 'Base crucks in Somerset and allied roof forms', *Proceedings of Somerset Archaeological and Natural History Society*, vol 125, 1981, pp 65–6.

75. Briggs, M. S. *The English Farmhouse*, 1953, pp 85–6; Hussey, C. 'Heronden, Kent', *Country Life*, 11 August 1960, pp 285–6; Thirsk, J. ed, *The Agrarian History of England and Wales*, vol 4, 1967, p 723; McRae, S. G. and Burnham, C. P. *The Rural Landscape of Kent*, 1973, pp 192–3; Henderson, J. B. 'The eighteenth century dairy farmsteads of Appletree Hundred', *Derbyshire Miscellany*, vol 7, no 5, 1976, p 232; Essex County Council, *The Essex Countryside, Historic Barns*, 1978, p 17; Reynolds, J. *The Hampshire Barn*, unpublished thesis, Architectural Association, 1978, pp 22–3, also pp 7, 20 for brick infilling of timber-framed barns. In East Sussex, however, where flint and timber were plentiful, brick was not regularly used until the eighteenth century (Caffyn, L. *A Study of Farm Buildings in Selected Parishes of East Sussex*, unpublished MA thesis, Manchester University, 1981, p 88.) For the use of brickwork to form dates on barns see Fowler, P. *Farms in England*, 1983, plate 54 (1666), and Pitford, F. P. *The Book of Bere Regis*, privately printed by the Dorset Publishing Co, 1978, p 12 (1748).

76. Wiliam, E. *Traditional Farm Buildings in North-East Wales, 1550–1900*, 1982, p 73. The substantial and highly exceptional courtyard farmstead at Bachegraig, Tremeirchion, Flintshire (modern Clwyd), built by Sir William Clough about 1567, was the earliest brick farmstead in Wales and one of the earliest in Britain (Wiliam, E. 'Traditional farm buildings in Wales', *Amgueddfa*, no 15, Winter 1973, p 13). Bricks were used for barns in Shropshire as early as 1700 (Weller, J. B. *Farm Buildings of Shropshire before 1837*, 1952, p 6–7, unpublished, kindly lent by author.)

77. Raglan, Lord and Fox, Sir Cyril, *Monmouthshire Houses*, pt 2, 1953, p 100. For another local account of the same general process see Davies, D. C. G. *Historic Farmstead and Farmhouse Types in the Shropshire Region*, unpublished MA thesis, Manchester University, 1952, pp 65–6.

78. For local examples of change to more durable materials during this period see Brooksby, H. 'The houses of Radnorshire – farm buildings', *Transactions of the Radnorshire Society*, vol 43, 1973, p 64 (stone instead of timber); Williams, M. *The South Wales Landscape*, 1975, p 205 (increased use of stone, though this was due to shortage of timber); Countryside Commission, *A Study of the Hartsop Valley*, 1976, p 6 (stone and slate instead of clay, timber and thatch); Raistrick, A. *Buildings of the Yorkshire Dales*, 1976, p 43 (slates instead of thatch); Martin, D. and Martin, B. 'Wall framing in barns', *Historic Buildings in Eastern Sussex*, vol 1, no 1, 1977, pp 12–18 (weather-boarding in place of wattle-and-daub); Wiliam, E. *Traditional Farm Buildings in North-East Wales, 1550–1900*, 1982, pp 102–3.

79. Brooksby, H. 'The houses of Radnorshire – farm buildings', *Transactions of the Radnorshire Society*, vol 43, 1973, p 75.

80. Laurence, E. *The Duty and Office of a Land Steward*, 1731, p 176.

81. Tyson, B. 'Construction schedules for some seventeenth century farm buildings in Cumbria', *Postmediaeval Archaeology*, vol 15, 1981, pp 219–24.

# 4 THE AGRICULTURAL REVOLUTION: THE AGRARIAN PHASE, 1750–1820

### Reclamation and Enclosure

The Agricultural Revolution was a vast and incoherent movement which sprawled across most of our countryside and more than a century of our history. It changed alike crops and stock, the systems and equipment of farming and much of the physical landscape itself; and in many areas it created the form and pattern of the farmsteads we see today. It did not, of course, begin neatly in the middle of the eighteenth century. Indeed, many of the improvements traditionally ascribed to the reign of George III were apparent in the previous hundred years. But the later Hanoverians developed and expanded them with a new urgency and more drastic consequences, for the times were demanding.

On the one hand, population was rising rapidly. In the 1750s there were over 6 million people in England and Wales; by 1801, the date of the first census, nearly 9 million, and by 1821 12 million. Further, a growing proportion of these new consumers were concentrated in towns of a size and number unknown in earlier ages. By the turn of the century, for instance, London alone offered a market of nearly a million people. There was no precedent for increases of this scale at this speed.

On the other hand, the most obvious traditional way of increasing the supply of food was now failing, for the reclamation of new farmland from forest, marsh or hill was nearing its practicable end. The men of the time continued the work of their ancestors energetically, winning, it has been estimated, 2 to 3 million acres, more than a twentieth of the entire land surface of the country, from the surviving waste. But by the end of this period little virgin land worth cultivating remained. In 1816, the Duke of Portland began a huge irrigation scheme in the Nottinghamshire sands; in 1820, John Knight started his epic attack on Exmoor Forest; and the extreme physical difficulties they overcame showed clearly that they were winning the last exploitable reserves of the ancient waste.

The alternative to more farming was better farming. In the hills this meant the steady decline of transhumance and the replacement of summer grazings for cattle by permanent farms. In northern England, seasonal migration to the uplands ceased in this period and many of the shielings were converted to steadings for the new farms. The system left as relics the remains of deserted shielings and the more recent stackstands; dry, level platforms, surrounded by a bank or ditch, for the storage of winter fodder, which were built in the eighteenth and early nineteenth centuries in the intermediate stages of reclamation when the pastures were first grazed all the year round. It also left its traces in placenames. The shepherd's cottage at Batailshieling in the Usway Valley in Northumberland was originally the summer home of Henry Bataille in the thirteenth century, while the Norse element 'erg', meaning summer pastures, is found in Hawkshead, which was once Hawkr's shieling, and in Sholver, which was once Skolg's shieling; and 'booth' in Derbyshire and Lancashire probably recalls herdsmen's summer settlements which later became permanent farms.[1]

In the Welsh uplands, most of the traditional seasonal cattle grazings were gradually occupied all the year round by the flocks of sheep which supplied the mills of the Industrial Revolution. So the summer dwellings of the *hafod* system were replaced by sheepfolds in which the flocks which grazed the mountain pastures in common were collected and segregated.[2] Some of the old summering houses were converted into permanent farmsteads which often preserved the word *hafod* in their names, but many were abandoned, 'left to the sheep, the mists, the whistling winds and the memory of a way of life departed'.[3]

In the arable lowlands, however, the most obvious way of increasing production was the more general use of certain innovations already established on advanced farms: on the one hand, a new implement, the drill, on the other, new grasses, clovers and root crops for feeding livestock. The drill sowed seeds in rows, which allowed hand-hoeing and horse-hoeing between them, thus enabling the farmer for the first time to control weeds on land that carried a crop. This ended the necessity for the wasteful bare fallow and made possible the development of new and more productive rotations. The new fodder crops, of course, greatly increased the number of livestock that farms could carry. Less obviously, they also opened new possibilities of improving the quality of livestock. Previously, the prevailing low level of nutrition had concealed the genetic capacity of farm animals. But now improved feeding enabled the farmer 'to assess the true, unrestricted potentialities of his stock . . . and perpetuate those desirable traits which had hitherto lain under the cloak of mediocrity'.[4] It was no accident that the breeder, Bakewell, was one of the major figures of this period.

These innovations offered the arable farmer improved rotations and the stock farmer great scope for selective breeding as well as larger and healthier flocks and herds. But the new crop rotations demanded radical changes in the traditional open-field cropping systems, while selective breeding required a degree of control over the movement and mating of livestock which was incompatible with communal grazing. The old order was considerably more adaptable and progressive in methods and organisation than was formerly believed, and the enclosure of open-field ploughland and common into individually managed holdings had been a continuing agricultural theme since the Middle Ages. But improvement was slow, the needs of the time pressing and opportunities tempting. So the change came in the more drastic form of land distribution which we call the Parliamentary enclosure movement.

The purpose of this movement was the replacement of the inherited farming system by one which allowed greater and easier exploitation of the new possibilities. Its principal instruments were, legally, Acts of Parliament authorising the re-allocation of land, and, physically, the hedges which divided new farm from new farm and new field from new field. Its outcome was the farming pattern we know today.

In the early years of this period, when the movement was beginning in earnest, the typical farm in much of lowland England consisted of arable strips scattered in the open-fields and grazing rights on the stubbles and on common land. Law, custom and physical necessity bound the farmer in inescapable partnership with his fellow villagers. Sixty years later, when the movement was nearing its end, the typical farm consisted of a compact holding of hedged fields farmed as the individual owner or occupier thought best.

## Landlords, Tenants and Farm Buildings

The leaders of this rural revolution were the landed aristocrats and gentry and the rising class of professional men who served them as advisers and managers. They were also the propagandists who, in their efforts to hasten and extend the benefits of the new farming methods, produced the mass of pamphlets, manuals, accounts of travels and experiences, and varied publications by farming societies which form the first considerable body of specialised agricultural literature in our history. Typically, the Board of Agriculture, which was founded in 1793 and dissolved in 1822, was primarily a State-financed information bureau, and its main memorial is a magnificent and comprehensive series of county reports in which its officials gave 'general views' on agricultural practice and developments in their particular areas. The tradition thus established continued and from the later eighteenth century onwards the agricultural industry tells its own history in its own contemporary publications.

One of the constant themes of the new literature in this period was the planning and construction of farm buildings. For this there was an obvious general reason. The new farms created by reclamation or enclosure needed new farmsteads, the old farmsteads needed extension and improvement to meet the demands which agricultural change thrust on them. Consequently, building and rebuilding became a major preoccupation of the farming industry. Indeed, this period is the first agricultural age which has left us a comprehensive and readily identifiable structural legacy. But there was also a more particular reason for the increasing interest of landowners and their agents in the buildings of the farm. By this time, the landlord and tenant system dominated the countryside and the varied arrangements of earlier times were hardening into various forms of the familiar division of functions whereby the landlord, in return for a cash rent, provided the land and its fixed equipment which the tenant farmer stocked and worked. The erection and maintenance of farm buildings was now the prerogative of the landlord, and therefore among the main responsibilities of his agent.

In Hanoverian times, therefore, few farmers owned the farms they cultivated. They leased the land and the buildings on it from landowners. The terms of agreement between the two partners in agriculture varied in detail from area to area, from estate to estate, but they all assumed the distinction between the provider and the user of farm buildings.[5] In practice, tenants who enjoyed little security in law but a good deal in practice sometimes erected buildings at their own cost, trusting the landlord would not give them notice until they had recovered the value of their investment. Bakewell, for instance, was prepared to build new sheds and convert an old barn for livestock at his own expense.[6] But such convenient arrangements did not alter the accepted principle. The advantages of a system which divided the heavy burden of raising agricultural capital were obvious. So, less agreeably, were its disadvantages, for it failed to ensure any necessary connection between the needs of the farm, as identified by the man who worked it, and the ability or willingness of the landowner to meet them.

In general, of course, expenditure on farm buildings depended on the fortunes of agriculture. But expenditure on any particular farmstead depended on the policy, resources and personality of a particular landlord. And a landlord might be rich or poor, wise or foolish; he might employ a shrewd agriculturist or an attorney ignorant of farming matters to manage his estate, he might or might not have the estate staff, the home-produced bricks and the home-grown timber to undertake building work on his own account as he wished.[7] At one end of the scale were such wealthy and progressive magnates as the Duke of Bedford, the Duke of Northumberland and Coke of Holkham, at the other were backwoods squires, idlers and wastrels.[8] Between such extremes existed a mass of men of varying means and different outlooks, including some who preferred appearance to utility.[9] All these differences were reflected in the buildings of the farms for which they were responsible. Significantly the author of the first substantial treatise on farm buildings felt justified in referring on the first page to farmers who declared that 'they would willingly pay 5 per cent or more on expenses laid out on commodious buildings, over and above the rent of the farm, than occupy for nothing those they at present possess', and reminding landowners that good buildings attracted good tenants.[10]

## Home Farms and Model Farms

An interesting byproduct of the system was the home farm. Few landlords farmed commercially on any considerable scale. But many kept a farm in hand for prestige, pleasure, household supplies and, possibly, profit. They also often intended these farms, at least in theory, to provide an example of progressive farming to their tenants, hence the term and sometimes the name of Model Farm. They equipped these farms with appropriate steadings, sometimes including spectacular buildings designed not by their agents, who were generally responsible for the buildings on their estates, but by architects, including some from the outside world of fashion and elegance, notably Soane and Wyatt. Such steadings and buildings, however, were exceptional, the prerogative of wealthy landowners. At their best, they served the substantial acreages of the home farms in the grand manner though at a high cost; at their worst, they met the criteria of the landscape gardener rather than the farmer.[11]

## New Farms, New Farmsteads

Some of the land reclaimed from the uncultivated waste was added to existing holdings. But most of it was divided into new farms and equipped with new farmsteads, thus continuing the system of isolated farms which had long been familiar in the hillier, pastoral areas of the north and west, where environment favoured them and history had established them. In Northumberland, for example, Lord Delaval in the later eighteenth century reclaimed 7,000 acres of upland and equipped them with 'thirteen solid grey stone farmsteads'; in

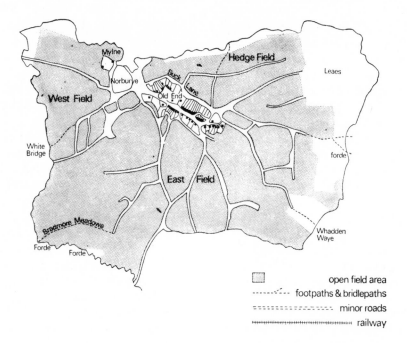

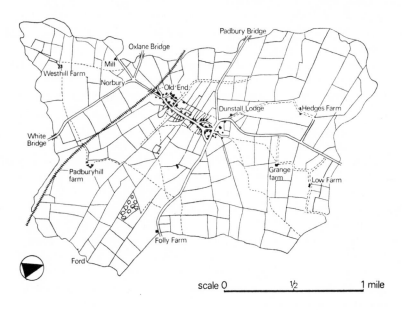

9   The effects of Hanoverian enclosure: (above) The Open Field parish of Padbury in Buckinghamshire, from a map of 1591; (below) the parish today, showing the outlying farmsteads built after the enclosure of 1796 (Based on Beresford, M. W. and Joseph, J. K. S., *Mediaeval England, An Aerial Survey 1958*, pp30, 33, 256–7) (*The Warden and Fellows of All Souls College, Cambridge University Press, Professor M. W. Beresford*)

Cumberland, the enclosure of the common grazings in the Nicol Forest area and their division among farmers with grazing rights produced 'many medium-sized farms'; in mid-Wales conifer shelter-belts marked the sites of new farms created after the enclosure between 1815 and 1818 of the Great Forest of Brecon; and 1,100ft (330m) high on the Yorkshire uplands the massive steading of Cordilleras Farm, created after the enclosure of Marske Moor in 1809 and worked until requisitioned by the army during the Second World War, still stands against a background of seemingly endless moors as 'a large and lonely landmark' and 'one of the finest testimonials to enclosing zeal which the north of England produced'. As it was in the hills, so it was in the wetlands; during the drainage of the Somerset Levels from the 1770s onwards, farmsteads were built away from the existing villages to serve the new farms on the reclaimed land. The reclamation of the Mendip Hills, where between 1771 and 1813 some 24,000 acres of rough grazings were converted to enclosed farmland, served by some forty farmsteads built during or shortly after this period, provides a well-documented example of this general process.[12]

In the open-field areas, however, the new needs created a radically new pattern of settlement. Traditionally, the lowland farmsteads clustered in the villages from which the farmers went out to their daily work on their scattered strips. But the compact farms created by the enclosures required farmsteads standing on their own land. Distances for men and stock and haulage were shorter, movement was simpler, control and inspection easier. The advantages were manifest. Indeed, they were among the main reasons for the enclosures, and those responsible for the new order naturally sought the maximum advantage from it. And so, as the years of George III's reign passed and more and more parishes were enclosed, new farmsteads appeared among the newly hedged fields which replaced the old patchwork of arable strips and common grazings[13] (see Fig 9).

The benefits of this replanning of the countryside were a common theme of the Board of Agriculture's surveyors who toured their counties between 1793 and 1815 to compile the series of county reports which give us the first systematic account of the farm buildings of England and Wales. They continually contrasted the traditional village steadings separated from their distant fields with the new steadings, such as those built by Jonathan Ackom of Wiseton in Nottinghamshire and the Rev Mr Lloyd of Aston in Shropshire, 'in a centrical part of the farm'.[14] The point is well illustrated by the criteria for siting a farmstead given by the Board's surveyor for Carmarthen and Pembroke, now in Dyfed, in 1794 and applauded by his successor in 1814.[15] Water inevitably came first, for it was still easier to take the farmstead to the water than water to the farmstead –

significantly, his colleague in Wiltshire noted that the lack of water in his county helped to maintain the old system of farmsteads 'crowded in villages'.[16] Shelter, a general need of all farmsteads but a particular need of farmsteads sited in the treeless expanses of former open-fields or common grazings, came next: in the more exposed areas trees were frequently planted round the homestead. Then came 'centricity', the need for the farmstead to stand in the middle of the fields it served.

The enclosures offered the first general opportunity since the original settlement of re-siting farm buildings in positions convenient for the working of the farm, and there were many reasons why the farmstead should be convenient to its fields, few why it should be near a road. The farmer was concerned greatly with 'dispatch in conveying home the crops and carrying the manure to the fields',[17] little with the periodical sale off his farm of his staple products, corn and meat, for a few hundred yards of farm track made little difference to the lumbering waggons or plodding oxen on their way to market. The days when he would sell milk off his farm every day, and receive in exchange so many necessities of his trade from the road which linked him to factory and port were still far ahead.

The change, of course, was neither immediate nor complete. Some new farms could be worked from the old homesteads. Some landlords followed the advice of the official surveyor of Northamptonshire and built new farmsteads in the centre of the new fields only when the old ones in the village were no longer worth repairing.[18] Others persisted in building new farmsteads in the villages, thereby perpetuating the inconveniences of the old system.[19] Thus, at Wold Newton in Yorkshire, three isolated farmsteads were built shortly after the enclosure of 1776 and two more by 1850, but six farms continued to be worked from farmsteads in the village, while at Upton in Huntingdonshire, now in Cambridgeshire, which was enclosed in 1812, only one farm stands outside the village, and at Salford in Bedfordshire, enclosed in 1808, only two.[20] Also, of course, the effects of the reclamations and enclosures of this period varied greatly from area to area. On the Yorkshire wolds, for example, nearly all the isolated farmsteads outside villages date from these years. In lowland Staffordshire, on the other hand, where by the early eighteenth century nearly a third of the farmsteads stood on isolated sites, the increase in the number of farmsteads outside villages was less rapid, from 112 in 1754 to 183 in 1817.[21] Rates of change differed from area to area, from parish to parish, but the general result was the same. By the end of this period the new pattern was established in most lowland areas.

In the open countryside, the new buildings slowly mellowed into the landscape until they came to look as if they had been there all the time.

71

Sometimes, however, they betray their origins by their names, which commemorate a victory such as Quebec or a hero such as Wellington, or recall the Northfield, the Town Pastures or some other feature of the system they replaced.[22] Sometimes, too, they can be identified by the materials of which they are built. At Elford in Staffordshire which was enclosed in 1766, for instance, the buildings in the core of the village are half-timbered, and those in the fields are of Georgian or Victorian brick, while in the Somerset Levels the farmsteads built on the land reclaimed after the 1770s are commonly of brick, not of the stone traditional in the older settlements of the area.[23]

In the villages, some of the old farmsteads survived. Many of the farmhouses became cottages occupied not by farmers but by hired men working for wages, while the old barns, byres and yards were converted into outhouses or allowed to fall into decay. A few survive, the last structural relics of a system which lasted over a thousand years and has now, except in the single parish of Laxton in Nottinghamshire, gone down into history.[24]

### Farmstead Design

The new farming system increased the demands of the farmer on the farmstead. As a crop grower, he needed more storage for more produce. He also needed the maximum quantity of good-quality manure to maintain and improve the fertility of his expanding and exacting arable acreage, and he looked to the farmstead to conserve with a minimum of waste the animal and vegetable residues which collected there. As a stock breeder, he needed more housing for more beasts. The new fodder crops allowed farms to carry more cattle and sheep, while the livestock improvers were developing new breeds which required better accommodation than their rougher ancestors. In addition, the conversion of forest to farmland and game preserve was now compelling the last of the woodland pigs to seek the permanent hospitality of the farmstead, particularly the dairy farmstead, where they fattened happily on the waste products of the farmhouse manufacture of butter and cheese.[25]

These demands were new in intensity but familiar in principle and they wrought no revolutionary change in the components of the farmsteads. Steadings remained essentially permutations and combinations of buildings selected from the familiar stock of barns and granaries, stables or oxhouses for work beasts, cowhouses, piggeries, cartlodges and henhouses which Young in 1770 regarded as 'absolutely necessary to the common practice of business'.[26] But the buildings were now arranged systematically according to a set of widely accepted and widely applied principles. The farmsteads of this age were the first to be based on a standardised design published and discussed in a substantial technical literature.

The origins of this design are obscure, though it was presumably derived from earlier courtyard patterns. It appeared suddenly and in developed form in the middle of the eighteenth century. The first illustrations of the system appeared in 1747 in the first book to be devoted solely to farm buildings,[27] and the first two datable examples of farmsteads of this type occur in the next fifteen years.[28] A sensible and, with hindsight, obvious way of meeting the agricultural needs of the time, it spread so rapidly that it became common practice by the end of the eighteenth century.[29] It was later continued by the Victorians and its long and successful life bears impressive witness to the competence of the men who originated it.

The achievement was considerable. Comparisons between the casual chaos of the old farmsteads, apparently built 'at random, without order or method, whose buildings have accumulated over the generations' and the more planned and purposeful layouts of the new order were a commonplace of this period.[30] The distinction between old and new was briskly expressed in the next age in a comment on Northumberland: 'A large proportion of the farm buildings [of this county] are of quite recent structure and almost wholly free from the incommodiousness and patchwork irregularity of their predecessors.'[31] There was no need to add an explicit 'therefore' at the beginning of the second part of the sentence.

The main criteria of farmstead planning in this period were the convenience of arrangement for routine chores, notably the feeding, littering and mucking-out of livestock and the effectiveness with which manure could be accumulated. But labour was cheap and plentiful throughout these years, whereas the demands for the means of fertility were insatiable. Consequently, the importance of the farmstead as a muck-factory, as a 'reservoir' of manure,[32] took precedence and forms a pervading theme in the practice and literature of farming of these years.

Thus in 1814 the official surveyor of Lancashire criticised the farmsteads of his county for their inconvenience 'for collecting manure, feeding stock or preserving corn'.[33] The order is significant. By the same token, his colleague in Monmouthshire, now Gwent, noted in 1812 that 'the increased quality of dung produced by good farmstead management is the sheet-anchor of the cultivator', [34] while William Marshall regarded 'the loss of the vegetative strength of animal manures' as an 'index of the improper form' of farmstead design.[35] Typically, the installation of gutters and downpipes was approved because it decreased the dilution by rainwater of manure in the yards,[36] and replacement of thatch by other materials partly

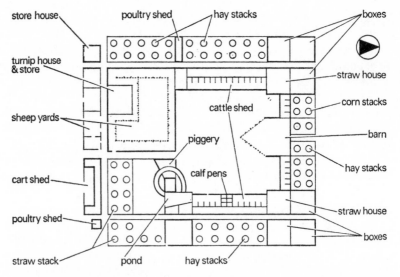

store house

poultry shed

hay stacks

boxes

turnip house & store

straw house

corn stacks

sheep yards

cattle shed

barn

piggery

hay stacks

cart shed

calf pens

straw house

poultry shed

boxes

straw stack

pond

hay stacks

10 The first advisory drawing of a model farmstead, published in 1770. It contains various unusual or impracticable features but illustrates the general layout so typical of the time

because it ended the diversion to roofs of straw required for the midden.[37] It was this preoccupation with manure, and therefore with yards, that determined the basic pattern of the Hanoverian farmstead. For into the yards went straw, into the stockbuildings around them went hay, straw and roots. Out of the buildings came manure to join the straw litter which the cattle, confined in winter in the yards, trampled into more manure. The yards were as central to the farming system as they were to the farmstead which surrounded them.[38]

Essentially, this type of farmstead consisted of three parts. The first was the barn, in which corn from the stackyard was threshed and from which straw was distributed. The second was the collection of livestock buildings, including buildings for work beasts, in which straw and hay were processed into manure. The third was the yard, formed by the barn and the livestock buildings, where stock exercised and manure accumulated. This functional relationship was described with classic brevity in a publication of the Board of Agriculture: 'The fodder consumed on the farm goes progressively forward from the barnyard through the cattle to the dunghill, without the unnecessary labour generally occasioned by carrying it backwards and forwards', while the hay stacked behind the cattle buildings 'followed the same progressive course to the dunghill'.[39] And then, in due course, the dung was carted to the fields to grow the corn which returned to the barn and so continued the cycle of farmstead operations.

The farmsteads of this period therefore took the form of a series of

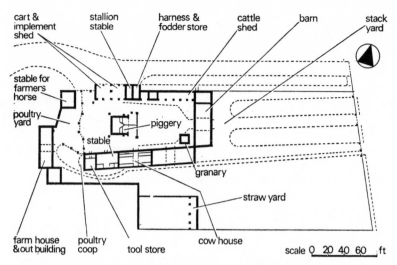

cart & implement shed | stallion stable | harness & fodder store | cattle shed | barn | stack yard

stable for farmers horse

poultry yard

piggery

stable

granary

straw yard

farm house & out building | poultry coop | tool store | cow house

scale 0 20 40 60 ft

11    The first contemporary plan of a new farmstead, published in 1783. This steading was built in 1775 to serve a 500 acre farm at Croydon (see page 115)

buildings round open yards, sometimes in a square but more usually on three sides of a square, some with one yard forming a U-pattern, some with two yards forming an E-pattern. The farmhouse, commonly to the south of the steading, completed this agricultural factory (see plates 13, 14). On all dairy farms it housed the substantial, stone-floored dairies where, with laborious traditional skills, the farmer's wife, daughters and maidservants processed milk into butter or cheese. On cheese-making farms it also included a ventilated chamber or loft where the cheeses ripened in storage.[40] On cider-making farms it included storage for barrels.[41]

On all well-planned farms the farmhouse was sited to allow the farmer a good view of the buildings 'for servants and stock cannot be too much under the eye of the master'.[42] An improved system of farming demanded a higher standard of supervision and management, particularly at its operational centre. Even more significantly, in this period references first occur to the farm office, a room in the farmhouse with an external as well as internal door, where the farmer could interview, give instructions, pay wages and keep his records without bringing work into his family home.[43] This new distinction between the private and working rooms of the farmhouse suggests the beginnings in agriculture of the change from the domestic to the factory system.

The yards faced south to catch the sun and avoid some of the rain-bringing south-west winds. They were sheltered on the north by the most substantial building on the farm, the barn – on larger farms by

75

two or three barns, ideally one for each type of grain – and by the north-facing sheds for carts and implements, whose timber required protection from sun and rain alike. Sometimes, too, they included lean-tos or other types of open-fronted shedding along the walls, under which the cattle could shelter and feed. Two examples of such shedding, dating from the late eighteenth or early nineteenth century, can be seen at the Weald and Downland Open Air Museum. In Devon a common type of shedding was the two-storey linney, with hay stored in the upper storey or 'tallet'; these increased in both number and size during this period.[44]

Into the barns from the rickyard immediately to the north of them came corn for threshing and winnowing on the central floor. Out of them came grain, occasionally still stored in the farmhouse but by the end of this period usually stored in a free-standing granary on staddles or in a room over the cartshed.[45] Out of them, too, came straw for littering the various livestock buildings and, above all, the yards. From this north range and at right-angles to it ran the wings which formed the yards and contained a medley of buildings, some for storage but most for livestock, and preferably arranged in accordance with this need for straw. Fattening cattle which required most straw stood nearest to the barn, then young cattle, and finally cows, working oxen and horses, the latter commonly in stables facing east to catch the early morning sun; the small recesses in the walls of some old stables to hold rushlights or candles, recall the winter hours when horsemen groomed their charges in the dark.[46] Pigs, housed in the familiar pen-and-run sties which had now become standard practice, lived near the farmhouse because they depended on dairy by-products and household waste. So did poultry, traditionally the concern of the farmer's wife. Sometimes their housing was combined in a two-storey building with a poultry loft over a pigsty.[47] Convenient to the cattleyards, sometimes in a barn, sometimes in stacks, stood the haystore. In its combination of arable buildings and livestock buildings, the Hanoverian farmstead proclaimed the nature of the mixed farming system it served.

On larger farms this simple pattern was complicated by the variety of enterprises and functions it was required to include. Sheep were now seldom housed, but yards and sheds for the flocks were still found on some farms; for instance, Ellman of Glynde, the creator of the modern Southdown, used to house his ewes in bad weather.[48] Then there was a miscellany of minor buildings, some of them semi-domestic, such as the 'nag stable' for the farmer's riding horse, housing for his gig, housing for a cider-press in apple-growing areas, possibly a smithy, usually served by a visiting blacksmith, and a slaughterhouse, all reflecting the local self-sufficiency of the rural economy of the time.[49]

Occasionally, too, there were local specialities. Thus, in Devon it was customary to store wood ash from farmhouse fires, for use as fertiliser, in small stone structures with corbelled roofs which were sometimes fitted with roosts for poultry, whose droppings were also conserved.[50] These ash-houses illustrated the frugal use of all available local materials which was so typical of the older order (see Plate 29). So did the gorse-mills of north Wales which processed this natural harvest into fodder for horses or, less commonly, for cattle. But such mills also illustrated the coming of mechanisation. For they were waterpowered or horsedriven products of the later eighteenth century and they replaced the traditional and laborious manual chopping and pounding of this fibrous material into edibility.[51]

Thus, the steading of a 600 acre Norfolk farm at the end of this period contained no less than fifty-five buildings, in addition to the farmhouse.[52] This was of course exceptional, and a number of them served the household rather than the farm. Nevertheless, the figure illustrates the multiplicity of demands made on the farmstead by the farming system of the Agricultural Revolution.

In two respects, however, the new order reduced the number of minor buildings a farmer might require. Improved communications and the consequent weakening of the necessity for self-sufficiency in the remote areas enabled farmers in the wet uplands to abandon the growing of cereals and with it the kilns required for drying their crops. The only recorded new kiln in this period formed part of a highly exceptional Yorkshire farmstead built above the 1,000ft (328m) contour to dry oats grown on reclaimed moorland.[53] In these years, too, the improved farming system and the demands made upon it combined to decrease the value of pigeons as a form of livestock and make their cost in food from the field less acceptable. On the one hand, the new fodder crops ended the need for the autumnal culling of cattle and therefore increased the supply of fresh meat, thus reducing the importance of pigeon pie as a welcome relief to a winter diet of salt beef. On the other hand, Board of Agriculture reporters in Napoleonic times emphasised the losses pigeons caused to crops rather than the value of the meat and manure they produced, and one contemporary proposed a tax on dovecotes to save grain for human consumption. The general arguments, though not the particular recommendation, were apparently successful. By 1808, for example, few pigeons were kept in Staffordshire because of the damage they did to standing crops. Many farmers continued to keep them as domestic assets, but in this period most dovecotes ceased to house an economic enterprise.[54]

Many of these minor buildings, however, were in the nature of 'optional extras' to the familiar and basic repertoire of buildings from which landowners and farmers chose according to the size and type of their farms. At one end of the scale, the buildings of small dairy farms in Cheshire were catalogued in the 1770s in terms of 'cowhouse for six cattle, stable, three-bay barn with carthouse', a 'good old timber barn, stable and cowtyeing for fifteen cattle', and 'a very low, mean old barn, six feet on the wall with cowtyeing, altogether five bays, and a little stable for two horses'.[55] The buildings of a typical Cumberland farm in the next generation were similarly listed as 'a barn, a byre for housing cattle in winter, and a small stable'.[56] At the other end of the scale, the steadings of the large farms in southern England were described as 'magnificent series of buildings, stables, cowhouses, granaries or barns . . . mixed with smaller habitations for pigs, dogs and poultry';[57] those in north-east Northumberland and in the Holderness area, more succinctly, as 'self-contained hamlets' and 'small villages'.[58] Between these extremes stood such steadings as the 'two barns, a good stable, cowhouse, woodhouse, yard and garden and a carthouse or hayhouse' which in the 1750s served a 152 acre farm 'pleasantly situated near Hendon Church';[59] the 'barn, stable, cowhouse, carthouse and hoghouse' of a 250 acre farm in Suffolk in 1774;[60] the 'three barns, two stables, cartshed and cowhouse' of a Sussex farm twenty years later;[61] 'the barn, stable, three cowhouses and carthovel' of a 103 acre farm in Caernarvonshire, now in Gwynedd, in 1800;[62] and, more generally, the 'barn with two floors, the stable, oxhouse, cowhouse and carthouse which constituted every necessity of most Dorset farms'.[63]

Such were the types of buildings which, in varying combinations, were formed into the general standardised pattern of north range and south-facing yards which throughout these years was so widely accepted, at least in the lowlands. There was, of course, an infinity of differences in detail to meet local needs and local circumstances. But in principle the hypothetical farmsteads shown in the advisory literature of the time and the new farmsteads described by the Board of Agriculture's surveyors in counties as different as Berkshire, Dorset, Lancashire, Northumberland and Yorkshire were virtually interchangeable.[64] The courtyard plan had triumphed.

Of course, there were exceptions to this general rule. Certain areas developed local types of building for their particular needs, such as the large 'warehouselike' granaries of Herefordshire.[65] More generally, in the uplands the tradition of the all-under-one-roof steading, inherited from the longhouse and forgotten in the lowlands, continued.[66] Indeed, longhouse-type steadings were still being built in parts of the north of England in the early nineteenth century.[67] At one extreme, this produced the occasional linear farmstead,[68] at the other, such two-storey 'vertical longhouses' as the 'byre houses' of Durham and

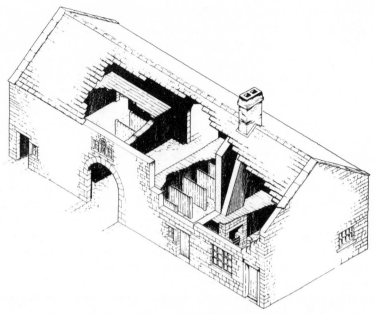

12 A typical eighteenth-century laithe house, showing the housing for livestock, the central passage from which hay and straw were unloaded into the loft above the stalls, and the dwelling house (Mercer, E. *English Vernacular Houses*, 1975, p46) (*Royal Commission on Historical Monuments, England*)

the descendants of the bastles of Northumberland, with cattle on the ground floor and the farmer and his family above them.[69] In between, laithe houses (see Fig 12) increased in number, largely, it seems, because they were peculiarly suited to serve as steadings for farms created from enclosed and reclaimed hill grazings.[70] Bank barns became an established feature of the Lake District, because they suited the exacting needs of the area, and were occasionally being introduced elsewhere;[71] and various other forms of 'combination barn', such as the 'Lancashire barn', which contained a barn and lofted cowhouse, made their appearance.[72] But such deviations were localised and exceptional.

Thus, in some areas of upland Yorkshire the all-under-one-roof farmstead continued, while in others from the mid-eighteenth century onwards an increasing number of farmhouses were built separate from their buildings. In the valleys, however, rebuilding in the new pattern replaced the old system.[73] On the other side of the Pennines, a survey of part of the Lowther estates in 1811 found three types of steading; those with scattered buildings, the result of piecemeal additions over the years; various forms of the linear type in the longhouse tradition; and the more recent steadings on three or four sides of a central yard.[74] The change is summarised in a case study of a longhouse converted into a cottage and incorporated into one of the new type of farmstead in Napoleonic times.[75] Even in Wales, where tradition was strong, the new order was establishing itself: in north-east Wales in the early nineteenth century most farmsteads were either L-shaped or consisted of a single or double row of buildings, while most yards were collecting areas for manure dropped in cowhouses and stables, rather than means of inwintering cattle to tread straw into manure.[76] But the Board of Agriculture surveyor for south Wales saw no point in giving descriptions of the new farmsteads he saw: 'It would be useless,' he wrote in 1814, 'as they are on plans and principles known and adopted in every part of the kingdom where improvements have taken place; that is, a main body or corn barn having a tangent wing at each side for stables, cowtyes, pen sheds etc, the yard opening to the milder points, the south or the south-east.'[77]

In process of time, the systematic plan of many Hanoverian farmsteads was obscured by additions and alterations until they came to resemble the disorderly accumulations condemned by their designers. Yet the strength of the tradition thus formalised was shown a century and a half later when an assessment of farm building needs after the Second World War started with the justified assumption that 'the ordinary farm building layout in England is generally three or four sides of a quadrangle with offshoots'.[78] You cannot go far in the modern countryside without seeing something of the standardised pattern first developed by our tireless great-grandfathers, the masterful men of the Agricultural Revolution.

## Outlying Buildings

Not all buildings, however, stood in the central farmstead where these principles ruled. On a number of farms it was economic to site isolated buildings for inwintering livestock in fields some distance from it. They are generally called 'barns' or 'field barns', but from function and design they should more accurately be called 'field cattlesheds', for the yards or other cattle shelters they included proclaimed their purpose better than the barns which stored litter and fodder. They were built as centres for the accumulation of manure for the surrounding fields in order to save the haulage of hay and straw to the main yards and then the haulage back again of the manure into which they had been converted.[79] Significantly, in the Yorkshire dales 'cowhouse is a term synonymous with barn'.[80]

The isolated barns and yards, most of them now abandoned, which are found on the chalk uplands of Dorset, Hampshire, Sussex and Wiltshire, generally date from the conversion of these upland sheepwalks to ploughland in Napoleonic times[81] (see Plate 17). They were built to maintain the fertility of the new cornfields that lay too far for proper manuring from the central farmsteads, which were usually sited on streams in the valleys. There must have been many reports in these areas during this period like the 1799 survey of a 1,000 acre farm in Hampshire which recommended the building on a distant part of the farm of 'a cottage for a carter and a shepherd, a good barn and stable and fold to serve land which at this time lies too far from home to receive a due return in manure for its produce' and make possible the further reclamation of the furze-covered upland.[82] The names of many of these units recall their origins. Some were called after their parent farms in the valleys, some were given such names as Down, Warren or New Barn; a series of barn walks near the Seven Sisters Park Centre in Sussex passes no less than five New Barns.[83] In the same period similar barns and yards, often called by such names as High Barn or Wold Barn, were erected on the higher and more remote parts of large Yorkshire farms.[84]

On the downs and wolds the problem was distance, for these secondary steadings could stand a mile or so away from the homestead. In the Pennines and in parts of Wales the problem was the difficulty of transport on steep slopes. This produced the small, two-storey field barns so typical of some upland areas in the north, which housed inwintered cattle on the ground floor, with hay and straw above them. In the dales, for example, such 'field houses' dot the landscape, sometimes standing in every third or fourth field. Few have been dated, but most were probably built in the later eighteenth and early nineteenth centuries as the pattern of enclosure spread outwards and upwards from the valley settlements.[85] In 1800 a Board of Agriculture surveyor in Yorkshire commented on the value of these buildings in saving haulage, 'an important circumstance in these hilly counties', and on 'their particular use during the time of making hay in a country where the weather is very uncertain and attended by sudden, frequent and violent showers'. In 1975 his successors from the Ministry of Agriculture noted that accommodation for livestock and fodder on these farms might be adequate on paper but was insufficient in practice since so much of it consisted of small, isolated buildings: 'Utilisation of such scattered buildings is extremely time-consuming.' Times change and economics with them.[86]

Another type of isolated building which probably increased in numbers in this period was the 'hogg-house' of Cumbria and some other upland areas. Like the field houses, the hogg-houses contained space for livestock and for fodder. But, unlike the field houses, they sheltered young sheep, not cattle, and they provided little manure for the land around them. The ruins of these buildings in the Lake

81

District, often sited in the corner of a field and sheltered by a few trees, are as typical of their landscape as the field houses are of the dales.[87]

## Intensive Livestock Housing

Sometimes familiar types of farmstead contained such unfamiliar but prophetic types of buildings as the various housing systems designed to serve the intensive livestock enterprises which had arisen in certain areas. Among these were the slatted-floor calfpens of the Gloucestershire veal rearers, in which close confinement secured warmth and guarded against loss of expensively acquired flesh by excessive playfulness;[88] the pens in Essex which 'fitted a pig as near as may be' so that it would not waste energy by turning round;[89] the long, narrow, well-strawed houses on farms round London in which lambs were fattened for the Christmas market by ewes turned in at night;[90] and the yards where Herefordshire farmers housed their sheep in winter and sometimes in summer as well to make manure for their arable land.[91] All these represented different applications of the same principle. So does a remarkable survival, a late eighteenth-century egg-production building at Lowick Highstead Farm in Northumberland. This recalls a forgotten but once-flourishing local trade which in the time of George III exported eggs by the hundred thousand to London via Berwick-on-Tweed. After the end of the Napoleonic Wars, however, London found it cheaper to obtain supplies from Ireland and the Continent, and the Northumberland farmers turned to other enterprises. The building remains as a useful reminder that there is nothing new either in specialised livestock buildings or in overseas competition.[92]

More radically, in these years a new type of raw material made possible the general intensification of a traditional type of livestock enterprise, and therefore made necessary changes in traditional methods of livestock housing. The raw material was oilcake, a byproduct of the oilseed-crushing industry, which began to be used as stockfeed in the later eighteenth century. This protein-rich concentrate not only fattened cattle more efficiently than the traditional fodders but also greatly increased the value of the residual manure so that the farmer who purchased it improved the fertility of his fields as well as the performance of his stock. So began the development of systems of stalls or boxes for the intensive winter-fattening of cattle which the new cake made profitable.

Sometimes these stalls or boxes were installed in existing buildings. Sometimes new special-purpose fattening houses were built to exploit the new possibilities. As early as 1771, for instance, Young noted near Retford 'a most complete oxhouse' for twenty-six beasts with mangers served from outside the house, a water supply and a room for storing and breaking into manageable pieces the cake which reached the farm in 1in (2.5cm) thick, oblong slabs.[93] A generation later, enterprising farmers, such as Adam of Mount Nod in Surrey, were fattening several hundred head in buildings 'constructed with great regard to convenience'.[94] New materials created new systems of production, new systems of production called into existence new types of building and, on occasion, new types of equipment suitable for more intensive enterprises; the first reference to a weighing machine on the farm comes from a description of a fattening house in 1805.[95] The process will become increasingly familiar. There was, however, particular as well as general prophecy in this development. At first, the oilcake came from English factories. Later, it was imported from America; the removal of the duty on foreign oilcake in the 1790s was one of the few political achievements of the Board of Agriculture.[96] Thus was foreshadowed the coming a century later of an unprecedented agricultural partnership, in which the home farmer provided buildings and livestock and the overseas producer the steady supply of concentrate foodstuffs which passed through the farmstead to emerge as meat, milk and manure.

But this was for the remote future. In George III's time, the livestock on the farm depended for all but a very small proportion of their rations on the surrounding fields. Nevertheless, a more specialised system was already well advanced in the towns. Indeed, in this period the true home of intensive livestock husbandry was not the countryside but London.

There were two main types of livestock enterprise in the capital, the urban dairy herds on which the townsman depended for his milk, and the cattle and pigs which fattened on the starchy waste products of the brewing and distilling industries. Neither system was new. Cows had been kept in city streets ever since urban expansion separated their inhabitants from dairy farms, while distillers were undercutting pig farmers in contracts for supplying the Navy with pork in the first half of the eighteenth century.[97] Both enterprises, however, reached new peaks of importance in this period. Regency London, with its 8,500 dairy cows and its annual output of more than 50,000 pigs[98] and an unspecified but considerable number of fat cattle, was a major centre of livestock production.

The dairy cows, nearly half of which were concentrated in the Paddington, Tottenham Court Road, King's Cross and Gray's Inn Lane areas, spent their milking life tethered in stalls from which they were let out into yards for water and exercise for three or four hours a day, until the time came for slaughter. In general, sanitary conditions among these 'wretched beasts housed in dark sheds or hovels, standing ankle deep in filth' were indescribably bad.[99] So were the standards and methods of cleaning the dairy utensils. So was the quality of the milk by the time it reached the customer, frequently in adulterated form.[100]

Away in Glasgow, it is true, William Harley showed that good housing and good management could produce clean milk in the middle of an industrial city. When he found he could not obtain clean milk for the invalids who frequented his public baths from cows herded 'in narrow lanes and confined corners', he turned cowkeeper and evolved the first modern cowhouse of which record has survived. By 1814 he was milking 300 head in a huge shed of the familiar modern double-range type, complete with feeding passages, ventilation system and a dairy with equipment for the steam sterilisation of utensils. His cowhouse was one of the sights of the town; but it was a very long, long time before the standards of the 'Harleian system' became normal practice.[101]

The London fattening houses, run as subsidiaries of substantial manufacturing firms, were far better built and better managed than the London cowhouses. Even such potential nuisances as mass-production piggeries with an output of 3,000 head a year won only praise from the Board of Agriculture's surveyors. The pigs, they reported, were 'kept with all imaginable care . . . no pains were spared to keep them clean and sweet, which the superior construction of their very extensive premises enables [the distillers] to do'.[102] Little information about such 'extensive premises' has survived, though it is clear that their size was considerable, their design advanced. Messrs Hodgson & Co, distillers, of Battersea, erected a range of oxhouses 600ft (180m) long and 32ft (9.6m) wide, each housing two rows of individually stalled cattle separated by a feeding passage, and attempted to provide them with slatted floors which allowed the cattle to lie dry and clean on 'open trellises or gratings', held a few inches off the ground by blocks, the dung being removed from below by hoe. The attempt was unsuccessful and injuries to the beasts' feet compelled the replacement of this system by brick flooring.[103] Nevertheless, the experiment is interesting as an example of the contribution which men outside the traditional farming economy were beginning to make to the development of farm buildings.[104]

The intensive system of the towns probably contributed to contemporary interest in the possibilities of making more intensive use of the buildings on conventional farms. The practice of 'soilage', the cutting and carting of green fodder to permanently housed cattle which never set foot in a field, was inherent in urban dairy enterprises. It was now considered for dairy herds on normal farms, and trials inspired by the Board of Agriculture concluded that it was more

Plate 7  The pig was originally a woodland animal. Herds of pigs foraged for themselves in the forests under the care of swineherds, until the shrinking of the woodlands, from the Middle Ages onwards, made it necessary to house them in the farmstead. These seventeenth-century pigs, confined in a simple yard in the first stage of such housing, preserve the long legs and lean bodies of their semi-wild ancestors (see page 46) (*Museum of English Rural Life*)

Plate 8    A Tudor granary presented by the Marquis of Bath to Lackham School of Agriculture, where it was re-erected. The staddlestones on which it stands provide protection from rats and mice (*Lackham Agricultural Museum*)

profitable to keep cows in houses and feed them there than to pasture them in the fields.[105] Despite such encouraging evidence, the system failed to establish itself on any scale in the countryside, though in some areas it was used for horses in the summer.[106] The discussion nevertheless foreshadowed the future development of intensive methods of livestock production and the part that buildings played in them, just as a visionary reference of the time to the use of wheeled stockhouses on iron rails to transport the cattle to the fields which provided their soilage foreshadowed the mechanisation which helped to make such systems possible.[107]

### Experiments, Innovations and Improvements

Such railways were never built. Neither, apparently, was the 'improved granary', which today would be described as an aerated grain silo, proposed by Sir John Sinclair.[108] Nevertheless, the importance of such unrealised dreams was considerable, for they illustrate the search for improvement which was so characteristic of the age. This produced such minor but useful innovations as 'fother rooms' in stockbuildings for the collection of seeds from hay stored there and a 'chequer-board' floor which allowed calves to lie dry.[109] There were also various new developments to meet new needs. Potato cellars were built on some Dartmoor farms when the crop was first grown in Napoleonic times; steam boilers cooked potatoes for livestock; and turnip houses protected or thawed root crops for feeding to inwintered cattle.[110] More generally, scattered evidence of the increasing provision of cartsheds reflects the growing volume of crops which were moved on the farm and sold off it and the consequent improvement in farm transport, notably the appearance of massive four-wheeled waggons on corn-growing farms in the later eighteenth century.[111]

The greater use in this period of staddlestones for granaries and ricks may also illustrate specific historical change as well as more energetic reaction to a familiar and continuing hazard.[112] For the invasion of Britain by the black Norway rat which began about 1730 greatly increased the importance of such forms of pest control. It may also have encouraged the provision of owl holes which are such a pleasing feature of a number of barns; many owl holes date from the eighteenth or nineteenth centuries.[113] They can be seen in a barn, probably dating from the early eighteenth century, at the Manor Farm Museum, Cogges, Oxfordshire, and there are holes plus a little platform under the ridge as a nesting place in the barn at Arkley on the north-western outskirts of London. The tradition continues to this day. In 1982 a Lincolnshire farmer reckoned that the owls which settled in the First World War hangar which housed his grain saved him £150 a week and he included owl holes, landing stages and nesting boxes in the new store he was building.[114]

Another development of this period was the cornhole. This was a small, roofed brick room built inside the barn near the threshing floor to hold threshed grain before it was winnowed, which appeared in the middle years of the eighteenth century. But its working life was short. Early in the next century it was made obsolete by the new machines which both winnowed and threshed the corn harvest.[115] By contrast, the loosebox, which is first recorded a few years before the beginning of this period and mentioned frequently during it, had a long and continuing future. Originally used for calves or calving, it later developed into the invaluable general-purpose animal building without which no livestock farm is complete.[116]

The needs and spirit of the time also inspired more ambitious attempts to develop new types of building by trial and error on the farm. We hear, for instance, of such innovations as a cattleshed based on a north German model,[117] a movable barn built for one of the royal farms at Windsor,[118] an umbrella for covering haystacks,[119] and experiments with new forms of all-under-one-roof steadings[120]and circular or polygonal designs.[121] None of these novelties established themselves in general practice, but the spirit which produced them succeeded in adding to the farmstead repertoire the prototypes of two of the most familiar of all modern buildings.

The first of these was the skeleton structure of poles or pillars of stone or brick, roofed with thatch or tiles, which later developed into the familar metal Dutch barn. The idea from which these buildings evolved reached this country in Elizabethan times, but it was not until the later years of George III that they were widely used by farmers who found a permanent shelter a better proposition than the seasonal thatching of haystacks and cornricks.[122] The second was the cowhouse, which towards the end of this period changed on the better farms from a crude hovel to a recognisable version of its modern design. The process was gradual and piecemeal but, item by item, the familiar component parts made their appearance; sloping standings, chain-ties and divisions between cows, internal water supplies, feeding passages, and dung channels flowing to grated outlets. In plan and section, though not in construction, the improved cowhouse of 1820 differed little from its successors of our own time.[123]

## New Needs and New Problems

Such novelties, however, were exceptional, and the main theme of this period was the universal agreement on the general plan which all properly designed farmsteads should follow. Unfortunately, this was accompanied by equally universal agreement on the general failure of existing farmsteads to meet the demands which the farming system made on them. Young's references in 1770 to cows without cowhouses, carts and implements without shelter and steadings without central yards[124] were repeated with variations and expansions throughout the series of county reports which the Board of Agriculture issued in the following generation. Stabling for horses, which was becoming increasingly important as the horse replaced the ox, was the only type of building seldom mentioned by these critics. Presumably the proud place of the riding horse in the life of the time and the immediate effect of poor conditions on the performance of animals on which the farm depended for its day-to-day work combined to encourage the provision of proper housing.[125] Apart from this, however, condemnation was general. Agricultural change had brought great benefits. But it also brought great problems, in particular, a problem which from this time onwards forms a permanent part of the history of farm buildings.

Since farm buildings serve farm needs, changes in farm needs necessarily precede changes in farm buildings. Consequently, as it is quicker to apply new systems of growing plants and raising animals than to build or rebuild, there is bound to be a certain interval between the development of a new need and the creation of buildings to meet it. This interval can be limited by foresight. It can seldom be eliminated. The difficulty is inherent in any period of agricultural change.

No doubt similar difficulties arose in earlier times, but it was only in this period that they became sufficiently important to enter the written record. For the changes brought by the Agricultural Revolution were unprecedented in speed and scope and they made unprecedented demands on the farmstead. The point was neatly illustrated by the new doors cut into the massive walls of Buckland Abbey barn in 1792 'with a labour nearly equal to that of cutting solid rock'. The barn dated from the days of 'packhorse husbandry', when corn was brought from the hilly harvest fields on horseback, and the doors sufficient for such primitive transport were not sufficient for the waggons of a later age.[126] More generally, contemporary condemnation of the wastage of manure on ill-planned steadings[127] and the 'pernicious' practice of wintering cattle in fields to the detriment of soil and animals alike because there were insufficient yards to house them,[128] reflected the inability of the agricultural partnership in their capacity as farmstead builders to keep pace with the needs that they were creating in their capacity as producers of crops and stock. The new steadings they built required periodical improvement, the old steadings they inherited required more drastic modernisation.

In the abstract, a continuous process of reconstruction is the only conclusive answer to this problem, but for obvious reasons this is no more than a dream of ultimate efficiency. In practice, the landowners and farmers of Hanoverian times, like their successors, contented themselves with more modest, less radical remedies. They built anew when they could, but it is probable that throughout these years the building of new farmsteads was matched by the adaptation of old farmsteads, sometimes by the improvement of old or the addition of new buildings, sometimes by more comprehensive schemes of replanning and reconstruction.

There is little systematic evidence from which to estimate the extent of this practice, which is essentially a matter of piecemeal change in individual farmsteads and so makes little impression on historical literature, though it did produce the first known criticism of a farm building on aesthetic grounds.[129] Some indications of the processes involved, however, are given by two illuminating case studies of this period. The first is structural and can be seen at Manor Farm Museum, Cogges, Oxfordshire. In the later eighteenth century, a small seventeenth-century barn was converted to a stable with a hayloft, reflecting an increase in crop production which made the small barn inadequate and accommodation for more working horses necessary[130] (see Fig 13). The second is documentary, the first recorded 'before and after' report, which was used by Charles Waistell, a highly practical agriculturist, to demonstrate the benefits that could be secured by the rational rearrangement of farm buildings. He described the remodelling, apparently about 1820, of a sprawling old Surrey farmstead to which buildings had been added over the generations 'with no regard whatever to the situation of previously existing conveniences'. An unwanted barn was removed, new livestock accommodation, a waggonshed and a granary were built, and particular enterprises and therefore particular types of work, were concentrated in particular areas. This reconstruction enabled the farm to carry more stock and the farmer to run his farm with less effort. In general, these benefits were secured not by the development of a new system but by the literal reformation of an existing one. The change did, however, include one technical novelty, a new intensive fattening shed for cake-fed cattle. This example, with its mixture of reorganisation and modernisation, provides a useful introduction to a continuing theme in farmstead development.[131]

## Machinery comes to the Farmstead

A more spectacular sign of the changing times was the appearance of machinery on the farmstead. This began, innocently enough, with the

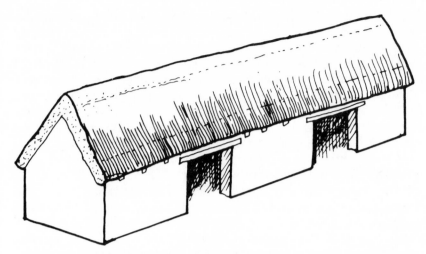

13   In the seventeenth century, a small barn for the storage of crops was built at the Manor Farm, Cogges, Oxfordshire. In the eighteenth century, corn production increased, the barn became too small for the new harvests, and the farm needed more working horses. So two new barns were built and the old barn was converted to a stable with a hayloft entered by stone steps. The small building added at the end of the stable may have originally been intended as a pigsty but later housed the farmer's gig, thus serving as the equivalent of a garage (Steane, J. M. ed, *Cogges, A Museum of Farming in the Oxfordshire Countryside*, 1978, published by the Oxfordshire County Council Department of Museum Services, pp19–21. The building can be seen at the Museum) (*Oxfordshire County Council, Dept of Museum Services*)

development in the later eighteenth century of small, hand-driven machines for cutting hay and straw into chaff to reduce wastage by cattle at feeding time, for grinding corn and beans for livestock and for winnowing by a system of sails on radial arms which replaced the wind on which the farmer had previously relied to separate grain from cavings.[132] Such simple forms of barn machinery could be installed with little difficulty in existing buildings, though the winnowing machine brought with it implications of change. It more than halved the floorspace required for threshing, which made the barn with a single threshing floor a better proposition than the larger and more expensive barn with two threshing floors. The output was the same, capital and maintenance costs were less. A Midland study shows that barns with single threshing floors became more popular than those with double threshing floors after 1800, when winnowing machines were in general use, and that three double–floor barns were adapted to the use of the new machine in or shortly after this period.[133] Meanwhile, a more drastic change was developing: the mechanisation of threshing, which in due course brought to the farm the unprecedented and revolutionary factor of inorganic power. From this time onwards it is buildings rather than men which arrange themselves around the new equipment.

The process of technical evolution, however, was gradual. The early eighteenth century had seen various attempts to mechanise threshing, one of the dreariest and most unhealthy chores of the farming year, by harnessing manpower, waterpower or literal horsepower to equipment which imitated the action of the human flailer. But it was not until 1786 that Andrew Meikle, a Scots millwright, hit upon the sounder principle which is still in use today. He built a drum fitted with pegs which revolved in a concave cover and rubbed and beat the grain off the straw as it turned. The grain fell into a container and the straw was carried away. This invention spread rapidly and within twenty years mechanical threshing had become established practice in most areas.[134] By 1800, 'common wrights' in Yorkshire villages were beginning to make threshing machines and in a few years' time the official surveyor of Northamptonshire 'wondered much' at their absence from his county.[135]

Most of these machines were driven by horses, originally up to six horses for the biggest machines, though mechanical improvement later reduced the number.[136] Some were driven by waterpower: readers of the delightful *Carrington Diary* will remember Mr Deacon of Tewin Bury who in the early 1800s 'turned the river by his wheat barn through the farme yarde for a thrashing machine'.[137] One or two, exceptionally, were driven by windpower.[138] A few were driven by steam.[139] And here was a portent indeed, for this was the first time man-made mechanical power entered the farmstead and its appearance marked the earliest definite break with the older tradition of rural self-sufficiency. The principles which the steam engine incorporated, the fuel it consumed and the technical knowledge required for its operation all came from the rising industrial economy that lay beyond the farm gate. It had no ancestors on the farm. But it had many descendants there.

In the early 1800s, however, the future of steampower on the farm was a matter for speculation. The implications of mechanisation presented more immediate questions. The most obvious was the development of a new type of barn smaller than its predecessors, since the threshing machine required less height than the swinging flail and could keep pace with a steady flow of sheaves from the rickyard, thus making unnecessary the storage of unthreshed corn in the barn. The changes in farmstead methods, caused first by the winnowing machine and then, more drastically, by the threshing machine, implied substantial changes in farmstead planning.[140]

Arthur Young, that percipient agricultural journalist, saw all this clearly. With his accustomed enthusiasm, he proclaimed that the mechanical thresher 'promised speedily to put an end to all barn building'; [141] . . . an over-simplified thought which a more cautious colleague rightly and amusingly modified to the probability that 'the gradual introduction of the threshing machine will render barns of the present size and number less necessary'[142] . . . and even foresaw the development of wheeled frames on iron rails to carry the stacks of corn to the thresher.[143] His appreciation of the opportunities offered by the new technique and their consequences was equally prophetic, and his suggestion that the prime-mover which drove the threshing machine should be harnessed to food-preparation equipment developed into one of the most penetrating paragraphs in the agricultural literature of the time. 'The position of the threshing mill,' he wrote in 1809, 'decides that of every other building, for it cuts, or ought to cut, all the hay of the farm into chaff, with much of the straw; and the house that immediately receives the chaff must be so placed as to admit a convenient delivery to the stables, stalls and sheepyards. Thus the straw-house, chaffhouse, stables, stalls, haystacks and sheepyard must be placed in consequence of the position of the threshing-mill, or waste and expense of labour must follow.'[144] Here was the first conscious statement of the principle that farm buildings are coverings for farm processes and that their relationship is determined by the demands of these processes. Young's understanding of contemporary change enabled him to see more clearly than any other man of his time the line of future farmstead development.

Indeed, he saw too far and too fast. The farmers for whom he wrote were content with the immediate benefits of the new technique – the saving of time and money, the reduced wastage of corn, the end of reliance on unreliable manual labour and the ability to market their crop earlier – and they found it easier to fit the machine into existing buildings than to adapt the buildings to the improved system made possible by the machine. In general, they replaced flail threshing by mechanical threshing and made little systematic attempt to secure the full advantage of the new process. It was simpler and, at least in the short run, cheaper to put the new machine in the old barn than to plan a rearrangement of much of the farmstead. Young was not the only official to comment sadly that most threshing machines stood in the barn where the flailers had worked not because the barn was the right place for it but because it was there.[145] The same preoccupation with immediate answers to immediate problems affected construction as well as adaptation. Waistell's model plans, published just after the end of this period, show barns specifically designed and sited for mechanical threshing. But apparently few such barns were built. A Midland study contrasted the many early threshing-machine barns which 'resembled the flail-thrashing barn in form and position' with the 'few ... which anticipated the designs that were to become common with High Farming' in the next generation.[146]

The new technique, however, did produce one new type of building. This was the wheelhouse, a single-storey round, square or polygonal building up to 30ft (9m) in diameter with a conical or pyramidal roof. These wheelhouses, standing adjacent to the barn, derived their name from their function. They protected the wheel, at first an overhead wooden wheel and later an iron wheel near the ground, the circumambulatory horses that turned it and the gear that transmitted through the barn wall the power they generated to the threshing machine, and sometimes other machinery, in the barn. Nearly all were built between the 1790s and the 1850s, the majority probably between 1800 and 1830, and they were found in many parts of the country, with concentrations in the north-east and in the Westcountry and few in Wales where waterpower was widely available. In the north they were called 'gin gangs', in the west 'pound houses' because the barn machinery they drove included the mills that crushed cider apples for which they were originally installed. Today, most of such horsegear as survives is preserved in museums, but a survey in 1973 in England, Wales and Scotland found some 1,300 of these unmistakeable little buildings still standing on farms[147] (see Plate 21, Fig 18).

## The End of an Old Tradition

The coming of machinery to the farmstead offered new possibilities of increased efficiency. It also raised new problems. But the implications of these were more obvious to later generations than they were to the men of the time and throughout most of this period the old assumptions continued.

Thus in 1770, Arthur Young, in his advice to prospective tenants, contented himself with listing the familiar principles of good farmstead planning and adding hints on the points of detail which made the difference between a good and a bad steading. The barn, for instance, should be floored not with clay but with oak plank, which gave a better and brighter sample of grain; the granary should contain sufficient space for the storage of two harvests lest the farmer be compelled to sell on a poor market; and the yard should be bottomed with stone or gravel and served by a pond.[148]

Similarly, in 1776 Nathaniel Kent wrote a manual of estate management called *Hints to Gentlemen of Landed Property*. Out of a total of 282 pages, only 13 were devoted to farm buildings, and even there he contented himself with a few casual hints on materials and maintenance. Twenty-eight years later, William Marshall wrote his comprehensive treatise, *On the Landed Property of England*, which allotted no more than half a chapter to 'the laying-out of the homestall'. For these writers still took it for granted that a general knowledge of farming practice and a particular knowledge of local building lore would enable any competent landowner, land agent or farmer to deal adequately with farm buildings. The first substantial

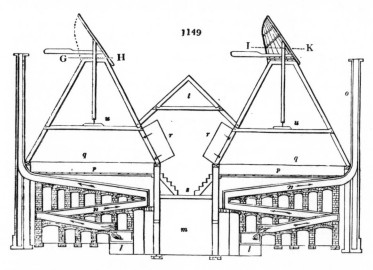

14   Section of a pair of cockle oasthouses built to the design of John Read in the early nineteenth century. The smoke and hot air from the cockle stoves were carried around the circular building in iron pipes and discharged through a chimney, thus drying the hops without contaminating them (Loudon, J. C. *An Encyclopedia of Cottages, Farm and Village Architecture*, 1836, p597)

publication to appear on this subject, a collection of four papers in the first volume of *Communications to the Board of Agriculture*, which appeared in 1797, accepted these assumptions without question and, in general, sought improvement not by urging innovations but by drawing attention to useful practices found on progressive farms.[149]

Such assumptions were reasonable when Young wrote, less reasonable when Marshall was writing, for men faced with the necessity of reorganising farmsteads to meet the implications of mechanical threshing required something more than traditional wisdom. New developments demanded new sources of information, new skills and new types of approach, but these were slow in coming. It was typical of the age that the major improvements in the most complicated farm structure then in use, the oasthouse, owed nothing to the engineer. In this period, its circular form was established by John Read, an ingenious gardener who turned his attention to hop-drying after experimenting with methods of heating hothouses and inventing the stomach-pump, while the pivoted conical cap by which the oasthouse was for so long instantly recognised was evolved by forgotten local craftsmen[150](see Fig 14). The old order still reigned. But the days when the knowledge that the farm taught would no longer be able to answer all the questions that the farm raised were not so very far ahead.

This period certainly saw the problem stated. Wedge's suggestion in the 1790s that the Board of Agriculture should sponsor the publication of farmstead plans 'in which utility, economy and neatness might be equally consulted' [151] illustrated the inadequacy of traditional sources to meet it and there must have been many besides Waistell who in these years tried in vain to obtain 'satisfactory information from books for arranging and executing (agricultural buildings) such as were required'.[152] But it produced no general remedy. The dream of the Board of Agriculture in 1797 of collecting and collating available information into 'a paper which would probably render any further discussion or additional publications on that branch of husbandry unnecessary'[153] remained a dream of a dying age, for it assumed that a review of approved contemporary practice would meet all needs indefinitely. The future, however, was to bring continuing change and development. The time was coming when the art and science of equipping a farm with efficient buildings would cease to be a normal part of the agricultural trade and become something of a specialist job. The self-sufficient rural technology of the old order was nearing its end, and the coming of the machine to the farmstead was one of the first clear breaks with this ancient tradition.

## The Last Age of Local Materials

The traditional use of local materials in farm buildings, however, still ruled. Significantly, the standardisation of the principles of farmstead planning in this period was not paralleled by the standardisation of farmstead construction which still reflected the physical variety of the English countryside. The builder's dependence on local products continued and even the tar used in Hampshire came as a byproduct from the local manufacture of gunpowder.[154] The continuing assumption that 'the materials of which a building is made must depend on local circumstances'[155] is illustrated by the materials listed in contemporary discussions of the best forms of construction for that crucial section of the barn, the threshing floor: oak embedded in masonry, timber on a layer of flints or cinders, flagstones from the 'argillaceous' hills, and a mixture of earth, clay and dung beaten and rolled till it was 'solid, hard and firm'.[156] The only manufactured material mentioned was brick;[157] and bricks in the earlier years of this period were made of clay from local pits and fired in local kilns.[158] Welsh farmers sometimes used more picturesque but equally local materials, burying upside-down cooking pots or the skulls of horses beneath the floor to give a better rhythm for the flail.[159] More generally, the arrangement whereby the landlord provided building materials, such as timber in the rough, for his tenants' repairs recognised that he would have little difficulty in finding them within the bounds of his estate.[160] Similarly, when one local material failed, others were used in its place. Thus, in certain areas of the Midlands and the north, good building timber became scarce in this period, so timber roof trusses were abandoned and walls of brick or stone carried up to support the purlins.[161] The effects of such limitations are interestingly shown on the Holkham estate. There is no stone in the area and therefore no source of staddlestones to protect stored grain from vermin. Consequently, grain was stored over cartsheds and not in free-standing granaries.

Typically, the new wheelhouses continued the old tradition. In Bedfordshire, they were built of ironstone, in Berkshire with weather-boarding, in Devon with granite pillars, in Norfolk with timber or flint, in Northumberland with sandstone and stone tiles, in Yorkshire with brick in the East Riding and with limestone in the West Riding.[162] The design of these structures was novel, the materials used in their construction ancestral.

Another important type of local material, in this as in other periods, was salvage from demolished buildings. Thus, sufficient new buildings were 'principally formed out of old materials from buildings pulled down' in Waistell's reconstruction of a Surrey farmstead, probably about 1820, to justify special tinting in the plan he provided to illustrate his case study. Again, the building accounts of the primitively named and domiciled Garth family of Crackpot in Yorkshire refer to pulling down old buildings but make little mention of felling trees or cutting new timbers, which suggests the common use of old timbers. Similarly, stones from buried Wroxeter, excavated when drought revealed the lines of Roman foundations, and from Hadrian's Wall, appear in local farmsteads; late sixteenth- or early seventeenth-century windows from a nearby house in an eighteenth-century stable in Flintshire, now in Clwyd; and medieval timbers in a barn on Humberside which was partly rebuilt after a fire in the same century. In another case, dating by structure would have assigned a cruck barn in Denbighshire, now in Clwyd, to the sixteenth or early seventeenth century, but sherds of a late eighteenth-century dish found under a footing course made necessary further investigation which identified the reused crucks. Less structurally, an ancient lead coffin made a useful pigs' trough on a Devon farm.[163] Indeed, the frugal ingenuity of the old rural builders has added appreciably to the problems of dating farm buildings. Few of these craftsmen were as obliging as W. Spears, presumably a worker in the estate brickyard, who wrote his name and the date, 1805, on a wet clay ridge tile removed a few years ago from a barn at Salisbury Hall in Hertfordshire.

Nevertheless, the county reports of the Board of Agriculture show a marked change in the choice of the particular local materials used. Brick and stone, where available, were beginning to oust the cruder traditional materials, and a number of the county surveyors contrasted the older buildings of timber, wattle-and-daub and thatch with the new ones of brick or stone and tiles[164] . . . incidentally, the need of brick barns for ventilation allowed the development of a new form of ornamentation by patterns of pierced brickwork.[165] In one area of lowland Shropshire, for example, the eighteenth century saw the final replacement of once traditional timber by stone; the last datable example of timber construction was built in 1784.[166] The same period also saw the end of the long history of the cruck, which in the form of the 'upper cruck', cruck blades seated in the end of first-floor beams to make trusses, was used in some Worcestershire farm buildings as late as the second half of the eighteenth century.[167]

Signs of the future, however, were already apparent. Imported timber was beginning to make its appearance on the farmstead, even in such an inland county as Staffordshire.[168] So, in a more radical break with tradition, was manufactured equipment: iron plates for mangers, milled lead as a substitute for ridge tiles,[169] threaded iron nuts and bolts for joining timbers,[170] lead for drinking troughs,[171] and metal eaves, gutters and downpipes to replace the hollowed fir poles or the more primitive rods sometimes used to carry water away from the eaves.[172] The new canals were now making available types of material unfamiliar in the areas they served: brick instead of stone in Warwickshire, slate in Staffordshire.[173] But as yet this was little more than prophecy. The particular hope expressed in 1800 by the official surveyor for the North Riding of Yorkshire that the canal being built between York and Stillington would carry building materials[174] did not receive general fulfilment until the next age brought a more revolutionary and a more comprehensive form of transport which symbolised the coming of a new technological age.

## NOTES

1. Royal Commission on Historical Monuments, *Shielings and Bastles*, 1970; Newton, B. *The Northumberland Landscape*, 1972, p 104; Richardson, C. G. B. 'Kings Stables, an early shieling on Black Lyne Common, Bewcastle', *Transactions of the Cumberland and Westmorland Antiquarian and Archaeological Society*, vol 79, 1979, pp 19–27; Pearsall, W. H. and Pennington, W. *The Lake District*, 1973, p 244 for Norse names; Thirsk, J. in a review of Cameron, K. *Placenames of Derbyshire*, 1959, in *Agricultural History Review*, 1960, p 120.

2. Trow-Smith, R. *A History of British Livestock Husbandry, 1700–1900*, 1959, pp 8–9.

3. Smith, P. *Houses of the Welsh Countryside*, 1975, pp 142–4. See also Peate, J. G. *The Welsh House*, 1944, p 127; Thomas, D. *Agriculture in Wales during the Napoleonic Wars*, 1963, p 179; Williams, M. *The South Wales Landscape*, 1975, pp 91–2; Wiliam, E. *Traditional Farm Buildings in North-East Wales, 1550–1900*, 1982, pp 23, 30.

4. Trow-Smith, R. *A History of British Livestock Husbandry to 1700*, 1957, p 258.

5. For the working of this system see Peters, J. E. C. *The Development of Farm Buildings in Western Lowland Staffordshire up to 1880*, 1969, pp 209–12; Wade-Martins, S. *A Great Estate at Work*, 1980; Tyson, B. 'Skirwith Hall and Wilton Tenement (Kirkland Hall). The rebuilding of two Cumbrian farmsteads in the eighteenth century', *Transactions of the Cumberland and Westmorland Antiquarian and Archaeological Society*, vol 81, 1981, pp 94–112; Wiliam, E. *Traditional Farm Buildings in North-East Wales, 1550–1900*, 1982, pp 258–60.

6. Pawson, H. C. *Robert Bakewell*, 1957, p 23.

7. Little systematic information is available on estate building resources in this period, but on some of the larger estates they were clearly very considerable. Holkham estate produced its own bricks and timber (Wade-Martins, S. *The Holkham Estate in the Nineteenth Century; with Special Reference to Farm Building and Agricultural Improvement*, unpublished PhD thesis, University of East Anglia, 1975, pp 276–7). Robert Salmon, the builder, engineer and inventor who was clerk of the works of the Duke of Bedford's estate, used the estate brickworks for experiments in brickmaking (Robinson, J. M. 'Estate buildings of the 5th and 6th Dukes of Bedford, 1787–1839', *Architectural Review*, vol 160, 1976, pp 276–81). A sawpit shed built in the early nineteenth century on Lord Sheffield's estate in Sussex can be seen at the Weald and Downland Open Air Museum.

8. On one Norfolk estate, lack of interest on the part of the owner compelled tenants to make their own improvements (Wade-Martins, S. *A Great Estate at Work*, 1980, p 5).

9. '[Some] designers gave more thought to symmetry and decoration than utility in the hope of pleasing the eye of the proprietor' (Messenger, P. 'Lowther farmplans: a preliminary survey', *Transactions of the Cumberland and Westmorland Antiquarian and Archaeological Society*, vol 75, 1975, p 339). An extreme example of such peculiar priorities was the 'series of wonderfully dotty farmbuildings' with which the Duke of Norfolk enlivened the landscape of an area near Greystoke Castle, Cumberland, after its enclosure in 1778. (Robinson, J. M. 'The follies of Solomon. Architecture of the 11th Duke of Norfolk', *Country Life*, 30 June 1983, pp. 1796–1800). See also note 11.

10. Beatson, R. 'On farm buildings in general', *Communications to the Board of Agriculture*, vol. 1, 1797, p. 1. See also Wade-Martins, S. *A Great Estate at Work*, 1980, p 85.

11. Farey, J. *General View of the Agriculture of Derbyshire*, vol 2, 1815, p 9, makes specific reference to William Martin, the architect who designed the Earl of Chesterfield's home farm, but does not mention the employment of architects for commercial farm buildings. See also Messenger, P. 'Lowther farm plans; a preliminary survey', *Transactions of the Cumberland*

and Westmorland Antiquarian and Archaeological Society, vol 75, 1975, pp 345–6; Robinson, J. M. 'Model farm buildings in the age of improvement', *Architectural History*, vol 19, 1976, pp 17–32; Robinson, J. M. 'Estate buildings of the 5th and 6th Dukes of Bedford, 1787–1839', *Architectural Review*, vol 160, 1976, pp 276–81; de la Ruffiniere du Prey, P. 'Oblivion for Soane's cowbarn?', *Country Life*, 8 January 1976, p 84. The haystores in the original plans of Soane's architecturally impressive structure in County Durham were 'small, dangerously under-ventilated and inaccessible from the outside' and were amended by a more agriculturally minded builder; Robinson, J. M. 'Remaking the Shugborough landscape', *Country Life*, 10 March 1977, pp 578–81; Robinson, J. M. *The Wyatts. An architectural Dynasty*, 1980, p 33; Robinson, J. M. 'In pursuit of excellence', *Country Life*, 21 June 1979, pp 2113–16 (The Harewood estate); Darley, G. *The National Trust Book of the Farm*, 1981, pp 97–99; Wiliam, E. *Traditional Farm Buildings in North-East Wales, 1550–1900*, 1982, p 264; Fowler, P. *Farms in England*, 1983, plate 33. The steading which Sir John Soane built in 1793–4 for the 3rd Earl of Hardwicke at Wimpole Hall, Cambridgeshire, now belongs to the National Trust and houses an agricultural museum, and a centre for rare breeds. See the National Trust leaflet *The History: Wimpole Home Farm*, 1983, which describes Soane's work here and elsewhere. The buildings of Shugborough Park Farm, designed by Wyatt and described by Pitt, W. *General View of the Agriculture of Staffordshire*, 1813, p 110, are now part of an agricultural museum. Wyatt's work at Holkham included three sets of farm buildings and the Great Barn, built between 1784 and 1792, where Coke held his 'sheepshearings' (Wade-Martins, S. *A Great Estate at Work*, 1980, pp 149–55). Wyatt's 'expensive projects built on a grand scale' made his period of employment at Holkham 'more extravagant' than the more economic regimes of previous and later estate managers (Wade-Martins, S. *The Holkham Estate in the Nineteenth Century; with Special Reference to Farm Building and Agricultural Improvement*, unpublished PhD thesis, University of East Anglia, 1975, p 296). Robinson, J. M. 'Estate buildings at Holkham', *Country Life*, 21 November 1974, pp 1554–7 and 28 November 1974, pp 1642–5, describes Wyatt's work and notes on p 1557 that two of his field barns were demolished in the mid-nineteenth century with unflattering references to 'specimens of such classes of building as were approved of in the days of Wyatt the architect'. An early well-developed example of a 'gothick' barn, built in 1757, survives in Hampshire (Reynolds, J. *The Hampshire Barn*, unpublished thesis, Architectural Association, 1978, p 75). Falconer, K. *A Guide to England's Industrial Heritage*, 1980, p 74, lists a battlemented farmstead built in Cumberland in the early nineteenth century by J. C. Curwen, a prominent agricultural improver, and designed 'to symbolise agricultural leadership'. See also note 9.

12. Newton, R. *The Northumberland Landscape*, 1972, pp 120–1; Forestry Commission, National Forest Park Guides, *Border Guide*, 1962, p 13 for Nichol Forest; Williams, M. *The South Wales Landscape*, 1975, p 143 for Brecon; Chapman, V. 'North country farms of the moorland fringe', *Beamish One, the First Report of the North of England Open Air Museum Joint Committee*, 1978, pp 41–60 for Cordilleras Farm and other Pennine reclamations; Havinden, M. *The Somerset Landscape*, 1981, p 164; Williams, M. 'The enclosure and reclamation of the Mendip Hills, 1770–1870', *Agricultural History Review*, vol 19, 1971, pp 65–81. See also Peters, J. E. C. *The Development of Farm Buildings in Western Lowland Staffordshire up to 1880*, 1969, pp 24–5; Wiliam, E. *Traditional Farm Buildings in North-East Wales, 1550–1900*, 1982, p 23.

13. For maps showing farmsteads in parishes before and after enclosure, see Beresford, M. W. and St Joseph, J. K. S. *Mediaeval England. An Aerial Survey*, 1958, pp 30, 33, 256–7 (see Fig 9); Harris, A. *The Rural Landscape of the East Riding of Yorkshire, 1750–1850*, 1961, pp 15–16, 71; Whiting, J. R. S. *History at Source, Agriculture, 1730–1832*, 1971, p 8; Roberts, B. K. *Rural Settlement in England*, 1977, p 93; The Arts Council, *Traditional Farm Buildings*, 1978, p 33; Havinden, M. *The Somerset Landscape*, 1981, pp 176–7.

14. Lowe, R. *General View of the Agriculture of Nottinghamshire*, 1978, p 8; Plymley, J. *General View of the Agriculture of Shropshire*, 1803, p 102.

15. Davies, W. *General View of the Agriculture of South Wales*, vol 1, 1814, pp 129–30.

16. Davis, T. *General View of the Agriculture of Wiltshire*, 1811, p 9.

17. Waistell, C. *Designs for Agricultural Buildings*, 1827, pp 10–11.

18. Pitt, W. *General View of the Agriculture of Northampton*, 1809, p 275; Hoskins, W. G. *Leicestershire*, 1957, p 99.

19. Wedge, T. *General View of the Agriculture of the County Palatine of Chester*, 1794, p 12; Pringle, A. *General View of the Agriculture of the County of Westmorland*, 1805, p 300.

20. Allison, K. J. *The East Riding of Yorkshire Landscape*, 1976, p 160, for Wold Newton; Bigmore, P. *The Bedfordshire and Huntingdonshire Landscape*, 1979, pp 179–80 for Upton; Beresford, M. *History From the Ground*, 1957, p 89 for Salford. For other examples of the delay between enclosure and the building of farmsteads for the new farms see Taylor, C. *The Cambridgeshire Landscape*, 1973, pp 184–5 and Steane, J. M. *The Northamptonshire Landscape*, 1974, p 239. For another example of the continuing use of steadings in the village

see Pye, N. *Leicester and its Region*, 1972, p 254. See also Harris, A. *The Rural Landscape of the East Riding of Yorkshire, 1700–1850*, 1961, pp 59, 70–2; Peters, J. E. C. *The Development of Farm Buildings in Western Lowland Staffordshire up to 1880*, 1969, pp 22–7; Brill, E. *Life and Tradition in the Cotswolds*, 1973, p 17.

21. Harris, A. *The Rural Landscape of the East Riding of Yorkshire, 1700–1850*, 1961, p 71; Peters, J. E. C. *The Development of Farm Buildings in Western Lowland Staffordshire up to 1880*, 1969, pp 18–27. In Shropshire the replacement of old farmsteads in villages by new farmsteads on new sites during the reorganisation of the estate of the Marquis of Stafford created additional isolated farmsteads by causing a number of hamlets to shrink to single farms (Rowley, T. *The Landscape of Shropshire*, 1972, p 148).

22. A Quebec Farm to commemorate Wolfe's victory of 1759 was built at Sileby in Leicestershire after the parish was enclosed in 1760. The same county also contains a Belle Isle Farm and a Moscow Farm as well as the less auspicious New York Farm and Bunkers Hill Farm (Hoskins, W. G. *Leicestershire*, 1957, p 99; Hoskins, W. G. *Fieldwork in Local History*, 1967, p 75). There is another Bunkers Hill Farm at Little Catworth in Huntingdonshire, now Cambridgeshire, which was enclosed in 1781 (Bigmore, P. *Bedfordshire and Huntingdonshire Landscape*, 1979, p 180). Waterloo Farms are fairly common and there is a Nelson Farm at Hart and an Elba Farm at Biddick in Durham (*Rural Durham*, Durham County Library Local History Publications, 1977, p 47), a St Helena Farm in the Brecklands (Postgate, M. R. 'The field system of Breckland', *Agricultural History Review*, vol 10, 1962, p 87), a Wellington Farm on the Mendips (Williams, M. 'The enclosure and reclamation of the Mendip Hills, 1770–1870', *Agricultural History Review*, vol 19, 1971, p 80), and a Quebec and a Hougomont Farm in Wiltshire (*A Guide to the Industrial Archaeology of Wiltshire*, published by the Wiltshire County Council Museum Service for the Wiltshire Archaeology and Natural History Society, 1978, p 55). Hallfields Farm and Hemploe Farm at Welford in Northamptonshire are named after two of the open-fields enclosed in 1778 (*Farmers Weekly Drainage Supplement*, 29 August 1980, pp 12–13). Town Pasture Farm at Barnard Castle, Northfield Farm at Billingham and Southfield Farm at Sedgefield in Durham also recall the open-field system (*Rural Durham*, Durham County Library Local History Publications, 1977, p 47). Whitsundole Farm at Salford in Bedfordshire, built outside the village after the enclosure of 1808, was named after the 'doles' or portions of meadowland which until 1769 were allocated among the villagers by drawing lots every Whitsun (Beresford, M. *History on the Ground*, 1957, p 89). Standalone Farm, Lonesome Hall and Seldom Seen Farm reflect the remoteness of some of the farmsteads built after the enclosures (*Rural Durham*, Durham County Library Local History Publications, 1977, p 47). The various Botany Bay farms provide evidence of date as well as remoteness from the settlements of the pre-enclosure countryside. In Oxfordshire the element 'fields' or 'grounds' in farm placenames identifies post-enclosure farmsteads (Emery, F. *The Oxfordshire Landscape*, 1974, p 100). More individually, Cordilleras Farm, built near Marske in Yorkshire between 1813 and 1824, recalls its founder's enthusiasm for the cause of Spanish-American freedom and the discoveries of Humboldt (Chapman, V. 'North country farms of the moorland fringe', *Beamish One, the First Report of the North of England Open Air Museum Joint Committee*, 1978, p 46). On the same principle but on a larger scale the whig Duke of Norfolk who supported the cause of the American colonists pleasingly named the farms which he established on land near Greystoke Castle in Cumberland enclosed in 1778 after events and personalities of the American War of Independence in order to annoy his tory neighbours. (Robinson, J. M. 'The follies of Solomon. Architecture of the 11th Duke of Norfolk', *Country Life*, 30 June 1983, p 1798).

23. Palliser, D. M. *The Staffordshire Landscape*, 1976, pp 122–3; Havinden, M. *The Somerset Landscape*, 1981, p 164. See also Roberts, B. K. *Rural Settlement in Britain*, 1977, p 190, for a similar distinction at Napton in Warwickshire, enclosed between 1779 and 1781.

24. A survey of a village in Berkshire showed that a third of the cottages were originally the homes of open-field farmers (Havinden, M. *Estate Villages*, 1966, p 23). A later survey in a Yorkshire village found pre-enclosure farmsteads hard to identify. 'All that is now left standing is the house . . . and the barn which is generally sufficiently substantial to have merited retention' (Popham, J. H. *Farm Buildings, Function and Form*, unpublished thesis for Diploma in Conservation Studies, Institute of Advanced Architectural Studies, York University, 1973, p 15). For other examples of village survivals of pre-enclosure farmsteads, see Crump, W. B. 'The little hill farm', *Proceedings of the Halifax Antiquarian Society*, vol 35, 1938, p 183; Henderson, J. B. 'The eighteenth century dairy farmsteads of Appletree Hundred', *Derbyshire Miscellany*, vol 7, no 5, 1976, p 232; Nicholson, P. 'Wiltshire farm buildings', *Wiltshire Folklife*, vol 1, no 3, 1977, p 44. Studies of surviving remains of pre-enclosure farmsteads in villages would make a valuable addition to agricultural literature.

25. In this period the use of woodland and scrub for pigs seems to have come to an end except in the New Forest (Trow-Smith, R. *A History of British Livestock Husbandry, 1700–1900*, 1959, p 218). In Cheshire, in the early nineteenth century, the use of pigsties was

regarded as an innovation (Davies, C. S. *The Agricultural History of Cheshire, 1750–1850*, 1960, p 137). Similarly, a contemporary in Shropshire noted the need for pigsties (Plymley, J. *General View of the Agriculture of Shropshire*, 1803, p 108). The necessary connection between milkhouse and pigsty was a commonplace of the time: 'From the dairy we are naturally led to the hogsty' (Priest, St J. *General View of the Agriculture of Buckinghamshire*, 1810, p 32).

26. Young, A. *The Farmer's Guide to Hiring and Stocking Farms*, vol 1, 1770, p 49. Stone, T. *An Essay on Agriculture*, 1785, p 245, gives a similar list.

27. Garret, D. *Designs and Estimates of Farmhouses etc for the County of York, Northumberland, Cumberland, Westmorland and the Bishopric of Durham*, 1747. Later editions appeared in 1759 and 1772 (Robinson, J. M. 'In pursuit of excellence', *Country Life*, 28 June 1979, p 2114).

28. Henderson, J. B. 'The dairy farmsteads of Appletree Hundred', *Derbyshire Miscellany*, vol 7, no 5, 1976, p 237, refers to 'some good examples' of this type of layout including Highfields Farm, Etwall, which has a barn dated 1749 and a cowshed dated 1760. The house is dated 1752. Peters, J. E. C. *The Development of Farm Buildings in Western Lowland Staffordshire up to 1880*, 1969, p 52, gives a 1762 example. The name of Courtyard Farm, Ringstead, near Hunstanton, which was built after the enclosure of the parish in 1781 (leaflet, *Welcome to Courtyard Farm*, 1983, available to visitors to the farm) may well record conscious pride in the new type of design.

29. Towards the end of the century the system reached remote upland Yorkshire, introduced by Francis Mewburn of the Howe, near Castleton, whose farmstead still stands (Hartley, M. and Ingilby, J. *Life in the Moorlands of North-East Yorkshire*, 1972, p 6). In Devon, though 'the hillsides were far from ideal for the courtyard layout, all save the smallest holdings endeavoured to adopt it' (Devon County Council, *Devon's Traditional Buildings*, 1978, p 26).

30. Dickson, R. W. *General View of the Agriculture of Lancashire*, 1814, pp 96–7. See also Morgan, G. B. *General View of the Agriculture of Cornwall*, 1811, p 242, and Pitt, W. *General View of the Agriculture of Staffordshire*, 1796, p 19. Similarly, Waistell, describing a Surrey farmstead he remodelled in the later years of this period, concluded that 'almost every building would have been better placed in some other situation than that in which it had been found'. Yet he did not choose this farmstead to illustrate the extreme consequences of generations of casual buildings 'at six or seven different periods'. He had seen many farms in his time and knew that 'few ancient farmyards were better, while many were worse arranged' (Waistell, C. *Designs for Agricultural Buildings*, 1827, pp 103–7).

31. Wilson, J. M. *Rural Encyclopaedia*, 1849, vol 2, p 227.

32. Billingsley, J. *General View of the Agriculture of Somerset*, 1798, p 203.

33. Dickson, R. W. *General View of the Agriculture of Lancashire*, 1814, p. 645.

34. Hassall, C. *General View of the Agriculture of Monmouth*, 1812, p 25. Francis Blaikie, Coke's agent, also called manure 'the farmer's sheet anchor' (*The Husbandry of Farmyard Manure*, 1818, p 7). This booklet includes advice on 'the proper form of dungyards'.

35. Marshall, W. *The Landed Property of England*, 1804, p 159.

36. Young, A. *General View of the Agriculture of Hertfordshire*, 1804, p 21.

37. Pitt, W. *General View of the Agriculture of Staffordshire*, 1796, p 21; Hassall, C. *General View of the Agriculture of Monmouth*, 1812, p 24; Farey, J. *General View of the Agriculture of Derbyshire*, vol 2, 1815, p 12. There was also criticism of the tax on tiles which, by increasing their price, encouraged the use of thatch for roofing (Young, A. *Annals of Agriculture*, vol 2, 1784, pp 314–15; Billingsley, J. *General View of the Agriculture of Somerset*, 1798, p 87). In practice, of course, as Marshall pointed out, the straw used for thatching was eventually replaced and much of the old material found its way into the yards and so back to the fields (*Rural Economy of the Southern Counties*, vol 2, 1798, p 9).

38. Peters, J. E. C. *The Development of Farm Buildings in Western Lowland Staffordshire up to 1880*, 1969, pp 134–8.

39. Beatson, R. 'On farm buildings in general', *Communications to the Board of Agriculture*, vol 1, 1797, p 56.

40. Twamley, J. *Essays on the Management of the Dairy*, 1816, describes dairy practice in this period with recommendations on dairy design on pp 4–21, 104–10. See also the Castle Museum, York, *The Dairy Catalogue*, 1979, and Shropshire County Museum Information Sheet, *Aston Scott Working Farm Museum, The Dairy* n.d. A survey a few years ago found some 350 farmhouses in the Vale of Gloucestershire and 50 in Wiltshire which still contained cheese lofts, sometimes with the original louvered windows, and suggested that there were probably a number of similar survivals in Somerset, Herefordshire and Worcestershire (Nielsen, V. C. 'Cheesemaking and cheese chambers in Gloucestershire', *Industrial Archaeology*, vol 5, 1968, p 162–70). See also Brunskill, R. W. 'The development of the small house in the Eden valley', *Transactions of the Cumberland and Westmorland Antiquarian*

Plate 9   An early eighteenth-century Welsh longhouse. The lower building on the right is a later addition. This building is now in the Welsh Folk Museum, St Fagans, Cardiff (see Fig 8) (*The National Museum of Wales, Welsh Folk Museum*)

Plate 10   The building furthest from the camera is a longhouse, probably sixteenth century, at Lettaford in Devon. The building on its left is a small barn which includes masonry that could be contemporary with the longhouse. In the eighteenth and nineteenth centuries the addition of a stable (possibly when horses replaced oxen as workbeasts), a haybarn, a small cowhouse and a pigsty converted this longhouse farmstead which originally served a small mixed farm into a courtyard farmstead serving a more pastoral system of farming. A building on the left of the gate is the stable, the building on the right the haybarn (see page 57) (*Nigel Harvey*)

Plate 11  A farmstead about the year 1800. This engraving is probably impression-ist rather than precise, but it illustrates the varied enterprises of the traditional mixed farming system, the dependence on manual labour, and the use of local materials. For the explanation of the *DAIRY* inscription over the door near the beehives (see page 102) (*BBC Hulton Picture Library*)

Plate 12  This late eighteenth-century stable, now in the Avoncraft Museum of Buildings, continued in use until the 1950s. Hay was stored in the loft overhead and forked into the hayracks as required. The stall partitions, hayracks and manger are probably not original but are of traditional type (*Avoncraft Museum of Buildings*)

*and Archaeological Society*, vol 53, 1953, p 186; Brill, E. *Life and Tradition in the Cotswolds*, 1973, pp 39–47, plates 82–5. The importance of these farmhouse dairies is shown by the fiscal concessions granted to them. In 1795 an Act of Parliament (36 Geo 3 c117) exempted their windows from Window Tax provided they were made of wooden laths or iron bars and 'Dairy' or 'Cheeseroom' was painted on the door 'in large roman black letters, of two inches at least in height, and of proportionate width'. In 1808 and 1817 further Acts (48 Geo 3 c55 and 57 Geo 3 c25) extended this concession to wire and glass windows respectively. The exemption automatically ended when the Window Tax was abolished in 1851 (14 and 15 Vict c36; Personal communication from Mr T. R. F. Skemp). Surviving examples of such inscriptions are mentioned in Torr, C. *Small Talk at Wreyland*, 1927, p 171; Crump, W. B. 'The little hill farm', *Proceedings of the Halifax Antiquarian Society*, vol 35, 1938, p 139; Wood, C. B. 'Fascinating houses', *Farmers Weekly*, 2 October 1953, p 85; Barley, M. W. *The English Farmhouse and Cottage*, 1961, p 262; Nielsen, V. C. 'Cheesemaking and cheese chambers in Gloucestershire', *Industrial Archaeology*, vol 5, 1968, p 169; Devon County Council, *Devon's Traditional Buildings*, 1978, p 22. Examples can be seen at the Holly Tree Museum, Colchester and at the Manor Farm Museum, Cogges, Oxfordshire (see Plate 11).
41. Homes, I. 'The agricultural use of the Herefordshire house and its outbuildings', *Vernacular Architecture*, vol 9, 1978, p 12.
42. Waistell, C. *Designs for Agricultural Buildings*, 1827, p 17. Dickson, R. W. *The Farmer's Companion*, vol 1, 1813, p 98, gave similar advice. See also Peters, J. E. C. *The Development of Farm Buildings in Western Lowland Staffordshire up to 1880*, 1969, pp 58–60.
43. Homes, I. 'The agricultural use of the Herefordshire house and its buildings', *Vernacular Architecture*, vol 9, 1978, p 16.
44. Devon County Council, *Devon's Traditional Buildings*, 1978, p 18.
45. Peters, J. E. C. *The Development of Farm Buildings in Western Lowland Staffordshire up to 1880*, 1969, pp 194–9; Caffyn, L. *A Study of Farm Buildings in Selected Parishes in East Sussex*, unpublished MA thesis, Manchester University, 1981, pp 72–6; Brunskill, R. W. *Traditional Farm Buildings of Britain*, 1982, pp 88–91; Wiliam, E. *Traditional Farm Buildings in North-East Wales, 1550–1900*, 1982, pp 239–43.
46. Peters, J. E. C. *The Development of Farm Buildings in Western Lowland Staffordshire up to 1880*, 1969, p 119. Devon County Council, *Devon's Traditional Buildings*, 1978, p 20, refers to such 'keeping holes' in the walls of cowhouses. A relic of the less exacting side of the horseman's life can be seen at the Ryedale Folk Museum in Yorkshire, where the outline of a Nine Men's Morris board was carved by the stable boys on a corn bin.
47. Peters, J. E. C. *The Development of Farm Buildings in Western Lowland Staffordshire up to 1880*, 1969, p 203; Henderson, J. B. 'The eighteenth century dairy farmsteads of Appletree Hundred', *Derbyshire Miscellany*, vol 7, no 5, 1976, p 235; Wiliam, E. *Traditional Farm Buildings in North-East Wales, 1550–1900*, 1982, pp 246–7, 250. An example of such a two-storey building can be seen at the North of England Open Air Museum, Beamish, Durham.
48. Trow-Smith, R. *A History of British Livestock Husbandry, 1700–1900*, 1959, p 128.
49. Peters, J. E. C. *The Development of Farm Buildings in Western Lowland Staffordshire up to 1880*, 1969, pp 191, 206–7 for smithy, pp 179–80 for slaughterhouse. For cider-making equipment see Tucker, D. G. 'Millstone making at Penallt, Monmouthshire, *Industrial Archaeology*, vol 8, 1971, pp 233–4 and 321–3, which gives information on cider mills as well as on cider millstones; Brill, E. *Life and Tradition in the Cotswolds*, 1973, pp 47–51; Jenkins, J. G. *Life and Tradition in Rural Wales*, 1976, p 160. For the identification by Sir George Baker in 1767 of 'Devon colic' as poisoning from lead in cider dissolved from casks or presses see Oswald, N. C. 'Baker, Battie and Huxham', *Report and Transactions of the Devonshire Association*, vol 112, 1980, pp 119–21. For a case of lead poisoning in the 1970s caused by the use of an old lead-lined cider press for do-it-yourself cider see *New Scientist*, 20 December 1973, p 863 and 21 February 1974, p 520.
50. Harris, H. *The Industrial Archaeology of Dartmoor*, 1958, p 149; Devon County Council, *Devon's Traditional Buildings*, 1978, p 23; Spooner, G. M. ed, *Worth's Dartmoor*, 1967, pp 416–17; Brunskill, R. W. *Traditional Farm Buildings of Britain*, 1982, p 122. Ash-houses were in use within living memory when Worth, who died in 1950, collected material for his book.
51. Wiliam, E. *Traditional Farm Buildings in North-East Wales, 1550–1900*, 1982, p 249.
52. Bacon, R. N. *Report on the Agriculture of Norfolk*, 1844, pp 395–6.
53. Chapman, V. 'North country farms of the moorland fringe', *Beamish One, the First Report of the North of England Open Air Museum Joint Committee*, 1978, p 50. Little systematic information on the history of farm kilns is available and the argument for their abandonment in this period is based not on positive but on negative evidence – the lack of references to them in either contemporary or later literature – as well as on general probability. A study of the development, incidence and use of these kilns would fill a

noticeable gap in rural history.

54. Boys, J. *General View of the Agriculture of Kent*, 1805, p 188; Priest, St J. *General View of the Agriculture of Buckinghamshire*, 1810, pp 38–40, 332; Vancouver, C. *General View of the Agriculture of Devon*, 1813, pp 357–8; Robinson, D. H. 'A pigeon for the pot', *The Field*, 25 August 1951, p 298, including proposed tax; Peters, J. E. C. *The Development of Farm Buildings in Western Lowland Staffordshire up to 1880*, 1969, pp 204–6. Taylor, R. F., describing a dovecote probably dating from the seventeenth century in 'A cob dovecote at Durleigh', *Somerset Archaeology and Natural History*, vol 112, 1968, p 101, mentions that most dovecotes in the county 'appear to have gone out of use about 1800'.

55. Davies, *The Agricultural History of Cheshire, 1750–1850*, 1960, pp 167–75.

56. Bailey, J. and Culley, G. *General View of the Agriculture of Cumberland*, 1805, p 208.

57. Mitford, M. R. *Our Village*, 1904, p. 33. The sketches which were later collected into this book began to appear in a periodical in 1819.

58. Head, Sir George, *Home Tour Through the Manufacturing Districts of England in 1835*, 1836, p 255, quoted in Harris, A. *Rural Landscape of the East Riding of Yorkshire, 1700–1850*, 1961, p 11; Newton, R. *The Northumberland Landscape*, 1978, p 138.

59. *Church Farm House*, a guide issued by the Borough of Hendon, 1962, p 3.

60. Evans, G. E. *Ask the Fellows who Cut the Hay*, 1956, p 83.

61. Callen, W. H. 'Crypt farm, Cocking', *Sussex Notes and Queries*, vol 16, November 1963, p 49.

62. Roberts, R. O. *Farming in Caernarvonshire around 1800*, 1973, p 37. This book contains a detailed contemporary report on all the buildings of the Vaynol Estate.

63. Claridge, J. *General View of the Agriculture of Dorset*, 1793, p 31.

64. This pervading similarity is illustrated by the conclusions of architectural students competing in 1952 for the Bannister Fletcher silver medal offered for an area study of pre-Victorian farmsteads. A typical Surrey steading was described by the prize-winner as a barn, a yard, a few open shelters for cattle and a granary; a typical Shropshire steading by another competitor as a barn, usually with a granary above, a yard, cattle shelters, a cartshed, a few outbuildings and pigsties (West, C. T. *Farm Buildings in South-East Surrey*, 1952, in typescript in RIBA library, pp 10–11; Weller, J. B. *Farm Buildings of Shropshire before 1837*, 1952, in typescript, kindly lent by the author, pp 12, 17). See also Peters, J. E. C. *The Development of Farm Buildings in Western Lowland Staffordshire up to 1880*, 1969, pp 48–64; Weller, J. *History of the Farmstead*, 1982, pp 47–54. On a Yorkshire estate twenty of the twenty-four post-enclosure farmsteads followed the standard pattern and in twelve of these the barn stood on the north of the yard. In all other cases there was some physical reason for deviation from this plan (Popham, J. H. *Farm Buildings, Function and Form*, unpublished thesis for the Diploma in Conservation Studies, Institute of Advanced Architectural Studies, York University, 1975, pp 17–18. For descriptions and plans of the new standardised pattern of farmstead see Loudon, J. C. *Designs for Laying Out Farms and Farm Buildings in the Scotch Style*, 1811; Loch, J. *Account of the Improvements on the Estates of the Marquis of Stafford*, 1820, pp 180–1, Appendix IX, pp (69)–(103); Burke, J. B. *British Husbandry*, vol 1, 1834, pp 85–111. Wade-Martins, S. *A Great Estate at Work*, 1980, describes in detail the farm buildings of this period on Holkham estate, 'an ideal estate on which to study the development of farm building design and its effectiveness as an aid to improved agriculture' (pp 134–47). This magnificent and possibly unique chronological series of farmsteads includes Waterden Farm, which was praised when new by Arthur Young in 1784 and described by Blaikie, Coke's agent, in 1816 as 'perhaps the finest set of farm premises in Great Britain' (pp 143–4). It remains, little altered, as one of the best early examples of the Hanoverian plan.

65. Homes, I. 'The agricultural use of the Herefordshire house and its outbuildings', *Vernacular Architecture*, vol 9, 1978, p 14.

66. Marshall, W. *The Rural Economy of Yorkshire*, vol 1, 1788, p 127, was presumably thinking in lowland terms when he expressed surprise at seeing 'an instance of the entire farmery of a small upland farm being composed under one roof', though he was apparently seeing nothing more unusual than a recently built laithe house. Weller, J. B. *Farm Buildings of Shropshire before 1837*, 1952, in typescript, kindly lent by the author, p 12, quotes a case of a farmstead with granary, cowhouse and farmhouse all under one roof; but even in a county so near the longhouses of Wales, this was 'unusual'.

67. Newton, R. *The Northumberland Landscape*, 1972, p 137; Mercer, E. *English Vernacular Houses*, 1975, p 38. 'Some northern villages, such as Milburn in Westmorland, consist wholly of little farms of longhouse type built in the eighteenth and nineteenth centuries' (Cook, O. *English Cottages and Farmhouses*, 1982, p 134). But in such buildings the farmer's dwelling and the cowhouse were 'wholly divided'. It was the end of a long story. 'By the late eighteenth century the longhouse was as outdated in the North as in the South-west' (Mercer, E. *English Vernacular Houses*, 1975, p 42).

68. Messenger, P. 'Lowther farmsteads; a preliminary survey', *Transactions of the*

# The Agricultural Revolution: The Agrarian Phase, 1750–1820

*Cumberland and Westmorland Antiquarian and Archaeological Society*, vol 75, 1975, pp 341–3.

69. Atkinson, F. *Life and Traditions in Northumberland and Durham*, 1977, pp 55–7; Durham County Council Library, Local History Publications, *Rural Durham*, 1977, pp 45–7; Brunskill, R. W. *Traditional Farm Buildings of Britain*, 1982, pp 108–9.

70. Crump, W. B. 'The little hill farm', *Proceedings of the Halifax Antiquarian Society*, vol 35, 1938, pp 143–9; Davies, C. S. *The Agricultural History of Cheshire, 1750–1850*, 1960, p 67; Stell, C. 'Pennine houses, an introduction', *Folklife*, vol 3, 1965, pp 20–1; Davies, N. W. I. *Barns and Barn Conversion in Cumbria*, unpublished BSc thesis, Brunel University, 1979, p 31; Mercer, E. *English Vernacular Houses*, 1975, pp 45–9; Darley, G. *The National Trust Book of the Farm*, 1981, pp 198–9, 224–5; Brunskill, R. W. *Traditional Farm Buildings of Britain*, 1982, pp 107–8.

71. Brunskill, R. W. *Vernacular Architecture of the Lake Counties*, 1974, p 86; Brunskill, R. W. *Traditional Farm Buildings of Britain*, 1982, pp 112–15; Wiliam, E. *Traditional Farm Buildings in North-East Wales, 1550–1900*, 1982, pp 122–3.

72. Brunskill, R. W. *Traditional Farm Buildings of Britain*, 1982, pp 109–11.

73. Raistrick, A. *Buildings in the Yorkshire Dales*, 1976, p 98, which notes considerable replacement or extension of valley farm buildings between the 1770s and 1820s or 1830s which was the time when 'farmyards surrounded by buildings were accepted as a normal farm plan'; Hartley, M. and Ingilby, J. *Life in the Moorlands of North-East Yorkshire*, 1972, pp 5–6, for separation of farmhouse and buildings after the mid-eighteenth century. William Marshall commented on the standardised farmsteads built in the East Riding of Yorkshire after the enclosures, 'barns and stables on the north, stock hovels and implements on the east, dwelling houses to the west, the whole forming a square strawyard open to the south saving a high brick wall and tall boarded gates' (*The Rural Economy of Yorkshire*, 1788, vol 1, p 127; vol 2, p 251).

74. Messenger, P. 'Lowther farmstead plans; a preliminary survey', *Transactions of the Cumberland and Westmorland Antiquarian and Archaeological Society*, vol 75, 1975, pp 330, 335, 338, 343.

75. Durham County Library, Local History Publications, *Rural Durham*, 1977, p 43.

76. Wiliam E. *Traditional Farm Buildings in North-East Wales, 1550–1900*, 1982, pp 185–6, 268.

77. Davies, W. *General View of the Agriculture of South Wales*, vol 1, 1814, p 129.

78. Portsmouth, Earl of, 'The fixed equipment of the farm', *Journal of the Royal Agricultural Society of England*, vol 107, 1946, p 100. A survey in Shropshire a few years later found 139 irregular, formless or abnormally sited farmsteads. But of the 357 steadings of classifiable patterns, 181 were built on three sides of a square, and 41 on four sides of a square (Davies, D. C. G. *Historic Farmstead and Farmhouse Types of the Shropshire Region*, unpublished MA thesis, Manchester University, 1952, p 88). A survey in Staffordshire found that of 212 classifiable plans of farmsteads as they were in 1880, 88 were on three sides of a square and 23 on four sides of a square. All these dated from the latter half of the eighteenth century onwards. There were 65 L-shaped farmsteads and 36 farmsteads consisting of a single row of buildings; the former dated from the late seventeenth century onwards, the latter from 1600 onwards (Peters, J. E. C. *The Development of Farm Buildings in Western Lowland Staffordshire up to 1880*, 1969, p 49). A survey of 68 farmsteads in Sussex found 5 farmsteads built on three sides of a square, 18 on four sides, 17 L-shaped and 28 consisting of 'scattered' buildings (Caffyn, L. *A Study of Farm Buildings in Selected Parishes in East Sussex*, unpublished MA thesis, Manchester University, 1981, p 38). A survey of 363 farmsteads in Wales found 101 built on three sides of square, 18 on four sides of square, 111 L-shaped, 12 unclassifiable and the remaining 121 single-row or double-row (Wiliam, E. *Traditional Farm Buildings in North-East Wales, 1550–1900*, 1982, p 37). In three of the surveys, therefore, 'Hanoverian pattern' farmsteads formed the largest single group of classifiable farmsteads. Even in Wales, where older traditions were stronger, they formed a third of the total and were only just outnumbered by single- and double-row steadings.

79. Peters, J. E. C. *The Development of Farm Buildings in Western Lowland Staffordshire up to 1880*, 1969, pp 27, 31–5. In Devon such isolated units often consisted of a traditional linney with a yard attached (Devon County Council, *Devon's Traditional Buildings*, 1978, p 20). See also Caffyn, L. *A Study of Farm Buildings in Selected Parishes of East Sussex*, unpublished MA thesis, Manchester University, 1981, pp 78–9.

80. Hartley, M. and Ingilby, J. *Life and Tradition in the Yorkshire Dales*, 1968, p 29.

81. Davis, T. *General View of the Agriculture of Wiltshire*, 1811, pp 10, 12; Jones, E. L. 'Eighteenth century changes in Hampshire chalkland farming', *Agricultural History Review*, vol 8, 1960, p 15; Taylor, C. *Dorset*, 1970, p 152; Brandon, P. *The Sussex Landscape*, 1974, p 194; East Sussex County Planning Department, *Barn Trails*, 1979. Descriptions of two of these secondary steadings, one over a mile from its homestead, are given in Pilkington, P. *Sussex Downland Farms*, an unpublished thesis on a survey in the Alfriston area submitted to

107

the Architectural Association School of Architecture in 1962.

82. Milner, A. B. *The History of Micheldever*, 1924, pp 243–4.

83. East Sussex County Planning Department, *Barn Trails*, 1979.

84. Popham, J. H. *Farm Buildings, Function and Form*, unpublished thesis for Diploma in Conservation Studies, Institute of Advanced Architectural Studies, York University, 1973, p 17; Allison, K. *The East Riding of Yorkshire Landscape*, 1976, p 164.

85. Long, W. H. and Davies, G. M. *Farm Life in a Yorkshire Dale, an Economic Study of Swaledale*, 1948, pp 47, 62; Hartley, M. and Ingilby, J. *Life and Tradition in the Yorkshire Dales*, 1968, pp 29, 32; Long, W. H. *Survey of the Agriculture of Yorkshire*, 1969, pp 54–5; Raistrick, A. *The West Riding of Yorkshire*, 1970, p 92; D'Arcy, J. 'Stone barns for better or worse', *Farmers Weekly*, 24 September 1971, p 111; Harris, H. *Industrial Archaeology of the Peak District*, 1971, p 146; Brunskill, R. W. *Vernacular Architecture of the Lake Counties*, 1974, pp 86–7; Smith, P. *Houses of the Welsh Countryside*, 1975, p 153; Brunskill, R. W. *Traditional Buildings of Britain*, 1982, pp 115–20; Wiliam, E. *Traditional Farm Buildings in North-East Wales, 1550–1900*, 1982, pp 31–2; Davies, N. W. I. *Barns and Barn Conversion in Cumbria*, unpublished BSc thesis, Brunel University, 1979, pp 17–22, 62, 82–3, refers on p 17 to field barns standing on large farms before the enclosure of the commons, though their numbers increased greatly when the former common grazings were brought into cultivation.

86. Tuke, J. *General View of the Agriculture of the North Riding*, 1880, p 34–5; Agricultural Advisory and Development Service, Ministry of Agriculture, Fisheries and Food, *Farm and Socio-economic Studies: 1, The North Pennines. 2, The Yorkshire Pennines*, bound together, 1975, p 14.

87. Brunskill, R. W. *Vernacular Architecture of the Lake Counties*, 1974, p 80; Countryside Commission, *A Study of the Hartsop Valley*, 1976, pp 26–8; Brunskill, R. W. *Traditional Farm Buildings of Britain*, 1982, pp 78–9.

88. Trow-Smith, R. *A History of British Livestock Husbandry, 1700–1900*, 1959, p 189.

89. Young, A. *General View of the Agriculture of Essex*, vol 2, 1807, p 343.

90. Middleton, J. *General View of the Agriculture of Middlesex*, 1813, pp 46, 453–7. The breed used was the Dorset Horn, which is remarkable in that the ewes will take the ram practically the whole year round, thus making autumn lambing possible.

91. Trow-Smith, R. *A History of British Livestock Husbandry, 1700–1900*, 1959, pp 210–11.

92. Atkinson, F. *Industrial Archaeology of the North-East*, vol 2, 1974, p 247.

93. Young, A. *A Farmer's Tour Through the East of England*, vol 1, 1778, pp 404–6. See also Peters, J. E. C. *The Development of Farm Buildings in Western Lowland Staffordshire up to 1880*, 1969, pp 160–1.

94. Stevenson, W. *General View of the Agriculture of Surrey*, 1809, pp 523–4.

95. Boys, J. *General View of the Agriculture of Kent*, 1805, p 32. See also Stevenson, W. *General View of the Agriculture of Lancashire*, 1814, p 190, where a farm-made weighing machine receives a separate section which suggests that it was unusual. A little later Sir John Sinclair described a weighing machine as 'an expensive article . . . but where it can be afforded of much consequence' in securing the proper rationing of fatstock (*The Code of Agriculture*, 1821, p 136).

96. Clarke, Sir Ernest 'The Board of Agriculture, 1793–1822', *Journal of the Royal Agricultural Society of England*, 3rd ser, vol 9, 1898, p 19.

97. Mathias, P. 'Agriculture and the brewing and distilling industries in the eighteenth century', *Economic History Review*, 2nd ser, vol 5, 1952–3, p 252.

98. Middleton, J. *General View of the Agriculture of Middlesex*, 1813, pp 417, 579. See also Atkins, P. J. 'London's intra-urban milk supply c1790–1914', *Transactions of the Institute of British Geographers*, 1977, pp 383–9; Stout, A. 'Three centuries of London cowkeeping', *Farmers Weekly*, 18 August 1978, pp v–xiii. There was also a town dairy enterprise in Liverpool, where between 1794 and 1824 the number of cowkeepers rose from about 70 to 149, the number of cows from 600 to 1,192 (Grundy, J. E. *The Origins of Liverpool Cowkeepers*, unpublished MA thesis, Lancaster University, 1982, p 30).

99. Drummond, J. C. *The Englishman's Food*, 1957, p 193.

100. Middleton, J. *General View of the Agriculture of Middlesex*, 1813, pp 422–4.

101. Harley, W. *The Harleian System*, 1829; Anon, 'William Harley and his dairy system', *Quarterly Journal of Agriculture*, vol 24, 1863–5, pp 207–19.

102. James, W. and Malcolm, J. *General View of the Agriculture of Surrey*, 1794, pp 34–7.

103. James, W. and Malcolm, J. *General View of the Agriculture of Surrey*, 1794, pp 31–2; Stevenson, W. *General View of the Agriculture of Surrey*, 1809, pp 522–3. This was not, however, the first reference to the use of slatted floors, which had been described nearly a century earlier as a traditional practice in oxstalls in Kent, where the urine was collected for manuring fruit trees (Mortimer, J. *The Whole Art of Husbandry*, vol 2, 1721, pp 282–3). Loudon, J. C. *Encyclopaedia of Agriculture*, 1866 ed, p 1025, describes a poorly designed

fattening house for 600 head of cattle at Brentford. He gives no date for its construction, but the reference to its gaslights suggests it was later than those previously mentioned.

104. By the same token, Bakewell copied the dung channels in the floors of his bullock fattening houses from the better type of London cowhouse (Trow-Smith, R. *A History of British Livestock Husbandry, 1700–1900*, 1959, pp 55, 193).

105. Curwen, J. C. *Hints on Agricultural Subjects*, 1809, pp 181–91; Sinclair, Sir John, *The Code of Agriculture*, 1821, p 487.

106. Young, A. *General View of the Agriculture of Hertfordshire*, 1804, p 198; Young, A. *General View of the Agriculture of Essex*, vol 2, 1807, pp 346–9.

107. Adams, G. *A Treatise Upon a New System of Agriculture*, 1810.

108. Sinclair, Sir John. *The Code of Agriculture*, 1821, pp 150–1.

109. For fother room, see Lowe, R. *General View of the Agriculture of Nottinghamshire*, 1798, p 10; for calf floor see Young, A. *General View of the Agriculture of Essex*, vol 1, 1807, p 45.

110. For potato cellars see Spooner, G. M. ed, *Worth's Dartmoor*, 1967, pp 416–17; Harris, H. *Industrial Archaeology of Dartmoor*, 1968, p 150. For steam boilers see Beatson, R. 'On farm buildings in general', *Communications to the Board of Agriculture*, vol 1, 1797, p 41; Stevenson, W. *General View of the Agriculture of Lancashire*, 1814, p 381; Architects in Agriculture, *Coleshill Model Farm, Oxfordshire*, 1981, p 18; for turnip houses see Peters, J. E. C. *The Development of Farm Buildings in Western Lowland Staffordshire up to 1880*, 1969, pp 167–8; Messenger, P. 'Lowther farmstead plans. A preliminary survey', *Transactions of the Cumberland and Westmorland Antiquarian and Archaeological Society*, vol 75, 1975, pp 343–4; Wade-Martins, S. *A Great Estate at Work*, 1980, p 156.

111. Davies, C. S. *The Agricultural History of Cheshire, 1750–1850*, 1960, p 122; Peters, J. E. C. *The Development of Farm Buildings in Western Lowland Staffordshire up to 1880*, 1969, pp 187–90; Martin, D. and Martin, B. *Historic Farm Buildings in Eastern Sussex*, 'Ancillary farm buildings', vol 1, no 3, 1979, pp 67–8; 'Agriculture', vol 1, no 4, 1979, pp 102–3; Caffyn, L. *A Study of Farm Buildings in Selected Parishes of East Sussex*, unpublished MA thesis, Manchester University, 1981, pp 76–7; Tyson, B. 'Skirwith Hall and Wilton tenement (Kirkland Hall). The rebuilding of two Cumbrian farmsteads in the eighteenth century', *Transactions of the Cumberland and Westmorland Antiquarian and Archaeological Society*, vol 81, 1981, p 95.

112. Rudge, T. *General View of the Agriculture of Gloucestershire*, 1807, p 43; Young, A. *General View of the Agriculture of Essex*, vol 1, 1807, pp 47–8; Young, A. *General View of the Agriculture of Sussex*, 1808, p 20; Vancouver, C. *General View of the Agriculture of Hampshire*, 1810, p 64. See also Sinclair, Sir John, 'Account of corn staddles at Woburn Abbey', *Communications to the Board of Agriculture*, vol 1, 1797, pp 2–3; Reynolds, J. *The Hampshire Barn*, unpublished thesis, Architectural Association, 1978, p 24; Nicholson, P. 'Wiltshire buildings', *Wiltshire folklife*, vol 2, no 3, Spring 1979, pp 49–54; Powell, G. H. 'Granaries on staddle stones in the Isle of Wight', *Proceedings of the Isle of Wight Archaeological Society*, vol 7, 1981, pp 259–63.

113. Jones, E. L. 'The bird pests of British agriculture in recent centuries', *Agricultural History Review*, vol 20, 1972, p 115.

114. Rogers, A. 'Flyers on the nightshift', *Farmers Weekly*, 5 February 1982, p 97. Reynolds, J. *The Hampshire Barn*, unpublished thesis, Architectural Association, 1978, p 11, noted owl holes in the gable ends of several barns.

115. Peters, J. E. C. *The Development of Farm Buildings in Western Lowland Staffordshire up to 1880*, 1969, pp 97–8.

116. Wiliam, E. *Traditional Farm Buildings in North-East Wales, 1550–1900*, 1982, p 203 for early reference, though in this area looseboxes are mainly nineteenth century; Peters, J. E. C. *The Development of Farm Buildings in Western Lowland Staffordshire up to 1880*, 1969, pp 158–62.

117. Mavor, W. *General View of the Agriculture of Berkshire*, 1809, pp 68–9.

118. Mavor, W. *General View of the Agriculture of Berkshire*, 1809, p 69.

119. King-Hele, O. G. 'The Lunar Society of Birmingham', *Nature*, vol 212, no 5059, 15 November 1966, p 231.

120. Boys, J. *General View of the Agriculture of Kent*, 1805, p 32; Morgan, G. *General View of the Agriculture of Cornwall*, 1811, p 24.

121. Such designs were common in that 'extraordinary flood' of expensive albums on *la ferme ornée* which appeared in the latter years of this period (Briggs, M. S. *The English Farmhouse*, 1954, pp 199–203). But these publications merely suggested picturesque accessories to tasteful homes for the nobility and gentry and form no part of agricultural history. There was, however, a limited agricultural interest in the possibilities of such unorthodox systems and the case for a polygonal farmstead was stated by William Marshall, one of the most practical farming writers of the time. (*The Landed Property of England*, 1804, pp 161–3). He knew of no set of buildings constructed on this principle, though a few

circular or semi-circular buildings or steadings were built about this time (Billingsley, J. *General View of the Agriculture of Somerset*, 1798, p 88; Young, A. *Annals of Agriculture*, vol 20, 1798, pp 449, 502; Young, A. *General View of the Agriculture of Sussex*, 1808, Figs 1–3; Dickson, R. W. *Practical Agriculture*, vol 1, 1805, pp 70–3; Robinson, J. M. *The Wyatts, an Architectural Dynasty*, 1980, p 33). But the fashion never established itself in general practice for reasons given by a realistic contemporary. Designs 'fantastically planned, in sweeps, semi-circles, octagons and pentagons . . . look pretty on paper, but when you come to construct them a good deal of difficulty occurs in roofing and a great deal of room is thrown away which cannot be applied to any beneficial purpose' (Hassall, C. *General View of the Agriculture of Monmouth*, 1812, p 25). A large, existing crescent-shaped cowhouse built by Sir John Soane at Burn Hill in Co Durham in the 1780s is described by de la Ruffiniere du Prey, P. 'Oblivion for Soane's cowbarn?', *Country Life*, 8 January 1976, p 84. See, however, note 11.

122. The ancestor of the Dutch barn was the 'hanging roof upon postes' that could be raised or lowered 'with pinnes and winches' which Sir Hugh Plat noticed in Holland in the sixteenth century. He built such a barn on his farm in Hertfordshire and may possibly have founded a local tradition there, since Peter Kalm saw a similar type of building in the same area in 1748 (Fussell, G. E. 'Low Countries' influence on English farming', *English Historical Review*, vol 74, 1959, p 521; see also Thirsk, J. ed, *The Agrarian History of England and Wales*, vol 4, 1967, p 744). A little later, T. Lightoler showed such structures and described them as 'Dutch barns' in his wildly impracticable album of farm building designs (*Gentleman and Farmer's Friend*, 1774, plates 3, 22, 33). Dutch barns with adjustable roofs were found in Wales in the early 1800s (Davies, W. *General View of the Agriculture and Domestic Economy of North Wales*, 1810, p 224). But elsewhere by this time farmers had adopted a more practical type of design in which the cumbersome and relatively fragile adjustable roof was replaced by a fixed roof, and the 'open', 'skeleton' or 'Dutch' barn, similar in principle, though not in construction, to the most familiar of all buildings on the modern farm was established practice in many parts of the country (Marshall, W. *Rural Economy of the Southern Counties*, vol 2, 1798, p 105; Young, A. *General View of the Agriculture of Essex*, vol 1, 1807, p 48; Mavor, W. *General View of the Agriculture of Berkshire*, 1809, p 69; Pitt, W. *General View of the Agriculture of Staffordshire*, 1809, p 20; Gooch, W. *General View of the Agriculture of Cambridgeshire*, 1811, p 30). An example of one of these early Dutch barns is shown in *Country Life*, 23 June 1955, p 1683. See also Peters, J. E. C. *The Development of Farm Buildings in Western Lowland Staffordshire up to 1880*, 1969, p 93–5; Smith, P. *Houses of the Welsh Countryside*, 1975, pp 145–6, 152. A form of the original Dutch barn with a roof that could be lowered was 're-invented' early this century by a Warwickshire farmer, but this was no more than a curiosity (Haggard, Rider H. *Rural England*, 1902, p 412).

123. Fussell, G. E. *English Dairy Farmer*, 1966, p 141; Marshall, W. *Rural Economy of the Midland Counties*, 1790, p 32; Lowe, R. *General View of the Agriculture of Nottinghamshire*, 1798, p 10; Marshall, W. *Rural Economy of the West of England*, vol 2, 1796, pp 353–4; Priest, St J. *General View of the Agriculture of Buckinghamshire*, 1810, pp 33–4; Waistell, C. *Designs for Agricultural Buildings*, 1827, pp 39–41; Peters, J. E. C. *The Development of Farm Buildings in Western Lowland Staffordshire up to 1880*, 1969, pp 141–6, 150–8; Brunskill, R. W. *Traditional Farm Buildings of Britain*, 1982, pp 60–6; Wiliam, E. *Traditional Farm Buildings in North-East Wales, 1550–1900*, 1982, pp 186–93, 196–203.

124. Young, A. *The Farmer's Guide to Hiring and Stocking Farms*, vol 1, 1770, pp 51, 53–4.

125. Stevenson, W. *General View of the Agriculture of Surrey*, 1809, p 30; Murray, A. *General View of the Agriculture of Warwickshire*, 1813, p. 80. For a summary of recommended practice at the end of this period see Waistell, C. *Designs for Agricultural Buildings*, 1827, pp 43–6. See also Peters, J. E. C. *The Development of Farm Buildings in Western Lowland Staffordshire up to 1880*, 1969, pp 110–29; Caffyn, L. *A Study of Farm Buildings in Selected Parishes in East Sussex*, unpublished MA thesis, Manchester University, 1981, pp 65–72; Wiliam, E. *Traditional Farm Buildings of North-East Wales, 1550–1900*, 1982, pp 160–77. Brunskill, R. W. *Vernacular Architecture of the Lake Counties*, 1974, p 76, notes the increasing importance of the stable in the eighteenth century. In a very different area, Martin, D. and Martin, B. 'Ancillary farm buildings', *Historic Buildings in Eastern Sussex*, vol 1, no 3, 1979, p 63, found evidence of increased buildings of stables in the later eighteenth century.

126. Marshall, W. *Rural Economy of the West of England*, vol 2, 1796, pp 307–13.

127. Batchelor, T. *General View of the Agriculture of Bedfordshire*, 1803, p 19; Rudge, T. *General View of the Agriculture of Gloucestershire*, 1807, p 300; Mavor, W. *General View of the Agriculture of Berkshire*, 1809, p 64; Dickson, R. *General View of the Agriculture of Lancashire*, 1814, p 96.

128. Young, A. *The Farmer's Guide to Hiring and Stocking Farms*, vol 2, 1770, p 443. See also Pomeroy, W. *General View of the Agriculture of Worcestershire*, 1794, pp 24–5; Billingsley, J. *General View of the Agriculture of Somerset*, 1798, p 32; Murray, A. *General View of the Agriculture of Warwickshire*, 1813, p 30; Davies, W. *General View of the Agriculture of South Wales*, vol 1, 1814, pp 131, 157.

129. This was Wordsworth's denunciation of the 'huge, unsightly barn, built solely for convenience and violating all the modesty of rustic proportions' which Mr K, the substantial Leicestershire farmer who moved to the Lake District for such distressingly personal reasons, tactlessly built on his farm at Grasmere (De Quincey, T. *Reminiscences of the English Lake Poets*, 1834, Everyman ed 1929, p 312). Such standards of judgement would have been considered irrelevant or, more probably, perverse by most of his agricultural contemporaries who assessed their farmsteads solely in terms of 'convenience' and seldom considered their appearance a matter even worth mentioning in their professional literature.

130. Steane, J. M. ed, *Cogges, a Museum of Farming in the Oxfordshire Countryside*, Oxford County Council, Department of Museum Services, 1980, pp 19–20.

131. Waistell, C. *Designs for Agricultural Buildings*, 1827, pp 103–7. William Marshall mentions an earlier case of farmstead improvement but gives few details and no plans (*Rural Economy of the Midland Counties*, vol 2, 1790, pp 52–60).

132. Fussell, G. E. *The Farmer's Tools*, 1952, pp 158–9, 180–2, 185.

133. Peters, J. E. C. *The Development of Farm Buildings in Western Lowland Staffordshire up to 1880*, 1969, p 77.

134. For the development of mechanical threshing see Fussell, G. E. *The Farmer's Tools*. 1952, pp 152–79; Fussell, G. E. 'Thrashing and barn machinery', *Journal of the Chartered Land Agents Society*, February 1960, pp 61–71; Collins, E. J. T. *Sickle to Combine*, 1969, pp 35–41; MacDonald, S. 'The early thrashing machine in Northumberland', *Tools and Tillage*, vol 3, 1978, pp 168–84; Collins, E. J. T. 'The diffusion of the thrashing machine in Britain, 1790–1880', *Tools and Tillage*, vol 1, 1972, pp 16–33; MacDonald, S. 'The progress of the early thrashing machine', *Agricultural History Review*, 1975, pp 63–77; Brunskill, R. W. *Traditional Farm Buildings of Britain*, 1982, pp 48–55; Wiliam, E. *Traditional Farm Buildings in North-East Wales, 1550–1900*, 1982, pp 126–7. For a comparison of costs of threshing by flail and horse-driven threshing machine see Stevenson, W. *General View of the Agriculture of Lancashire*, 1814, pp 167–8.

135. Tuke, J. *General View of the Agriculture of the North Riding of Yorkshire*, 1800, p 82; Pitt, W. *General View of the Agriculture of Northamptonshire*, 1809, p 55.

136. Peters, J. E. C. *Discovering Traditional Farm Buildings*, 1981, p 29. See also note 134.

137. Branch-Johnson, W. *The Carrington Diary*, 1956, p 26. For waterpower see also Warren, D. 'Waterpower on farms in West Somerset', *Somerset Industrial Archaeological Journal*, no 1, 1976, pp 5–12. A waterpowered barn installation built in the first decade of the nineteenth century can be seen at Park Farm, Shugborough, Staffordshire, now an agricultural museum. At Honington Grange, Lilleshall, in the same county a waterwheel installed by 1820 to drive barn machinery was powered by water from a system of ponds which may have originated as medieval fishponds and were used in the sixteenth century to power a blast furnace (information given during an Institute of Archaeology course visit to the farm in 1982). For a surviving 1804 waterwheel installation which originally drove a threshing machine see Reynolds, J. *The Hampshire Barn*, unpublished thesis, Architectural Association, 1978, p 26.

138. A windmill apparently built for driving a threshing machine survives on the outskirts of Brighton. A photograph of it appears in Jones, S. R. *English Village Homes*, 1936, p 82. Loudon, J. C. *Encyclopaedia of Cottage, Farm and Villa Architecture*, 1836, pp 471–3, shows a proposed farmstead which includes a threshing machine and other barn machinery powered by a windmill. See also Falconer, K. *A Guide to England's Industrial Heritage*, 1980, pp 74, 172; Brunskill, R. W. *Traditional Farm Buildings of Britain*, 1982, pp 51–3. See also note 139.

139. In Northumberland, 51 of the threshing machines installed between 1796 and 1820 whose source of power is known were driven by horses, 28 by water and 2 by wind (MacDonald, S. 'The early thrashing machine in Northumberland', *Tools and Tillage*, vol 3, 1978, p 175). Nearly all the 37 new farmsteads built on the Midland estates of the Marquis of Stafford in this period were equipped with threshing machines. Waterpower was used when available, steampower otherwise. Two steam engines were installed on the Shropshire estates of the Marquis in 1812 and 1816 (Loch, J. *An Account of the Improvements on the Estates of the Marquis of Stafford*, 1820, pp 180–1; Peters, J. E. C. *The Development of Farm Buildings in Western Lowland Staffordshire up to 1880*, 1969, p 104). In one area of Staffordshire, the first installation was a waterpower scheme in 1808, and what was probably the first horsepower scheme in 1820 (Peters, J. E. C. *The Development of Farm Buildings in Western Lowland Staffordshire up to 1880*, 1969, pp 102–4). The first agricultural steam engine

in the country and probably in the world was installed in 1798 by Wilkinson the ironmaster, who used steam for threshing on his Denbighshire farm, now in Clwyd (Davies, W. *General View of the Agriculture of North Wales*, 1810, p 122) and by 1810 a Durham quarry owner had harnessed for threshing a steam engine used for pumping water from his workings (Bailey, J. *General View of the Agriculture of Durham*, 1810, p 81). The industrial connection is obvious. In 1811 Trevithick installed a steam engine for threshing in Cornwall (Coleman, J. 'Report on exhibition of implements, award of medals etc at the International Meeting at Kilburn', *Journal of the Royal Agricultural Society of England*, 2nd ser, vol 15, 1879, p 732). This engine, the oldest agricultural steam engine in the world, is now in the Science Museum, London (see Plate 19). It is not, however, wholly original, as its boiler was replaced in 1856. It was built for Sir Christopher Hawkins and gave such good performance that another Cornish landowner, Lord Dedunstanville, ordered an engine from Trevithick. The boiler of this second engine is also in the Science Museum (Titley, A. *Richard Trevithick*, 1934, pp 130–1). The true ancestor of general farmstead mechanisation, however, was a steam plant installed in 1804 on a Norfolk farm, where it drove a grinding mill and chaff-cutter as well as a threshing machine (Young, A. *General View of the Agriculture of Norfolk*, 1804, p 73).

140. Peters, J. E. C. *The Development of Farm Buildings in Western Lowland Staffordshire up to 1880*, 1969, pp 86–7.

141. Young, A. *General View of the Agriculture of Essex*, vol 1, 1807, p 47.

142. Mavor, W. *General View of the Agriculture of Berkshire*, 1809, pp 66–7.

143. Gooch, W. *General View of the Agriculture of Cambridgeshire*, 1811, p 31.

144. Young, A. *General View of the Agriculture of Oxfordshire*, 1809, p 20.

145. Young, A. *General View of the Agriculture of Oxfordshire*, 1809, p 20; Dickson, R. *General View of the Agriculture of Lancashire*, 1814, p 97.

146. Peters, J. E. C. *The development of Farm Buildings in Western Lowland Staffordshire up to 1880*, 1969, pp 86–7. See also Sweetland, P. *The Barns of Bredon Hill*, unpublished thesis, Birmingham School of Architecture, 1979, p 30.

147. Hutton, K. 'The distribution of wheelhouses in the British Isles', *Agricultural History Review*, vol 24, 1976, pp 30–5, which gives the number of existing wheelhouses on p 30. For wheelhouses and horse-driving gear see Hellen, J. A. 'Some provisional notes on wheelhouses and their distribution in Northumberland', *Journal of the Geographical Society of the University of Newcastle-upon-Tyne*, vol 18, 1970, pp 19–28; Rowland, J. H. 'Horsepower on the farm', *Country Life*, 29 January 1970, p 254; Hellen, J. A. 'Agrarian history unobserved', *Country Life*, 11 November 1971, pp 1325–6; *Country Life*, 23 December 1971, p 1792; Wright, P. A. *Salute the Carthorse*, 1971, p 46–8; Hartley, M. and Ingilby, J. *Life in the Moorlands of North-East Yorkshire*, 1972, p 67; Hellen, J. A. 'Agricultural innovations and detectable landscape margins; the case of wheelhouses in Northumberland', *Agricultural History Review*, vol 20, 1972, p 140–54; Harrison, A. and Harrison, J. K. 'The horsewheel in North Yorkshire', *Industrial Archaeology*, vol 10, 1973, pp 247–64, 337–9; Atkinson, F. *Industrial Archaeology of the North East*, vol 1, 1974, pp 186–92 and entries to wheelhouses in gazette in vol 2; Brunskill, R. W. *Vernacular Architecture of the Lake Counties*, 1974, p 87–9; *Country Life*, 17 July 1975, p 150; Atkinson, F. *Life and Tradition in Northumberland and Durham*, 1977, pp 71–6; Brunskill, R. W. *Traditional Farm Buildings of Britain*, 1982, pp 48–54; Weller, J. *History of the Farmstead*, 1982, pp 135–9; Wiliam, E. *Traditional Farm Buildings in North-East Wales, 1550–1900*, 1982, pp 151–2. For wheelhouses serving cidermaking machinery see Laycock, C. H. 'The Roundhouse or Machinehouse', *Devon and Cornwall Notes and Queries*, vol 11, 1920, pp 285–7; Laycock, C. H. 'The old Devon farmhouse', *Report and Transactions of the Devonshire Association*, vol 52, 1920, pp 165, 189; Sheldon, L. 'Devon Barns', *Report and Transactions of the Devonshire Association*, vol 64, 1932, p 391; Reed, M. 'Poundhouses and cider presses', *Devon and Cornwall Notes and Queries*, vol 33, 1974–7, p 90; Hook, B., Ward, A. P. and Murless, B. I. 'Horse gins in Somerset', *Journal of the Somerset Industrial Archaeological Society*, no 1, 1976, pp 31–4; Devon County Council, *Devon's Traditional Buildings*, 1978, pp 22–3.

148. Young, A. *The Farmer's Guide to Hiring and Stocking Farms*, vol 1, 1770, pp 50–5. Stone, T. *An Essay on Agriculture*, 1785, pp 243–51, gave similar 'hints and tips' advice.

149. Garret's book of 1747 (see note 27) was the first book solely concerned with farm buildings, but this consisted of plans without explanatory text. Most of the other publications on farm buildings between 1747 and 1797 were concerned with the imaginary possibilities of *la ferme ornée* and cannot be regarded as agricultural literature. See note 121.

150. Loudon, J. C. *An Encyclopaedia of Cottage, Farm and Villa Architecture*, 1836, 592–9, includes an account of Read and his work; his bust stands in the church at Horsemonden, where he died in 1847. See also Parker, H. H. *The Hop Industry*, 1934, pp 76–8; Burgess, A. H. 'Hopdrying', *Agriculture*, vol 46, September 1939, pp 524–31; Locke, P. E. 'Landscape with oasts', *House of Whitbread*, vol 19, no 1, Spring 1959, pp 17–19; McRae, S. G. and Burnham, C. P. *The Rural Landscape of Kent*, 1973, pp 193–5; Burgess,

112

A. H. *Hops*, 1964, p 8; Cronk, A. 'Oasts in Kent and East Sussex', *Archaeologia Cantiana*, vol 94, 1978, pp 241–54; Homes, I. 'The agricultural use of the Herefordshire house and its outbuildings', *Vernacular Architecture*, vol 9, 1978, pp 13–14; Kent County Council Education Committee, *Traditional Kent Buildings*, no 1, 1980, pp 12–15.

151. Wedge, T. *General View of the Agriculture of the County Palatine of Chester*, 1794, p 65.

152. Waistell, C. *Designs for Agricultural Buildings*, 1827, p 2. This book was published after the end of this period, but it appeared posthumously and represented the views Waistell formed in the course of a lengthy agricultural career which apparently began in the 1770s. Waistell became a member of the Royal Society of Arts in 1792 and was chairman of the Society's Committee on Agriculture from 1815 to 1825. In 1808 he was awarded the Society's gold medal for a paper on valuing timber. He also invented a corn dibble (personal communication from the Librarian of the Royal Society of Arts; *Transactions of the Royal Society of Arts*, vol 26, 1808, pp 19, 45–70; vol 27, 1809, pp 79–84; vol 29, 1812, pp 50–1).

153. *Communications to the Board of Agriculture*, vol 1, 1797, p ii.

154. Vancouver, C. *General View of the Agriculture of Hampshire*, 1810, p 70.

155. Morgan, G. *General View of the Agriculture of Cornwall*, 1811, pp 25–6. For descriptions of materials in particular areas as an introduction to the agricultural use made of them see Peters, J. E. C. *The Development of Farm Buildings in Western Lowland Staffordshire up to 1880*, 1969, pp 1–5; Ebbage, S. *Barns and Granaries*, 1977, pp 21–42 (Norfolk); Devon County Council, *Devon's Traditional Buildings*, 1978, pp 1–6; Reynolds, J. *The Hampshire Barn*, unpublished thesis, Architectural Association, 1978, pp 6–10; Sweetland, P. *Barns of Bredon Hill*, unpublished thesis, Birmingham School of Architecture, 1979, pp 34–9; Wiliam, E. *Traditional Farm Buildings in North-East Wales, 1550–1900*, 1982, pp 61–101. For the use of ling, a typical local material, for thatching some of the buildings of a massive new farmstead in the 1770s see Chapman, V. 'North country farms on the moorland fringe', *Beamish One, the First Report of the North of England Open Air Museum Joint Committee*, 1978, p 42. For a surviving farm building of 'mud', a mixture of earth and straw traditional in certain Midland areas, see McCann, J. 'Mud buildings of the East Midlands', *Country Life*, 11 November 1982, p 1473. The date of this building is unknown, but this material was used in the area in this period.

156. Farey, J. *General View of the Agriculture of Derbyshire*, vol 2, 1815, p 17, for oak; Davies, T. *General View of the Agriculture of Wiltshire*, 1811, p 11, for timber or flints; Davies, W. *General View of the Agriculture of North Wales*, 1810, p 182, for flagstones; Adam, J. *Practical Essays in Agriculture*, vol 2, 1786, p 221, for mixture. For surviving or recorded threshing floors illustrating the use of local materials see *Postmediaeval Archaeology*, vol 7, no 3, 1973, p 110; Nicholson, P. 'Wiltshire farm buildings', *Wiltshire Folklife*, vol 1, no 3, Autumn 1977, pp 46–7; vol 2, no 1, Spring 1978, pp 25–6; vol 2, no 3, Spring 1979, p 54; Reynolds, J. *The Hampshire Barn*, unpublished thesis, Architectural Association, 1978, pp 9, 26; Sweetland, P. *The Barns of Bredon Hill*, unpublished thesis, Birmingham School of Architecture, 1979, p 39; Wiliam, E. *Traditional Farm Buildings in North-East Wales, 1550–1900*, 1982, pp 139–41.

157. Farey, J. *General View of the Agriculture of Derbyshire*, vol. 2, 1815, pp 17–19.

158. In Staffordshire, where brick earths were plentiful, temporary kilns were usually established on building sites until the later eighteenth century. The first permanent kilns appeared by 1770, 'at first serving only their immediate neighbourhood and so operating only intermittently' and temporary kilns continued on isolated sites. By 1820, however, most bricks came from permanent kilns 'which, as a result of improved road transport, served a much wider area than before' (Peters, J. E. C. *The Development of Farm Buildings in Western Lowland Staffordshire up to 1880*, 1969, pp 3–4). See also Henderson, J. B. 'The eighteenth century dairy farmsteads of Appletree Hundred', *Derbyshire Miscellany*, vol 7, no 5, Spring 1976, p 233. See also note 7.

159. Wiliam, E. 'A guide to old farm buildings', in *The Re-use of Redundant Farm Buildings*, published by the Welsh Office Agriculture Department, 1982, p 23.

160. Peters, J. E. C. *The Development of Farm Buildings in Western Lowland Staffordshire up to 1880*, 1969, p 210; Tyson, B. 'Skirwith Hall and Wilton Tenement (Kirkland Hall). The rebuilding of two Cumbrian farmsteads in the eighteenth century', *Transactions of the Cumberland and Westmorland Antiquarian and Archaeological Society*, vol 81, 1981, pp 94–112.

161. Peters, J. E. C. 'The wall as a truss in farm buildings', *Vernacular Architecture*, vol 11, 1980, pp 17–21.

162. Hutton, K. 'The distribution of wheelhouses in the British Isles', *Agricultural History Review*, vol 24, 1976, p 35.

163. Waistell, C. *Designs for Agricultural Buildings*, 1827, p 105; Raistrick, A. *Buildings of the Yorkshire Dales*, 1976, pp 61–3, for the Garth family; Rowley, T. *The Shropshire Landscape*, 1972, p 39, for Wroxeter; Newton, R. *The Northumberland Landscape*, 1972, p

138, for Hadrian's Wall; Wiliam, E. 'Traditional farm buildings in Wales', *Amgueddfa*, no 15, 1973, p 13, for Flintshire example; Society for the Protection of Ancient Buildings, *Annual Report 1979–80*, p 8, Humberside example; Wiliam, E. 'A cruck barn at Hendre Wen, Llanwrest, Denbighshire', *Transactions of the Ancient Monuments Society*, vol 21, 1976, pp 23–31; Bidgood, R. F. *Two Villages*, published by the author, 'Twyford', Beach Rd, Woolacombe, North Devon, (?1977), p 9–10, for trough. On Holkham estate, Peterstone Farm incorporated part of a medieval abbey and Waterden Farm material from a deserted medieval village (Wade-Martins, S. *A Great Estate at Work*, 1980, p 160; Wade-Martins, S. at 1980 Oxford University Department of External Studies conference on Studies of Farm Buildings). On a Cheshire estate in the 1770s an old house was converted into a barn (Davies, C. S. *The Agricultural History of Cheshire, 1750–1880*, 1960, p 167).

164. Wedge, T. *General View of the Agriculture of the County Palatinate of Chester*, 1794, p 12; Lowe, R. *General View of the Agriculture of Nottingham*, 1798, p 9; Rudge, T. *General View of the Agriculture of Gloucestershire*, 1807, pp 44–5; Young, A. *General View of the Agriculture of Lincolnshire*, 1808, p 39; Hassall, C. *General View of the Agriculture of Monmouth*, 1812, p 24; Murray, A. *General View of the Agriculture of Warwickshire*, 1813, p 29; Farey, J. *General View of the Agriculture of Derbyshire*, vol 2, 1815, p 12. For other local examples of change in building materials in this period see Popham, J. H. *Farm Buildings, Form and Function*, unpublished thesis for Diploma in Conservation Studies, Institute of Advanced Architectural Studies, York University, 1973, pp 11–13, for a Yorkshire study; Roberts, R. O. *Farming in Caernarvonshire Around 1800*, 1973, p 13; Allison, K. J. *The East Riding of Yorkshire Landscape*, 1976, pp 161–2; Weller, J. B. *Farm Buildings of Shropshire Before 1837*, 1952, pp 6–7, unpublished, kindly lent by the author; Wiliam, E. *Traditional Farm Buildings in North-East Wales, 1550–1900*, 1982, pp 70, 73 79–80.

165. Peters, J. E. C. *The Development of Farm Buildings in Western Lowland Staffordshire up to 1880*, 1969, p 214; Reynolds, J. *The Hampshire Barn*, unpublished thesis, Architectural Association, 1978, p 10; Peters, J. E. C. *Discovering Traditional Farm Buildings*, 1981, pp 15–16.

166. Davies, D. C. G. *Historic Farmstead and Farmhouse Types in Shropshire*, unpublished MA thesis, Manchester University, 1952, pp 47–8, 113.

167. Charles, F. W. B. *Mediaeval Cruckbuilding and its Derivatives*, 1967, p 17. 'Curved principals', a type of truss recognisably in the cruck tradition, were used in Shropshire in the eighteenth century. (Personal communication, Mrs Carol Ryan, Planning Department, Shropshire County Council, 1983.) For surviving crucks see Alcock, N. W. *Cruck Construction. An Introduction and Catalogue*, 1981, published by the Council for British Archaeology, which includes farm buildings, mostly barns.

168. Leatham, I. *General View of the Agriculture of the East Riding of Yorkshire*, 1794, p 24, notes that 'as the district adjoins the sea, [Baltic] timber and deals are available'; Peters, J. E. C. *The Development of Farm Buildings in Western Lowland Staffordshire up to 1880*, 1969, p 3.

169. Young, A. *General View of the Agriculture of Norfolk*, 1804, pp 20, 22.

170. Hewett, C. A. *Abbot's Hall Barn*, published by the Museum of East Anglian Life, 1975, p 6. Such nuts and bolts were apparently first used by Wren in 1710 in the nave roof of St. Paul's.

171. Boys, J. *General View of the Agriculture of Kent*, 1805, p 32.

172. Young, A. *General View of the Agriculture of Hertfordshire*, 1804, pp 20–1; Farey, J. *General View of the Agriculture of Derbyshire*, 1815, pp 14–15.

173. Roberts, B. K. *Rural Settlement in Britain*, 1977, p 190, for Warwickshire; Peters, J. E. C. *The Development of Farm Buildings in Western Lowland Staffordshire up to 1880*, 1969, p 5.

174. Tuke, J. *General View of the Agriculture of the North Riding of Yorkshire*, 1800, p 306.

# 5 HANOVERIAN FARMSTEADS:

### The First Case Studies

In this period the general history of farmstead development can for the first time be illustrated in detail by plans of particular sets of farm buildings and descriptions of the functions they fulfilled. Their appearance in the literature of the late eighteenth century reflected the spirit of informed improvement which was so typical of the time. The men of the Agrarian Revolution were proudly conscious that they knew better methods of equipping as well as cultivating their land than their forefathers, and they made their principles and techniques clear by demonstrating them on the printed page.

Some of these drawings represented actual farmsteads, others summarised general or local experience. But both types were presented as examples of recommended design. The first drawing of an imaginary model farmstead appeared in 1770, the first plan of a named farmstead 'offered as a mirror in which others may see the advantages and disadvantages of their own farmeries' thirteen years later,[1] and in the next generation these were followed by a variety of plans showing different types of farmsteads suitable for different types of farms (see Figs 10 and 11). Of course, the sets of buildings described were not typical of the time – *ex hypothesis*, they were better than average. But they were all examples of commercial designs chosen by men with professional reputations to lose for the consideration of men with money to invest. As such, they provide an invaluable series of case studies illustrating contemporary assumptions and practice.

### A Staffordshire Farmstead

The first example illustrates Staffordshire practice and was published in 1796,[2] though steadings of this general type were built in most counties throughout this period (see Fig 15).

The steading was described as suitable for 'a respectable farm of 200 to 500 acres' and assumed a mixed-farming system producing corn, milk and meat. It was planned on the familiar U-pattern round two large yards which lay open to the southern sun but provided little

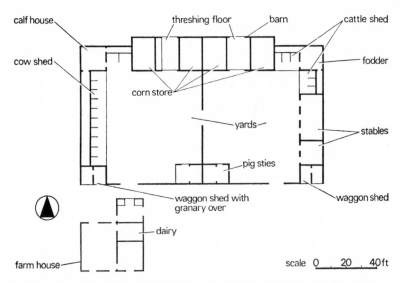

15  Plan of a steading designed in 1796 for a mixed Staffordshire farm of 200 to 500 acres

protection from the rain that in winter probably turned them into quagmires. The two barns, one for the wheat which was sold off the farm, and the other for the oats and barley which were fed on it, formed the bulk of the north range. Each contained a hard central floor where flailers threshed the corn which was stored in the barn or brought in from the stackyard to the north of the buildings, the straw going to the livestock houses and the yard, the corn to the granary over one of the cartsheds. The north range was flanked by two ranges of livestock buildings, the east wing housing fattening cattle and working horses or oxen, and the west wing the dairy herd whose milk was processed into butter and cheese in the farmhouse dairy. Waggons and carts were housed in shelters at the south ends of these wings, which was convenient for service in the fields but left them exposed to the warping effects of sun and rain.

These were all commercial buildings. But the tradition of domestic self-sufficiency was maintained by a few pigs and poultry for family use, housed near the farmhouse where the farmer's wife could feed them on domestic scraps and on the dairy residues.

## A Yorkshire Farmstead

The Midland steading illustrated in Fig 15 served a mixed-farming system. So did this North Riding farmstead serving a 300-acre holding,[3] though here livestock were more important than corn, and fattening cattle than dairy cattle (see Fig 16). Again, it illustrates the

116

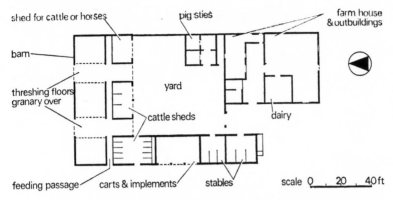

16    Plan of a steading designed in 1800 for a Yorkshire farm of 200 acres

same general principles of design – the barn on the north, the cattle buildings near the barn from which they received their straw, and the pigsties near the dairy in the farmhouse. But the differences in the climate, the size of holding and the economy of the farm were reflected in differences in detail. The barn was proportionately smaller and housed livestock as well as corn so that cattle, the main consumers of straw, could be fed and littered without crossing cold and possibly snowbound yards. Yet the basic pattern had not been changed. It had merely been adapted to particular circumstances.

Like its Staffordshire predecessor, this farmstead was dependent on human power for all operations. But these were the last years when totally unmechanised steadings could be presented as examples of good practice. From this time onwards one of the themes of farmstead history is the gradual introduction of machinery first for static work, then, much later, for the movement of materials.

### Steadings for Large Farms

The general standardisation of farmstead design in this period is strikingly illustrated by a comparison of two steadings for large farms, one in the south, one in the north (see Figs 17 and 18). The first was built in Sussex, apparently about the year of Trafalgar, to serve the 1,400 acre home farm of a great landowner who paid 'some attention to symmetry and appearance but in general rejected every improvement that could not come within reach of the common farmer'.[4] The second, probably prepared a few years later, was hypothetical. But it represented the views of the experienced Waistell, and may well have been based on a farmstead he had helped to plan.[5]

Both designs assumed mixed-farming systems and both accepted the conventional basic pattern, differing only in scale from the smaller

117

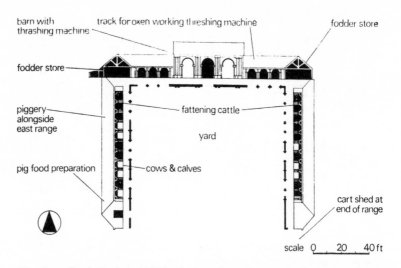

17  A steading built about 1805 for the home farm of a great landowner in Sussex

steadings of the time, and only in detail from each other. In general, these two sets of buildings, planned for areas probably more than two hundred miles apart, are almost interchangeable. The only obvious regional characteristic is the circular shelter, so typical of certain northern areas, which protected the horse and gear that drove the threshing machine.

Both designs include threshing machines driven by animal power, by literal horsepower in the north, by oxen in Sussex, which long prized the working qualities of its local breed. But a reference in the description of the southern steading to grinding, chaff-cutting and other food-preparation equipment in the barn illustrates an early stage in its change from a building in which corn was stored and threshed to one in which grain and straw, roots and cake were processed with the aid of machines for delivery to livestock. The barn continued to dominate the farmstead. Nevertheless, the truth of Arthur Young's prophecy was already becoming apparent. Mechanisation was beginning to change its function.

## Missing Information

Significantly, none of the publications from which these drawings are taken gives any information on the construction of the farmsteads they describe. For their writers knew that all farm buildings were built of local materials and saw no point in detailing the methods of one area for readers elsewhere who could only use such products of woodland, quarry or pit as were available near their homes. So, partly

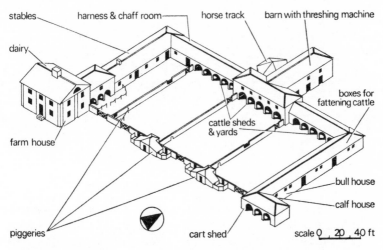

stables

harness & chaff room

horse track

barn with threshing machine

dairy

boxes for fattening cattle

cattle sheds & yards

farm house

bull house

calf house

piggeries

cart shed

scale 0  20  40 ft

18    Steading designed about 1815 for a large northern farm. Note the small circular horsetrack or 'gingang' which sheltered the horses that drove the threshing machine

by statement and partly by omission, these case studies strikingly illustrate the combination of similarity of general design and diversity of particular methods of construction which was so typical of the farmsteads of their age.

## NOTES

1. Young, A. *The Farmer's Guide to Hiring and Stocking Farms*, vol 2, 1770, p 467; Marshall, W. *Minutes of Agriculture*, 1783, pp 21–2. The latter, describing the steading built on his Croydon farm eight years earlier, referred feelingly to 'the anxieties and attendance which the immediate superintendance (of its construction) occasioned' and his minute of 11 August 1775 records a *cri de coeur* with which many of those concerned with building work on farms with sympathise. 'The carpenters have done building, jobbing, gate-making and tarring and, thank my stars, they are off!' Builders are pleasant people, but their completed work is commonly preferable to their company.

2. Pitt, W. *General View of the Agriculture of Staffordshire*, 1796, plate opposite p 18.

3. Tuke, J. *General View of the Agriculture of the North Riding of Yorkshire*, 1800, plate 4, p 46. The farmstead described was intended for a farm rented at £300 a year. Rents in the county averaged 15s to 21s per acre (p 49), so the farm is assumed to be 300 acres.

4. Young, A. *General View of the Agriculture of Sussex*, 1808, pp 464–71, 468–9.

5. Waistell, C. *Designs for Agricultural Buildings*, 1827, plates 7 and 8.

# 6 THE AGRICULTURAL REVOLUTION: THE INDUSTRIAL PHASE, 1820–80

## The Intensification of Farming

In this period the demand for food increased steadily. The population of England and Wales rose from 12 million in 1821 to 16 million in 1841, 20 million in 1861 and 26 million in 1881; and throughout most of this period it was the responsibility and profitable privilege of the British farmer to feed this growing market with little help or competition from overseas. The result was a major economic achievement in British history: the development of a farming system which raised the art and science of food production to a pitch never before seen, so that visitors from the Old and the New Worlds alike marvelled at the efficiency, the prosperity and the professional pride of the British agricultural industry. Towards the end of the period, however, even this 'High Farming', as it was so rightly called, failed to keep pace with the demands made on it. By 1880 Britain was importing half its bread and a quarter of its meat. Nevertheless, so great was the faith in the continuation of agricultural progress that men as sensible as Caird never doubted that most of Britain's food would continue to come from Britain's farms.

It was, however, clear from the beginning of this period that the resources and methods of the Agrarian Revolution could no longer keep the growing population fed. Reclamation continued; but it could only make a limited and ever-shrinking contribution to the national food supply. Enclosures, too, continued; but here also the end was in sight as open-field parishes gradually became first anomalies, then rarities. By the time of Queen Victoria's accession it was obvious that any large increases in food production could only come from the more intensive exploitation of existing farmland, a change symbolised by the end of that ancient but extensive system, transhumance.[1] So the building of new farmsteads on new farmland, which had been such a conspicuous feature of George III's time, now dwindled to a minor agricultural theme. A number of new steadings, it is true, were built some to serve farms created by belated enclosures and others to serve farms created by enclosures a generation earlier but worked from

Plate 13   An Essex example of the standard Hanoverian pattern of farmstead design, probably late eighteenth century. The barn where corn was threshed is in the north range, two ranges of livestock buildings form the south-facing yard where cattle trod straw into manure, and the farmhouse is to the south, in a position which allowed the farmer convenient supervision of work in the farmstead (*BBC Hulton Picture Library*)

Plate 14   A Nottinghamshire example of the Hanoverian pattern, probably from the 1820s or 1830s (*Aerofilms Ltd*)

Plate 15  The general transport of such a perishable commodity as liquid milk was impossible until the coming of the railways. Farm-produced milk was therefore processed into butter or cheese by the farmer's wife and daughters, whose workshops were rooms in the farmhouse (*Museum of English Rural Life*)

Plate 16  A late eighteenth-century granary now in the Avoncroft Museum of Buildings. The grain upstairs was protected from damp and from rats and mice, while the ground floor was used as a cartshed. The stairs recall the demands of pre-mechanical farming on human muscles – the corn harvest was carried upstairs, a sack at a time, on men's backs. Note the kennels under the stairs for the dogs, which discouraged thieves and vermin (*Avoncroft Museum of Buildings*)

village homesteads which were now falling into decay.[2] This, however, was no more than the completion of an inherited task. The new age faced a new need, the development of farmsteads on existing farms to meet the demands of a more sophisticated, more productive and more demanding farming system.

The basic problem was summarised in a letter which Caird wrote to Sir Robert Peel in 1850. 'It would be vain,' he said, 'to drain the land and fit it for the culture of green crops if no suitable housing is provided for economically converting these into a marketable form and for preserving and accumulating manure.'[3] The improvement of fertility by drainage, better tillage, and the use of purchased manures and the residues of purchased feedstuffs; more crops, including more stockfeed; more stock and therefore more corn, meat, butter and cheese to sell; and more byproducts of stock and crops to go back to the land to maintain and improve fertility . . . such was the circle of Victorian farming. So the farmstead became the workshop wherein an increasing weight of crops was either prepared for market or converted by an increasing number of stock into saleable products and manure.[4]

The growing demands on the farmstead, however, reflected an improvement in the quality as well as an increase in the quantity of the equipment, crops and stock which were housed, stored or processed there. The point was neatly illustrated in a question raised in 1841. 'As the cost and wear and tear of implements have now become a serious consideration in the farmer's outlay . . . might not every farmer have a suitable shed with a hard, clean floor . . . within which each implement should have its proper place?'[5] Clearly, the complicated and expensive equipment which the farmer was now buying from the manufacturer merited better protection than the cruder products of the old order. Equally clearly, the same argument applied more forcibly in the wider world of livestock which are inherently more likely to respond to better treatment than inorganic equipment. The improved cattle of the period required improved housing if they were to repay the time and skill which had been invested in them.[6] And obviously such needs could not be met by the traditional type of steading with its obsolescent barn, dark, dirty and ill-ventilated stables and cowhouses, inadequate implement housing and open central yard where water from the spoutless buildings washed away so much of the value of the manure which accumulated there.[7]

## The Industrial Farmstead

The Victorian farmer met the new problems of the farmstead in the same way as he met the new problems of the farm. He sought new technical allies who could provide him with means of producing more food from a limited acreage. He found them in the new urban economy created by the Industrial Revolution. As the years passed, he came to rely increasingly on the engineer for the new techniques of deep drainage, on the manufacturer for implements, on the chemist and the merchant for the guano, superphosphate and other purchased plant foods which were beginning to reinforce the traditional dungheap. So the farmer turned specialist, a specialist in the growing of crops and the rearing of stock, and delegated to other specialists many of the new forms of old technical responsibilities once undertaken on the farm or in the village.

In particular, he delegated many of his traditional responsibilities for the design, equipment and erection of the more complicated buildings demanded by a more exacting farming system to the specialist who provided some of his knowledge, to the engineer who provided much of his equipment and to the manufacturer who provided most of the building materials he required. The implications were obvious and accepted. The farmer who called to his aid the resources of industry came to consider the problems of his farmstead in industrial terms. It was, therefore, in the early Victorian period that the familiar modern concept of the farmstead as an agricultural factory was first consciously established.

'Agriculture has most properly come to be regarded as a manufacture and the benefits arising from a perfect adaptation of the farm buildings to the various operations conducted in them are now generally admitted . . . In other mechanical arts we find no difficulty in distinguishing one building from another. Nobody would mistake a flour mill for a spinning mill or a factory for a warehouse. So ought we to be able to distinguish the system of farming by the structure of the steadings.' This passage combines quotations from two textbooks of the 1860s.[8] But its cohesion illustrates the strength of the common doctrine. Contemporaries repeated the same assumptions in different words, referring to the homestead as 'the farmer's manufactory'[9] and urging the use of the machine 'to make the business of the farm approximate more closely to that of the factory'.[10] The men of the steam age were proudly conscious of the improvements which the developments of their time made possible, and their buildings still bear witness to the conviction and skill with which they applied the equipment and techniques made available to them by expanding industry. The strength of the industrial environment in which they worked is curiously illustrated by the loans which land improvement companies were empowered by an Act of 1849 and various subsequent Acts to make for capital investment in agriculture, including investment in farm buildings. For these loans were in large measure designed to placate landowners and farmers for the repeal of the Corn Laws in 1845 which deprived them of their traditional tariff protection in the interests of a triumphant industrialism.[11]

Nevertheless, the new industrial approach did not change the general principles of farm-building design. Caird's criteria of a good farmstead – the degree to which it provided stock with warmth and shelter, allowed ease of working and made possible the conservation of rich manure[12] – were those of his grandfather, though the next generation gave rather higher priority to economising labour.[13] Neither did it revolutionise the application of these principles.

Thus, it made little difference to the siting of new farmsteads. 'Centricity' was still as important as it was in the days of the Hanoverians, and the need for a reliable supply of water as vital as it was in the days of the Saxons. Neither did it affect the basic needs and relationships of men, materials and livestock. It was still necessary to convert stacked corn into grain and straw. It was still necessary to store the grain safely and pass the straw to the yards and stockbuildings for conversion into manure. It was still necessary to face yards south to catch the sun, and cartsheds north to protect timber from sun and rain. It was still convenient to site stables near cartsheds and piggeries near the farmhouse. Even the changes in the function of the barn were not sufficient to affect its proud inherited position. Many eighteenth-century arguments and recommendations on planning were repeated in nineteenth-century books, and many eighteenth-century decisions in nineteenth-century steadings. So the Victorian farmstead was essentially an industrialised version of its predecessors. It was built of factory-produced materials and fitted with factory-produced equipment, but it accepted and continued the basic Hanoverian design.[14]

Similarities and differences are shown at their most obvious and spectacular in some of the more monumental farmsteads with which Victorian landowners, continuing the tradition of their fathers and grandfathers, equipped their 'model' home farms. At first sight, these massive sets of buildings, incorporating the most advanced technologies of their time, frequently topped by factory-type chimneys and sometimes covering over an acre of ground, have little in common with the cruder and more countrified Hanoverian steadings from which they were descended. But they served familiar needs in a familiar way and continued into the new age the old pattern of the north range with wings of livestock buildings forming south-facing yards.[15]

## New Men, New Books

Yet the implications of this industrialisation were considerable. In particular, the pressure of technical change and the possibilities and problems involved soon made it increasingly clear that local experience and inherited lore were no longer sufficient qualifications for the designer of farm buildings. There were too many new ways of building and equipping farmsteads, too many new ideas and proprietary products, too many decisions on new issues requiring new technical knowledge for the traditional estate manager to remain master of the subject. More specialised men were needed, more specialised men duly appeared, and changes in their professional characteristics and in the technical literature they produced for the guidance of their more general-purpose brethren illustrated the growing complexity of the subject they served.

Thus Waistell, whose posthumous treatise on farm buildings appeared in 1827, was the last representative of the old tradition. He was a farmer giving other farmers the benefit of his personal experience and observations.[16] In the next decade, Loudon combined the old and the new. He was a farmer and a land agent, but he enlisted the services of a team of architects, engineers, farmers and surveyors in compiling the massive encyclopaedia of rural buildings he published in 1833.[17] A generation later the change was complete. In 1861, Burn, co-author of a substantial volume which included illustrated descriptions of ten model and five actual farmsteads, described himself as an engineer.[18] Two years later, Denton appeared on the title page of his classic series of studies of *The Farm Homesteads of England* in full formality as MInstCE and 'Engineer to the General Land Drainage and Improvement Company'.[19] Agriculturists who specialised in farm buildings were replaced by technical men who specialised in agriculture; and the influence of their work and writings, though impossible to quantify, was clearly considerable and pervading.[20]

Traditional local skills, like traditional local materials, were no longer sufficient to meet the needs of the farmstead, for the cost and complexity of the work now necessitated a far more rigorous and informed analysis of the problems involved and a far more conscious application of established principles to obtain specified results. So the new literature set forth with a mass of detail the grammar of the subject from the determination of building requirements, via the procedures for siting and planning farmsteads to the criteria for choosing building materials. In so doing, it equipped the farming industry with its first sound and comprehensive guides to the design and construction of farm buildings.[21] Denton was over optimistic in his conclusion that, 'under the stimulation of an imperious necessity', local tradition and casual empiricism had been replaced by a 'collection of well-recognised axioms'.[22] No technology serving such a complex of variables as the needs of the farm can be completely or decisively codified. But, like James Small's famous treatise on the plough half a century earlier, these new textbooks 'concentrated and clarified what other men had been thinking in a muddled and indefinite manner'.[23] They also marked the end of an age. Here as elsewhere, the farm was no longer technically sufficient unto itself.

## Landowner, Agent and Architect

The new technology, however, operated within the framework of the old rural order. It was the landowner who made the final decisions and, as in the past, he exercised his power according to his personal character, abilities and resources.[24] Individually, landowners were responsible for the buildings on their farms. Collectively, therefore, they controlled the course of farmstead development.[25]

The landowner generally worked through his agent, who was, in effect, the general manager of the estate.[26] The qualifications and experience of such men varied greatly but, in principle, their functions were similar. All were concerned with the maintenance and improvement of the estate as well as its routine administration. Farm building work had long been part of their professional responsibilities. In this period the importance of such work increased considerably. Technically, development and innovation created new problems of information and decision. Economically, buildings became more substantial, more complicated and consequently more expensive.

In many cases, probably in most, the agent designed new farm buildings himself.[27] He also made arrangements for their construction and, later, for their maintenance and repair. Sometimes he used direct labour, calling on the resources of the estate yard which with its associated brickworks, quarries and woodlands played such an important part in the economy of the larger properties.[28] Sometimes, at least for new work, he employed a local builder under contract. Garth, who earned the praise of his employer for 'making such a capital plan for my buildings', represented the system in fiction. The agent of Littleton estate in Staffordshire who in 1825 met the bricklayer and carpenter to set out the buildings at Yew Tree Farm and his successor in 1864 who 'was expected to be able to draw out plans for farm buildings' represented it in fact.[29]

Sometimes, however, the agent followed the advice of Ewart who in 1851 recommended that the construction of big farmsteads should be supervised by 'an architect or competent building surveyor'.[30] Thus, the extensive buildings of the Coleshill Model Farm in Oxfordshire were 'arranged by Mr Moore, Lord Radnor's agent, and erected from the plans and under the superintendence of Mr George Lamb, architect'.[31] Lamb does not seem to have continued with this type of work, but a few of his professional colleagues developed appreciable agricultural practices.

One of the most conspicuous was Frederick Chancellor, for many years surveyor to the Diocese of St Albans and also first Mayor of Chelmsford, who left an album of plans of twenty-five farmsteads he had designed in Essex and neighbouring counties. Many North Londoners will have seen one of his steadings, College Farm in Finchley, which he designed in 1882 for G. T. Barham, founder of the Express Dairy Company, 'as a model of what a dairy farm serving a growing population ought to be'.[32] William Wilkinson, remembered mainly for his planning of later Victorian North Oxford, also designed a number of substantial farmsteads for major landowners, including two which in 1863 received the accolade of an appearance in Denton's album of *Farm Homesteads of England*.[33] Various other architects, too, among them Gilbert Scott, concerned themselves from time to time with farm buildings.[34] But the architectural contribution to the development of farm buildings was small. Only a few architects took much interest in this type of work, while many landowners and their agents feared to employ members of a profession untrained in agriculture and suspected of a tendency to sacrifice efficiency to appearance.[35] Significantly, one of the most effective of these practitioners was the more specialised G. A. Dean who in his book, *The Land Steward*, emphasised his agricultural credentials and described himself as an 'agricultural architect and engineer'. His monument still stands at Egmere Farm, near Walsingham, in Norfolk, an impressive set of buildings he designed in the early 1850s for the second Earl of Leicester, Coke's son and successor. With its orderly plan, massive structures and carefully designed fittings, including cast-iron uprights and thresholds, ramps for wheelbarrows, stockproof latches and wooden lintels continuing the brick pattern over the doors in an unexpected agricultural *trompe-l'oeil*, it proclaims the resources and attention to detail of the industrial age.[36]

The use of such outside expertise, however, was exceptional and generally confined to the design and construction of large farmsteads, particularly those of home farms. Most farm buildings were planned by the agents of the estates they served, and the designers identified in Denton's album show that some land agents at least were capable of undertaking very substantial projects without architectural assistance.[37] Typically, the farmsteads built to serve the farms created by the major reclamation enterprise of this period were designed not by an architect but by the landowner with the assistance of his agent: Frederic Knight of Exmoor was his own architect.[38]

## The Landowner and Farmstead Development

The task before the landowner and his advisers and executives was considerable, for the steadings which they inherited from the Agrarian Revolution were no more capable of meeting the needs of the changed times than those inherited by the men of the Agrarian Revolution had been a century earlier. Nothing less than a general modernisation was required. Some landowners, notably such leaders of the industry as the Duke of Bedford and the Duke of Northumberland, who employed skilled staff to build and repair their farmsteads, erected massive steadings on their home farms, maintained large and highly equipped estate yards and over the years invested huge sums in farm buildings and other improvements, were both equipped and prepared to meet their responsibilities. In particular, they appreciated that good buildings were necessary to attract the good tenants on whom depended the long-term prosperity of their estates.[39] But others, such as the Buckinghamshire landowner who received £1,500 a year in rent from a farm yet refused to provide proper accommodation for his tenant's cattle, were less able or less willing to meet their responsibilities.[40] The latter was exceptional, but unfortunately, as Caird's report of 1852 on his agricultural tour of the country made clear, the former were not typical. He saw many new farmsteads, well designed, well built and well equipped, the rural equivalent of the factories which were making his country the workshop of the world, and he gave praise where praise was due. But in his final judgement he quoted the general state of the buildings he had seen as evidence of the low standards of estate management that prevailed.

'The inconvenient, ill-arranged hovels,' he wrote, 'the rickety wood and thatch barns and sheds devoid of any known improvement for economising labour, food and manure, which are to be met with in every county in England and from which anything else is exceptional in the southern counties, are a reproach to the landlords in the eyes of all skilful agriculturists who see them. One can scarcely believe that such a state of affairs is permitted in an old and wealthy country'. The British farmer, he concluded, was meeting the necessities of the present with the equipment of the past.[41] Nearly thirty years later the more generalised review of landowners and landownership which he gave to an international congress was considerably more favourable. He referred to a general improvement in farm buildings and his main criticism was not neglect but the extravagant expenditure caused by insufficient assessment of agricultural needs and poor planning.[42]

Even so, the year after he spoke, another prominent agriculturist commented on the landlords' responsibility for the 'want of adequate buildings which at present impedes the progress of improved dairy husbandry'.[43] The farmsteads of Victorian England reflected the shortcomings as well as the virtues of the landlord and tenant system of the time.

Nevertheless, the Victorian achievement was considerable and impressive. Many surviving buildings and an immense technical literature bear witness to the confidence, skill and tireless application to the matter in hand of the designers and builders of this period. But, of course, it was the innovations and the new constructions which aroused the interest of contemporaries and were duly recorded in book and journal. The obsolete, the historical and the localised inevitably attracted less attention. Yet they persisted. Longhouses continued in use, occupied by cattle as well as families;[44] a study of farm buildings in north-east Wales found that a third of the farmsteads consisted of a single or a double range of buildings;[45] the last wheelhouse was built in the late 1870s or early 1880s;[46] primitive forms of roofing as hedge clippings or twigs piled pyramidwise and sometimes thatched were still occasionally used for simple buildings;[47] and in the north laithe houses and bank barns were still built – a number of laithe houses were built to serve newly reclaimed upland near Cragg Vale in the 1830s and the last datable example was not built until the last year of this period.[48] Such anomalies and survivals remind us that for every Victorian farmer who worked in a Victorian farmstead a dozen worked in Hanoverian, Stuart or Tudor buildings.

Indeed, the distinction between industrial and pre-industrial farmsteads was already so obvious that the old buildings were beginning to acquire a period charm evocatively illustrated by an early Victorian novelist's description of a farmstead of the old tradition. 'The outhouses, which had been built up by successive generations of tillers of the soil, each of whom had some special fancy in the way of stables, breweries, granaries or barns, are various, solid and quaint. They surround a yard which covers half an acre of ground paved with flint around the sides . . . but otherwise soft bottomed and full of straw in which fat heifers stand . . . and munch out of racks, and saucy calves disport themselves and bully the younger generation of small-limbed, fat-sided pigs . . . Lots of poultry are picking and scratching around the barn doors and pigeons are fluttering among them . . . The rickyard, full of long stacks of hay and round stacks of corn, lies beyond.'[49] The picture of tranquil and varied plenty was attractive. But it deceived. Such farmsteads belonged to the past. The needs of the industrial age required the application of industrial resources and industrial criteria to the buildings of the farm.

130

## More Housing for More Cattle

The most obvious weakness of the early Victorian farmstead was insufficient accommodation for cattle as expansion had failed to keep pace with the increase of horned stock made possible by the new cropping system. 'There is scarcely a farmer of stability in the country,' wrote Dean in 1851, echoing the conclusion of Beatson a lifetime before, 'who would not pay an additional rent of from 7 to 9 or, in some instances, 10 per cent on the cost of a first-rate homestead, provided the outlay be judicious, rather than have a miserable one such as farmers are now compelled to put up with . . . It would pay him well to give such a percentage, as the homestead would enable him to feed a large number of livestock through the winter.'[50] A mass of local evidence provides a detailed commentary on his generalised conclusion. In the north and south, in arable and pastoral districts alike, the general story was the same: too few buildings for too many cattle. The consequences for both stock and soil were plain to see, for the outwintering of cattle in the fields meant the loss of condition in wet and cold, the poaching of soggy pasture and the dropping on grassland of manure more urgently required by the hungry ploughlands.[41]

Here, indeed, was one of the limiting factors in contemporary agricultural development. At one end of the scale, it prevented progressively minded farmers from adopting improved techniques. The conservation of manure remained one of the primary functions of the farmstead yet, for example, a visitor to Northamptonshire in 1852 lamented that 'it was vain for the tenant to endeavour to improve the quality of his manure' by the intensive indoor feeding of cattle, for he lacked bullock hovels.[52] At the other end of the scale, it enforced almost archaic standards on the less advanced. Half a century after the turnip had helped to revolutionise the system of fodder production, the farmers of south Wales answered those who recommended this crop to them with a simple question. 'What is the use of growing turnips when we have no sheds to feed them in?'[53] Seldom has the importance of farm buildings in the agricultural economy been summarised more succinctly.[54]

But it was not just a question of more accommodation. It was also a question of better accommodation. In Napoleonic times, progressive men had urged that cattle should be wintered in buildings and not left to fend for themselves in fields. Half a century later, their successors were arguing that cattle should be kept not in open yards but under cover. The change reflected important advances in their methods and managerial standards. For one thing, the growing use of expensive oilcake and other purchased concentrates for fattening cattle increased the incentive to provide livestock with conditions which encouraged the efficient conversion of feed into meat. It was noted in this period that farmers were 'beginning to see that warmth and shelter are equivalent to food', and one enthusiastic pioneer even suggested that a thermometer should be fitted in every cattleyard.[55] For another, this new form of expenditure made necessary the better protection of manure to prevent the wastage of the residues of these rich rations by exposure to rain. Once again, improved techniques required improved buildings if the full benefits they offered were to be secured.

The development of cattle accommodation was, therefore, a major feature of this period. One novelty was the hammel, a loosebox with a run which allowed the animal free access to the open air. But such buildings were expensive in both capital and labour.[56] Yards remained the main type of cattle housing, growing in size until they often covered far more floor space than all the rest of the farmstead. At first, they were either open or, at most, provided with shelters. Under pressure of informed opinion, however, covered yards gradually became more common. Open yards continued to hold their own in rearing districts, since young stock require sunshine, in areas such as East Anglia, where rainfall was light and straw for litter plentiful and, inevitably, on the less-advanced farms elsewhere. But by the 1860s the roofing of yards was established or at least approved practice in most parts of the country.[57]

The provision of roofing enabled the yard to provide both cattle and manure with better protection. But it did not alter its essential character. It remained a mass-production unit, housing a large number of animals in a manner which enabled the master cattle 'to drive the weak about and allow them little rest' and rendered feeding 'slovenly, wasteful and imperfect', since the strongest 'consume the choicest parts of the food'.[58] The improvement of yards, therefore, was accompanied by an increase in more intensive systems of boxes or stalls which made possible the individual treatment of stock, each animal being confined or tethered in a 'place of its own so that bullying was eliminated and the cattle allowed to eat and rest undisturbed, while feed could be carefully rationed and manure properly conserved.'[59]

Such a system provided cattle with the most favourable conditions for meat production, and the farmer with the most effective methods of manure conservation, so far devised. But these were achieved only at heavy cost in both capital and labour. In particular, they involved expensive buildings which continued in their own way the tradition of the specialised 'oxhouses' of the later eighteenth century. The fattening house which Read visited in Buckinghamshire in 1855 differed little in concept from that which Young visited in Nottinghamshire in 1771.[60] But it was very different in detail. In the Victorian building the cattle were fed from trolleys running on a small railway up the central gangway and their water was pumped by steam. Of course, few houses were as elaborate as this. Nevertheless, the degree of technical and financial investment in this particular building illustrated in extreme form the general level of intensification represented by this method of housing and explains the awed admiration of a shrewd French visitor. 'Nothing is bolder, more ingenious and more characteristic of the spirit of enterprise among the English,' he wrote in 1855, 'than [this system] which tends to extend itself everywhere.' He was wrong when he described such housing as 'at variance with all habits', for there was nothing new in principle in the intensive fattening of livestock in special-purpose buildings. But he was right in his appreciation of the energy and uninhibited industrial logic with which this principle was developed and applied.[61]

Such developments reflect the rising price of meat in this period. The effects of this trend are illustrated on the Holkham estate in the traditionally arable county of Norfolk which in these years increased its expenditure on yards and boxes and evolved improved systems of communications between buildings to allow the easier movement of feedstuffs.[62] Normal practice, however, lagged far behind the advances of the enterprising minority and, though on the whole the cattle of 1880 were considerably better housed than those of 1820,[63] the general deficiency in the quantity and quality of cattle accommodation continued. Meanwhile, the cattle population of the country was steadily rising. In the last decade of this period, the first years for which official statistics are available, the number of cattle rose from $4\frac{1}{4}$ million to over $4\frac{3}{4}$ million; and there must have been many areas like Westmorland where it was clear by 1878 that building was failing to keep pace with breeding.[64]

Deficiencies in the quality of housing were equally obvious, though more difficult to assess. The provision of guttering and downpipes, however, can be taken as a practical index of the varying standards of accommodation, since yards and the cattle in them are the principal beneficiaries of such protection against the concentrated fall of rainwater from the roofs of surrounding buildings. In some areas, guttering came to be regarded in the later years of this period as normal equipment. In others, 'spoutless buildings' bore witness to the general inefficiency of the local farmsteads which was reflected in the poor condition of the stock they housed.[65]

At first sight, the story of the cattleyard in this period continues the familiar tradition of practical men meeting practical needs with such resources as were readily available. In general, this was true. But the mid-Victorian covered yard also reflected the coming of a new and revolutionary form of knowledge, for it was the first type of agricultural building to be influenced by the findings of scientific research. Farmers had long known that unprotected manure lost much of its value. The Victorians were the first who could measure this loss and draw informed financial and structural conclusions from it. In the 1850s, Voelcker had shown in detail by a series of experiments the degree to which cover preserved the nutritive value of farmyard manure,[66] and a few years later Denton in his textbook on farm buildings quoted the evidence of chemical analysis on this point as well as Voelcker's generalised opinion that 'manure made in covered yards was worth fully half more than manure made in open yards'.[67] Significantly, too, one of the champions of the covered yard was Sir Henry Thompson, the railway magnate and improving landlord, who was apparently led to a belief in its advantages by his interest in soil chemistry.[68] Here, indeed, was prophecy. Traditionally, the designer of farm buildings had relied exclusively on experience and observation. Now, for the first time, he was beginning to pay heed to the findings of scientific research.

Indeed, he was even beginning to call for research on problems created by new developments. The first such suggestion dates from 1857. 'The writer regards the subject [of the comparative advantages and disadvantages of yard and box systems for fattening cattle] as sufficiently important to warrant a suggestion that the Royal Agricultural Society of England should get some well-attested experiments on the subject'.[69] Admittedly, this was no more than prophecy, for it was a long time before the scientist made a substantial and continuing contribution to the knowledge required in farmstead planning. But Voelcker and Thompson showed the way which many were to follow and the historical importance of their work is as obvious to later generations as its practical importance was to their contemporaries.

## Dairy Buildings in Country and Town

Until the middle years of the nineteenth century, the inherited dairy system continued unchallenged. The milk-producing farm sold its milk as butter or cheese and the urban cowkeeper provided the townsman with his liquid milk.

In early Victorian times, as in Hanoverian times, the traditional dairy areas produced their traditional specialities – butter in the Vale of Aylesbury, for instance, cheese in Cheshire and Leicestershire – in traditional types of building. The familiar cowhouse, with its rows of individual stalls in which cows were tied in the winter and milked all the year, was now the accepted and satisfactory form of housing. It was found, with endless local variations, in all milking areas and the designs recorded by Loudon in the 1830s and Denton in the 1860s were merely improved versions of those which the Board of Agriculture's surveyors had found on advanced farms a generation earlier.[70] Reformers like Joseph Harding might complain in detail of damp, badly ventilated dairies standing too close to the farmyard, and occasional enterprising farmers might attract attention by harnessing horsepower to the cream churn, but there was no suggestion that the principles on which the dairies were planned and built needed more than sensible and conscientious application.[71]

Neither, at first, was there any great change in urban dairying. The number of cows in London increased as the population grew until in the early 1860s they totalled some 24,000.[72] But the general standards of urban milk production remained those of the eighteenth century, as descriptions in the 1840s of 'the half-underground dens and cellars in which cows were kept for the greater part of the year, standing knee-deep in filth, with little or no ventilation' and the condemnation of the London milk supply by the *Lancet* in 1847 showed.[73] Nevertheless, future developments were already apparent. As early as 1846, a Romford farmer, who sent his milk to London on the Eastern Counties Railway, won from a London dairyman the contract for supplying St Thomas's Hospital by quoting a price of 9d to 10d a gallon against his rivals' 12d a gallon.[74] For the first time the urban milk producer faced competition from his country cousin. Even so, the amount of 'railway milk' reaching the cities was small and the rate of increase slow until 1865, when the cattle plague devastated the cattle population of this country. Within a year, nearly a quarter of a million cattle died of this plague or were slaughtered to prevent its spread, and losses were proportionately higher among the crowded herds of the towns than on the farms.[75]

The first effect of this was, of course, a great increase in the volume of milk brought to London by rail to make good the deficiency. The second was less predictable but equally important. For the inspectors appointed to supervise the measures taken to control the cattle plague were the first officials to penetrate the London cowhouses and their revelations encouraged both the consumption of railway milk by the urban public and the enactment of sanitary legislation by the municipal authorities. Within a year or two, such effects of the new regulations as the exclusion of cowhouses from the more congested areas and the establishment of minimum space requirements per beast were noted as welcome novelties.[76] Thus did the legislative control of building design come to the London cowhouse. It was soon to come to all cowhouses and ultimately, in various forms, to all types of farm building. The inspectors appointed under the Cattle Disease Prevention Act of 1866 had many successors and from this time onwards 'the requirements of the regulations' were among the factors affecting the planning and construction of farm buildings.

However, all this was for the future. The immediate consequence was a general improvement in urban standards. There were still plenty of 'filthy holes' but the changing times favoured such 'patterns of neatness and convenience' as Mr Drewell's establishment in Upper Weymouth Street, Marylebone, which included a quarantine room for newly arrived cows, and Mr Veal's 'clean, dry, warm and airy' cowshed in Acacia Road, St John's Wood.[77] Nevertheless, the days of even the best urban cowhouses were numbered.

At the height of the cattle plague, milk came to London by rail from as far away as 200 miles. When the plague ended the London cowhouses were restocked and the maximum distance fell to 95 miles.[78] But the lesson had been learnt and the rattle of the milk trains sounded the knell of the old order. By the late 1870s the figure was back to 150 miles.[79] Caird, who as early as 1851 foresaw the possibility of farms in Hampshire and Essex providing London with liquid milk, proved a true prophet.[80]

The railways enabled the Victorian farmer to take the first step towards the modern dairy system. A combination of foreign competition and industrial development compelled him to take the second. In the 1860s American factory-made cheese began to beat the produce of the English farmhouse so decisively in both price and quality that the Royal Agricultural Society of England, after due inquiry, sponsored the establishment of a cheese factory under an American manager. This opened in 1870 and within six years ten such factories were in operation, between them processing the milk of 7,000–8,000 cows.[81] The economic advantages of the new order were obvious and, as one of the last rural survivals of the domestic system yielded to the factory system, it did not need much prescience to see that butter-making would soon follow.[82] The farmer of the coming age would no longer process milk. He would sell it as a liquid.

One result of this change was the end of the farmhouse dairy. A survey in Gloucestershire found that the last datable dairy of this type was built in 1863; a survey in north-east Wales which did not investigate survivals inside farmhouses found two butter or cheese dairies outside farmhouses built in 1860 and 1862 and one, possibly the last of its race, apparently built after 1888.[83] Another consequence of the new trade was the abandonment of pig-keeping in dairy areas, for the end of butter-making and cheese-making on the farm meant an end of the rich byproducts which provided cheap and convenient feed for pigs. By the later years of this period there were many farmers besides Mr

George in Wiltshire who 'had no pigs to sell because . . . he has nothing upon which to feed them, the milk being sold. The pigsties are full of weeds.'[84]

### Other Livestock Buildings

Like the yard and the cowhouse, the stable in these years changed little in principle but greatly in detail, and its higher standards of flooring, drainage and ventilation illustrated both the application of new materials and fittings and the growing appreciation of livestock needs. Typically, it is in this period that we meet the first detailed advice on desirable environments in animal houses to appear in technical literature. Loudon's recommendation that the temperature in stables should be 50°F (10°C) in winter and from 60° to 65°F (16–19°C) in summer was based on experience rather than research.[85] Yet it foreshadowed the development of that codified knowledge of the physiological requirements of livestock which is one of the scientist's greatest contributions to farmstead development.

There was, however, little interest in new forms of piggery. In this period the woodland pig herd passed into history, though in early Victorian times the pigs of the New Forest commoners still grazed on beechmast in the pannage months obedient to the swineherd's horn, and in Shropshire in 1868 a combination of a good acorn year and a poor grain harvest revived old tradition and sent children to collect acorns for the pigs.[86] So pigs fattened in the farmstead, usually in some form of the traditional pigsty with pen and run, though there were occasional and prophetic references to intensive and labour-saving pig fattening houses 'which have some resemblance in form and disposition to cattleboxes on a smaller scale'.[87] Similarly, apart from premature mention in the 1860s of the large-scale production of eggs and table poultry in 'a greenhouse-looking affair' over 300ft (90m) long,[88] poultry were housed in yards or lofts or expected to continue the immemorial practice of finding their own homes among the buildings of the farmstead. There was now little interest in any form of sheep housing, for the sheep had become almost wholly an animal of the fields. The fattening of lambs for the Christmas market in buildings which had once been such a feature of agriculture in Middlesex had now ceased and, except in occasional upland areas, only a few experimentally minded farmers, among them J. J. Mechi and 'Mr Lawes of Harpenden in Hertfordshire', housed either breeding or fattening sheep.[89]

### Intensive Livestock Housing

Apart from the box system of fattening cattle described on p 132, therefore, the general intensification of agriculture was not accompanied by any general intensification of livestock housing. In his report on his agricultural tour, for instance, Caird mentions only one or two cases of soilage systems,[90] and there are no further references to the London fattening houses, which had presumably closed by Victorian times. Such traditions, it is true, were continued in the 1870s by an enterprising Berkshire landowner who fattened tied cattle on the waste products of the sugarbeet he grew for his distillery in the first concrete farm building ever built (see Plate 28). But this was the highly exceptional system of a highly exceptional man.[91] Throughout this period, the town cowhouse remained the only common example of the use of a building to make possible an intensive system of livestock husbandry divorced from the fields.

## Outlying Buildings

The general intensification of farming and the particular need to maintain fertility ensured the continuation of 'field barn' or barn-and-yard units remote from central farmsteads where inwintered cattle trod straw into manure for the surrounding fields. On the downs and wolds, in the dales, in remote cornfields on large arable farms, wherever distance or terrain made impracticable the regular transport of straw inwards to the main yards and manure outwards to the land that needed it, the men of this period, like their predecessors, established suitable forms of these subsidiary manure-factories.[92] Sometimes these buildings were served by a stockman from the main steading, sometimes by a stockman living in a cottage attached to the unit, though the slow improvement in rural standards was reflected by the difficulty of obtaining workers for such lonely jobs. Respectable men were not prepared to live in such isolated cottages, particularly as their children would lose any chance of education.[93] Today, few of these units are used, but many still stand to bear witness to the reclaiming and consolidating energies of our Hanoverian and Victorian forefathers in the last age of the moving agricultural frontier.

## The Steam-engine and the Barn

After a lifetime of change livestock houses were still immediately recognisable versions of the types of building from which they were descended. But the traditional barn was required to adapt itself to the more radical demands of new equipment and new processes, and it could only do so by abandoning its traditional assumptions and designs. Thus, in one generation, an ancient type of building became obsolete, and its epitaph was written by the mid-Victorian farmers who lamented the superfluous barns inherited from the past or, more

Plate 17 Outlying buildings and the fields they served. This remote barn-and-yard unit was a 'muck-factory' where straw from the surrounding fields was thrashed and stored in the barn for use as litter in the yard. Inwintered cattle trod the straw into manure to maintain the fertility of land too far from the central farmstead to receive a supply from its yards. This unit was probably built during the Napoleonic Wars when large areas of rough upland grazings were converted to cornfields (*Aerofilms Ltd*)

Plate 18 Thrashing by flail about the year 1800. A similar picture could have been painted at any time in the previous millennium. The 'basket' on the left is a winnowing fan. It was used for casting the thrashed grain into the air to separate it from the chaff in the draught provided by opening the doors of the barn (*Museum of English Rural Life*)

Plate 19  The oldest agricultural steam engine in the world. It was built in 1811
by Trevithick, and drove a thrashing machine on a Cornish farm. The original
boiler was replaced in 1856. This engine is now in the Science Museum (see
page 112) (*The Science Museum*)

Plate 20  An early Victorian thrashing machine. Such gear could be fitted quite
easily into existing farmsteads, but it rendered new barns of traditional size and
design unnecessary. Horsegear similar in principle was often housed in small
circular buildings called wheelhouses or gingangs (see Plate 21) (*Museum of
English Rural Life*)

practically, converted them to cattlesheds.[94] On many farms the new technologies could, in practice, be fitted into existing barns with reasonable efficiency and economy. Nevertheless, in principle they demanded a new type of building.

The cause of this drastic change was the combination of an eighteenth-century invention and a nineteenth-century power unit. By the 1820s, mechanical threshing was widespread, as the Luddite riots of the labourers whom it deprived of their precious winter work as flailers showed so pathetically.[95] For some years horses, water and steam competed as prime-movers for threshing machines and other barn machinery.[96] But steampower finally triumphed, and in 1867 the machinery judges of the Royal Agricultural Society of England recommended the abolition of prizes at the Royal Show for horsedriven threshing gear, 'since we think it a mistake to encourage by prizes machines that ought to be bygones in English agriculture'.[97] The victory of steam, however, was neither immediate nor absolute. The 'Royal' judges in 1880, despite their predecessors, thought fit to award a prize to a horsegear exhibit, and the horse still had many years of work in the farmstead before it.[98] Waterpower, too, continued in service, now turning Pelton wheels and, exceptionally, turbines as well as traditional wheels.[99] Nevertheless, by mid-Victorian times the steam engine was common on large arable farms and 'smoking chimneys were to be seen in all parts of the country'.[100] A number, long smokeless, still stand with apparent incongruity in the farmlands as memorials to the new technical order which arose when the oldest of trades accepted the first great achievement of the new mechanical age.

The appearance on the farm of the sweet and mighty power of steam fascinated the men of the time, and the new chimneys achieved an almost aggressively symbolical importance. Loudon, who in 1836 had commended the 'remarkable elegance' of Glasgow factory stacks to the attention of the rising generation of agricultural architects and dreamed of chimneys enriching the landscape of Northumberland,[101] foresaw the kind of delight with which Ruegg ten years later hailed 'the tall chimney and extensive range of buildings' of an advanced farm that brought 'activity and animation to a somewhat desolate district' of Dorset.[102] The contemporary hope of repeating in agriculture the steam-driven triumphs of the Industrial Revolution was epitomised by the smoking chimney which dominated the idyllically aristocratic estate shown in the frontispiece of a textbook of the 1860s.[103]

At first, the new power more than fulfilled the claims made on its behalf. Predictably, it greatly reduced the cost of threshing.[104] Less predictably, it soon began to serve the stockman as well as the corn

141

grower by continuing in new form the minor processing revolution which sought to make the varied range of fodders available for the growing livestock population more digestible and palatable. Grey was not the only farmer of the time to see that 'the erection of a steam engine affords a good opportunity for constructing apparatus for steaming potatoes and other foods for cattle'.[105] For the power of the steam engine could grind or crush corn and beans, break oilcake and cut chaff and roots, while its heat could steam potatoes and chaff, boil linseed and cook pigfeed. So the machinery introduced for one major task was harnessed with equal success to a number of minor ones.[106]

Few farmers could attain the complicated and expensive efficiency of the Yorkshire manufacturer turned farmer 'within whose barn are fitted every imaginable machine for converting the corn and vegetable produce of the farm into food for man and beast'.[107] But by the 1850s there must have been a number like Sir John Conroy of Berkshire whose barn contained steam-driven equipment for breaking cake, grinding corn and slicing roots.[108] A more general tribute to the consequences of the introduction of the steam engine to the farmstead came a few years later from Nottinghamshire, where 'the erection of suitable buildings for cutting fodder and straw, pulping roots and grinding corn for consumption by livestock' was classed among major recent improvements in agriculture.[109]

The new equipment and the new processes made new buildings necessary. They also made necessary the adaptation of old ones. Two Midland studies found that a number of fodder-processing barns had begun life as more traditional types of barn but had been converted to the new function. The changes generally involved the addition of a loft to allow the installation of a gravity-feed system in which, for example, chaff from a chaff-cutter in the loft fell to a heap or container on the ground floor where it was mixed with roots processed by a slicer or pulper.[110] One sign of the development of fodder processing was the replacement in cattle buildings of hay racks by the mangers required for holding sliced roots, chaff and other chopped fodder.[111] Another was the abandonment in 1866 of what was probably the last of the Welsh gorse mills, for by this time such cumbersome installations were superseded by small and simple machines.[112] The processing of even this primitive fodder was improved by the technologies of the industrial age.

Contemporary interest in the possibilities of mechanising farmstead processes was considerable.[113] But the steam engine did not prove a satisfactory agent for such mechanisation. In particular, it could not readily distribute the power it produced or apply it to haulage work. Consequently, it remained harnessed to certain limited static operations, and in the rest of the steading human arms and legs continued to provide the power for transport and handling. Indeed, within a decade of its general appearance in the farmstead, it began to lose its major responsibility there.

For the obvious convenience of taking the threshing machine to the cornstacks instead of bringing all the corn to the barn encouraged the development of portable threshing machines. These were driven at first by portable steam engines which were also hauled to their place of work by horses but later by self-propelled traction engines which could pull as well as drive. From the middle of the century onwards, the use of such outfits spread rapidly and, as the years passed, more corn was threshed in the fields and fewer steam engines were installed in the buildings.[114] The replacement of the barn's old primary function by its new secondary one was symbolised by a barn built in Staffordshire in 1851 which included accommodation for hay, straw and feed preparation 'but no signs of a stationary threshing machine or memory of one'.[115] Significantly, the original design for Coleshill Model Farm in Oxfordshire, completed in 1853, included a stationary steam engine with a chimney. But this was replaced during construction by a small building for a portable steam engine.[116]

So, in a generation, the barn lost its ancient function as the centre for the processing and storage of the corn crop and became a centre for the storage and processing of livestock feed. 'In place of the hall-like interior of the barn, the scene of great assemblies for shearing and dancing, there was now only the workshop-like interior of the mixing house with its ranks of cutting, grinding, breaking, stirring machines driven by flapping belts to the steady beat of the steam engine'[117] (see Plate 24). The final stage of the change in this period is shown in a comparison of the entries in the farmstead competitions organised by the Royal Agricultural Society of England in 1849 and 1879. In the former, the steam engine, the proud prime-mover of the threshing machine, dominated the farmstead from the barn. In the latter, steam power was seldom more than an agent for the preparation of fodder, for the competitors assumed that corn was threshed in the field.[118]

Meanwhile, here as elsewhere, older ways lingered. Partly from conservatism, partly to provide winter work, flail-type barns were still occasionally built in the last years of this period and even into the next,[119] while threshed corn was sometimes stored in Welsh farmhouses until late in the nineteenth century.[120] There are byways as well as highways in agricultural history.

## Buildings for Storage and Processing

Even humble storage buildings illustrated the intensification and complication of Victorian agriculture. Thus, increasing production and rising values encouraged expenditure on the protection of farm produce, as references to Dutch barns show.[121] Again, implements were increasing in number, complexity and cost. In advanced areas, therefore, landowners provided improved implement shedding, sometimes including rooms, occasionally lockable, for tools and paint. In less-advanced areas they provided implement shedding for the first time. It was in this period, for example, that sheds for carts and implements established themselves in north-east Wales, often combined, as in English practice, with a granary overhead. Sometimes, too, they pleasingly incorporated another English tradition: the space below the stairs to the granary provided a good site for kennelling of the sheepdogs introduced from Scotland in the later years of this period.[122] Another sign of the times was the first appearance of the fertiliser store on farmstead plans.[123] Greater production per acre meant increased reliance on purchased resources and this, in turn, meant more capital outlay on buildings.

It also meant greater attention to the various processing enterprises of the farm. New forms of cider mill appeared,[124] while on hop farms the availability from the 1830s of near-smokeless anthracite coal ended the need to protect hops from the combustion products of their drying fuel and enabled the cockle kiln to be replaced by a simpler oast without a chimney. Such was the origin of the oasts which, together with their adjacent 'stowage' buildings where the dried hops were stored and packed into long sacks called 'pockets', came to be regarded as 'traditional' features of the hop-growing landscape.[125] It is salutary to remember that they date only from early Victorian times and were, in part, a byproduct of the Industrial Revolution.

The same general pressures and possibilities were reflected in the various efforts made at the end of this period to develop equipment for drying hay and corn.[126] None of these was successful but they foreshadowed the future reliance of the farmer on the industrialist for the mechanical means of conserving his harvested crops which brought such great changes to the operations and appearance of the farmstead in the next century.

### Building Materials and Equipment

The industrial age wrought even greater changes in the fabric and fittings of farm buildings than in their design. The brickfield and the slate quarry greatly increased the production of familiar materials, the factory added a steady flow of new types of material and equipment and the railways, fulfilling the promise made by the canals in the previous century, carried old and new alike throughout the length and breadth of the country.[127] The 'newly dug stones' and the 'native timber in the rough' which the Earl of Radnor's agent provided for the contractor who built the massive steading of Coleshill Model Farm in 1852, and the stems of the wild clematis with which a forgotten farmer bound the thatch of the adapted longhouse at Castle Farm Folk Museum near Bath, represented a dying tradition.[128] The ancient dependence on local resources came to an end.

The change was rapid. In 1836, for instance, Loudon could still write that 'the materials with which farm buildings are constructed are commonly those which are most abundant in the locality'. Significantly, however, he added in a later paragraph that 'in all the more advanced districts of Britain, thatched roofs have given way to tiles and slates'.[129] A generation later the emphasis was very different. In 1863 Denton thought it necessary to warn his readers against the assumption that purchased materials were invariably better than home-produced ones, adding magisterially that 'local materials should not hastily be set aside'. But he emphasised that purchased bricks and imported timber were sometimes better and cheaper than local stone and home-grown timber, while few of the materials he recommended could have been provided from local sources or manufactured by local skills.[130] The general point was aptly illustrated in the 1840s by Frederic Knight when he was building farmsteads to serve the new land he was so laboriously reclaiming from the Exmoor wilderness. 'No English fir for me', he wrote on the bottom of one of his specifications. Even in one of the most remote farming areas in the kingdom the timber used in new farmsteads came from the Baltic.[131]

The most obvious consequence of these changes was the widespread use of the better traditional materials. Brick, tiles and slates, hitherto only available in areas which produced them or which happened to lie convenient to river or canal, increasingly replaced the less durable mud, timber and thatch of the older order. Sometimes the general improvement encouraged local improvement in the type of locally produced material used. Thus, from 1840 to the mid-1850s the brickyard of the Ashburnham estate in Sussex took few outside orders as all the bricks it produced were required for rebuilding the estate's old timber farmsteads.[132] Indeed, estate brickyards probably met much of the increased demand for bricks. Garth, the agent in *Middlemarch* in the 1830s, thought happily of 'the fine bricks we can get out of the clay at Bott's Corner . . . it would cheapen the repairs', and Curtis, his flesh-and-blood successor forty years later, repeated the implied advice. Bricks made on the estate, he wrote, were much cheaper than purchased bricks and he included a chapter on brickmaking in his treatise.[133] Sometimes, too, materials traditional in one area were imported into other areas where they were hitherto unknown. In the Bredon district of Worcestershire, for example, brick and slates only became common materials for farm buildings after the railway came in 1866.[134]

Similarly, by the 1840s, slates were becoming a normal roofing material in counties as different as Devon and Northumberland,[135] incidentally creating academic problems for the future as they did so. On buildings of their own age these new roofing materials provide the modern historian with a conspicuous and convenient means of setting a limit to their earliest date of construction. But when used to re-roof older buildings, they may add to his difficulties, for the replacement of thatch by slate often included the replacement of the old timbering by new. Thus, in Devon, original roof timbers earlier than the seventeenth century are rare, as nineteenth-century improvers destroyed many old roof structures and with them the timberwork clues they could give to the age of the buildings of which they formed part.[136]

In the early 1850s, therefore, Caird frequently contrasted the barns and hovels of local materials 'requiring constant repair, a fruitful source of inconvenience and waste' with the new buildings of neater and more lasting type erected by such landowners as Lord Derby, the Duke of Wellington and Sir James Graham.[137] Even such a traditional type of building as the Downland barn, formerly built of local flints, timber and thatch, now used bricks, imported softwood trusses with bolted connections, and slates or mass-produced tiles.[138] Already, therefore, the new system was establishing itself. The days when farm buildings appeared to grow out of the soil of their parish were passing. From this time onwards, the materials of which they were built had no necessary connection with the land on which they stood.

Less immediately important but more prophetic was the appearance on the farm of new materials created or developed by the factory system. Creosote was used for preserving timber in the 1840s[139] asphalt for dampproof courses and flooring in the 1860s[140] and, more important, during the same period glazed windows became normal practice.[141] Two basic materials of the future, galvanised corrugated iron sheeting and concrete, also entered agricultural service in these years. The former established itself as a recognised roofing material, valued for its cheapness and lightness but disliked for the poor insulation it provided and its liability to rust,[142] while the latter soon became 'the invariable material for the foundations of all good buildings'.[143] A little later, it was also used for walls. But the failure of attempts to make it available in the convenient form of concrete blocks limited its uses for above-ground work, and it seems to have remained to the end of this period 'an auxiliary material to use when usual building materials must be brought from a distance and those adapted to making concrete are readily obtained on the spot.[144] By the end of this period both materials were sufficiently common to earn a place in an aesthetic lament over the replacement in farm buildings of 'lichencovered walls ... of ashengrey stone or ruddy brick, snug thatch and warm many-tinted tiles' by 'muddy-brown stock brick and the still more colourless and uninteresting concrete ... and corrugated iron'.[145]

Many other factory products, too, were now influencing the construction and equipment of farm buildings. Some, such as metal heelposts, stall divisions and mangers, were new forms of traditional fittings.[146] Some, such as ventilation cowls, hollow bricks to improve insulation, and rails and rollers for sliding doors, were new devices from the technical world beyond the village workshop.[147] Some, such as cast-iron pillars and iron trusses which bridged wide spans more economically than timber, were structural parts which foreshadowed prefabricated systems to come.[148] Others, more novel, offered new ways of doing old jobs. There was no precedent on the farm for the gas lighting or the gas engines which appeared in occasional advanced steadings in the 1860s[149] or for the iron railways on which trollies carried stacks to the threshing machine or fodder to the troughs of housed cattle.[150]

Indeed, one of the signs of the times was the increasing frequency with which proprietary names and illustrations of proprietary products appeared in the technical literature. The cast-iron stalls of Messrs Cottam & Hallen,[151] the pig-troughs of the Shotts Iron Company,[152] Dean's linseed mill[153] and Beedon's patent eaves tiles,[154] all showed that the age of local craftsmen and local materials was passing. The day of the manufacturer and the merchant had come.

But not entirely. The Ashridge estate staff who in 1830 rebuilt Pitstone Green Farm in Buckinghamshire at a cost of £896 14s 3d used timbers from the old steading they pulled down for the new cartshed.[155] The contractor who in 1852 built the steading of Coleshill Model Farm in Oxfordshire at a final cost of £2,939 16s 4d used bricks and stones from demolished cottages and farm buildings which had previously occupied the site.[156] No doubt many others made similar but unrecorded use of materials similarly obtained. For not all the revolutionary changes of this period could end that most enduring and pleasing tradition of the agricultural builder, his frugal and ingenious use of whatever lies to hand, including that most local of resources, material salvaged from old buildings.[157]

## NOTES

1. The last 'summering' took place in 1862 (Roberts, A. *National Park Forest Guide, Snowdonia*, HMSO, 1963, p 16).
2. See p 71. Victoria Farm and Upper Canada Farm on the Mendips date by their names

a stage in this process (Williams, M. 'The enclosure and reclamation of the Mendip Hills, 1770–1870, *Agricultural History Review*, vol 19, 1971, p 80). So does New Zealand Farm in Wiltshire – New Zealand was declared British territory in 1840 (*A Guide to the Industrial Archaeology of Wiltshire*, published by Wiltshire County Council Museum Service for the Wiltshire Archaeology and Natural History Society, 1978, p 55). For the farmsteads built in this period by the Knights to serve their Exmoor estate see Orwin, C. S. *The Reclamation of Exmoor Forest*, 1929, pp 53–6 and Havinden, M. *The Somerset Landscape*, 1981, p 184; for a farmstead built in 1858 to serve one of the farms created by the reclamation of Wychwood in Oxfordshire see Higgs, J. *The Land*, 1964, photo 175; for a farmstead built in 1849 to serve a warren area converted to farmland see Allison, E. J. *The East Riding of Yorkshire Landscape*, 1976, p 161. See also Peters, J. E. C. *The Development of Farm Buildings in Western Lowland Staffordshire up to 1880*, 1969, pp 18, 224–8.

3. Spring, D. *The English Landed Estate in the Nineteenth Century*, 1963, p 117. Coke of Holkham put the same point in more particular terms when he said to a tenant, 'if you will keep an extra yard of bullocks I will build you a yard and sheds free of expense' (Bacon, R. N. *Report on the Agriculture of Norfolk*, 1844, p 394).

4. The importance of the farmstead in this period as a 'manure factory' is illustrated by the considerable interest in the possibilities of conserving and using liquid manure. See, for example, Love, P. 'On the best method of applying liquid manure to the land in a liquid state', *Journal of the Royal Agricultural Society of England*, vol 20, 1859, pp 22–30; Blackburn, J. T. 'On the economical application of the liquid manure of a farm', *Journal of the Royal Agricultural Society of England*, vol 23, 1862, pp 1–15. Schemes for the collection of liquid manure in tanks and its distribution to the fields by pipes or carts were included in a number of advanced farmsteads but results were seldom satisfactory. 'Great disappointment has been experienced by farmers generally in the want of profit resulting from the distribution of liquid manure; experience and careful calculation having proved that where it necessitates the several operations of raising, carting and spreading, the benefit does not equal the cost of application' (Denton, J. B. *The Farm Homesteads of England*, 1863, p 158). The subject occurs frequently in the literature of the time but the practice never became general. For surviving Victorian liquid manure tanks see *Farmers Weekly*, 21 February 1975, p 47 and 31 July 1981, p 89; Fowler, P. *Farms in England*, 1983, plate 37. The remains of a remarkable liquid manure irrigation scheme of the 1850s can be seen at the home farm of Leighton estate, near Welshpool, Powys, which is now the property of the County Council. Streams and a cut from the Severn were channelled to drive a turbine which pumped plain water or water mixed either with guano or with manure from the steading to a tank on a hill above the farm from which a system of pipes distributed it to the fields.

5. Crosskill, W. 'On the necessity of care in the preservation of agricultural implements', *Journal of the Royal Agricultural Society of England*, vol 2, 1841, p 150. His words were heeded. See p 144.

6. The consolidation of new breeds of cattle was a major feature of the times. The *Shorthorn Herdbook* appeared in 1822, the *Hereford Herdbook* in 1846, the *Devon Herdbook* in 1851 and the *Aberdeen-Angus Polled Herdbook* in 1862. The publication of a herdbook, of course, implies both a considerable degree of development and a desire for further improvement.

7. Andrews, G. H. *A Rudimentary Treatise on Agricultural Engineering. I. Buildings*, 1852, pp 2–4, 75–7, 105.

8. Stephens, H. and Burns, R. S. *The Book of Farm Buildings*, 1861, p vi; Denton, J. B. *The Farm Homesteads of England*, 1863, p vi. The same point was later repeated even more forcibly by a commentator on the plans submitted in a farm buildings' competition. 'Until a competitor can put himself in the position of a manufacturer wanting the best for his factory, totally regardless ... of any considerations beyond the best and cheapest way of manufacturing his goods, he will be unlikely to succeed as a planner of farm buildings' (*The Builder*, vol 37, no 1903, 26 July 1879, p 840).

9. Wilson, J. *British Farming*, 1862, p 83. Compare 'The modern farmstead is an establishment for the manufacture of mutton, beef and pork' (Morton, J. C. *The Prince Consort's Farms*, 1863, p 83).

10. Thompson, H. S. 'Farm buildings', *Journal of the Royal Agricultural Society of England*, vol 11, 1850, p 187. See also Wade-Martins, S. 'The industrial archaeology of High Farming', *Journal of the Norfolk Industrial Archaeology Society*, Special Conference edition, 1981, pp 7–16; Brigden, R. 'Industrial archaeology in rural areas', *Journal of the Norfolk Industrial Archaeology Society*, Special Conference edition, 1981, pp 17–25.

11. 12 and 13 Vict c16; 16 and 17 Vict c154, with amendments 18 and 19 Vict c84 and 26 and 27 Vict c140; 23 and 24 Vict c169 (personal communication from Mr A. D. M. Phillips and Miss J. L. Jones of Keele University, 1982, currently working on 'The spatial adoption of farm buildings in England, 1850–1899' Social Science Research Council). See also Floud, Sir Francis, *The Ministry of Agriculture and Fisheries*, 1927, pp 251–5.

12. Caird, J. *English Agriculture in 1850–1*, 1852, p 489. See also Grey, J. 'On farm buildings', *Journal of the Royal Agricultural Society of England*, vol 4, 1843, p 1.

13. Throughout this period wages remained low, but after 1850 they rose perceptibly and regularly. Hence the mid-Victorian comment that 'so much of the cost of all farming operations is reducible to labour, and so much of this labour is connected with the homestead, that the arrangements of the latter should be especially framed to economise time' (Elliot, J. 'Farm buildings', *Journal of the Royal Agricultural Society of England*, vol 23, 1862, p 473).

14. See, in addition to the textbooks of this period listed on p 271, Donaldson, J. *A Treatise on Manures*, 1842, pp 374–87; Grey, J. 'On farm buildings', *Journal of the Royal Agricultural Society of England*, vol 4, 1843, pp 4–16. For a summary analysis of this basic pattern see Morton, J. *Cyclopaedia of Agriculture*, vol 1, 1855, pp 790–1. The same basic plan is recommended for small farms and for upland farms in Sturge, J. Y. and Isaac, T. W. P. 'On farm buildings for small farms', *Journal of the Bath and West of England Society*, vol 7, 1859, pp 191–205, and Poundley, J. *Designs for Two Sets of Steadings . . . Mainly Adapted to the High Districts of Wales*, 1857. For the varying incidence of this type of farmstead in this period see Peters, J. E. C. *The Development of Farm Buildings in Western Lowland Staffordshire up to 1880*, 1969, pp 49–59; Wiliam, E. *Traditional Farm Buildings in North-East Wales, 1550–1900*, 1982, pp 35–59, 268. An interesting illustration of the acceptance of the new system is given in Durham County Library Local History Publication *Rural Durham*, 1977, p 42. A farmstead of linear plan in 1768 had become a U-type courtyard steading by 1838.

15. For the place of 'model farms' in the agricultural system of the time and the part played by their buildings in it see MacDonald, S. 'Model farms', in Mingay, G. E. ed, *The Victorian Countryside*, 1981, pp 214–26. He quotes a contemporary view that 'few [model farms] can be considered as proper examples to be copied by others' and concludes that most were 'essentially a fashion . . . and expensive, trivial and, ultimately, ephemeral'. The farmsteads which served them were certainly expensive but neither trivial nor ephemeral. For examples see Morton, J. C. *The Prince Consort's Farms*, 1863; Jones, J. L. 'Farming under a Victorian roof', *Country Life*, 12 October 1972, pp 919–20, and Fowler, P. *Farms in England*, 1983, plates 37–9 (Eastwood Manor Farm, East Harptree, Somerset); Popham, J. H. *Farm Buildings, Function and Form*, unpublished thesis for Diploma in Conservation Studies, Institute of Advanced Architectural Studies, York University, 1973, pp 20–2 (Home Farm, Birdsall estate, Yorkshire, which included poultry houses, since the farm provided for the needs of the owner's house); Woodhams, L. *The Story of an Agricultural Building*, published by the Ministry of Agriculture, Fisheries and Food, Wolverhampton, 1976, pp 3–4 (Home Farm, Abberly, Worcestershire); Lincolnshire and Humberside Arts, St Hughs, Newport, Lincoln, unpublished *Survey of Agricultural Buildings Group*, produced to accompany lecture at Oxford University Department for External Studies conference, February 1980. This describes Scopwick House Farm, Lincolnshire, built in 1868, which included a steampowered distribution system and, incidentally, a brick chicken coop; Architects in Agriculture, *Coleshill Model Farm, Oxfordshire*, 1981; Fowler, P. *Farms in England*, 1983, plates 30, 43. Taine expressed surprise that a model farm he visited in 1862 was making money 'and the nobleman who started it in the public interest now finds it profitable' (Mingay, G. E. *Rural Life in Victorian England*, 1977, pp 58–9). But this particular steading appears to have been unusually economically designed, which suggests an unusually economically managed home farm. The remains of a remarkably advanced and experimental home farm of the 1850s can be seen on the Leighton estate, near Welshpool, Powys, now the property of the County Council. Its massive buildings, which include two radial piggeries, now serve six small farms. For its turbine-driven liquid manure irrigation scheme see note 4.

16. See p 113.

17. It is, however, fair to add that the astonishing J. C. Loudon (1783–1843) the only designer of farm buildings to win a place in the *Dictionary of National Biography*, would have found no particular technical difficulty in replacing any or all of his contributors. He was an agriculturist and horticulturist, an architect and a town planner; he wrote his way through the entire corpus of rural knowledge, at one time editing no less than five journals simultaneously. He found time for a form of professional Grand Tour during which he accompanied the Russian forces which followed the despairing Grande Armée on the retreat from Moscow; and he left as his memorials five massive encyclopaedias and much of the enduring delight of Great Tew in Oxfordshire, one of the most beautiful of all English villages, where he replanned the landscape as well as the farming system when he was agent for a local landowner.

18. Stephens, S. and Burn, R. S. *The Book of Farm Buildings*, 1863.

19. J. B. Denton (1814–93) trained as a surveyor under a land agent and began his career as a surveyor for enclosure schemes. He later became a civil engineer concerned with railway construction, water supplies and sewage disposal. But he maintained an interest in

agriculture throughout his professional life and was for a time a director of a land company as well as a land-drainage engineer (*Minutes of Proceedings of the Institution of Civil Engineers*, vol 15, 1894, pp 386–9).

20. See, for example, Dean's work for the Holkham estate (see p 128) and the effects on cowhouse design of published recommendations, including prize entries in the Royal Agricultural Society of England's 1849 competition for farmstead plans (Peters, J. E. C. *The Development of Farm Buildings in Western Lowland Staffordshire up to 1880*, 1969, p 163).

21. It also recorded the end of the unhappy tradition of *la ferme ornée*. In this period Loudon was influenced by this curious fashion though it affected the domestic rather than the agricultural sections of his *Encyclopaedia of Cottage, Farm and Village Architecture*. Its epitaph was written crushingly in 1863 by Denton, who dismissed in a phrase those who 'regarded farm architecture as a mere matter of taste' before turning to the adult and practical question of 'the adaptation of farm buildings to the various operations conducted within them' (Denton, J. B. *The Farm Homesteads of England*, 1863, p vi). See also the austere comments of J. Ewart on 'the sacrifice of utility to ornament' in *A Treatise on the Arrangement and Construction of Agricultural Buildings*, 1851, p 27. The Victorians stood no nonsense from Regency affectations.

22. Denton, J. B. *The Farm Homesteads of England*, 1863, p vi. Few of his contemporaries, however, would have quarrelled with the twelve 'golden rules . . . generally recognised in the arrangement of the best buildings' which he listed on pp 145–7.

23. Fussell, G. E. *The Farmer's Tools*, 1952, pp 48–9.

24. The purely personal element in landownership was considerable. 'It is very noticeable [on the Holkham estate] that the greatest irregularities in the expenditure curve [on farm buildings] are caused not by the national or international economy but by family affairs' (Wade-Martins, S. *A Great Estate at Work*, 1980, p 96).

25. Wade-Martins, S. *A Great Estate at Work*, 1980, gives a detailed account of the policy and management of a major estate (Holkham). See also Peters, J. E. C. *The Development of Farm Buildings in Western Lowland Staffordshire up to 1880*, pp 208–18; Wiliam, E. *Traditional Farm Buildings in North-East Wales, 1550–1900*, 1982, pp 258–66.

26. For the land agent of this period see Richards, E. 'The land agent', in Mingay, G. E. ed, *The Victorian Countryside*, 1981, pp 439–56.

27. In 1826 Cobbett praised 'the most complete farmyard I ever saw' on Lord Folkestone's estate at Coleshill in Oxfordshire and described it as 'the contrivance of Mr Palmer, Lord Folkestone's bailiff and steward . . . The master gives all credit to the servant, but the servant ascribes a good deal of it to the master' (Cobbett, W. *Rural Rides*, vol 2, 1893, p 123). The degree of interest taken by the owner varied, of course, with the individual. An interested landowner, like Lord Folkestone, would probably discuss the scheme with his agent, who would then prepare draft plans. These would in turn be discussed, after which the agent would prepare final plans of the approved scheme.

28. Little systematic information is available on the origin and development of estate yards and their associated brickyards, quarries and timberyards. But the importance of these numerous and sometimes very substantial centres must have been considerable. In early Victorian times the Duke of Bedford's yard employed a hundred men (Caird, J. *English Agriculture in 1850–1*, 1852, p 439), and the Marquess of Bath's yard at Longleat more than sixty (Thompson, F. M. L., *English Landed Society in the Nineteenth Century*, 1963, p 171). The former, which included steam-driven machinery for sawing timber, was described by Peel in 1849 as 'more like a dockyard than a domestic office' (Spring, D. *The English Landed Estate in the Nineteenth Century*, 1963, p 45). In the 1830s the 55,000 acre Yarborough estates in Lincolnshire had five brickyards (Darley, G. *The National Trust Book of the Farm*, 1981, p 176). For Holkham estate yard, woodlands and brickyards see Wade-Martins, S. *A Great Estate at Work*, 1980, pp 78–84 and Manning, K. 'Longlands Farm, Holkham estate', *Journal of the Norfolk Industrial Archaeology Society*, vol 2, no 5, 1980, pp 17–20. The steampowered yard included a foundry apparently capable of producing cast-iron pillars, windows and door thresholds (Wade-Martins, S. 'Factory farming in the 1850s', *Country Life*, 6 July 1978, p 623). For the timberyard of an estate which prided itself on using only its own timber in its own buildings see Fleming, M. 'Earsham timberyard', *Journal of the Norfolk Industrial Archaeology Society*, vol 2, no 5, 1980, pp 27–32. In 1894 a land agent in Wales reported that all the buildings on his 8,000 acre estate were built of brick made on the estate. In the same area, however, estate saw mills only became common after the mid-nineteenth century (Wiliam, E. *Traditional Farm Buildings in North-East Wales, 1550–1900*, 1982, pp 74, 94). A history of estate yards would fill a noticeable gap in rural history.

29. See George Eliot, *Middlemarch*, chapter 58 for Garth (the novel is set in the 1830s); Peters, J. E. C. *The Development of Farm Buildings in Western Lowland Staffordshire up to 1880*, 1969, p 212. The 'architects' who were employed, temporarily and exceptionally, in the Holkham estate office early in this period were probably draughtsmen who drew the agent's

plans (Wade-Martins, S. *A Great Estate at Work*, 1980, pp 73, 148).
    30. Ewart, J. *A Treatise on the Arrangement and Construction of Agricultural Buildings*, 1851, p 1.
    31. Architects in Agriculture, *Coleshill Model Farm, Oxfordshire*, 1981, p 14.
    32. Essex County Council, *The Essex Countryside, Farm Buildings*, 1974, p 6; Essex Record Office Publication 67, *Agriculture in Essex, c1840–1900*, 1975, plate 10; Grafton Green, B. *Milk for the Millions*, Barnet Libraries Local History Publications, 1983, p. 5.
    33. Sant, A. 'Three Oxford architects', *Oxoniensia*, vol 35, 1970, pp 35–102. This gives a list of all Wilkinson's work, including his farm buildings; Brockman, H. A. N. *The British Architect in Industry, 1841–1940*, 1974, pp 37–9, 77.
    34. Brockman, H. A. N. *The British Architect in Industry, 1841–1940*, 1974, pp 37–9, including reference to George Godwin, editor of *The Builder*, who designed farm buildings; Wiliam, E. *Traditional Farm Buildings in North-East Wales, 1550–1900*, 1982, pp 247, 264, including reference to Gilbert Scott.
    35. *The Builder*, vol 7, 3 November 1849, p 517; Wilson, J. *British Farming*, 1862, p 84; *The Builder*, vol 23, 5 March 1865, p 146; Dean, G. A. *The Land Steward*, 1851, pp 180, 183, 187, who refers to the design and supervision of construction by an architect but adds that 'a practical knowledge of agriculture, and great experience in constructing such buildings are absolutely necessary'. 'When the earliest issues of *The Builder* began to publish designs for farm buildings in the 1840s, the authors bent over backwards to reassure the reader that these were sensible plans, thought up by men knowledgeable in agricultural matters and little concerned with aesthetic minutiae' (Darley, G. *The National Trust Book of the Farm*, 1981, p 99). See also the advice to architects given by *The Building News* in 1860, quoted in Brockman, H. A. N. *The British Architect in Industry, 1841–1900*, 1974, p 40.
    36. Wade-Martins, S. 'Factory farming in the 1850s', *Country Life*, 6 July 1978, pp 62–3; Wade-Martins, S. *A Great Estate at Work*, 1980, pp 170–2.
    37. Denton, J. B. *Farm Homesteads of England*, 1863.
    38. Orwin, C. S. *The Reclamation of Exmoor Forest*, 1929, pp 53, 68.
    39. Grey, J. 'On farm buildings', *Journal of the Royal Agricultural Society of England*, vol 4, 1843, pp 1–3; Caird, J. *English Agriculture in 1850–1*, 1852, p 2; Spring, D. 'A great agricultural estate. Netherby under Sir Charles Graham, 1820–1845', *Agricultural History*, vol 20, April 1955, p 96; Wade-Martins, S. *A Great Estate at Work*, 1980, p 97.
    40. Caird, J. *English Agriculture in 1850–1*, 1852, p 2. Wiliam, E. *Traditional Farm Buildings in North-East Wales, 1550–1900*, 1982, pp 262–3, contrasts the substantial expenditure on farm buildings of such improving landlords as the Duke of Westminster and an estate so neglected first by an absentee landlord, then by his alcoholic widow, that tenants had to undertake their own repairs.
    41. Caird, J. *English Agriculture in 1850–1*, 1852, pp 490–1. See also Donaldson, J. *A Treatise on Manures*, 1842, p 371, and Grey, J. 'On farm buildings', *Journal of the Royal Agricultural Society of England*, vol 4, 1843, p 1. 'The mossy thatch of the cowshed, the broken grey barn doors ... the uneven, neglected yard' of Freeman's End Farm were not confined to fiction or to the 1830s in which the novel was set (George Eliot, *Middlemarch*, chapter 39).
    42. Caird, J. 'British agriculture', *Journal of the Royal Agricultural Society of England*, 2nd ser, vol 14, 1878, p 312.
    43. Murray, G. 'Report on the trial of dairy implements and machinery at Bristol', *Journal of the Royal Agricultural Society of England*, 2nd ser, vol 15, 1879, p 136.
    44. Mercer, E. *English Vernacular Houses*, 1975, p 38.
    45. Wiliam, E. *Traditional Farm Buildings in North-East Wales, 1550–1900*, 1982, p 37.
    46. Harrison, A. and Harrison, J. K. 'The horsewheel in North Yorkshire', *Industrial Archaeology*, vol 10, 1973, p 253 for late wheelhouse. Hutton, K. 'The distribution of wheelhouses in the British Isles', *Agricultural History Review*, vol 24, 1976, p 32, mentions three wheelhouses built between 1845 and 1868.
    47. Smedley, N. *Life and Tradition in Suffolk and North-East Essex*, 1976, p 20; Peters, J. E. C. 'The solid thatch roof', *Vernacular Architecture*, vol 8, 1977, p 825.
    48. For laithe houses see Stell, C. 'Pennine barns. An introduction'. *Folklife*, vol 3, 1965, pp 20–1; Mercer, E. *English Vernacular Houses*, 1975, pp 45–9; Brunskill, R. W. *Traditional Farm Buildings of Britain*, 1982, pp 104–9. For bank barns see Brunskill, R. W. *Vernacular Architecture of the Lake Counties*, 1974, p 86; Brunskill, *Traditional Farm Buildings of Britain*, 1982, pp 113–15.
    49. Hughes, T. *The Scouring of the White Horse*, first published 1858, 1892 ed, p 21, and *The Ashen Faggot*, first published 1862, included with it, p 285. A generation later, a commentator compared the businesslike new farmsteads with the 'casual scattering of farm buildings' and general haphazard mess of the old order. But he regretted that the change meant the loss of 'all the picturesqueness of one of the most picturesque elements in the English landscape.' (*The Builder*, 9 February 1884, p 216).

50. Dean, G. A. *The Land Steward*, 1851, p 177. For Beatson see pp 68, 99.

51. Raynbird, H. 'On the farming of Suffolk', *Journal of the Royal Agricultural Society of England*, vol 8, 1848, p 320; Acland, T. D. 'On the farming of Somerset, *Journal of the Royal Agricultural Society of England*, vol 11, 1850, pp 743, 745; Rowley, J. J. 'On the farming of Derbyshire', *Journal of the Royal Agricultural Society of England*, vol 14, 1853, p 49; Read, C. S. 'On the farming of Oxfordshire', *Journal of the Royal Agricultural Society of England*, vol 15, 1854, p 255; Moscrop, W. J. 'On the farming of Leicestershire', *Journal of the Royal Agricultural Society of England*, 2nd ser. vol 2, 1866, p. 334; Bowstead, T. 'Report on farm prize competition' (in South Wales), *Journal of the Royal Agricultural Society of England*, 2nd ser, vol 8, 1872, p 279; Harding, J. 'Recent improvements in dairy practice', *Journal of the Royal Agricultural Society of England*, vol 21, 1860, p 84, commented on the increase in the yields of grass and hay which followed investment in yards and other stockbuildings which kept cattle off the land in winter.

52. Bearn, W, 'On the farming of Northamptonshire', *Journal of the Royal Agricultural Society of England*, vol 13, 1852, p 36.

53. Read, C. S. 'On the farming of South Wales', *Journal of the Royal Agricultural Society of England*, vol 10, 1849, p 147. The same point was made by Grey, J. 'On farm buildings', *Journal of the Royal Agricultural Society of England*, vol 4, 1843, p 4, who quoted the case of a farmer who bought a high quality bull but had no safe and suitable building in which to house it.

54. Progressive landlords, of course, were well aware of this. In 1842 the Duke of Bedford's auditor in Devonshire urged local agents to encourage tenants to 'make manure, grow green crops and keep cattle in all the winter, all points they are defective in' (Horn, P. *The Rural World, 1750–1850*, 1980, p 240).

55. Bravender, J. 'The farming of Gloucestershire', *Journal of the Royal Agricultural Society of England*, vol 11, 1850, p 176; Mechi, J. J. *A Series of Letters on Agricultural Improvement*, 1845, p 70, for thermometer.

56. Peters, J. E. C. *The Development of Farm Buildings in Western Lowland Staffordshire up to 1880*, 1969, p 162; Wiliam, E. *Traditional Farm Buildings in North-East Wales, 1550–1900*, 1982, pp 209–12.

57. Blundell, J. 'Farm buildings', *Journal of the Royal Agricultural Society of England*, vol 23, 1862, pp 475–6. For yards in this period see Peters, J. E. C. *The Development of Farm Buildings in Western Lowland Staffordshire up to 1880*, 1969, pp 134–41.

58. Glover, 'On box-feeding cattle' in Anon, *The Farmer's Friend*, published by Smith, Elder and Co, 1847, p 21.

59. Almack, B. 'On the agriculture of Norfolk', *Journal of the Royal Agricultural Society of England*, vol 4, 1845, p 319. See also Bell, T. G. 'A report on the agriculture of the county of Durham', *Journal of the Royal Agricultural Society of England*, vol 17, 1856, p 109; Read, C. S. 'Recent improvements in Norfolk farming', *Journal of the Royal Agricultural Society of England*, vol 19, 1858, p 295; Peters, J. E. C. *The Development of Farm Buildings in Western Lowland Staffordshire up to 1880*, 1969, p 160.

60. Read, C. S. 'Report on the farming of Buckinghamshire', *Journal of the Royal Agricultural Society of England*, vol 16, 1855, p 297. See pp 82–3. Wade-Martins, S. 'Factory farming in the 1850s', *Country Life*, 6 July 1978, pp 62–3, describes fattening boxes of this period at Egmere Farm near Walsingham, Norfolk, and notes that the size of the boxes is a reminder that cattle were slaughtered much older and much larger than they are today.

61. de Lavergne, L. *The Rural Economy of England, Ireland and Scotland*, 1855, pp 184–5.

62. Wade-Martins, S. *A Great Estate at Work*, 1980, pp 166–7, 177.

63. Readers of Richard Jefferies will remember his incidental references to the improvement of cattle housing in this period. 'In those days [the 1820s] cattle for the most part – except those that were fattening – remained in the fields throughout the winter, roughing it in the shelter of great hawthorn bushes. Cattle are now sheltered far better than they ever were before ... For modern scientific farming [in 1883] depends much upon improved sheds and careful housing of cattle. The old farmers preferred cattle that could stand any weather out of doors' (*Field and Farm*, Looker, S. J. ed, 1957, pp 32, 80, 85). See also Jefferies' *Hodge and his Masters* (Rossabi, A. ed, 1979, pp 296–7), which refers to improvements in cattle housing 'since [liquid] milk selling commenced'. This book was first published in 1880. See also Darby, J. 'The agriculture of Pembrokeshire', *Journal of the Bath and West of England Society*, 3rd ser, vol 19, 1887–8, p 108, who noted that improved accommodation for cattle 'enabled farmers to keep an improved breed instead of the rough but hardy runts that were able to live out in all weathers'.

64. Garnett, F. W. *Westmorland Agriculture*, 1912, p 191. Similarly, Darby, J. 'The agriculture of Pembrokeshire', *Journal of the Bath and West of England Society*, 3rd ser, vol 19, 1887–8, p 108, noted that large sums had been expended on livestock buildings 'but there is still much to be done'. See also Darby, J. 'The farming of Dorset, *Journal of the Bath and*

*West of England Society*, 3rd ser, vol 4, 1872, pp 38–40.

65. In 1845, J. J. Mechi listed guttering and downpipes among the items of expenditure against which he was 'warned, entreated and dissuaded' by his farming friends. Early in the next decade Caird made special reference to 'the spouting to carry off rainwater' on a model farm in Berkshire, so he presumably regarded it as exceptional, and Andrews remarked that 'nine-tenths of the farm steadings of England are without guttering' (Mechi, J. J. *Letters on Agricultural Improvement*, 1845, p 1; Caird, J. *English Agriculture in 1850–1*, 1852, p 106; Andrews, G. H. *Rudimentary Treatise on Agricultural Engineering. I. Buildings*, 1852, p 2). See also Rowley, J. 'The farming of Derbyshire', *Journal of the Royal Agricultural Society of England*, vol 14, 1853, p 63. A few years later, however, Read found that spouting was normal practice in Norfolk (Read, C. S. 'Recent improvements in Norfolk farming', *Journal of the Royal Agricultural Society of England*, vol 19, 1858, p 295). Nevertheless, Wilson found it necessary to urge the importance of providing farm buildings with spouting (Wilson, T. *British Farming*, 1862, p 96). Such variations continued in the next decade. A committee awarding prizes in a farm competition specifically commented on the lack of guttering on a Shropshire farm and ascribed it to a whim of the owner, whereas a similar committee a year later reported that 'spoutless buildings' were common in south Wales (Wheatley, J. 'Report of the farm prize competition', *Journal of the Royal Agricultural Society of England*, 2nd ser, vol 7, 1871, p 319; Bowstead, T. 'Report on the farm prize competition', *Journal of the Royal Agricultural Society of England*, 2nd ser, vol 8, 1872, p 322). As late as 1948 a National Agricultural Advisory Service farm buildings officer had to argue the case with the agent of a small Westcountry estate for including guttering and downpipes on some farm buildings under reconstruction (personal experience).

66. Voelcker, A. 'On the composition of farmyard manure', *Journal of the Royal Agricultural Society of England*, vol 17, 1856, pp 213–59.

67. Denton, J. B. *The Farm Homesteads of England*, 1863, pp 130–1. The first reference to the findings of research as a factor in the design of buildings for the farm, however, occurred a few years earlier when J. C. Morton quoted the opinion of 'the French Academicians' on the desirable cubic airspaces for horses and cattle (*Cyclopaedia of Agriculture*, 1885, vol 1, p 798).

68. Fussell, G. E. 'Sir Harry Stephen Moysey Thompson', *Journal of the Land Agents Society*, vol 49, December 1950, p 541.

69. Bennett, W. 'The farming of Bedfordshire', *Journal of the Royal Agricultural Society of England*, vol 18, 1857, p 25.

70. For cowhouses in this period see Peters, J. E. C. *The Development of Farm Buildings in Western Lowland Staffordshire up to 1880*, 1969, pp 143–6, 150–8, 163–78; Caffyn, L. *A Study of Farm Buildings in Selected Parishes of East Sussex*, unpublished MA thesis, Manchester University, 1981, pp 65–7; Wiliam, E. *Traditional Farm Buildings in North-East Wales, 1550–1900*, 1982, pp 186–93, 196–7, 212–14.

71. Cheke, V. *The Story of Cheesemaking in England*, 1959, p 162; Caird, J. *English Agriculture in 1850–1*, 1852, p 4. See also Harding, J. 'On the construction and heating of dairy and cheese rooms', *Journal of the Bath and West of England Society*, vol 16, 1868, pp 190–9 and for butter-making and cheese-making methods and equipment The Castle Museum, York, *The Dairy Catalogue*, 1979; Shropshire County Museum Information Sheet, *Acton Scott Working Farm Museum, The Dairy*. Horses, donkeys and dogs were used to drive gear for churning milk in Wales (Jenkins, J. G. *Life and Tradition in Rural Wales*, 1976, pp 51, 131, 155; Wiliam, E. *Traditional Farm Buildings in North-East Wales*, 1982, p 223). An example of horsegear for churning, which was installed in the early nineteenth century and used until 1879, can be seen in the Science Museum in London.

72. Morton, J. C. 'Dairy farming', *Journal of the Royal Agricultural Society of England*, 2nd ser, vol 14, 1878, p 670. See also Atkins, P. J. 'London's intra-urban milk supply c1790–1914', *Transactions of the Institute of British Geographers*, N.S. vol 2, 1977, pp 383–9; Stout, A. 'Three centuries of London cowkeeping', *Farmers Weekly*, 18 August 1978, pp v–xiii. For the town dairies in Liverpool in this period see Grundy, J. E. *The Origins of Liverpool Cowkeepers*, unpublished MA thesis, Lancaster University, 1982, pp 18–36.

73. Drummond, J. C. *The Englishman's Food*, 1957, pp 299–300.

74. Burnett, J. *Plenty and Want*, 1966, p 6.

75. In all, 5,357 of the 9,531 cows in the Metropolitan Board of Works area were attacked by the plague. Of these only 325 recovered (Burnett, J. *Plenty and Want*, 1966, p 156).

76. Whetham, E. G. 'The London milk trade 1860–1900', *Economic History Review*, 2nd ser, vol 17, 1964, p 372; Morton, J. C. 'Town milk', *Journal of the Royal Agricultural Society of England*, 2nd ser, vol 4, 1868, p 85; Clutterbuck, J. C. 'The farming of Middlesex', *Journal of the Royal Agricultural Society of England*, 2nd ser, vol 5, 1869, p 21. There were, however, some admirable urban cowhouses before this time. The 'model' cowhouse shown in Plate 26 was apparently built in the 1850s. It stood at the junction of Melbury Rd and High Street Kensington (Sheldon, J. P. *Dairy Farming*, 1881, pp 345–9).

153

77. Morton, J. C. 'Town milk', *Journal of the Royal Agricultural Society of England*, 2nd ser, vol 4, 1868, p 83–6. See also Loudon, J. C. *Encyclopaedia of Agriculture*, 6th ed, 1866, pp 1028–9.

78. Morton, J. C. 'Town milk', *Journal of the Royal Agricultural Society of England*, 2nd ser, vol 4, 1868, p 97.

79. Morton, J. C. 'Dairy farming', *Journal of the Royal Agricultural Society of England*, 2nd ser, vol 14, 1878, p 670.

80. Caird, J. *English Agriculture in 1850–1*, 1852, pp 94, 142, 227–8. George Barham, who founded the Express Dairy Company in 1864 chose the name because of the trains on which the milk would travel. The trademark of the Company was a locomotive and its first offices were at 28 Museum St, convenient for King's Cross mainline terminus. (Grafton Green, B. *Milk for the Millions*. Barnet Libraries Local History Publications, 1983, p 3.)

81. Morton, J. C. 'On cheesemaking', *Journal of the Royal Agricultural Society of England*, 2nd ser, vol 2, 1875, pp 261–300.

82. Chester, H. 'The food of the people', *Journal of the Royal Agricultural Society of England*, 2nd ser, vol 4, 1868, p 119.

83. Nielsen, V. C. 'Cheesemaking and cheesechambers in Gloucestershire', *Industrial Archaeology*, vol 5, 1968, p 169; Wiliam, E. *Traditional Farm Buildings in North-East Wales, 1550–1900*, 1982, pp 223–4.

84. Jefferies, Richard. *Hodge and his Masters*, Rossabi, A. ed, 1979, p 94. This book was first published in 1880.

85. Loudon, J. C. *An Encyclopaedia of Cottage, Farm and Village Architecture*, 1836, p 375. Frere, P. H. 'The improved construction of stables', *Journal of the Royal Agricultural Society of England*, vol 25, 1864, pp 364–8, quotes the evidence of an army report on the ventilation of cavalry stables and recommends improved ventilation. See also Peters, J. E. C. *The Development of Farm Buildings in Western Lowland Staffordshire up to 1880*, 1969, pp 113–28; Kent County Council Education Committee, *Traditional Kent Buildings*, no 2, 1981, pp 9–10 (surviving Victorian stable); Caffyn, L. *A Study of Farm Buildings in Selected Parishes of East Sussex*, unpublished MA thesis, Manchester University, 1981, pp 67–72; Wiliam, E. *Traditional Farm Buildings in North-East Wales, 1550–1900*, 1982, pp 160–77.

86. Anon. *English Forests and Forest Trees*, 1853, p 168; Spooner, W. C. 'The agricultural capabilities of the New Forest', *Journal of the Royal Agricultural Society of England*, 2nd ser, vol 7, 1871, p 228, which refers to the autumn pannaging of an average of 4,000 pigs annually in the 1860s; Shropshire County Museum, *Information Sheet 2*, p 3.

87. Dean, G. A. *The Land Steward*, 1851, p 205. See also Stephens, H. and Burns, R. S. *The Book of Farm Buildings*, 1861, p 493; Peters, J. E. C. *The Development of Farm Buildings in Western Lowland Staffordshire up to 1880*, 1969, pp 200–1; Wiliam, E. *Traditional Farm Buildings in North-East Wales, 1550–1900*, 1982, pp 245–7; Youatt, W. *The Pig*, 1847, pp 137–42, refers only to fattening buildings based on the sty. The 1860 edition of his book, edited by S. Sidney, describes a more intensive type of enclosed fattening house, pp 53–7, but this was clearly exceptional. Long, J. *The Book of the Pig*, 1885, pp 205–13, included descriptions of some elaborate piggeries for large-scale production but they were all based on the principle described in Youatt's 1847 book.

88. Clarke, J. A. 'On increasing our home production of poultry', *Journal of the Royal Agricultural Society of England*, 2nd ser, vol 2, 1866, pp 356–7. See also Peters, J. E. C. *The Development of Farm Buildings in Western Lowland Staffordshire up to 1880*, 1969, pp 201–4.

89. Clutterbuck, J. 'on the farming of Middlesex', *Journal of the Royal Agricultural Society of England*, 2nd ser, vol 5, 1869, p 19. Mechi housed his sheep in yards with sheds for shelter (Mechi, J. J. *A Series of Letters on Agricultural Improvements*, 1845, p 71). Lawes used portable houses with slatted floors run on rails laid in the fields to save treading on the soil and provide the sheep with a dry bed (Caird, J. *English Agriculture in 1850–1*, 1852, pp 463–4). Movable sheds were also used on the Quantocks (Acland, T. D. 'On the farming of Somerset', *Journal of the Royal Agricultural Society of England*, vol 11, 1850, pp 694–5). The Prince Consort used a more intensive system on one of his Windsor farms. He housed fattening sheep in a building with a slatted floor and found that they 'throve fast compared with the progress made out of doors' (Morton, J. C. *The Prince Consort's Farms*, 1863, p 87). Coleshill Model Farm in Oxfordshire, completed in 1853, included sheepyards and a fat sheephouse with a slatted floor (Architects in Agriculture, *Coleshill Model Farm, Oxfordshire*, Occasional Paper no 1, 1981, p 19). But the practice was exceptional. Sheep were, however, inwintered in Derbyshire in this period (Rowley, J. J. 'The farming of Derbyshire', *Journal of the Royal Agricultural Society of England*, vol 14, 1853, p 47), while Poundley, J. *Designs for Two Sets of Farm Buildings ... Mainly Adapted to the High Districts of Wales*, 1857, included accommodation for inwintered sheep.

90. He also mentions a few slatted floor systems (Caird, J. *English Agriculture in 1850–1*, 1852, pp 69, 121, 141, 275, 375). For this system, which was only found on the farms of

occasional pioneers, see also de Lavergne, L. *The Rural Economy of England, Scotland and Ireland*. 1855, p 185. He refers to soilage on p 241; Morton, J. C. *The Prince Consort's Farms*, 1863, p 87; Hyams, E. ed, *Taine's Notes on England*, 1957, p 132; Copeland, J. 'Nothing new in slats', *Farmers Weekly*, 7 July 1961, pp 88–9; Architects in Agriculture, *Coleshill Model Farm, Oxfordshire*, 1981, p 19.

91. Robert Campbell built this house of mass concrete walls and a tile roof on his Faringdon estate about 1870 (Gray, J. R. 'An industrial farm estate in Berkshire', *Industrial Archaeology*, vol 8, 1971, pp 171–85). From internal evidence it seems possible that this was the farmstead where Taine saw a slatted floor system (Hyams, E. ed, *Taine's Notes on England*, 1957, p 132).

92. Hartley, M. and Ingilby, J. *A Yorkshire Village*, 1953, p 249, for the replacement of small field cowhouses by the familiar two-storey field barns after the Askrigg enclosure of 1819; Peters, J. E. C. *The Development of Farm Buildings in Western Lowland Staffordshire up to 1880*, 1969, pp 32–3; D'Arcy, J. 'Stone barns for better or worse', *Farmers Weekly*, 24 September 1971, p 111, for later nineteenth-century dale field barns; Thorndyke, M. A. 'Havens from wintry weather', *Country Life*, 17 January 1980, p 189, for Northumberland outbuildings; Wade-Martins, S. *A Great Estate at Work*, 1980, pp 147, 157, for Holkham outbuildings; Armstrong, J. R. 'Hampers Barn', *Sandgate Preservation Society Newsletter*, Spring 1982, pp iv–v, for Sussex outbuildings.

93. Spearing, J. B. 'On the agriculture of Berkshire', *Journal of the Royal Agricultural Society of England*, vol 21, 1860, p 33.

94. A useful 'bench-mark' date in this process is 1837, the year the last barn was built on Holkham estate (Wade-Martins, S. *A Great Estate at Work*, 1981, p 157), though occasional barns of traditional type continued to be built until the closing years of this period (Peters, J. E. C. *The Development of Farm Buildings in Western Lowland Staffordshire up to 1880*, 1969, p 98) and even later (see p 195). For laments and reconstructions see Read, G. S. 'On the farming of Oxfordshire', *Journal of the Royal Agricultural Society of England*, vol 15, 1854, p 255; Blundell, J. 'Method of converting old barns into cattleboxes', *Journal of the Royal Agricultural Society of England*, vol 25, 1884, p 250–3; Read, C. S. 'On the farming of Buckinghamshire', *Journal of the Royal Agricultural Society of England*, vol 16, 1853, p 309; 'Mr Little's report on the western and southern counties', *Journal of the Bath and West of England Society*, 3rd ser, vol 14, 1882, p 84.

95. By 1827 attacks on threshing machines were sufficiently common to make necessary an Act imposing a penalty of seven years' transportation on those who damaged them. Nevertheless, their destruction was a 'prominent feature' of the labourers' rising of 1830 (Hammond, J. L. and Hammond, B. *The Village Labourer 1760–1832*, 1911, pp 249, 273). See also Hobsbawm, E. J. and Rudé, J. *Captain Swing*, 1969, pp 74, 198, 288–99, 359–65, and Horn, P. *The Rural World, 1750–1850*, 1980, pp 88–93.

96. See also Peters, J. E. C. *The Development of Farm Buildings in Western Lowland Staffordshire up to 1880*, 1969, pp 102–5; Wiliam, E. *Traditional Farm Buildings in North-East Wales, 1550–1900*, 1982, pp 151–2. In Northumberland between 1820 and 1850 the number of horsepowered installations among those whose source of power is known rose from 41 to 86, of waterpowered installations from 24 to 28 and of steampowered installations from 5 to 10 (MacDonald, S. 'The early thrashing machine in Northumberland', *Tools and Tillage*, vol 3, 1978, p 175, which also mentions one driven by windpower).

97. Coleman, J. 'General report on the implement show at Bury St Edmunds', *Journal of the Royal Agricultural Society of England*, 2nd ser, vol 3, 1867, p 593.

98. Royal Agricultural Society of England, *Award of Prizes for Implements at the Annual Show*, 1880, p 3.

99. See *Farmers Weekly*, 3 June 1966, p 49, for a late nineteenth-century turbine installation on a Shropshire farm which replaced a waterwheel and continued in service until 1951 (personal communication, Mr Rowland Ward, during 1982 Institute of Industrial Archaeology conference visit); Gray, J. R. 'An industrialised farm estate in Berkshire', *Industrial Archaeology*, vol 8, 1971, pp 171–85. See also note 4. For waterwheels see Peters, J. E. C. *The The Development of Farm Buildings in Western Lowland Staffordshire up to 1880*, 1969, pp 102–3; Atkinson, F. *Industrial Archaeology of the North-East*, vol 1, 1974, p 186; Jenkins, G. *Life and Tradition in Rural Wales*, 1976, pp 50–1; Warren, D. 'Waterpower on farms in West Somerset', *Journal of the Somerset Industrial Archaeological Society*, no 1, 1979, pp 5–12; Pitkin, M. *The Farm Wheel and Machinery at Temple Balsall*, unpublished thesis, Birmingham School of Architecture, 1982, which describes a mid-Victorian waterwheel installation which drove a threshing machine and a range of other machinery and continued in service until 1945–6; Wiliam, E. *Traditional Farm Buildings in North-East Wales, 1550–1900*, 1982, pp 149–51, which includes Pelton wheels. See also the watermill publications of the Wind and Watermill Section of the Society for the Protection of Ancient Buildings. For the waterwheel shown on p 173 see Bidgood, R. F. *Two Villages*, published from 'Twyford', Beach Rd, Woolacombe, Devon (? 1977), pp 21, 30.

100. de Lavergne, L. *The Rural Economy of England, Scotland and Ireland*, 1855, p 184, which notes a considerable increase in the use of steampower in the previous few years. An unpublished report on *The New Bingfield Project*, prepared by students of the Mechanical Engineering Department of Newcastle University in 1967, describes the reconditioning of a steam engine installed about 1830 on a Northumberland farm to drive a threshing machine, a grinding mill and possibly also a chaff-cutter. This engine continued in use until shortly after the First World War (personal communication and loan of typescript report from Mr John Moffitt, CBE, who was responsible for preserving this engine in his Westside Museum).

101. Loudon, J. C. *An Encyclopaedia of Cottage, Farm and Village Architecture*, 1836, p 662.

102. Ruegg, L. H. 'The farming of Dorsetshire', *Journal of the Royal Agricultural Society of England*, vol 15, 1854, p 410.

103. Stephens, H. and Burn, R. S. *The Book of Farm Buildings*, 1861. See also Atkinson, F. *Industrial Archaeology of the North-East*, vol 1, 1974, pp 191–2, and site references in gazetteer in vol 2 which lists surviving farm chimneys in Durham, Northumberland and Yorkshire.

104. Wilson, J. *British Farming*, 1862, p 155, reckoned it reduced the cost of threshing by three-quarters. A flailer could thresh 0.2 tons of wheat per day, a two-horse threshing machine 5 tons, excluding winnowing, and a 12 hp steam-driven threshing machine 15 tons, including winnowing and dressing (Collins, E. J. T. 'The age of machinery', in Mingay, J. E. ed, *The Victorian Countryside*, 1981, p 210).

105. Grey, J. 'On farm buildings', *Journal of the Royal Agricultural Society of England*, vol 4, 1843, p 7.

106. The waste heat of the steam engine could also be used to dry corn either as sheaves or as grain (Stephens, H. and Burn, R. S. *The Book of Farm Buildings*, 1861, pp 494–507), but in this period grain drying in any form was highly exceptional. These authors also discussed on pp 507–8 a prophetic contemporary suggestion that grain could be stored safely in airtight containers, apparently unaware of French experiments with this technique a generation earlier (Jenkins, H. M. 'Report on the practice of ensilage', *Journal of the Royal Agricultural Society of England*, 2nd ser, vol 20, 1884, pp 129–32). See also *Silos for Preserving British Fodder Crops*, by the sub-editor of *The Field*, 1884, pp 1–18.

107. Caird, J. *English Agriculture in 1850–1*, 1852, p 305.

108. Caird, J. *English Agriculture in 1850–1*, 1852, p 104.

109. Parkinson, J. 'On improvements in the county of Nottingham since 1800', *Journal of the Royal Agricultural Society of England*, vol 22, 1861, p 165; de Lavergne, L. *The Rural Economy of England, Scotland and Ireland*, 1855, p 184, put threshing corn as the first use of steam engines and then listed various forms of fodder processing, including the use of the heat produced, and pumping.

110. Peters, J. E. C. *The Development of Farm Buildings in Western Lowland Staffordshire up to 1880*, 1969, p 89–90; Sweetland, P. *The Barns of Bredon Hill*, unpublished thesis, Birmingham School of Architecture, 1979, pp 30–1.

111. Peters, J. E. C. *The Development of Farm Buildings in Western Lowland Staffordshire up to 1880*, 1969, pp 172–3; Wiliam, E. *Traditional Farm Buildings in North-East Wales, 1550–1900*, 1982, p 216.

112. Wiliam, E. *Traditional Farm Buildings in North-East Wales, 1550–1900*, 1982, p 249. The building is now in the Welsh Folk Museum.

113. Ritchie, R. *The Farm Engineer*, 1849, pp 209, 213, 223, 257. Significantly, the volumes on *Motive Powers and Machinery of the Farmstead* and on *Buildings* in Andrews, G. H. *A Rudimentary Treatise on Agricultural Engineering*, 1852 were of equal length.

114. Harvey, J. *The Industrial Archaeology of Farming*, 1980, pp 102–3.

115. Peters, J. E. C. *The Development of Farm Buildings in Western Lowland Staffordshire up to 1880*, 1969, p 92.

116. Architects in Agriculture, *Coleshill Model Farm, Oxfordshire*, 1981, p 19.

117. Brunskill, R. W. *Traditional Farm Buildings of Britain*, 1982, p 59.

118. 'Essays on the construction of farm buildings', *Journal of the Royal Agricultural Society of England*, vol 11, 1850, pp 186–310; 'Report by judges of the farm buildings competition', *Journal of the Royal Agricultural Society of England*, 2nd ser, vol 15, 1879, pp 774–836. See also Peters, J. E. C. *The Development of Farm Buildings in Western Lowland Staffordshire up to 1880*, 1969, pp 84–93.

119. Peters, J. E. C. *The Development of Farm Buildings in Western Lowland Staffordshire up to 1880*, 1969, pp 69, 72, 98; Sweetland, P. *The Barns of Bredon Hill*, unpublished thesis, Birmingham School of Architecture, 1979, pp 18–19, in which it is suggested that such barns might have been used for threshing in bad weather, since a portable threshing machine could work inside them. They could well have been used for such a purpose, but it is improbable that they would have been built for it; Wiliam, E. *Traditional Farm Buildings in North-East Wales, 1550–1900*, 1982, pp 111, 156, 269.

120. Wiliam, E. 'A guide to old farm buildings', *The Re-use of Redundant Farm Buildings*, published by the Welsh Office Agriculture Department, 1982, p 24; Wiliam, E. *Traditional Farm Buildings in North-East Wales, 1550–1900*, 1982, p 239.

121. 'If there is one improvement required more than another at the present time, it is the use of Dutch barns instead of ricks' (Spearing, J. B. 'On the agriculture of Berkshire', *Journal of the Royal Agricultural Society of England*, vol 21, 1860, p 34). Denton, J. B. *The Farm Homesteads of England*, 1863, p 162, described Dutch barns as 'deservedly growing in favour, though at a low rate'. The nineteenth-century haysheds with pillars of local slate that can be seen at the Welsh Folk Museum were built to house the increased haycrop which followed the draining of the Dwyryd valley. In some other areas of Wales, however, haybarns were only built in this period on the more progressive estates (Wiliam, E. *Traditional Farm Buildings in North-East Wales, 1550–1900*, 1982, p 154).

122. Caird, J. *English Agriculture in 1850–1*, 1852, p 104, for a shed on a Berkshire farm where 'the more intricate machines' were kept under lock and key. In 1851 only 5 per cent of the farms on such an advanced estate as Holkham had implement sheds, but from the 1860s onwards more implement sheds were provided (Wade-Martins, S. *A Great Estate at Work*, 1980, pp 175, 177, 179). In an area of Staffordshire the first special-purpose implement shed appeared in 1855, the first lockable toolshed for small tools, paint and spare parts in 1857, though a Shropshire estate provided such toolsheds from 1811 (Peters, J. E. C. *The Development of Farm Buildings in Western Lowland Staffordshire up to 1880*, 1969, pp 188–94). The Holkham estate also provided more farm smithies after the 1860s. The Staffordshire survey found that most farm smithies were built after 1840 or 1850 (Wade-Martins, S. *A Great Estate at Work*, 1980, pp 177, 179; Peters, J. E. C. *The Development of Farm Buildings in Western Lowland Staffordshire up to 1880*, 1969, pp 206–7). For developments in Wales see Wiliam, E. *Traditional Farm Buildings in North-East Wales, 1550–1900*, 1982, pp 228–39, 242.

123. Plan illustrating article by T. Sturgess on 'Farm buildings', *Journal of the Royal Agricultural Society of England*, vol 11, 1850, pp 288–91.

124. Cadle, C. 'Essay on the manufacture and preservation of perry and cider', *Journal of the Royal Agricultural Society of England*, vol 25, 1864, pp 76–81; Quinion, M. B. *A Drink in its Time*, published by the Museum of Cider, 1979, pp 9–10, which ascribes the slow spread of the mechanically powered rotary mill in Herefordshire in Victorian times partly to the heavy capital investment in stone mills. 'At least 2,000 [stone mills] still exist in the county.'

125. Buckland, G. 'On the farming of Kent', *Journal of the Royal Agricultural Society of England*, vol 6, 1845, pp 289–90; Whitehead, C. 'On recent improvements in the cultivation and management of hops', *Journal of the Royal Agricultural Society of England*, 2nd ser, vol 6, 1870, pp 362–4, which notes on one hand the survival of a few cockle kilns, on the other, the replacement of 'rule-of-thumb' by 'research confirmed by experience' in the design of oasthouses; Burgess, A. H. 'Hopdrying', *Agriculture*, vol 46, 1939, pp 524–31; Locke, P. E. 'Landscape with oasts', *House of Whitbread*, vol 19, no 1, Spring 1959, pp 17–19; McRae, S. G. and Burnham, C. P. *The Rural Landscape of Kent*, 1973, pp 193–5; Cronk, A. 'Oasts in Kent and East Sussex', *Archaeologia Cantiana*, vol 95, 1978, pp 241–54; Homes, I. 'The agricultural use of the Herefordshire house and its outbuildings', *Vernacular Architecture*, vol 9, 1978, pp 13–14, which includes reference to the installation of kilns in some of the old 'warehouse type' granaries of the area.

126. Fussell, G. E. *The Farmer's Tools*, 1952, p 179.

127. The positive effect of the railways is strikingly illustrated by negative examples of the effects of their absence or limitation. Smith, P. *Houses of the Welsh Countryside*, 1975, p 324, notes that Ruabon brick, 'the most characteristic factory-produced building material of this age [in Wales] . . . is never found far from the station yard'. See also Wiliam, E. *Traditional Farm Buildings in North-East Wales, 1550–1900*, 1982, p 75.

128. Architects in Agriculture, *Coleshill Model Farm, Oxfordshire*, 1981, pp 14–15.

129. Loudon, J. C. *An Encyclopaedia of Cottage, Farm and Village Architecture*, 1836, pp 416, 418. In the previous year thatch was described as 'properly abolished' in Yorkshire (Allison, K. J. *The East Riding of Yorkshire Landscape*, 1976, p 162).

130. Denton, J. B. *The Farm Homesteads of England*, 1863, p 147.

131. Orwin, C. S. *The Reclamation of Exmoor Forest*, 1929, p 54. In 1851 the agent of the Holkham estate referred to 'bad English timber' (Wade-Martins, S. *A Great Estate at Work*, 1980, p 158). Grey, J. 'On farm buildings', *Journal of the Royal Agricultural Society of England*, vol 4, 1843, p 9, and Ferguson, J. D. 'An all-under-one-roof farmstead', *Quarterly Journal of Agriculture*, vol 20, 1857, p 64, specified 'Memel fir' for farm buildings. See also Low, D. *Landed Property*, 1844, p 119; Ewart, J. *Treatise on the Arrangement and Construction of Agricultural Buildings*, 1851, p 5; Denton, J. B. 'On the use of home-grown timber', *Journal of the Royal Agricultural Society of England*, 2nd ser, vol 4, 1868, p 208; and Denton, J. B. 'Report of judges of farm plans sent in for competition at the London International Exhibition', *Journal of the Royal Agricultural Society of England*, 2nd ser, vol

15, 1879, p 783. The East Sussex County Planning Department, *Barn Trails*, 1979, trail 1, a guide to barns in or near the Seven Sisters Country Park, notes the contrast between the original oak roof framing and the softwood used in the nineteenth-century repairs of one barn.

132. Woodford, J. *Bricks to Build a House*, 1976, p 167. One consequence of the increased use of bricks in this period was the ornamentation of the larger and more important new buildings by multi-coloured brickwork (Peters, J. E. C. *The Development of Farm Buildings in Western Lowland Staffordshire up to 1880*, 1969, p 214; Caffyn, L. *A Study of Farm Buildings in Selected Parishes of East Sussex*, unpublished MA thesis, Manchester University, 1981, p 88). Another was the use of different coloured bricks to date new buildings. A brick barn at West Ilsley in Berkshire, for instance, bears the date 1858 in blue brick. A third may have been the appearance after about 1825 of circular instead of the traditional rectangular pitching-holes through which carts could be unloaded into barns. Sheaves of corn were less likely to strike against the edges of round than straight-edged openings and shed grain and such windows were more easily built in brick than in traditional materials (Peters, J. E. C. *The Development of Farm Buildings in Western Lowland Staffordshire up to 1880*, 1969, p 214; Peters, J. E. C. *Discovering Traditional Farm Buildings*, 1981, p 14; Wiliam, E. *Traditional Farm Buildings in North-East Wales, 1550–1900*, 1982, p 176, 267).

133. George Eliot, *Middlemarch*, chapter 40. This novel is set in the 1830s; Curtis, C. E. *Estate Management*, 1879, p 270.

134. Sweetland, P. *The Barns of Bredon Hill*, unpublished thesis, Birmingham School of Architecture, 1979, p 38.

135. Grey, J. 'A view of the past and present state of agriculture in Northumberland', *Journal of the Royal Agricultural Society of England*, vol 2, 1841, p 190; Tanner, H. 'The farming of Devon', *Journal of the Royal Agricultural Society of England*, vol 9, 1849, p 488. The slates used in Northumberland came from Westmorland and Wales. The source of those used in Devon is not given. Probably they were shipped across from Wales, like those which roofed John Knight's new farmsteads on Exmoor (Orwin, C. S. *The Reclamation of Exmoor Forest*, 1929, p 52). See also East Sussex County Planning Department, *Barn Trails*, 1979, trails 2, 3 and 6. Slate 'probably became popular' in East Sussex in the early nineteenth century (Caffyn, L. *A Study of Farm Buildings in Selected Parishes of East Sussex*, unpublished MA thesis Manchester University, 1981, p 89). The large-scale production of Welsh slate began about 1820 (Rural Industries Bureau, *The Thatcher's Craft*, 1961, p 2) and slate roofs soon became 'fairly universal' in some areas of Wales (Wiliam, E. *Traditional Farm Buildings in North-East Wales, 1550–1900*, 1982, p 95).

136. Devon County Council, *Devon's Traditional Buildings*, 1978, p 18.

137. Caird, J. *English Farming in 1850–1*, 1852, p 152.

138. Reynolds, J. *The Hampshire Barn*, unpublished thesis, Architectural Association, 1978, p 22.

139. In this period a variety of substances and processes for the preservation of timber were suggested and some were patented. The only one to survive was creosote, which was patented by Bethell in 1838 (Richardson, N. A. 'Creosote as a wood preservative', *The Journal of the Chartered Land Agents Society*, vol 65, March 1966, p 112).

140. Denton, J. B. *The Farm Homesteads of England*, 1863, p 157.

141. Loudon, J. C. *Encyclopaedia of Cottage, Farm and Village Architecture*, 1836, pp 376, 386; Low, D. *Landed Property*, 1844, p 125; Stephens, H. and Burn, R. S. *The Book of Farm Buildings*, 1861, pp 346, 352. The first refers to glazing in stables and cowhouses only, the second and third to glazing in granaries and barns as well. See also Ewart, J. 'On the construction of farm buildings', *Journal of the Royal Agricultural Society of England*, vol 11, 1850, pp 234, 238. For the development of glazing in farm buildings see Peters, J. E. C. *The Development of Farm Buildings in Western Lowland Staffordshire up to 1880*, 1969, pp 126, 176, 199, 217–18; Peters, J. E. C. *Discovering Traditional Farm Buildings*, 1981, p 64; Wiliam, E. *Traditional Farm Buildings in North-East Wales, 1550–1900*, 1982, pp 175, 220, 242.

142. Ewart, J. *A Treatise on the Arrangement and Construction of Agricultural Buildings*, 1851, p 6; Elliott, J. 'Farm buildings', *Journal of the Royal Agricultural Society of England*, vol 23, 1862, p 475; Evershed, H. 'Agriculture of Hertfordshire', *Journal of the Royal Agricultural Society of England*, vol 25, 1864, p 301; Denton, J. B. 'On the comparative cheapness and advantages of iron and wood in the construction of roofs for farm buildings', *Journal of the Royal Agricultural Society of England*, 2nd ser, vol 2, 1866, p 120; Tuckett, P. D. 'On the comparative cheapness and advantages of iron and wood in the construction of roofs for farm buildings', *Journal of the Royal Agricultural Society of England*, 2nd ser, vol 2, 1866, p 140.

143. Denton, J. B. *The Farm Homesteads of England*, 1863, p 147. See also Caird, J. *English Agriculture in 1850–1*, 1852, p 439; Tebbut, C. P. 'On the construction of farm buildings', *Journal of the Royal Agricultural Society of England*, vol 11, 1850, p 303; Dean,

G. A. *The Land Steward*, 1851, p 195.

144. Hunt, G. 'On concrete as a building material for farm buildings and cottages', *Journal of the Royal Agricultural Society of England*, 2nd ser, vol 10, 1874, pp 211–32. Concrete blocks were used experimentally in the 1860s and proved cheaper than brickwork (Clark, F. J. 'A cheap material for farm buildings', *Journal of the Royal Agricultural Society of England*, vol 24, 1863, pp 552–3), but some at least proved 'very deficient in durability of transverse strength' (Stephens, H. and Burn, R. S. *The Book of Farm Buildings*, 1861, p 142) and there is no mention of such blocks in Hunt's general article quoted above. The first concrete farm building in this country was probably the highly unusual feeding shed, 160ft (48m) long, 60ft (18m) wide and 12ft 6in (3.75m) to the eaves, with mass-concrete walls and an insulated tile roof which Robert Campbell built about 1870 for an intensive cattle fattening enterprise on his Faringdon estate (Gray, J. 'An industrial farm estate in Berkshire', *Industrial Archaeology*, vol 8, 1971, pp 171–85). See page 138 and Plate 28. At the end of this period, concrete was used normally for foundations, sometimes for mass-concrete walls (Curtis, C. S. *Estate Management*, 1879, p 219; Wade-Martins, S. *A Great Estate at Work*, 1980, p 181).

145. *The Builder*, 9 February 1884, p 218.

146. Stephens, H. and Burn, R. S. *The Book of Farm Buildings*, 1861, pp 336, 419, 422.

147. Andrews, G. H. *A Rudimentary Treatise on Farm Buildings. I. Buildings*, 1852, pp 135–40; Morton, J. C. *Cyclopaedia of Agriculture*, vol 1, 1855, p 797; Stephens, H. and Burn, R. S. *The Book of Farm Buildings*, 1861, p 418; Denton, J. B. *The Farm Homesteads of England*, 1863, p 152.

148. Tebbut, C. P. 'On the construction of farm buildings', *Journal of the Royal Agricultural Society of England*, vol 11, 1850, p 309; Dean, G. 'On the cost of agricultural buildings', *Journal of the Royal Agricultural Society of England*, vol 11, 1850, p 568; Ferguson, J. D. 'An all-under-one-roof steading', *Quarterly Journal of Agriculture*, vol 20, 1857, pp 58–64, proposed a large farmstead covered by a single roof 'supported on castiron pillars . . . in some respects similar to a railway station'. The analogy is significant.

149. For gas lighting see Moscrop, W. J. 'On the farming of Leicestershire', *Journal of the Royal Agricultural Society of England*, 2nd ser, vol 2, 1866, p 312; Jenkins, H. M. 'Eastburn Farm, near Driffield, Yorkshire', *Journal of the Royal Agricultural Society of England*, 2nd ser, vol 5, 1869, p 415; for gas engine see Popham, J. H. *Farm Buildings, Function and Form*, unpublished thesis for Diploma in Conservation Studies, Institute of Advanced Architectural Studies, York University, 1973, p 22.

150. Dean, G. A. *The Land Steward*, 1851, pp 184, 190–1; Read, C. S. 'Report on the farming of Buckinghamshire', *Journal of the Royal Agricultural Society of England*, vol 16, 1855, p 309; Elliott, J. 'Farm buildings', *Journal of the Royal Agricultural Society of England*, vol 23, 1862, pp 43, 473; Denton, J. B. 'Report of the judges of farm plans sent in for competition', *Journal of the Royal Agricultural Society of England*, 2nd ser, vol 5, 1879, pp 780–1; Architects in Agriculture, *Coleshill Model Farm*, 1981, p 19.

151. Dean, G. A. *The Land Steward*, 1851, p 202.

152. Stephens, H. and Burn, R. S. *The Book of Farm Buildings*, 1861, p 422.

153. Marshall, J. 'A report on the feeding of stock with prepared food', *Journal of the Royal Agricultural Society of England*, vol 7, 1847, p 392.

154. Denton, J. B. *The Farm Homesteads of England*, 1863, p 152.

155. Pitstone Local History Society, Pitstone Green Farm, Buckinghamshire, *In Pitstone Green There is a Farm*, 1979, p 17.

156. Architects in Agriculture, *Coleshill Model Farm*, Oxfordshire, 1981, p 16.

157. Ewart, J. *A Treatise on the Arrangement and Construction of Agricultural Buildings*, 1851, p 27, refers to the reuse of old materials; Reynolds, J. *The Hampshire Barn*, unpublished thesis, Architectural Association, 1978, p 8, to the use of iron tyres from discarded waggon wheels in the repair of timber roof-members; Caffyn, L. *A Study of Farm Buildings in Selected Parishes of East Sussex*, unpublished MA thesis, Manchester University, 1982, p 88, to the transfer of an old railway warehouse to a farm where it was used as a store.

# 7 VICTORIAN FARMSTEADS: SOME EXAMPLES

## New Times, New Standards

The Victorians, like the Hanoverians, published their farmstead case studies to illustrate practical examples of good commercial design. But their task was more difficult for they were concerned with the introduction of new equipment and techniques as well as the application of agreed principles. Moreover, their readers were considerably more sophisticated and critical than those of Arthur Young's time, so that their work was different in form as well as in content. It was more detailed, more technical, more professional both in preparation and presentation, and its quality and character remind us immediately that we are in the age of the engineer. Farmsteads were now industrial installations designed on industrial principles, and those who described them conformed to industrial standards.

## A Corn-and-Meat Farmstead

The farmstead shown in Fig 19 was planned in 1849 for a typical corn-and-meat farm of 250–300 acres.[1] In basic design, it continued the traditions of the Agrarian Revolution, but the improvements in detail it included were numerous.

Thus, the yards were better planned than those previously illustrated, allowing the easier distribution of fodder and the housing of cattle in small groups. The fattening shed was fitted with a tramway for trollies to reduce the labour of feeding. Louvred ventilators were provided for the enclosed livestock buildings. Drainage, too, was carefully considered and an underground tank provided for liquid manure storage, while one of the sheds was used as a store for the fertilisers which advanced farmers were now beginning to buy in increasing quantities. Still, there was no drastic change in the system and, typically, the most conspicuous innovation, the introduction of steam threshing, did no more than substitute a more efficient for a less efficient form of prime-mover. The barn altered its position to suit the new routine, but there was little attempt in this particular steading to

160

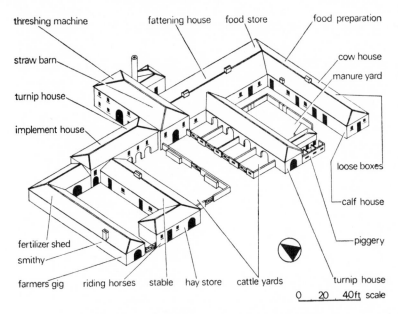

threshing machine    fattening house   food store    food preparation

straw barn

turnip house

implement house

fertilizer shed
smithy

farmers gig    riding horses    stable   hay store    cattle yards

cow house

manure yard

loose boxes

calf house

piggery

turnip house

0   20   40ft  scale

19    Steading designed in 1849 for a mixed farm of 200 to 300 acres

use the new power to create a fodder-preparation centre – the buildings contained five separate rooms for storing and processing fodder, each serving a particular group of animals. Essentially, therefore, this farmstead is a Victorian version of its predecessors.

## A Dairy Farmstead

The needs of the dairy farm were very different from those of the corn-and-meat farm. Nevertheless, as this dairy farmstead (see Fig 20), designed in 1851 for a farm of 100–150 acres carrying a herd of twenty-eight milkers, showed, its buildings conformed to the same general pattern.[2]

There were, of course, modifications. In particular, the barn decreased in importance and size and, since there was little corn to thresh, horsegear was preferred to the more efficient but more expensive steam engine. Again, a farm of this type needed only a small stable and implement shed. More generally, the dairy enterprise added a southern range, consisting of a cowshed adjacent to the farmhouse, where the milk was made into butter, a calfhouse and bullpens, which in turn made necessary a row of sties for the pigs that fattened on the dairy wastes. But there was no radical change in plan: the steading remained a recognisable version of that found on the mixed farm previously illustrated.

161

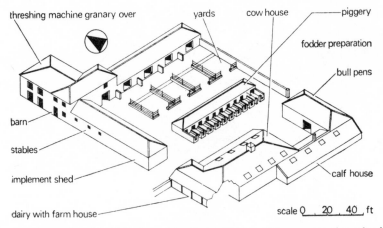

threshing machine granary over    yards    cow house    piggery

fodder preparation

bull pens

barn

stables

calf house

implement shed

dairy with farm house    scale 0   20   40 ft

20  Steading designed in 1851 for a dairy farm of 100 to 150 acres, carrying a herd of twenty-eight milkers

## An Advanced Farmstead of the Steam Age

One of the most remarkable sets of buildings of this period was erected in Herefordshire in 1861 to serve an arable and fattening farm of 614 acres which reared its own young stock[3] (see Fig 21). In general plan, it followed tradition, though the roofing of the yards to protect the cattle and manure was advanced rather than general practice. But its aggressively industrial equipment and manner of operation, illustrated how a wealthy and progressive landowner could adapt the technology of the steam age to the purposes of the farm.

The mechanical heart of the farm was a 12hp steam engine 'in a handsome Doric frame'. Its main task was driving the threshing machine, which was served by a miniature railway terminus of tramlines down which the stacks rolled by gravity on their timber trucks when the time came, and handling the grain and straw thus produced. After threshing, the grain went either to a sacking apparatus 'actuated by the beam of the weighing-machine', which not only ceased to pour when the sack was full but obligingly rang a bell as well, or else was carried to the granary by an auger and poured into any one of sixteen bins from swivel spouts. The straw was mechanically elevated, transported along a passage under the roof of the central range and dropped to the boxes and yards below.

In addition to processing the corn harvest, the engine also served the cattle enterprise. Its power was harnessed to a variety of cutting and grinding equipment, and its heat to cooking apparatus, so that the barn area included a central workshop for fodder preparation. Indeed, this steading represents one of the most ambitious attempts ever made to exploit the power of steam for farmstead work. But it illustrates the

162

limitations as well as the achievements of the new prime-mover. The steam engine could not readily transmit power around a range of buildings and so failed to provide a basis for a satisfactory system of materials-handling. The grain auger and straw conveyor emphasised by contrast the dependence of even this farmstead on manual effort for the bulk of its internal transport.

## Choice of Building Materials

These case studies show that the industrial age brought many improvements but few fundamental changes to farmstead design. They also show, however, that its effects on farmstead construction were more revolutionary, more comprehensive. The references in the specifications and descriptions of these buildings to cast-iron spouting, cast-iron pillars, asphalt and galvanised-iron sheeting demonstrated the use the builder was now making of factory products. The wider and more decisive implications of the Industrial Revolution were illustrated by the summaries of the advantages and disadvantages of such major materials as brick or stone for walling, and tiles or slates for roofing, given by the authors of the first two examples. For it was the railway age which, by ending dependence on local materials, first made such choices standard practice.

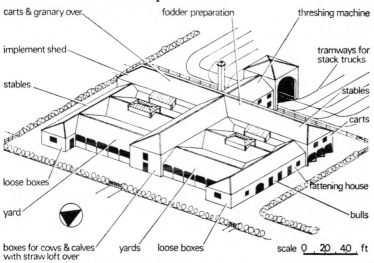

21   An advanced farmstead built in 1861 to serve a mixed farm of 614 acres in Herefordshire

## NOTES

1. Sturgess, T. 'Farm buildings', *Journal of the Royal Agricultural Society of England*, vol 11, 1850, pp 288–300.
2. Ewart, K. *A Treatise on the Arrangement and Construction of Agricultural Buildings*, 1851, pp 5–6, 18–20.
3. Denton, J. B. *Farm Homesteads of England*, 1863, pp 57–9, 92–4.

# 8 DEPRESSION, ADAPTATION AND IMPROVISATION: 1880–1939

## Competition from Overseas

In 1866, some 16,000lb of canned meat from Australia reached British ports. In 1871, the figure was 22 million.[1] This sudden appearance of a new source of food for the British consumer foreshadowed the more general combination of two factors which were soon to overthrow the traditional farming system of this country. The first was the exploitation of new lands overseas by colonising farmers, the second the development of cheap and reliable means of bringing their products to the British market.

The next generation saw the fulfilment of this prophecy. The mechanical reaper redeemed the prairie wheat-grower's lack of human labour, the wire fence came to the aid of the rancher on the treeless plains, and the railway was reinforced by the steamship equipped with refrigerated chambers. By the end of the century, the British farmer's ancient monopoly of the home market had gone down into history and he was striving to justify an economic activity whose obvious necessity had never before been questioned. The overseas producer, whom Caird in 1878 had welcomed as an ally in the task of feeding the growing population of these crowded islands where little land of agricultural value remained unoccupied, had turned rival, and for a lifetime there was little respite for the British farmer.

The flood of cheap corn from North America which between the 1860s and the 1890s nearly halved the average price of wheat was merely the precursor of a steadily increasing mass of imports. Grain and meat, butter and cheese, from countries as varied as Australia and the Argentine, Denmark, New Zealand and the USA, undersold the British farmer in his home market. The Englishman's economic adversaries were powerful and he could expect little encouragement and few favours from his free trade countrymen. In the 1870s the home farmer had supplied the home market with some three-quarters of its food. In the first decades of the twentieth century, he supplied about a quarter, and it was the imports which fixed the prices he received. Foreign competition, rather than a growing population, was now the decisive factor. The depression had come.

## Agricultural Adjustment

So this period saw the gradual and painful adaptation of the farming system to the new conditions. Hence the change from brown to green as the farmer abandoned an arable system, whose costs and losses were becoming intolerable, and allowed the defeated ploughland to go down to grass. Hence a steady rise in the importance of the livestock with which the farmer exploited the new pastures and the cheap grain which had suddenly been thrust upon him – a change neatly and structurally illustrated at Manor Farm Museum, Cogges, Oxfordshire, by a late Victorian cattleshed with the wooden uprights of its open front standing on the redundant staddlestones which had once supported and protected cornricks. Hence, above all, the development of the liquid milk industry for, alone among farmers in Great Britain, the milk producer feared no competition from overseas.

The extent of the change is shown in the figures. In the later 1860s, it has been estimated, the British farmer derived some 45 per cent of his income from his arable crops and 55 per cent from his livestock. By the later 1930s, the figures were 27 per cent and 73 per cent respectively. More particularly, in the same period, the proportion provided by wheat sank from 15 per cent to 2 per cent, the proportion provided by milk rose from 15 per cent to 29 per cent.[2] By the end of this period the farmer earned more from his milk than from all his arable cash crops put together, and the establishment in 1933 of the Milk Marketing Board, the farmer's first appearance in the unfamiliar world of Big Business, reflected the new agricultural order.

The growing predominance of livestock brought with it other economic changes. Grass and hay could not feed all the animals all the time, so the farmer came to rely increasingly on imported fodder, particularly on imported concentrates which provided the protein necessary for the efficient production of meat and milk. This was nothing new in principle. But, as the volume of imported foodstuffs grew until by the late 1920s they provided about half the food, except for grass, consumed by British livestock, the change in scale produced a new form of agricultural industry. The farmer, who bought so much of his raw materials from overseas and converted them via the stomachs of his stock into human food, was turning manufacturer. By 1939 it was easy and even necessary to describe our farming system in crudely industrial terms of input, output and end product.

## Neglect and Deterioration in the Farmstead

Such changes in the farming system implied corresponding changes in the farmstead to meet the new technical needs. But the fall in agricultural prices was inevitably followed by a fall in the rent of agricultural land. The income on which the landlord depended to maintain and improve his property shrank; the rents of the depression times were commonly 10 per cent to 20 per cent lower than those of the mid-Victorian period, yet building costs steadily increased with the general rise of prices.[3] There was now little point in reclaiming such small areas of the waste as remained, so no new farmsteads were required to equip new farmland. As a matter of routine, textbooks continued to include plans of versions of the familiar E-pattern and U-pattern farmsteads, but they remained on paper.[4] Significantly, in this period model farms, 'justly discredited as only instructive in their expensiveness', came to an end, leaving their massive buildings 'as monuments to the lavish expenditure which was customary half a century ago',[5] and the only new class of homestead built served the smallholdings created for social rather than economic reasons under the 1892 Act and later legislation.[6] There was no incentive to reconstruct existing farmsteads to meet the changing needs. Soon there was no economic possibility of doing so.[7] Finally, as hopes and resources slowly failed, even their maintenance was neglected. This was an age of steady deterioration, at best checked by patchwork and repairs on the cheap.

So the first general theme of this period was the abrupt end of two lifetimes of continuous development. The effects of this were gradual, though, as the years passed, the limitations on production caused by 'the buildings that weren't there' became increasingly obvious. By the early twentieth century there were many farmers facing the same sort of constraint as the Berkshire tenant who could not farm his hungry downland fields properly because his landlord could not provide upland yards where bullocks could tread straw into manure.[8]

The second general theme was the steady decay of the inherited stock of farm buildings. Here, too, the results were slow in coming. Hall, in his agricultural tour just before the First World War, did not comment explicitly on the lack of new construction, for by his time men had come to take this for granted. But he found the farmsteads of the Hanoverians and Victorians in fair order. In some areas, buildings were good, in others bad, depending mainly on the type of material used. Farmsteads in stone districts naturally showed less wear and tear than those in districts which used clay, flints with mortar or bricks.[9] But, as the years passed, the cumulative effect of human neglect and the steadily destructive power of nature began to turn the steadings which had served the most advanced farming system of its day into a collection of industrial slums.

Gradually, tirelessly, the rain seeped through roofs of decaying thatch or slipping slates, through holes where the wind had torn away tiles that were not replaced, and rotted the supporting timbers. Water from choked or falling guttering crumbled away walls and undermined foundations. Unpainted woodwork failed to hold window panes or door hinges. There was no end to it. Year by year, the patient processes of decay and disintegration probed for weaknesses in the unmaintained buildings. Year by year, they found less resistance and the slow, pervading degeneration they wrought became more obvious, less redeemable. As early as 1918 it was noted that many farmsteads in Berkshire had deteriorated too far for repair at economic cost,[10] and in the following decades the inefficiency of farm buildings became an accepted weakness in the rural economy. In 1939, a former Minister of Agriculture described their general condition as 'dreadful'. It was difficult, he added, to 'exaggerate the extent of their dilapidation or the handicap it constitues to good husbandry'.[11] Detailed local studies in this period provided a painful commentary on his generalisation.

Thus, in the 1930s, when milk was the main source of the farmer's income, a survey of cowhouses in the Midlands reported that nearly a quarter of those visited needed complete reconstruction, and nearly a third substantial alteration if they were to be judged fit to produce clean milk.[12] Again, in East Anglia, once one of the most advanced and prosperous farming areas in the world, another study in the same decade showed that the buildings of 46 per cent of the farms investigated were inadequate or inconvenient, 25 per cent in poor repair and 16 per cent inadequate or inconvenient *and* in poor repair.[13] As it was in this area of large-scale arable farming, so it was among the small livestock farms of Carmarthen, now in Dyfed. Here most of the farms had most of the buildings they needed, but the buildings were old-fashioned and in poor condition. 'The cowsheds are very inadequate, the most prevalent faults being insufficient light and ventilation . . . Stables are in many cases badly constructed . . . Many of the pigsties are small and so badly built that it is very difficult to keep them even moderately clean . . . Another serious defect is the almost entire absence of any adequate accommodation for farmyard manure.'[14] Here, as elsewhere, any general attempt at improvement had ceased and farmers were living patiently on their structural capital.

The agricultural costs of this pervading farmstead inefficiency were varied, considerable and obvious. Stored produce, manure, equipment, labour, livestock health and performance – there were few farming resources on which it did not levy toll. The more subtle personal costs were described in the 1920s by a Cambridgeshire farmer who considered his sodden morass of a yard, his century-old sheds and his dark, dank barn rendered just habitable for pigs by the addition of windows and half-doors, and reflected that his holding was typical of many thousands in England. 'We sometimes forget,' he wrote, 'the large part of the life of the farm worker and farmer which is spent "somewhere round the yards". Much of this work is done in places which are dark, damp and draughty . . . Poor as some of our urban factories may be, one would have to go down to the sweatshops of the East End of London to find anything as inefficient and uncomfortable as old-fashioned farm buildings. Farming with bad buildings is such a squalid job that until this question is tackled agriculture is bound to be a backward industry.' But the times offered little hope that it would be tackled, and he concluded sadly that farming had got into a vicious circle. 'We dare not build because the industry will not stand it, and the industry gets worse because of the badness of the buildings.'[15]

### Improvers and Improvements

Nevertheless, the pressures on the farmstead of the changing needs of the farm continued. New forms of enterprise, new equipment and techniques and, above all, the necessity of housing and feeding an increasing head of livestock, made direct and indirect demands on steadings designed for obsolete systems of farming.[16] Frequently, these pressures were ignored: it was cheaper to suffer loss from wastage, cheaper to accept the limitations imposed by an obsolete framework, than to rebuild. But there was a good deal of piecemeal and individual adaption of old farmsteads to new purposes. The process is poorly documented, for it was essentially a matter of personal enterprise, particular farms and limited objectives: the conversion of an old building to a new purpose on one farm, the remodelling of a range of buildings on another. It was also inherently inefficient. For one thing, the proud and confident men of the Agricultural Revolution had assumed the permanence of the farming economy for which they planned and their steadings made little provision for the possibility of future change or expansion. For another, some of the older buildings were too unsound, some too solidly constructed, to allow easy or effective adaptation. But the times allowed no option. The farming community did its best with such resources as were available to it and sought no more than immediate answers to immediate problems.[17] In this period, therefore, the inclusion in the textbooks of sections on modernising individual buildings or remodelling farmsteads became standard practice.[18]

Another sign of the times was the growing use of secondhand materials to meet the pressing need for economy. The first reference to the value of railway sleepers for walls for yards or sheds occurred as early as 1896; Nissen huts appeared on farms after the First World

War; in the next decade converted goods vans and railway carriages were common features of the agricultural landscape; and an enterprising man could even find a profitable place in the farmstead for the funnels of an obsolete cruiser which he used as silos.[19] In these years, under relentless economic pressure, the farmer developed and expanded his inherited taste for structural improvisation with other people's discards.

Inevitably such conditions destroyed any hope that the farm-building designer would establish himself as a recognised ally of the farmer, alongside the soil chemist, the veterinary surgeon, the agricultural engineer, the plant breeder and the other professionals who were by now accepted members of the agricultural system. The days of general development were past and there was no place for such men in a world of patchwork and slow degeneration.[20] Neither landowner nor farmer needed outside assistance in meeting the routine problems of minimum maintenance and minor improvements. Almost alone among the various branches of agricultural technology, the planning of farm buildings remained entirely a matter for the local general practitioner.

Traditionally, this general practitioner was the land agent who administered the estate on behalf of the owner and employed either the staff of his estate yard or a local contractor for building work on the farms for which he was responsible. But the changes wrought by the depression brought into being a new and important figure in the history of farmstead development. This was the pioneering farmer. Of course, the views and needs of farmers had always affected building design, but from Hanoverian times onwards, they had only done so indirectly, via the landlord who made the final decisions. Under the increasing economic pressures of the time, however, landowners were now increasingly prepared to sell land to farmers, thus creating a growing class of owner-occupiers. At the end of the nineteenth century, such men were rare. By the time of the First World War they occupied some 10 per cent of the agricultural land of the country, by the time of the Second World War some 30 per cent. As owners, they carried the responsibility for the fixed equipment of their farms which had formerly been undertaken by their landlords. But they also enjoyed full managerial independence.[21]

The impoverished landlord might not be able or willing to raise the capital for substantial investments in new or improved buildings. As early as 1891 one of the Scotsmen who established themselves as dairy farmers in the hitherto arable county of Essex commiserated with landlords expected to finance the 'additions and adaptations required for the new style of farming'.[22] More particularly in uncertain times when, in the words of a textbook on farm buildings, 'rotations once regarded as almost as fixed as the stars have passed away and in their place is little that can be regarded as permanent',[23] landowners were seldom prepared to sink capital in buildings which might meet the needs of the particular tenant then in occupation of the farm but not those of his unknown successor. The complaints in 1916 of the Oxfordshire land agents who had invested in dairy buildings at the insistence of their tenants only to find that the tenants who followed them did not continue in the milk business illustrated this general problem.[24] The owner-occupier, however, cared for none of these things. He could build, demolish, improvise or adapt as his interests suggested and his resources allowed. He could also, if he wished, innovate or experiment. He had nobody to consider but himself.

Admittedly, few owner-occupiers were able to take much advantage from this theoretical freedom. The burden of the depression was too great: 'the better you farm, the more you spend, and the more you spend, the more you lose' was a familiar saying of the time. But the tenurial changes offered unprecedented opportunity to enterprising men. A generation later, in a famous phrase, Sir George Stapledon proclaimed the need for 'mad farmers', by which he meant farmers capable of abandoning tradition and enthusiastically introducing new systems, unproved but promising techniques, anything which appeared remotely hopeful of success, before conventional wisdom had time to prove its impossibility. Now, for the first time, such men could apply their peculiar talents to the buildings on their farms. Farmstead development had gained a new and valuable source of ideas.

### Barn and Grainstore

Throughout this period, the barn continued to dominate the farmstead. But it was now little more than an historical relic. There was less corn to be harvested; the decreased crop was no longer threshed indoors but ricked in the open and threshed by portable machines moved and driven by traction engines; and by the 1890s the adaptation of these obsolete buildings to new purposes had become a standard problem for the landowner and the farmer.[25] Some were converted to implement houses or various forms of livestock buildings, some continued a reduced form of their original function as stores for bagged grain and straw, others degenerated into dignified dumps for anything that could not conveniently be housed elsewhere. Some, more symbolically, became fodder stores and mixing-rooms from which the livestock which had replaced the corn enterprise were supplied with their concentrate rations. But nearly all of them shared a common neglect, for their design and construction, in particular their huge roof surfaces, made them the most expensive and least remunerative buildings on the farm to maintain. They survived not because the farmer needed them but because they were the most substantial structures he had inherited.

At the end of this period, however, a few barns recovered something of their ancient purpose. For in 1928 a new machine appeared in the English cornfields. This was the combine-harvester, a fusion of the reaper and the threshing machine which cut and threshed the corn in one mobile operation, excreting the straw behind it on the land it stripped. It offered considerable savings in the labour and cost of harvesting. But it offered them at a capital cost which only substantial corn-growers could afford, and by 1939 there were no more than 150 'combines' in the country. Even so, the effects on the farmstead of this new harvesting technique were already visible.

For the combine brought problems as well as economies. It delivers the crop as grain, not as sheaves of unthreshed corn, and therefore eliminates the rick from the harvest routine. But it does not eliminate the needs met by the rick, which is essentially a form of aerated store that both protects the corn it houses and allows the wind and atmosphere to dry it. The combine produces a sudden mass of grain which always needs storage and generally needs drying as well to prevent heating and the development of moulds. The Norfolk farmer who in 1931 invested in two combines and in 1932 found himself forced to further expenditure on a grain-drying installation was only one of the first of those who turned to the engineer for new and complicated equipment to meet the new needs – drying plants of various types and sizes to rid the grain of its surplus moisture, bins to hold it and conveyors to move it from place to place in the plant.[26] The combine, true to its inorganic origins, had sired a sort of mechanical rick.

Since the new grain-drying and storage plants necessarily served large arable farms, there was often no need to provide them with new housing, for the old barns commonly stood empty or half-used. So part of the harvest routine returned to its ancient home and the dryer and its associated bins stood where the Hanoverians had installed their threshing machines and forgotten generations of flailers had toiled in dusty discomfort. But we must beware of any sentimental assumption of continuity in these changes. It was mere structural accident that a building designed for the processes of one age happened to be available and suitable for the processes of another.

Such changes, however, were highly exceptional. On most corn-growing farms traditional methods and traditional buildings continued in service. One feature of this contrast typifies the variations in stages of technical development which were so characteristic of this period. The decade which saw the first British

171

cornfield harvested by a combine also saw the construction of the last of the granaries-over-cartsheds which had originated three centuries earlier on farms where the corn harvest had outgrown attics and corn chambers in the farmhouse.[27]

## Change in the Dairy Farmstead

It was, however, a sign of the times that the greatest single cause of change in the farmstead in this period was not connected with grain production. It was the expansion of the liquid milk industry first made possible by the railways and later encouraged by the development of road transport. One sign of its triumph was the increase in the number of dairy cows in England and Wales from under 2 million in the early 1880s to over 3 million in the late 1930s. Another was the steady decline of the ancient farmhouse trades of butter-making and cheese-making, the result of competition from the new form of dairy enterprise as well as from home and overseas factories. By 1914, butter-making on the farm survived in only a few areas where communications did not allow the marketing of liquid milk.[28] By 1939 barely a thousand farms continued cheese production.[29] A third reason was the end of the dairy farmer's urban rival. The old system died slowly and as late as 1930 there were just over 1,000 cows in inner London, including a herd of 85 head in Bermondsey, and nearly 5,000 in 280 cowhouses in Liverpool, where the stocking rate in terms of cows per acre was higher than that of the dairy county of Somerset.[30] But its days were numbered. The urban cowkeeper could not resist indefinitely the competition of the farmer whose standards of hygiene and marketing improved so markedly in the 1930s, while the development of bottling and pasteurisation required investment uneconomic for small producer-retailers. In the next age the town dairy was to become first a curiosity, then a memory.

More cows meant more cowhouses on more farms, but there was no radical change in the design inherited from the mid-Victorians. There was, however, a good deal of improvement in detail, mainly as the result of the steady pressure of a new set of influences on the planning of dairy farmsteads. Rules and regulations had come and with them a new figure on the agricultural landscape, the inspector, 'the man from the council', who enforced them.

The increasing importance of milk as an item in urban diet was welcomed by reformers as well as producers. But the legislators of an age in which Disraeli took *'Sanitas sanitatum, omnia sanitas'* as the text of one of his most famous speeches were not likely to overlook the dangers inherent in the increased consumption of a highly perishable commodity peculiarly susceptible to contamination. Consequently, a

Plate 21   From manpower via horsepower to steampower. This farmstead at the Beamish North of England Open Air Museum was built in the late eighteenth century on the standard Hanoverian plan. In 1799 thrashing by flail was replaced by horse-driven mechanical thrashing. The horsegear was housed in a wheelhouse or gingang, the small building with the polygonal roof in the yard nearest the camera. About 1850, horsepower was replaced by steampower. The farmhouse stands in the left-hand corner of the farmstead. Beyond it is the piggery, convenient for the farmer's wife who fed the pigs on household wastes and possibly also on dairy byproducts (*Beamish North of England Open Air Museum*)

Plate 22   From horsepower to waterpower. The waterwheel on this Devon farm was probably installed in early Victorian times. It replaced the horses which worked in the Hanoverian wheelhouse on the left, to drive thrashing and fodder processing machinery in the barn. The wheel was scrapped when metal was needed in World War II (*Mrs R. F. Bidgood*)

Plate 23    By early Victorian times pre-industrial farmsteads were beginning to acquire a period charm. This engraving was published in 1846 (see page 130) (*BBC Hulton Picture Library*)

Plate 24    In mid-Victorian times, the barn lost its ancient function as a centre for the storage and processing of corn, and became a centre for the storage and processing of livestock feed, 'with ranks of cutting, grinding, breaking, stirring machines driven by flapping belts to the steady beat of the steam engine' (see page 143). (From Copland, S. *Agriculture, Ancient and Modern*, 1866, Vol. 1, page 571) (*Museum of English Rural Life*)

series of measures, beginning with the Dairies, Cowsheds and Milkshops Order of 1885, made local authorities responsible for issuing bylaws regulating the design and construction of dairy buildings to secure 'the health and good condition of the cattle therein, the cleanliness of milk-vessels therein and the protection of the milk therein against infection'. The phrasing was general, the application particular and detailed, and over the years the various local authorities gradually developed codes and precedents to determine the standards of lighting, ventilation, drainage and water supply acceptable in their jurisdiction.

The dairy presented a general problem, for most farmers naturally continued to use the dairy at the back of the farmhouse where their mothers had once made butter and cheese. Such dairies were commonly some distance from the cowhouse and the milk was too often exposed to contamination from the yards across which it was carried in pails. It took many regulations, many arguments and many years to end this old tradition and establish the new type of dairy adjacent to the cowhouse it served. The change is difficult to follow in detail, but it was apparently the replacement of the older regulations by the more demanding Milk and Dairies Order of 1926 that finally established the familiar dairy with its corrugated cooler, its washing troughs and its steam-sterilising chest, as a necessary part of the cowhouse on the better milk-producing farm[31] (see Fig 22).

In the cowhouse itself the new authorities required 'proper and necessary' standards of ventilation, window lighting and air space per beast in the cowhouse. They preferred concrete floors to cobble or earthen floors, dung channels to hopeful slopes, external to internal

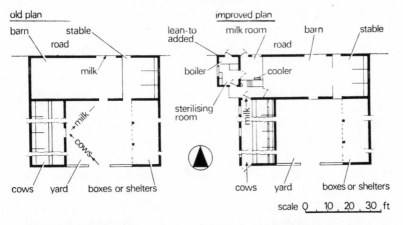

22   Typical inter-war example of the improvement of a milk production system by the addition of a dairy (Based on *The Construction of Cowhouses*, HMSO 1929, p19) (*The Controller of HMSO*)

drain inlets. Taken separately, none of their demands was revolutionary, indeed, they asked no more than accepted good practice which, in many cases, made possible easier working as well as a higher standard of hygiene. None involved substantial structural change. None, except the gradual insistence that the cattle in double-range houses should stand tail to tail instead of head to head to avoid cross-infection, even necessitated major changes in internal rearrangement. Taken together, however, they created a new form of an old building (see Fig 23). In 1924, for instance, a visitor to the dairying county of Cheshire commented on the difference between the older houses, in which the stalls stood across the width of the building, and those constructed in the past twenty years, in which they stood along the length of the house, thus simplifying the feeding routine and allowing better supervision of the herd in addition to improving lighting and ventilation.[32] Much of the credit for such improvements must go to the bylaws and those who administered them.[33] It is no accident that some of the farm buildings textbooks of this period included appendices which quoted the model regulations in full.[34]

These improvements in the milking environment were soon accompanied by improvements in milking technique. In the early 1900s, nearly a century of inventions, patents and peculiarities finally produced a practicable form of milking machine, which for the first time enabled one man to milk more than one cow simultaneously.[35] The benefit was considerable, but acceptance was slow and cautious. In 1919, an official committee reported that the machines gave good performance but that many farmers preferred manual labour if it was available.[36] The proviso was important. The agricultural labour force was shrinking and under sheer demographic pressure the vacuum pump and pipes, the teat-cups and milk containers of the 'bucket' type of milking machine, gradually established themselves in the cowhouse. By 1939, some 8 per cent of herds and 15 per cent of cows were milked mechanically.[37]

The new machines greatly decreased the labour of milking in the cowhouse. But they did not remedy the inherent economic weaknesses of the cowhouse system. For a building in which each cow has a substantial stall of her own and men bring food and litter to her and take milk and manure away from her is necessarily expensive in both capital and labour. Economic pressures made a new system desirable, technical development made it possible; and the later years of the period saw the first break with the inherited tradition of the cowhouse.

The agent of this change was the bucket plant's more sophisticated successor, the 'releaser' type of milking machine, which appeared on the market in the early 1920s. For the bucket plant was literally a milking machine and only a milking machine. It did no more than

176

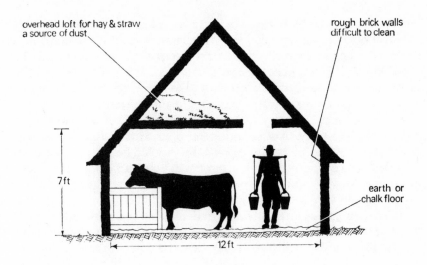

overhead loft for hay & straw
a source of dust

rough brick walls
difficult to clean

7ft

earth or
chalk floor

12ft

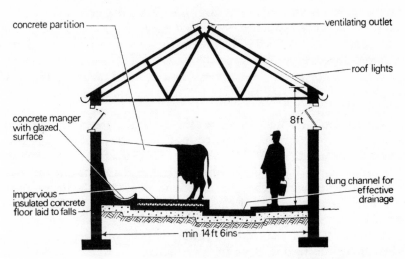

concrete partition

ventilating outlet

roof lights

concrete manger
with glazed
surface

8ft

impervious
insulated concrete
floor laid to falls

dung channel for
effective
drainage

min 14ft 6ins

23   The development of the cowhouse: (*above*) a typical mid-Victorian cowhouse; (*below*) a
typical cowhouse of the 1930s

transfer the milk from the udder to the bucket. But the releaser plant
also carried the milk from the udder to the dairy in an overhead
pipeline. It could not as yet operate satisfactorily in a building as large
as a cowhouse, for the distance it could carry milk was limited.
Nevertheless its scope was sufficient to make it the mechanical basis of
a new and revolutionary type of dairy building.

   The possibilities it offered were first grasped by A. J. Hosier, a
Wiltshire farmer faced with the problem of establishing a large dairy
enterprise on 1,000 acres of chalk with no adequate buildings. Hand-

milking of a herd the size he planned was out of the question. So was the cost of building the necessary cowsheds. With radical simplicity, therefore, he distinguished between the housing function and the milking-room function of the cowhouse. His cows, he decided, needed winter housing neither for their own sake nor, since his well-drained soil could stand concentrated treading in the winter months, for the sake of the land. But they still needed milking and it was cheaper to take a milking-point to a large number of cows than to bring a large number of cows to the milking-point. So in 1922 he constructed from bits and pieces of discarded machines a releaser plant on wheels, complete with a light roof and portable dairy equipment, which a tractor could tow to the cows in the fields.

In so doing, he secured advantages denied to those who followed the older tradition. For in the cowhouse the farmer with a bucket plant continued to milk each cow in her stall. His machine enabled him to milk several cows at once, but it did not enable him to reduce the number of stalls his herd required. Hosier, however, needed only a few stalls. At milking time, the cows filed through them one after the other, each cow remained in them only long enough to be milked and then making room for her successor. So each of his stalls served eight, ten, or twelve cows. The milking machine reduced the labour costs of all who used it. But Hosier was the first for whom it also reduced capital costs.[38]

Neither Hosier's invention nor the system of open-air dairying which it made possible commended itself to local tradition. But both were successful and in 1927 Hosier was able to form a small company for the commercial manufacture of the portable 'bails' he had invented. Nevertheless, these bails were no more than the forerunners of a more general technical change, for they could only be used in certain exceptional areas where the soil would not suffer excessively from the hooves of outwintered cattle. This change began in 1932, when Hosier decided to establish a permanent milk-point on his farm and so created the prototype of the specialised dairy building we now call a 'milking parlour'.[39]

Physically, a milking parlour is best described as a bail in a building ... a set of stalls to hold the cows while they are being milked, a releaser plant to milk them and a dairy to process their milk, with a floor beneath them, walls around them and a roof above them. Economically, it provided the dairy farmer with a new and efficient means of fulfilling one of the main functions of the traditional cowhouse. But it was cheaper to build, since a farmer with a parlour could milk as many cows as his neighbour with a cowhouse several times the parlour's size. It was also cheaper to run, because the releaser plant mechanised more operations than the bucket plant.

Technically, however, it owed its importance neither to its origins nor to its competitive advantages but to its own peculiar characteristics. For in essence the parlour is a 'housed mechanical process', one of the most unequivocal and successful examples of a farm building planned around a machine and in accordance with the routines it dictated. Its development heralded the revival in new form of the tradition created by the engineers of the steam age a century earlier.[40]

This, however, was for the future. The immediate impact of the parlour on the dairy farmstead was limited to areas where cows required no winter housing ... or, more accurately, to such few farmers in such areas who were either starting a dairy enterprise or were prepared to abandon their existing cowhouses and invest in parlours. In most of the country, where the needs of stock and soil combined to make the winter housing of the dairy herd necessary, the single-purpose parlour, which offered an improved method of milking, presented no real challenge to the dual-purpose cowhouse in which the farmer could house as well as milk his herd.

Even in these areas, however, economic pressures were already suggesting future developments. In 1926 an enterprising Northamptonshire farmer named W. S. Abbot converted an old barn into a cowhouse but, wishing to economise, built only sufficient stalls for milking his cows in batches, as in a bail or parlour. In the winter he housed them in one of the strawed yards traditionally occupied by fattening bullocks. Economically, this farmstead adaptation reflected the growth of the dairy herd at the expense of the grain and meat enterprises. Technically, it unknowingly foreshadowed the answer to a problem which had not yet arisen. The innovation established itself in limited practice towards the end of this period but attracted little attention.[41] In the next generation, however, a substantial and increasing proportion of the national milk supply was to come from cows housed in yards and milked in parlours.

## Silage and Silos

The expansion of the national dairy herd created problems of feeding as well as problems of housing. Pasture provided grazing in the summer months, and the merchant provided concentrates all the year round. But the supply of bulk fodder for the winter months was a more difficult matter. Traditionally, the farmer relied for this on hay and roots. Now, however, the changing times were emphasising the disadvantages of both crops. On the one hand, the dairy farmer needed a supply of hay reliable in both quantity and quality if he was to get the best out of his herd. But hay-making, however delightful in literary or artistic retrospect, is inevitably a chancy process when

179

cutting, drying and stacking are all at the mercy of a singularly unpredictable climate. On the other hand, he also wanted his fodder cheap. But the root crops were the most costly part of the intensive ploughland system on which the depression had fallen so heavily and the rate of decline of the root acreage was even greater than that of the other arable crops.

Here again, however, a combination of agricultural need and technical development produced an alternative to the inherited systems. This was silage-making, a process evolved on the Continent in the middle years of the nineteenth century.[42] Essentially, this is a crude form of canning, the cut grass or other green crop being stored undried in an airtight pit or structural container, which gives it an independence of the weather denied to hay-making. It therefore offered the farmer a way of producing a new form of bulk fodder less hazardous than making hay and cheaper than growing roots. But it offered these benefits only to those who understood the problems involved, and the manner of its introduction to Great Britain provides an instructive commentary on the implications of technological change in this period.

The story began conventionally enough in the 1880s when the first campaign to introduce silage into the country followed the familiar pattern of the Agricultural Revolution. Its sponsors were the traditional leaders of the farming industry, notably the Duke of Bedford and Lord Walsingham, its technical centres their estates and the farms of their more substantial tenants, its literature mainly surveys of practice and reports of individual experiences. But behind the façade of the old order the shape of the future was already apparent.

For one thing, the British farmer was accustomed to develop his own improvements in his own way with little help from foreigners. But this time he necessarily relied for much of his original information on Continental sources. More strikingly, interest in the new possibilities produced in 1883 the first book to offer the home farmer the lessons of American research and development.[43] The days of the old insularity were numbered, and one of the major sources of new technical knowledge made its first tentative appearance on the historical scene. For another, the private-enterprise system of communication on which the industry relied for the spread of new ideas and information could not meet the sudden demand for advice on this complicated innovation, and the balance was redressed, prophetically, by the administrative resources of the state. The two substantial reports issued in this decade which recorded the findings of a comprehensive survey of all the silos in the kingdom by the Agricultural Department of the Privy Council and the proceedings of a Royal Commission on the possibilities and problems of silage helped to make the early practice of silage-making one of the best documented of all farmstead developments. They also marked the first modern appearance of the government in its now familiar role of agricultural investigator and adviser.[44]

To contemporaries, however, all this was merely part of the triumphant progress of the new system. The interest it aroused was considerable, extensive and fashionable – in 1884, for instance, the Prince of Wales publicly commended silage at an agricultural meeting[45] – and within a few years an astonishing variety of assorted silos, some 2,600 structures in all, with another 1,200 primitive but cheaper silage stacks under strained rope wires, had appeared on British farms.[46] There was, of course, no standard design for such a novel type of building and each man built as he thought fit. Some of these silos were below ground, either as lined pits or in the simpler form of 'holes to bury hay stacks in'. Some were above ground as clamps or towers, some partly above and partly below ground. Some were formed within existing buildings, such as 'barns whose occupation is to a great extent gone';[47] some were unprecedented types of structure specially designed for the new purposes and some were equipped with hydraulic presses and other mechanical gadgets for the necessary consolidation of the material, while others relied on weights or treading by horses.[48] It was all very picturesque, but it was not the way of the future. Gradually, it became obvious that the results of these varied activities were not sufficiently attractive to win farmers from the familiar routines of the hayfield, and by the end of the century only the occasional enthusiast continued to make silage.[49] In 1912, for instance, it was noted that even in Westmorland, one of the counties where the climate most strongly favours silage, none of the fifty-seven silos built a generation before was still in use.[50]

There were various reasons for this failure. The technique was new, many mistakes were made and there was no general advisory service to provide guidance on right and wrong methods. More fundamentally, there was insufficient technical knowledge of the type that can only be obtained by research, for the men of the time did not realise that the processes which produced the 'sweet silage' they so prized also caused substantial losses in digestibility, particularly in the digestibility of protein.[51] The field was yielding to the laboratory as a source of agricultural knowledge and the traditional combination of aristocratic patronage and the pooling of empirical observations was no substitute for recommendations based on prolonged scientific study.

In the new century, however, interest in silage revived as farmers sought new ways to exploit their grass crop and saw in silage a possible alternative bulk fodder to replace their increasingly uneconomic root

181

crops. The new attack on the problem was symbolised by the erection in 1901 of a new kind of silo on a new kind of farm. The former was a wooden tower silo of the American type, the first product of American technology to establish itself in the English farmstead. The latter was the experimental farm of Wye College, for it was now clear that the future of silage lay largely in the hands of the research workers.[52] As the years passed, scientific understanding of the complex problems of this method of crop conservation increased. So did the number of towers of wood, concrete, steel or brick which appeared in the farmlands and replaced the older and more improvised systems of making silage in disused buildings or trenches. The tower systems gave good performance but were too expensive in capital costs and in labour for general use. So the new technique and the new towers were only found on a minority of the larger and more advanced farms, notably in the Eastern Counties where farmers developed special mixtures of arable crops, such as oats and vetches, which were ensiled and fed in place of mangolds, swedes and turnips.[53]

Indeed, there were far fewer silos in the country in the 1930s than in the 1880s.[54] At first sight, therefore, silage in this period had done little more than establish itself as a possible means of green-crop conservation. But this is a superficial assessment. In sounder analysis, the farmer had mastered a new system whose value was to be made manifest in the next generation. But he had not done this on his own. He owed his success to the scientists who had learnt the principles of silage-making in their laboratories and field stations and to the engineers who designed the towers to hold the new material and the equipment to handle it.

The point is of more than specialised importance. For the story of silage in this half-century epitomises the weaknesses of the old system for securing agricultural innovation and the reasons for the development of more sophisticated procedures. The improvised Victorian silos represented one of the last technical developments pioneered by the traditional leaders of agriculture, the towers of the twentieth century one of the first research-based technologies to affect the design and construction of the farmstead.

## Grass Drying

The importance of the scientist and the engineer was even more obvious in the development of another method of grass conservation which made its appearance on the farm at the very end of this period. Farmers had long known from observation that young grass was a peculiarly rich feed. They also knew, however, that the only means open to them of ensuring a steady supply of young grass, intensive grazing or equally intensive cutting and feeding, were impracticable under normal conditions of management. But the scientists who investigated this problem in the 1920s showed that grass of this type could be preserved with little loss of feeding value by artificial drying, and in due course the engineers produced equipment, housed in simple industrial-type sheds, which dried young grass, cut continuously during the growing season, into a convenient and stable form of fodder. The first of these grass dryers started work in 1933 and by the outbreak of the Second World War over eighty of them were in operation on English and Welsh farms, not merely conserving grass at its most valuable stage of development but converting it from a bulky to a concentrate feed. Dryers were too expensive, the system of grassland management required to supply them too exacting, for the new technique to enter into general practice. But it did allow enterprising farmers to produce their own concentrates and sell the surplus of their industrially processed grass to other farmers, thus turning a forage crop into a cash crop. The grass-drying farmer was, in fact a part-time manufacturer.[55]

## Buildings for Beef Production

The depression favoured the dairy cow and therefore encouraged the buildings and technologies that her particular line of production required. But it dealt harshly with her beef-producing cousins which had fattened so contentedly in the yards and boxes of the mid-Victorians. They formed part of the failing arable system and their meat could not compete in price with the refrigerated products of overseas ranches. From the time of the First World War onwards there was no increase in beef cattle on British farms and even this static level was only maintained by farming habits which took little account of costings. By the 1930s, the intensive box system had gone down into history and the fattening of yarded bullocks ranked high among the more gentlemanly ways of losing money. Drink, it was admitted, might be simpler, horses quicker and women pleasanter, but none was so reliable or so respectable as the good old bullock in the good old yard.

So the farmers of the early twentieth century continued to fatten bullocks in the yards built by their nineteenth-century predecessors. Sometimes they roofed open yards to preserve the manure whose continuing importance is amusingly illustrated by an unexpectedly personal passage in an otherwise detached textbook: 'I have seen manure four to five feet thick cut out of the centre of a covered yard by a trussing knife, splendid stuff, resembling in section streaky bacon, for which hungry land would be grateful as a hungry man for the other.'[56] Indeed, the roofing of yards was one of the few improvements made to existing buildings in this period.[57] But often landowners and farmers could not even afford to reach such standards of approved Victorian practice and they took, and left, the yards as they found them . . . the buildings of one of the better Berkshire estates in 1918 'were almost invariably easily identified by their covered yards'.[58] The unhappy, unprofitable bullocks in a dilapidated yard bottomed with a soggy morass of wasting manure so typical of these times proclaimed the failure of a major Victorian enterprise.[59]

## More Pigs, New Piggeries

The pig was more fortunate, for the new age brought him cheap food as well as competition from overseas. Indeed, it is in terms of fodder that the development of the pig enterprise in this period is most convincingly analysed. The end of butter and cheese manufacture on the farm deprived the pig of the waste products which had secured him his traditional place on the dairy farm. But the coming of cheap grain and cheap imported concentrates encouraged new types of pig farming which made necessary new types of piggery. In the first decade of the twentieth century, the pig population continued at its old level and textbooks still recommended the Victorian pen-and-run system of housing derived from the traditional cottager's pigsty.[60] By the 1930s the number of pigs had increased by half, they were concentrated in larger numbers on fewer farms, and technical writers were talking of pig buildings in terms of 'plant' and detailing new and sophisticated designs based on overseas models.[61]

Nevertheless, there was no wholesale revolution. By the end of this period, only one of three main groups of pig producer made any general use of the new types of building. The smallholders and 'cottage garden men', whose pigs were a domestic asset rather than a source of cash income, were content with the familiar pen-and-run piggery, a simple and effective form of housing which came to be known as 'the cottager's pigsty'.[62] The general farmers who kept pigs in various degrees of economic intensity, sometimes as major enterprises, sometimes as mere sidelines to turn tail corn and chat potatoes into meat and manure, took a more commercial line. But they were well aware of the celebrated 'pig cycle' of alternate booms and slumps which affected prices with such painful regularity and were seldom prepared to sink capital in specialised buildings. On the contrary, they exploited the pig's domestic adaptability and improvised pig housing from any form of cover that happened to be available. Some, indeed, went further. They revived the old tradition of 'the open air pig' and reared their herds in woodlands, providing them only with huts or rough shelters.[63] Thus, a survey of pig housing in the 1930s found that pigs were farrowed in anything from huts in the field via dog kennels, railway carriages and goods vans to artificially warmed pens, and fattened in converted dwelling houses, poultry houses, looseboxes, implement sheds, cowsheds, cottagers' pigsties, barns, yards, malthouses and even a disused railway engine shed.[64] But the more specialist producers, including a number working in factory style with pigs as their processing plant and purchased fodder as their raw material, sought higher standards of efficiency in their buildings, particularly in their fattening houses. It was, however, typical of the empirical times that they neither made nor sponsored any general attempt to identify the type of environment which best suited the fattening pig and to design a building to provide it. Instead, they copied the most successful type of house available.

This was the 'Danish' or 'Scandinavian' house which established itself in Great Britain in the early 1930s, and soon became the standard piggery on advanced farms.[65] The principle on which this totally enclosed house was designed was sound, for it strove to keep the pigs warm by conserving their body heat and thus reducing the feed bill which was the main item in their production cost. So was its internal design, for it allowed the pigs separate living and dunging areas and the pigmen a convenient central feeding passage. Yet the performance of these houses in Great Britain varied wildly. At one extreme they allowed specialists to fatten pigs on a scale and with an efficiency never before seen. For example, they housed the pigs of R. P. Chester, the industrialist who converted a thousand acres of semi-derelict land in Hampshire into the largest pig enterprise in the country, complete with a substantial office and laboratory.[66] At the other, they proved less effective than the familiar improvised housing on general farms. The basic reason for this discrepancy provided a further illustration of the growing inadequacy of the practical tradition in the new technical times.

For the 'Danish' houses erected in Great Britain were not copies of their Scandinavian originals. They were adaptations to one climate of a type of building developed for another climate. Such adaptation was obviously desirable. It was the manner of the adaptation which was at fault. There was little attempt to devise a building which would reproduce in Great Britain the environment which their prototypes provided in their homeland. But there was a great deal of guesswork on the degree to which the unfamiliar overhead lofts and the expensive degree of insulation of the true Danish houses could be reduced. Some farmers chose wisely. Many chose unwisely and in the years ahead a section on methods of improving conditions in Danish-type houses by decreasing heat loss was to find a place in farm building textbooks.[67] But the next age would do more than offer remedies for such defects. It would also provide for the first time recommendations and specifications based on something firmer than personal opinion.

## Poultry Housing

The development of poultry housing in these years followed the general pattern of pig housing. For poultry, like pigs, benefitted from the new supply of cheap concentrates and offered alternative hopes of profit to farmers whose traditional lines were no longer paying.

For most of this period, however, poultry remained no more than a casual sideline of the mixed-farming system, by custom the responsibility of the farmer's wife who relied on eggs for pin-money. An interesting exception was the chicken cramming industry of the Sussex Weald with its roofed rows of pens on stilts along which two men pushed a sort of sausage-machine on wheels and forcibly fed the penned birds through a gutta-percha tube.[68] Between the wars, however, a minor agricultural revolution created a new and expanded form of poultry industry, based on egg production. The number of hens in the country doubled; the old dual-purpose type of bird was largely replaced by more specialised egg-producing breeds, the average egg production per bird rose rapidly; and in the last quarter of this period the barnyard flocks found themselves competing increasingly not only with a substantial poultry enterprise developed on many general farms but also, more prophetically, with the intensive systems of the specialist producers.

Traditional methods survived on many farms where a few dozen hens and a proud cock sheltered in simple timber huts fitted with perches or, like the birds of the Carmarthen smallholders which roosted in cartsheds,[69] found what homes they could in the buildings of the farmstead. But on others long lines of unfamiliar structures appeared in fields once dedicated to corn and cattle. Sometimes these were movable pens with attached runs, shifted regularly by hand or tractor,[70] sometimes small sheds, sometimes substantial timber houses, open-fronted in the southern counties, totally enclosed like the 'Lancashire cabin' in the harsher north, each as large as a conventional cowhouse and fitted with 'scratching quarters, nests and utensils for feeding, confinement of broody hens, etc'.[71] On many of these farms, however, the fields contributed little but space for exercise and sunlight to the thousands of birds concentrated on them. The intensive poultryman, like the intensive pigman, was buying his feed from the merchant and developing methods of production which had as much in common with the factory as with the traditional type of farm.

An even more radical break with tradition was now on the way. For the discovery that cod-liver oil could provide birds with the vitamin D for which they were otherwise dependent on the action of direct sunlight on their bodies enabled farmers for the first time to keep poultry permanently indoors. All that was needed for egg production, therefore, was a building, hens and food. There was no longer any need for fields. Soon even the limited factor of floor space was to be reduced. The early total confinement houses, like their less intensive predecessors, allowed the birds to run loose on the floor. But in the later 1920s experiments with cage systems to control such antisocial habits as feather-pecking and cannibalism produced an adaptation of the American battery system of three, four or even five tiers of hens in types of individual cage which allowed easy feeding, egg collection, egg recording and manure removal. Science and technology had devised a method of maintaining large numbers of birds in buildings independent of the farm.[72]

The immediate importance of the battery system was small, but the long-term significance of the principles it incorporated was immense. It was a major step in the intensification of livestock husbandry and, typically, it raised in the countryside a problem hitherto confined to the cattle enterprises of the towns. It is no accident that one of the questions discussed in the first book published on this system was the possibility of selling poultry manure.[73] Livestock enterprises had long been able to exceed the productive capacity of the particular farm which carried them. This was the first evidence that new systems of management incorporated in new systems of housing would also allow them to exceed its absorptive capacity.

## Mechanisation in Field and Steading

So the number of livestock on farms increased. But the number of men on farms steadily decreased as farm workers left their impoverished industry for better prospects elsewhere. At the end of this period there were as many farmers as at the beginning, but the labour force they employed had fallen by half; and there were limits to the possible economies from lower standards and less exacting systems of farming. So the farmer turned increasingly to forms of prime-mover cheaper and more readily available than human beings.

The most obvious change came in the fields. At first the farmer made greater use of four-legged horsepower and the number of horses used solely for agricultural purposes rose from 844,000 in 1881 to its peak of 937,000 in 1911 as the ancient combination of sickle, scythe or rake and human muscles finally yielded to the horse-drawn reaper and binder, the horse-drawn mower, swath-turner and side-delivery rake. Then he began to replace the horse by the more powerful and convenient tractor, and the throb of the internal combustion engine took its place among the normal sounds of the countryside. By 1939, there were still eleven horses to every tractor but the latter produced two-thirds of the total mobile power of the farm.[74]

The effects of such mechanisation on the central farmstead were slight. The new implements, like their predecessors, required only simple shelter and the additional horses only more stables of a long-established pattern, while the tractor was content with 'a disused coachhouse or similar building',[75] preferably with a concrete floor to ease the task of maintenance and repair, and a fuel store. All this was a matter of minor modifications and adjustments, though, as the arable acreage shrank and tractors increasingly replaced horses, stables joined corn barns as possibilities for conversion to milk-production buildings.[76] But the combination of decreased ploughland, the tractor and the increasing use of fertiliser rendered obsolete the traditional outlying buildings where inwintered cattle trod straw into manure for outlying fields. Many such fields now returned to the rough grazing from which they were originally reclaimed. Where cultivation continued, fertility was maintained at less cost by manure and fertilisers hauled from the homestead. So gradually the barn-and-yard units of the chalk and limestone uplands and the field barns of the Pennines were abandoned to become empty, lonely evidences of pervading agricultural change.

Meanwhile, an equally important, though less spectacular, revolution was developing behind the walls of the farmstead. The farmer was replacing organic power by mechanical power in the buildings as well as in the fields.

The first agent of this revolution was the internal combustion engine which lightened many farmstead chores long before it was harnessed to plough, drill or reaper. Gas engines were used on farms in the 1880s, but were soon superseded by the 'petroleum engine' which made its earliest agricultural appearance at the Royal Show in 1888 and was recognised in the following decade as a 'highly useful means of driving farm machinery' and a serious rival to the steam engine which had hitherto provided the only general alternative to manpower for indoor work.[77] In the next generation the progress of this new prime-mover was rapid.[78] In 1908, it has been estimated, static petrol and oil engines provided the farming industry with 46,000 hp; in 1913 with 108,000 hp; in 1925 with 370,000 hp and in 1939 with 540,000 hp.[79] Only in the middle 1930s did the mobile horsepower of the farmer's tractor fleet exceed that of the stationary engines which worked in his farmstead.

The nineteenth century had provided the farmer with means of producing power, first the steam engine, then the internal combustion engine which gradually replaced it. The twentieth century, more radical, provided him with ready-made power, manufactured centrally, distributed by wires and available at the flick of a switch. As far back as 1908 the agricultural possibilities of clean and quiet electrical power were recognised and proclaimed.[80] But such hopes were mere dreams until the general spread of powerlines into the countryside, and it was only at the end of this period that the farmer made any substantial use of electricity except for lighting.[81] In the 1930s, however, the increase of electrical equipment exhibited at agricultural shows,[82] the conversion of some of the last horse-threshers in Northumberland to electric drive[83] and the appearance of a section on electricity in a major agricultural annual[84] marked the acceptance of the new power as a normal tool of the farming trade. The farmstead improver had acquired an ally, the internal combustion engine a rival.

By the end of this period, therefore, static mechanical power, sometimes aided by stationary tractors, ground and mixed fodder, milked cows and pumped water in a substantial and increasing proportion of farmsteads. Yet it is more accurate to call this development the use of machinery rather than true mechanisation. For in general, the new prime-movers entered the farmstead on the farmstead's terms. They fitted themselves into existing buildings and took their place in existing routines. They were improved substitutes for earlier forms of power, for the power of men and horses, water and steam, and not means of creating new operational patterns. They saved the farmer time and energy, but they brought few major changes to the processes they powered or to the design of the buildings that housed them. The appearance of the farmstead was no guide to the amount of mechanical power used in it.

Nevertheless, there were limited but prophetic exceptions to this generalisation, for the implications of the pervading and versatile mechanical power now freely available to the farmer for the first time, were already becoming visible among the run-down steadings of the depression times. New mechanical processes made possible by the new forms of energy were beginning to create new types of farm building. In the 1930s, the milking parlour provided an actual, the grain-drying installation a potential, example of this development. Their numbers were small. So was their immediate importance. But they foreshadowed the future. In the next age, much of the old promise of the engineer of the age of steam was to be fulfilled by his successor of the age of oil and electricity.

## Hop Buildings

The effects of such technical changes were interestingly summarised in the development of the oasthouse in this period. At its beginning, the familiar kiln with the conical top and pivoted cowl which proclaimed its dependence on natural draught was in universal use. The only development was a change from round to square kilns, partly because it was found that round kilns, which were more expensive to build, gave no advantage in air flow, and partly because they allowed the introduction of 'roller hairs' by which hops could be moved on rollers from kiln to cooling room. But the coming of electric fans, which were introduced early in the century and became general after experiments in the 1920s had made it possible to specify the degree of forced draught required, ended the necessity for such cowls, which were replaced in new buildings by cheaper louvres. In the next decade, oil fuel began to oust coal, just as coal had once ousted charcoal. Together, the work of the scientist and the engineer produced a new form of kiln which was housed with its ancillary services in a single industrial-type building. The oasthouse was very different from most other buildings on the farm, but its changing equipment and design in these years told the same general story.[85]

## Building Materials

In these years the farmer became as dependent on the general economic system for the means of building and maintaining his farmstead as for his means of powering it. On the one hand, the old tradition of local self-sufficiency passed finally into history. Such time-honoured materials as 'clay lump' in Norfolk, 'clunch' in Cambridgeshire, sarsen stone in Wiltshire and ling thatch in the Pennines became mere survivals and home-grown timber could not compete with imported softwood.[86] Even traditional materials now often came from distant sources. The tiles which roof a late nineteenth-century cattleshed at Manor Farm Museum, Cogges, Oxfordshire, came from a Bridgwater factory and in the next generation the lorry completed the work of the railway. In the 1930s, for example, Ruabon bricks, formerly confined to areas near railway yards, found their way to more remote parts of Wales.[87]

On the other hand, the bricks, tiles and slates of the earlier nineteenth century were reinforced and in part supplanted by new and more sophisticated products peculiarly suited to the changed conditions. For the farmer was no longer interested in substantial new construction. He wanted cheap adaptations, cheap improvisation and cheap repairs.

In particular, he came to rely increasingly on two industrial products which, as we have seen, had appeared on the farm in mid-Victorian times and were now to establish themselves as standard

Plate 25    A cowhouse, probably fairly typical, of the early nineteenth century. The overhead loft makes it low and dark, the materials used make it difficult to clean (*BBC Hulton Picture Library*)

Plate 26    A 'model' mid-Victorian cowhouse built, improbably, in Kensington. Few town or country cowhouses were as advanced or as hygienic as this one, but it shows the standard which could be reached by proper planning and construction. The iron roof trusses, the cast-iron partitions between the cows and the labour-saving railway for moving fodder illustrate the influence of the industrial age on agricultural buildings (see page 153) (*Museum of English Rural Life*)

Plate 27   A Victorian example of the 'cottager's pigsty', the normal form of specialised housing for pigs from the late-eighteenth to the early-twentieth century. It met the needs of pigs of all ages well, but was expensive in capital and in labour. It generally stood near the farmhouse, where the farmer's wife could conveniently feed the pigs on the waste products of the household and the dairy (*Dr J. E. C. Peters*)

Plate 28   The first concrete farm building (on right). It was built of mass-concrete in Berkshire in about 1870 (see page 138) (*Mr John Gray*)

materials. Both were cheap to buy. Both were simple to use, since they required little skilled labour and could be handled by ordinary farm staff. Both were convenient for small jobs, for the immediate repairs, first-aid and patchwork with which he strove to 'minimise the effects of a certain amount of unavoidable neglect.'[88] Between them, they changed the appearance of British farmsteads.

The first of these materials was cement for the concreting which in this period became one of the recognised farm crafts. Few farmers were as fortunate as Geoffrey Garratt, whose farm lay only a mile from a cement works. But many found as he did that 'it is extraordinary what good work can be done by direct labour and a little courage,'[89] and in the twentieth century advice on making concrete became a normal feature of the farm building textbook. The farmer, however, could only use cement as an ingredient of the mass concrete suitable for such literally basic purposes as foundations, yard bottoms or floors, in particular the floors of the cowhouses for which sanitary inspectors were increasingly demanding impervious, easily cleaned surfaces and properly formed and laid dung channels. For its more sophisticated application he was dependent on the factory.

In 1911, for instance, a land agent had suggested the agricultural use of the new reinforced concrete in which steel rods overcame the material's weakness in tension and so allowed it to be formed into beams, posts and other structural members. Paying formal tribute to the lingering tradition of self-sufficiency, he considered the possible manufacture of such components in estate yards but concluded, inevitably, that the technical difficulties were too great.[90] When reinforced concrete units eventually came to the farm a generation later, they came prefabricated from the factory. The same point arose in more immediately practical fashion in the years between the wars, when farmers began building walls of solid concrete or, more promisingly, of concrete blocks.[91] Technically, the latter were preferable. Yet the change marked another break with the old order of dependence on local resources. It was possible to make concrete blocks on the farm. But it was generally wiser to buy them ready-made from the factory, where the manufacturing process was more precise and more reliable. The help which cement could offer the farmer anxious to help himself was considerable in scope but limited in kind.

The second do-it-yourself material was corrugated iron sheeting, which rapidly became the most conspicuous of all farm building materials. It appeared on the roofs of new buildings, it replaced tiles, slates or thatch on old buildings, it was thrust under thatch or nailed to boards to give decaying barns a few more years of life, and it provided walls as well as roofs for sheds and yards. Its weaknesses, notably its poor insulating properties and its need for protection from rust, were obvious. But they were not so obvious as its virtues of low cost and general utility, and there were soon few farms without corrugated iron somewhere or other in their buildings.[92]

Only at the end of this period was its dominance challenged by a new and equally convenient form of sheeting which offered better insulating properties and required no maintenance. This was asbestos-cement sheeting, which by the early 1930s was 'assuming very great importance in agricultural work',[93] and by the end of the decade was taken for granted as the normal roofing for new buildings.[94] Indeed, the new white roofing would eventually in large measure replace corrugated iron, just as corrugated iron had replaced the older materials.[95] But this lay in the future. The farmer of the depression times relied on mass concrete and corrugated iron to keep his obsolescent and decaying buildings operational.

### Prefabrication

The industrial system which provided the farmer with these materials for maintaining his buildings also provided him with an increasing range of fittings with which to equip them – rainwater goods of cast iron, galvanised iron and asbestos-cement, troughs of iron and glazed earthenware, automatic drinking bowls for cattle, metal window casements, sliding doors, cowls and louvre ventilators, overhead tracks for removing manure from cowhouses. Year by year, the list of such fittings lengthened and the trade catalogues grew in size. Few of the items listed were new in principle. It was their scope and variety which had changed. But they were only part of a more radical change. For the trade which produced prefabricated fittings now began to produce prefabricated buildings as component parts made in the factory for assembly on the farm.

The earliest prefabricated buildings were the proprietary portable silos and the more ambitious ready-made iron farmstead which appeared in the 1880s.[96] The manufacture of the former, however, ceased when the system for which they were designed was abandoned and the latter was no more than a curiosity. The future of this system of construction depended on the sale of a standardised product to a large and continuing market. Characteristically, it was first successfully applied to one of the commonest and simplest structures on the farm, the Dutch barn, which in this period provided a classic case of industrial response to agricultural opportunity.

When the depression reinforced the general need to protect corn and hay with the particular need to reduce costs, above all labour costs, industrially produced barns of steel members and corrugated iron sheeting began to establish themselves as normal features of the farming landscape.[97] By Edwardian times, they were 'rapidly making thatching a lost art' and in the next generation they were classed among the few types of building which landowners and farmers regarded as a reasonable investment.[98]

So the farmer who had once built his own buildings from such materials as his village offered was now able to buy not only materials but ready-made buildings. All he had to do was to 'excavate and prepare concrete foundations' for his new Dutch barn.[99] Everything else was done for him by the suppliers and their mobile gang of erectors. A new and prophetic type of factory product had come to the farm.

## Past and Future

Technologically, therefore, this was a decisive period. On the one hand, it saw the decline or end of many historical traditions hitherto preserved by the farmstead. In these years, natural water supplies ceased to determine the siting of farm buildings;[100] the last and wildly anachronistic barns for flail threshing were built;[101] the last datable bank barn was built in 1904, though it may have had successors up to 1914, and the last Durham 'byrehouse' was apparently abandoned in the 1920s;[102] pigeons finally lost their lingering value as farm livestock and the conversion of an occasional pigeoncote to a house or a smithy provided interestingly early examples of the re-use of redundant farm buildings for non-agricultural purposes;[103] farm butter, farm cheese and farm cider were replaced by factory-made products;[104] steam and water were replaced by new forms of power;[105] estate yards decreased in numbers as tenanted farms were sold to owner-occupiers and expenditure on farm buildings shrank;[106] the custom in parts of Wales of unmarried farm workers sleeping over the stables, which continued from the days when oxherds slept by their charges, came to an end;[107] and such flails,[108] such horse-driven barn machinery[109] and such liquid manure installations [110] as continued in service, such local building materials as were still used[111] and such longhouses as were still inhabited[112] became interesting historical relics. On the other hand, it also saw the establishment of a new agricultural system typified by the appearance in the textbooks of references to the fertiliser store for 'bag manure';[113] the cake store for purchased concentrate feed';[114] the loading bay for the growing volume of materials the farmer bought and sold;[115] and the office from which he administered his increasingly complicated business.[116]

The effects of these changes on the appearance of the farmstead were noted as early as 1912. 'There was a time ... when [farmsteads] lent a charm to rural scenery ... Now that the industry has become more serious, more exacting and more precise, the picturesque side . . . has given way to lines of formality and stiffness. The older order was coupled with waste . . . The new order accepts thrift and watchfulness as essential to success. These ideas are pronounced in the stiff, formal buildings of the new age.'[117] The observer overemphasised the extent and immediate consequences of the new order. But he prepared his readers for the literal shape of things to come.

Indeed, many developments in this period offered a preview of the future. Intensive systems of housing pigs and poultry, farmstead mechanisation, milking parlours and grain-drying installations, prefabrication, a new constructional pattern of concrete floors, walls of concrete blocks and roofs of asbestos-cement sheeting supported on steel and reinforced concrete members, were novelties in this age, but conventional practice in the next. More subtly, the conditions of the new age raised radical questions about the assumptions on which farm buildings should be designed. This period saw the appearance of the idea that the rate of agricultural change might make necessary buildings planned either for a limited life or for easy adaptation to different needs.[118]

Yet all these varied developments tell the same story. They all prepare us for the changes of our own generation. For they illustrate the growing integration of agriculture into the science-based industrial economy around it which is the fundamental theme of farming history in the twentieth century.

## NOTES

1. Drummond, J. C. and Wilbraham, A. *The Englishman's Food*, 1957, p 322.
2. Ojala, E. M. *Agriculture and Economic Progress*, 1952, p 208.
3. For the changing level of rents in this period see Orwin, C. S. and Whetham, E. H. *History of British Agriculture, 1846–1914*, 1964, chart III. According to the same authors (p 196), figures of expenditure under various Acts encouraging capital investment suggest that the national outlay on farm buildings improvement decreased by about three-quarters between 1873–82 and 1903–12. The figures for expenditure on improvements, mainly on buildings, on two Cambridgeshire estates in this period are probably typical of changes in the more hard-hit arable areas. Up to 1880, about 50 per cent of the rent revenue was spent on improvements. For the next forty years, the figure was 20 per cent. In the 1920s it increased to 40 per cent, but the average rent per acre was that of the 1880s and by this time the purchasing value of this income was greatly reduced (McGregor, J. J. 'The economic history of two rural estates in Cambridgeshire, 1870–1934', *Journal of the Royal Agricultural Society of England*, vol 98, 1937, pp 148–9). Changes in the predominantly livestock areas of the north and west were not so extreme as in the arable counties of East Anglia, but they showed the same general tendencies.
4. For example, Smith, H. H. *The Principles of Landed Estate Management*, 1898, pp 99–101; Curtis, C. E. *Farm Buildings*, 1912, p 106; Wrightson, J. and Newsham, J. C. *Agriculture, Theoretical and Practical*, 1915, p 332. In 1891 Holkham estate concluded a century's farmstead development with its last major rebuilding period (Wade-Martins, S. *A Great Estate at Work*, 1980, p 164). A generation later an architect wrote sadly 'modern farm buildings are so few . . . that they are almost non-existent' (Gunn, E. 'Recent farm buildings', *Architect's Journal*, vol 65, 1927, p 475). In the same period a land agent illustrated his article, significantly entitled 'The repair and reconstruction of farm buildings', with a traditional farmstead plan but added that 'it does not often fall to the lot of a land agent nowadays to complete a new farmstead except perhaps after a fire', continuing with a thought

familiar to many of the professional successors in the next generation. 'Many of us would possibly be not unduly perturbed if certain of the homesteads with which we come into contact were subject to such a catastrophe, provided that they were amply insured' (*Journal of the Land Agents Society*, vol 32, 1933, pp 224–8).

5. Hall, A. D. *A Pilgrimage of British Farming*, 1914, p 437; *Journal of the Land Agents Society*, vol 5, 1906, p 399. For a late example, apparently built for amenity and status rather than for agricultural reasons, see Hussey, C. 'Outbuildings at Barrington Court, Somerset', *Country Life*, 8 September 1928, pp 332–8. The title is instructive. The farm buildings were regarded as agreeable adjuncts to the Big House and not, as on a commercial farm, as part of the means of production whereby the farmhouse and its occupants were maintained. Descriptions of some later nineteenth-century architect-designed farmsteads in Brockman, H. A. N. *The British Architect in Industry, 1841–1940*, 1974, p 77, suggest that they were earlier examples of this genre.

6. These smallholdings were created and administered by the county councils under the supervision of the Board of Agriculture, later the Ministry of Agriculture and Fisheries. By the end of this period some 30,000 such holdings had been established, their average size being 15 acres. A number of these were horticultural holdings or specialised poultry holdings, but others were small mixed farms usually equipped with smaller editions of the types of farmstead found on larger farms but sometimes with the more technically interesting all-under-one-roof farmstead. Owing to the small size of the enterprises they served, however, such developments had little influence on general farmstead design (Taylor, S. *Modern Homesteads*, 1905, pp 60–4; Potter, T. *Buildings for Smallholdings*, 1909; Maule, H. P. G. 'Farm buildings for smallholdings', *Journal of the Ministry of Agriculture*, vol 29, May 1922, pp 113–18; June 1922, pp 230–4; and March 1923, pp 1099–1104; Gunn, R. 'Recent farm buildings', *Architect's Journal*, vol 65, 1927, pp 475–86).

7. Some landowners, such as Henry Chaplin, who became the first president of the (second) Board of Agriculture which was established in 1889, spent substantial sums on building and repairs in the early years of the depression in order to retain tenants. Incidentally, he 'drew heavily' on Land Improvement Company loans (see p 124) to finance this expenditure, which managed to include repairs to a pub (Report of the Lincolnshire and Humberside Arts, St Hughs, Newport, Lincoln, *Survey of Agricultural Buildings Groups*, issued at a lecture at Oxford University Department for External Studies conference on farm buildings, February, 1980). Such policies, however, could not be sustained for long at a time of falling rents.

8. Orr, J. *Agriculture in Berkshire*, 1918, p 103.

9. Hall, A. D. *A Pilgrimage of British Farming*, 1914, pp 80, 98, 116, 119, 129.

10. Orr, J. *Agriculture in Berkshire*, 1918, p 102.

11. Addison, Lord. *A Policy for British Agriculture*, 1939, p. 61.

12. Dixey, R. N. 'The condition of cowsheds', *The Farm Economist*, vol 2, January 1936, p 3.

13. Carslaw, R. M. and Graves, P. F. 'The condition of farm buildings', *The Farm Economist*, vol 2, January 1937, pp 101–3.

14. Thomas, E. *The Economics of Smallholdings*, 1927, pp 55–7. See also Howell, P. *An Economic Survey of a Rural Parish* (in Wales), published by the Institute for Research in Agricultural Economics, Oxford, 1923, pp 12–13.

15. Garratt, G. T. *Hundred Acre Farm*, 1928, pp x, 29, 30.

16. In this period only one type of livestock decreased its demands on the farmstead. References to sheephouses continued to appear for form's sake in textbooks, but sheep housing was no longer practised. A long, hard winter in the 1880s raised the question of shelter for the flock (Moore, H. F. 'The winter of 1885–6', *Journal of the Royal Agricultural Society of England*, 2nd ser, vol 22, 1886, pp 377–442), but it was not followed by any general revival of interest in housing systems.

17. By 1902 Henderson, R. *The Modern Farmstead*, p vii, commented on the 'promiscuous adding of building to building and the jamming of shedding into every available corner and the leaning of it against any clear space'. Such practices were not new, but the depression intensified them.

18. Malden, W. J. *Farm Buildings*, 1896, pp 105–29; Taylor, S. *Modern Homesteads*, 1905, pp 52–4; Wrighton, J. and Newsham, J. C. *Agriculture, Theoretical and Practical*, 1915, p 335; Lawrence, C. P. *Economic Farm Buildings*, 1919, pp 21–30; McHardy, D. N. *Modern Farm Buildings*, 1932, pp 182–8. Lawrence, p 21, described additions and alterations as 'the work which most often claims the attention of the agent'.

19. Malden, W. J. *Farm Buildings*, 1896, p 111; advertisement by the Government Surplus Property Disposal Board of Nissen huts 'suitable for housing, storage or workshops, or accommodation for pigs or sheep', in *Journal of Ministry of Agriculture*, vol 26, March 1926, p 1181; Price, W. T. and Ling, W. A. *Advisory Report on Pighousing*, 1936, pp 19–24, published by the Wiltshire County Council. For the use of the cruiser's funnels as silos see

Orwin, C. S. *Pioneers in Power Farming*, 1934, p 12. A textbook of 1915, Wrighton, J. and Newsham, J. C. *Agriculture, Theoretical and Practical*, includes advice on do-it-yourself 'extemporised' and temporary buildings, using such materials as sleepers, byproduct 'slabs' from saw mills, galvanised iron sheeting, straw, faggots and bracken (pp 335–42).

20. Significantly, H. W. Moore, an architect who in 1879 won the dairy farmstead prize competition at the Dairy Show, undertook no later agricultural work (Sant, A. 'Three Oxford architects', *Oxoniensia*, vol 35, 1970, p 79), though architects were employed on some Welsh estates in the late nineteenth century (Wiliam, E. *Traditional Farm Buildings in North-East Wales, 1550–1900*, 1982, p 264). Henderson, R. *The Modern Homestead*, 1902, p vii, observed that architects were seldom employed for farm buildings 'and when they are, their want of touch in rural matters leads them astray'. A generation later, a standard agricultural manual summarised with agreeable simplicity the accepted view. 'The proper arrangement(of farm buildings) greatly facilitates labour and may save the farmer immense expense in feeding and handling his stock and produce. Their planning should be entrusted to someone who understands these matters and not to a professional architect.' (McConnell, P. *The Agricultural Notebook*, 9th edition, 1919, p 69; 11th edition, 1930, p 69). Between the wars, the architectural influence on farm-building design was negligible. A leading article in the *Architect's Journal*, vol 65, 1927, p 469, noted the 'evident feeling almost general to all farmers that it was almost sacrilege for anybody but a practical farmer (with accent on the *practical*) to attempt to know anything of farm processes or the arrangement of farm buildings' but admitted that 'a large proportion of architect-designed farm buildings fail from non-acquaintance with simple essentials' and warned its readers that 'serious farm building design on a commercial basis was no primrose path'. Few attempted this path. (See note 21.)

21. In 1919, C. P. Lawrence assumed that farm buildings were solely a matter for land agents (*Economic Farm Buildings*, p viii). In 1935, when owner-occupiers were more numerous, E. Gunn addressed his book to 'farmers, land agents and architects', though he implied regretfully that architects were seldom employed on farm buildings (*Farm Buildings*, subtitle, p 60).

22. McConnell, P. 'Experiences of a Scotsman on the Essex clays', *Journal of the Royal Agricultural Society of England*, 3rd ser, vol 2, 1891, p 312.

23. Malden, W. J. *Farm Buildings*, 1896, p 13.

24. Orr, J. *Agriculture in Oxfordshire*, 1916, p 113.

25. Clarke, A. D. *Modern Farm Buildings*, 1899, pp 38–40.

26. Robinson, H. G. 'Messrs S. E. and J. F. Alley's mechanised farming', *Journal of the Royal Agricultural Society of England*, vol 93, 1932, p 163. He was not, however, the very first to do so. The first grain dryer in the country to meet the need created by the combine was built in 1929 (Cover, W. 'Electricity from grain drying', *Farm Mechanisation*, vol 1, no 4, January–February 1947, p 146). The dependence of the combine on the dryer was recognised very early. When Hosier bought his first combine in 1935, he took care that his dryer was installed before harvest time (Hosier, A. J. and Hosier, F. H. *Hosier's Farming System*, 1951, pp 41, 189).

27. Wiliam, E. *Traditional Farm Buildings in North-East Wales, 1550–1900*, 1982, pp 236–9.

28. Ernle, Lord. *English Farming, Past and Present*, 1941, p 389.

29. Cheke, V. *The Story of Cheesemaking in Britain*, 1959, p 272. As early as 1898 cheese-rooms in farmhouses 'were in many cases turned into applelofts' (Smith, H. H. *The Principles of Landed Estate Management*, 1898, p 87). Farmhouse cheese-makers who continued in production generally did so by developing small-scale cheese factories on their farms.

30. *Man and His Cattle*, issued by the Ministry of Agriculture, Fisheries and Food, 1967, pp 14–15. By 1938, however, there were only 151 cows in built-up London and the number of cows and cowhouses in Liverpool had dropped by a quarter (personal communication from the Public Relations Officer of the Milk Marketing Board; *Man and His Cattle*, issued by the Ministry of Agriculture, Fisheries and Food, 1967, p 15). See also Atkins, P. J. 'London's intra-urban milk supply, c1790–1914', *Transactions of the Institute of British Geographers*, NS vol 2, 1977, pp 383–9; Stoute, A. 'Three centuries of London cowkeeping', *Farmers Weekly*, 18 August 1978, pp v–xiii; Camden Historical Society, *From Primrose Hill to Euston Road*, 1982, p 47, for Brown's dairy, a large and ornate town dairy known as 'the cows' cathedral' which was demolished in 1903. It stood on the site of Camden Town Underground station. Long, J. *British Dairy Farming*, 1885, p 312, expressed 'disgust' at a town dairy he had recently visited. But the *Report of the Agricultural Department of the Privy Council Office on Eruptive Diseases of Teats and Udders of Cows in Relation to Scarlet Fever in Man*, HMSO, 1888, pp 72–4, concluded after an examination of 9,176 cows in the Metropolitan Board of Works area that the health of the cows would compare favourably with that of farm cows, mainly because of 'the improved sanitary conditions under which they are now kept' and noted that the regulations of the Dairies, Cowsheds and Milkshops Order 1885 (see p 175) was well administered. The success of the Liverpool cowkeepers, whose numbers reached

their peak in 1909, was largely due to the same reason. Dr E. W. Hope, who as Medical Officer of Health was responsible for enforcing the regulations from 1894 to 1923, compared the hygienic standards of milk production on farms unfavourably with those in the city. The typical Liverpool dairy consisted of a yard at the side or rear of a house-cum-shop around which stood the cowhouse with a loft above it, the stable, a shed for the milkfloat or, later, the van, a walled midden and a water trough. The Medical Officers of Health required cowhouses of well-maintained brick, 'the interiors lofty and well lit and with plenty of headroom, even when there were lofts'. After 1926 they insisted on the building of special cooling rooms for the milk (Grundy, J. E. *The Origins of Liverpool Cowkeepers*, unpublished MA thesis, Lancaster University, 1982, pp 36–41, 49–56). It was some time before the majority of dairy farmers reached such standards.

31. The 1923 edition of the bulletin on *The Construction of Cowhouses*, issued by the Ministry of Agriculture and Fisheries, made no reference to the dairy. The 1929 edition, however, gave detailed guidance on dairy design and construction, including suggestions on remodelling existing buildings to allow the addition of a dairy at one end of the cowhouse (pp 18–22). The improvement of the dairy was essentially a matter of the better application of existing resources. The familiar corrugated cooler, for instance, had been in use since the beginning of this period (Fussell, G. E. *The English Dairy Farmer*, 1966, pp 178–9).

32. Young, T. J. 'Agriculture in the county of Cheshire', *Journal of the Royal Agricultural Society of England*, vol 85, 1924, p 163. For the structural improvements required in existing cowhouses and the standards required in new ones, see Liversage, V. 'The economic aspects of Grade A (Tuberculin Tested) milk production', *Scottish Journal of Agriculture*, vol 9, July 1926, pp 1–9; Dixey, R. N. 'The cost of erecting cowhouses', *The Farm Economist*, vol 1, 1935, pp 197–9; Dixey, R. N. 'The cost of converting buildings into cowsheds', *The Farm Economist*, vol 1, 1935, pp 213–15; Dixey, R. N. 'The cost of improving cowsheds for Certified and Grade A (T.T.) milk', *The Farm Economist*, vol 1, 1935, pp 233–8.

33. 'The inspection of milk production premises is becoming more important' (Macewen, H. A. *The Public Milk Supply*, 1910, p 86). In 1898 Rider Haggard, farming in Norfolk, 'believed there existed inspectors of dairies, though I never saw or heard of one inspecting my dairy'. He spoke too soon. Next year, 'an inspector descended on me and requested me to alter a certain surface drain in one of my cowhouses' (Haggard, R. *A Farmer's Year*, 1906, pp 369–70). Progress, however, was slow. 'We had a visit from the inspector under the new Dairies Order and our buildings were passed, though I suspect they offend at least one bye-law. Literally enforced, the Order would stop milk production on most of our mixed farms' (Garratt, G. T. *Hundred Acre Farm*, 1928, p 5). See also Dixey, R. N. 'The cost of improving cowsheds for Certified and Grade A (T.T.) milk', *The Farm Economist*, vol 1, 1935, p 233. It took a long time for research findings on the importance of proper ventilation and temperature for milk yield (MacDonald, J. ed, *Stephens' Book of the Farm*, 5th ed, vol 3, 1909, pp 346–8) to reach the cowhouse. Two of the few articles on farm buildings which appeared in the architectural press in the 1920s were apparently inspired by the Milk and Dairies Order of 1926. The first was mainly concerned with dairy buildings and emphasised the importance of proper standards of design and construction. The second was wholly concerned with dairy buildings and specifically mentioned the Order (Gunn, E. 'Recent farm buildings', *Architect's Journal*, vol 65, 1927, pp 475–86; Darling, F. 'The modern dairy farm', *Architect's Journal*, vol 65, 1927, pp 486–90).

34. Clarke, A. D. *Modern Farm Buildings*, 1899; Haines, A. H. and Daniel, A. F. H. *Surveying and Building Construction for Agricultural Students*, 1915; Lawrence, C. P. *Economic Farm Buildings*, 1919. See also Macewen, H. A. *The Public Milk Supply*, 1910, pp 93–121 and Curtis, C. E. *Farm Buildings*, 1912, p 67.

35. For the history of the milking machine see Hall, H. S. 'The mechanisation of milk production', *British Agricultural Bulletin*, vol 4, June 1951, pp 75–9; Fussell, G. E. *The Farmer's Tools*, 1952, pp 194–8; Fussell, G. E. 'Dairy machinery', *Journal of the Chartered Land Agents Society*, March 1960, pp 117–20; Jannsson, T. *The Development of the Milking Machine. A Historical Review*, published by Alfa-Laval, Tumba, Sweden, 1973.

36. *Final Report of the Committee on the Production and Distribution of Milk*, 1919, HMSO, Cmnd 483, p. 60.

37. Bridges, A. 'The economics of machine milking', *Agriculture*, vol 46, April 1939, p 64.

38. Orwin, C. S. *A Pioneer of Progress in Farm Management*, 1931, pp 10–11, 17–18; Hosier, A. J. and Hosier, F. H. *Hosier's Farming System*, 1951, pp 10–11, 14–21.

39. The term was first used in the last years of this period. R. M. Currie in 1938 included the 'so-called parlour' on his list of milking systems ('The production of higher grades of milk', *Journal of the Farmers' Club*, February 1938, p 8). Mr Brooke's reference in chapter 2 of *Middlemarch*, first published in 1872, to 'making a parlour of your cowhouse' was purely coincidental.

40. Appropriately, a textbook of the time noted that 'the fullest present development' of the milking parlour was devised by one of the major milking machine firms (Gunn, E. *Farm*

*Buildings*, 1935, p 30).

41. Bridges, A. *The Flexibility of Farming*, 1933, p 30, for Abbot; Mansfield, W. 'Cambridge University farm', *Journal of the Royal Agricultural Society of England*, vol 97, 1936, p 107; Salter, R. G. 'Cowsheds or covered yards', *Journal of the Land Agents Society*, vol 38, 1939, pp 88–91.

42. Jenkins, H. M. 'Report on the practice of ensilage', *Journal of the Royal Agricultural Society of England*, 2nd ser, vol 20, 1884, pp 132–7; *Silos for Preserving British Fodder Crops* by the sub-editor of *The Field*, 1884, pp 1–18.

43. *Ensilage in America*, by Thorold Rogers, the economic historian. It included on p 86 a remarkable prediction of general as well as particular application by Dr George Thurber of the *American Agriculturist*. 'Much is yet to be done in *americanising* the whole matter [of silage],' he wrote, 'and we have no doubt that the experiments now being made will greatly simplify not only the building of the silo but every other step in this method.' The general point was appreciated by a contemporary who noted 'the cool effectiveness, as might have been expected' of an American pighousing system (*The Builder*, vol 46, no 2140, 9 February 1884, p 218). This was not, however, the first reference to the practical ingenuity of American farmers. A writer in the same journal had mentioned 'novelties' in American farm building design twenty years earlier (vol 20, no 992, 2 February, 1862, pp 92–3). 'Notes on silage', *Journal of the Bath and West of England Society*, 3rd ser, vol 14, pp 230–247, 1882, uses American evidence.

44. *Return of the Replies to Questions Relating to Silos and Ensilage*, Privy Council Office, 1885; *Report of the Private Ensilage Commissioners*, 1886. The contrast between the official professionalism of these papers and the casual amateurism of the Old Board of Agriculture publications in George III's time illustrates very strikingly the effects of the mid-Victorian reform of the Civil Service.

45. Haydn's *Dictionary of Dates*, 1885, p 301.

46. Rew, R. H. 'Effects and lessons of the wet summer of 1888', *Journal of the Bath and West of England Society*, 3rd ser, vol 20, 1888–9, p 150; Kersey, H. W. and Orwin, C. S. 'The comparative costs of silage and mangolds', *Journal of the Royal Agricultural Society of England*, vol 86, 1925, p 48, mentions that some of the winches for straining the wire ropes that were laid over the grass stacks of this period could still be found 'lying around the stackyard'.

47. Jenkins, H. M. 'Report on the practice of ensilage', *Journal of the Royal Agricultural Society of England*, 2nd ser, vol 20, 1884, p 232.

48. Jenkins, H. M. 'Report on the practice of ensilage', *Journal of the Royal Agricultural Society of England*, 2nd ser, vol 20, 1884, pp 126–246; *Silos for Preserving British Forage Crops*, by the sub-editor of *The Field*, 1884, which reached a third edition in the following year; Cox, H. *Silos for Preserving British Fodder Crops in a Green State*, 1885; Fry, G. *Sweet Ensilage*, 1885; Potter, T. *The Construction of Silos*, 1886; Smith, E. J. 'Grandfather's silage boom', *Farmers Weekly*, 31 December 1965, pp 44–6; Sutherland, R. M. and Haughs, M. A. *Economics of Silage Production*, North of Scotland Agricultural College, Economic Report 123, 1968, pp 5–6; McGregor, A. 'The answer to the farmer's terror', *Farmers Weekly*, 22 March 1968, pp viii–ix. The two last references mention a short-lived Silage Society. The title of the last reference is derived from an 1888 publication of this Society which claimed that silage-making could 'exorcise the farmer's terror' of losing a valuable crop when it was ready for harvesting. It was a valid argument, but premature. It was many years before technical development made this claim capable of fulfilment.

49. Everitt, W. S. *Practical Notes on Grasses and Grassgrowing in East Anglia*, 1897, p 82; Gaut, R. *History of Worcestershire Agriculture*, 1939, p 388. Long, J. *The Dairy Farm*, 1897, includes a chapter on silage, pp 35–8. A few years later another textbook, Puxley, H. L. *Modern Dairy Farming*, 1906, makes no mention of it.

50. Garnett, F. W. *Westmorland Agriculture*, 1912, p 209. An early silage pit now used as a grainstore survives on Lord Armstrong's Lower Trewhitt Farm, Northumberland (Darley, G. *The National Trust Book of the Farm*, 1981, p 103) and an 1885 covered silo on Town House Farm, Madley, Herefordshire (Brown, P. 'Up-to-the-minute covered silo, seventy-five years old', *Farmer and Stockbreeder*, 16 May 1961, p 86). The latter won first prize in a Royal Agricultural Society of England competition in 1886. ('The silo and silo stack competition, 1885–6', *Journal of the Royal Agricultural Society of England*, 2nd ser, vol 22, 1886, pp 271–5, 300, 304, which includes a description and drawing of the silo (see page 209).

51. Watson, S. J. 'The conservation of grassland herbage', *Journal of the Royal Agricultural Society of England*, vol 95, 1934, p 108; Watson, S. J. and Smith, A. M. *Silage*, 1956, pp 15–16; Franklin, J. B. *British Grasslands*, 1957, pp 161–2. Significantly, the 'reeking smell of butyric acid' was the main memory of silage-making in this period recalled by elderly Sussex farmers half a century later (Jesse, R. H. B. *A Survey of the Agriculture of Sussex*, 1960, p 125).

52. Largely but not entirely. Experiments with the Wye College silo showed a high loss in

the feeding value of the crop stored. In 1910, George Jacques, a Norfolk farmer, imported a taller type of American silo and obtained better results which helped to establish the practice in the eastern counties (Hall, A. D. 'Can silage be substituted for roots?', *Journal of the Farmers' Club*, March 1923, pp 20–1; Moore, S. *Silos and Silage*, 1950, p 11).

53. Smith, F. 'A note on the economy of silos in farm management', *Journal of the Royal Agricultural Society of England*, vol 79, 1918, pp 120–3; Oldershaw, A. W. 'Ensilage', *Journal of the Bath and West and Southern Counties Society*, 5th ser, vol 13, 1918–19, pp 54–86; Amos, A. 'Ensilage', *Journal of the Farmers' Club*, March 1923, pp 19–37; Oldershaw, A. W. 'Ensilage', *Yearbook of the Central Council of Milk Recording Societies*, 1925, pp 78–9; Watson, S. J. and Smith, A. M. *Silage*, 1956, pp 15–16; Jesse, R. H. B. *A Survey of the Agriculture of Sussex*, 1960, p 125; Mercer, W. B. *A Survey of the Agriculture of Cheshire*, 1963, p 81. Most of the steel and timber silos of this period have now disappeared but a small and decreasing number of brick and concrete towers still stand. Allison, K. J. *The East Riding of Yorkshire Landscape*, 1976, p 256, contrasts some decaying timber survivors of the inter-war years with the 'tall modern silos now to be seen everywhere'.

54. Oldershaw, A. W. 'Ensilage', *Journal of the Bath and West and Southern Counties Society*, 5th ser, vol 13, 1918–19, pp 57, 64, estimated the total number of silos in the country as rather over one hundred. There are no later figures but the increase in the next twenty years cannot have been very great.

55. Cheveley, S. W. *Grassdrying*, 1937, pp 11–16; Roberts, F. J. *Fodder Conservation*, 1939, pp 1–5.

56. Clarke, A. D. *Modern Farm Buildings*, 1899, pp 92–3.

57. Moscrop, W. J. 'On covered cattle yards', *Journal of the Royal Agricultural Society of England*, 3rd ser, vol 1, 1890, p 473.

58. Orr, J. *Agriculture in Berkshire*, 1918, p 103.

59. The condition of such yards was a common cause of complaint in this period. 'With regard to the yards where the bullocks are kept and where the straw is trampled into manure, everyone who knows a little about farming has lectured the farmers and landlords about the waste that goes on ... Those men will fare best who have the largest supplies of farmyard manure. Without exaggeration it may be said that the bullock yards where this is made and collected are absurdly arranged to serve the purpose. In most cases they seem to be constructed and situated rather as ponds or reservoirs to receive the water from quite wide catchment areas' (Orr, J. *Agriculture in Oxfordshire*, 1916, p 110). 'A few days rain ... and the open yards – nine-tenths of the yards in the eastern counties are wholly or partly uncovered – became ponds of sodden manure ... Farmers and farm workers mostly start young and get used to slipping about wet yards in six inches of mud. It is part of the regular routine' (Garratt, G. T. *Hundred Acre Farm*, 1928, pp 22–3). See also Haggard, R. *A Farmer's Year*, 1906, p 94; Russell, E. J. and Richards, E. H. 'On making and storing manure', *Journal of the Royal Agricultural Society of England*, vol 77, 1916, pp 1–36.

60. Malden, W. J. *Farm Buildings*, 1896, pp 76–80; Winder, T. *Handbook of Farm Buildings*, 1908, p 103. Clarke, A. D. *Farm Buildings*, 1899, p 107, preferred boxes to pigsties.

61. McHardy, D. N. *Modern Farm Buildings*, 1932, p 153; Gunn, E. *Farm Buildings*, 1935, pp 47–52.

62. Anyone familiar, directly or indirectly, with the older rural society will recall the almost ceremonial importance of the cottage pig in the life and conversation of the village. Flora Thompson, describing an Oxfordshire hamlet in the late Victorian and Edwardian times, referred to the lean-to pigsty at the back of each cottage. 'During its lifetime the pig was an important member of the family ... He was everybody's pride and everybody's business ... Men callers on Sunday afternoons came not to see the family, but the pig, and would lounge with its owner against the piggery door, scratching piggy's back and praising his points or turning up their noses in criticism' (*Lark Rise to Candleford*, 1948, pp 21–2). The number of cottagers' pigs, however, decreased as sanitary standards improved after the passing of the Public Health Act of 1875. The first sanitary inspector who visited Lark Rise about the turn of the century 'shook his head over the pigsties' (p 233). His successors were able to do more than shake their heads.

63. Lloyd, E. W. *Pigs and their Management*, 1950, pp 134–7.

64. Price, W. T. and Ling, W. A. *Advisory Report on Pighousing*, 1936, pp 19–24, published by Wiltshire County Council.

65. The first house of this type in this country was built in 1929 (Jackson, F.W. 'Intensive housing for pig feeding', *Pigbreeders Annual*, vol 14, 1934–5, pp 67–76). See also Stewart, W. A. 'Distinctive features of pig farming in Scandinavia', *Agriculture*, vol 38, October 1931, pp 689–93; Ministry of Agriculture and Fisheries, *Bulletin* no 32, 1931, pp 53–7 by the same author. Only a few years later there was 'probably greater agreement on the type of building suitable for fattening purposes than on any other point in pig housing. A fattening house should be built on what is generally known as the Danish or Scandinavian plan' (Rae, R.

'Systems of housing pigs', *Journal of the Royal Agricultural Society of England*, vol 97, 1936, p 132).

66. Lloyd, E. W. *Pigs and their Management*, 1950, pp 139–40.

67. *Postwar Building Studies no 17, Farm Buildings*, HMSO, 1945, pp 119–20; *The Housing of Pigs*, Bulletin 160 of the Ministry of Agriculture and Fisheries, 1953, pp 37–8.

68. Short, B. 'The art and craft of chicken cramming. Poultry in the Weald of Sussex, 1850–1950', *Agricultural History Review*, vol 30, pt 1, 1982, pp 17–30.

69. Thomas, E. *The Economics of Small Holdings*, 1927, p 57.

70. The movable pen system was first applied to the commercial housing of the egg-laying flock in 1930 (Denham, H. J. 'Notable farming enterprises, IV. A commercial experiment in poultry farming', *Journal of the Royal Agricultural Society of England*, vol 94, 1933, pp 83–4).

71. Elkington, W. M. 'Poultry in agriculture', *Journal of the Royal Agricultural Society of England*, vol 90, 1929, p 147.

72. Elkington, W. M. 'Poultry in agriculture', *Journal of the Royal Agricultural Society of England*, vol 90, 1929, pp 155–7, which includes reference to American influence; Robinson, L. *Battery Egg Production*, 1945, pp i–iii; Blount, W. P. *Hen Batteries*, 1951, pp 13–15; Short, B. 'The art and craft of chicken cramming. Poultry in the Weald of Sussex, 1850–1950', *Agricultural History Review*, vol 30, pt 1, 1982, p 26.

73. Robinson, L. *Battery Egg Production*, 1945, p 94. This book was published after the war but clearly refers to pre-war experience, since this intensive system was almost eliminated by wartime restrictions on feedstuffs.

74. Britton, D. K. and Keith, D. F. 'A note on the statistics of farm power supplies in Great Britain', *The Farm Economist*, vol 6, 1950, p 166.

75. McHardy, D. N. *Modern Farm Buildings*, 1932, p 150.

76. Dixey, R. N. 'The cost of converting buildings into cowsheds', *The Farm Economist*, vol 1, 1935, p 213.

77. Pidgeon, D. 'Report on miscellaneous implements at Newcastle', *Journal of the Royal Agricultural Society of England*, 2nd ser, vol 24, 1888, p 210–12, including a reference to the 'enormous sales' of gas engines on p 210; Pidgeon, D. 'Oil-engines in relation to agriculture', *Journal of the Royal Agricultural Society of England*, 3rd ser, vol 3, 1893, p 153; Malden, W. J. *Farm Buildings*, 1896, p 158. By the turn of the century the oil engine was 'rapidly taking the place of the steam-engine as a provider of motive power in the homestead' (Henderson, S. *The Modern Farmstead*, 1902, p 251). See also Scott Watson, J. A. S. *History of the Royal Agricultural Society of England*, 1939, p 100; Wiliam, E. *Traditional Farm Buildings in North-East Wales, 1550–1900*, 1982, p 153. A horse engine was replaced by a petrol engine on a Staffordshire farm as early as 1890 (Peters, J. E. C. *The Development of Farm Buildings in Western Lowland Staffordshire up to 1880*, 1962, p 105).

78. 'The success of the oil engine has been phenomenal – more so even than the gas engine' (MacDonald, J. ed, *Stephens' Book of the Farm*, 5th ed, 1908, vol 1, p 429).

79. Britton, D. K. and Keith, D. F. 'A note on the statistics of farm power supplies in Great Britain', *The Farm Economist*, vol 6, 1950, p 166. For static engines in this period see Hope, H. 'Bring out your old engines', *Farmers Weekly*, 11 June 1976, p v; Edginton, D. *Old Stationary Engines*, 1980; Bird, M. 'There's life in the old engine yet', *Farmers Weekly*, 5 October 1979, pp xv–xix. See also the monthly journal, *The Stationary Engine*, published by D. Edginton, Lodge Wood Farm, Hawkeridge, Westbury, Wilts.

80. Beauchamp, J. W. and Winder, T. *Handbook of Farm Buildings*, 1908, pp 155–71; McDonald, J. ed. *Stephens' Book of the Farm*, 5th ed, 1908, vol 1, pp 431–2.

81. For its use in advanced farming see Matthews, R. B. *Electro-farming*, 1928; see also Weller, J. *History of the Farmstead*, 1982, pp 169–70.

82. Wright, S. J. 'Farm implements and machinery', *Journal of the Royal Agricultural Society of England*, vol 96, 1935, p 243.

83. Pawson, H. C. *A Survey of the Agriculture of Northumberland*, 1961, p 37.

84. Wright, S. J. 'Farm implements and machinery', *Journal of the Royal Agricultural Society of England*, vol 97, 1936, pp 229–32.

85. Whitehead, C. 'Fifty years of hop farming', *Journal of the Royal Agricultural Society of England*, 3rd ser, vol 1, 1890, pp 336–7; Burgess, A. H. *Hops*, 1964, pp 11, 13, 16, 205–11; Burgess, A. H. 'Hopdrying', *Agriculture*, vol 46, 1939, pp 524–31; Cronk, A. 'Oasts in Kent and East Sussex' *Archaeologia Cantiana*, vol 95, 1978, pp 241–54; Cox, A. and Gallagher, P. 'A small oast house', *Traditional Kent Buildings*, no 3, 1983, pp 24–25, published by Kent County Council.

86. 'Clay lump', a traditional material in stoneless East Anglia was 'rarely used' in Norfolk by the turn of the century and last used in Suffolk in 1921 (Haggard, R. *A Farmer's Year*, 1906, p 263; Trist, P. J. O. *A Survey of the Agriculture of Suffolk*, 1971, p 66). By 1920 cobwalling in Devon 'had been discontinued for some years and was only remembered by the older generation' (Laycock, C. H. 'The old Devon farmstead', *Report and Transactions of the*

*Devonshire Association*, vol 52, 1920, p 172). Between the wars Geoffrey Garratt in Cambridgeshire followed local custom by bottoming his yards with another traditional local material, 'clunch', or hard chalk from the nearby hills, but without great success: 'it can be had from the village pit for nothing, but like most things which cost nothing, it is worth little more' (Garratt, G. T. *Hundred Acre Farm*, 1928, p xi). Appropriately, his words contain what is probably the last current reference to the 'village pit' on which so many generations had relied for some of their basic building materials. Grigson refers to the use of sarsen stone in a new farm building in Wiltshire as late as 1923, but in the parish he describes with such perceptive detail this stone had not been used within living memory (Grigson, G. *An English Farmhouse*, 1948, p 42). Curtis, C. E. *Farm Buildings*, 1912, pp 23, 85, gave the cost of thatch for the sake of completeness, though it was 'practically unused' Ling (heather) thatch was last used in this period (Hartley, M. and Ingilby, J. 'Roofs gathered from nature', *Country Life*, 13 April, 1978, pp 1022–4; Wiliam, E. *Traditional Farm Buildings in North-East Wales, 1550–1900*, 1982, pp 95, 239, 267. See also Walton, J. *Homesteads of the Yorkshire Dales*, 1979, p 53). Some surviving examples of 'bundle thatch' which are not 'earlier than the nineteenth century' may date from this period (Smedley, N. *Life and Tradition in Suffolk and North-East Essex*, 1976, p 20; Peters, J. E. C. 'The solid thatch roof', *Vernacular Architecture*, vol 8, 1977, p 825; Council for British Archaeology, Group 9, *Newsletter 12*, 1982, pp 107–8, for date estimate). Most textbooks of the period dismissed home-grown softwood as inferior and assumed that imported softwood would be used except for such rough work as homemade Dutch barns (Henderson, R. *The Modern Homestead*, 1902, pp 43, 359; Winder, T. *Handbook of Farm Buildings*, 1908, p 131; Lawrence, C. P. *Economic Farm Buildings*, 1919, pp 51–85; McHardy, D. N. *Modern Farm Buildings*, 1932, p 55). See also critical comment on native timber in McConnell, P. 'Experiences of a Scotsman on the Essex clays', *Journal of the Royal Agricultural Society of England*, 3rd ser, vol 2, 1891, p 312. The use of secondhand materials, however, continued; for example, a Welsh estate in the 1890s systematically demolished old buildings to provide materials for new ones (Wiliam, E. *Traditional Farm Buildings in North-East Wales, 1550–1900*, 1982, p 30).

87. Smith, P. *Houses of the Welsh Countryside*, 1974, p. 324.
88. Clarke, A. D. *Modern Farm Buildings*, 1899, p 176.
89. Garratt, G. T. *Hundred Acre Farm*, 1928, p xi.
90. Orwin, C. S. 'An investigation into the value of ferro or reinforced concrete for farm and estate purposes', *Journal of the Royal Agricultural Society of England*, vol 72, 1911, pp 122–39. There was no future in the crude do-it-yourself reinforced concrete described by a contemporary (Owen, T. 'Buildings in ferro-concrete', *Journal of the Land Agents Society*, vol 9, 1910, pp 58–61).
91. A query early in the century on the possible use of concrete blocks received an unenthusiastic answer (*Journal of the Land Agents Society*, vol 3, 1904, pp 38, 101). Lakeman, A. *Concrete Cottages, Small Garages and Farm Buildings*, 1918, described farm buildings with walls of concrete blocks, but their use at this time was clearly exceptional. Bennett, J. H. 'Practical characteristics of some new building materials and plant', *Journal of the Land Agents Society*, vol 24, 1925, pp 665–9, described only mass concrete systems.
92. Hall, C. P. 'The construction and arrangement of farm buildings', *Journal of the Royal Agricultural Society of England*, 3rd ser, vol 7, 1896, p 781; Smith, H. H. *The Principles of Landed Estate Management*, 1898, pp 92–3; Douglas, L. M. 'Swine husbandry', *Journal of the Farmers' Club*, January 1911, p 14; Curtis, C. E. *Farm Buildings*, 1912, pp 86–7; McHardy, D. N. *Modern Farm Buildings*, 1932, p 53. The life of this material could be prolonged by painting it. Few farmers, however, bothered to do so. They had no money to spare for jobs of this kind and in any case practical men doubted if such maintenance was economic – it was cheaper to let the sheeting rust away (Taylor, S. *Modern Homesteads*, 1905, p 49; Lawrence, C. P. *Economic Farm Buildings*, 1919, p 118).
93. McHardy, D. N. *Modern Farm Buildings*, 1932, p 51. As early as 1927 the *Architect's Journal* warned its readers that 'architects must not even jib at the use of asbestos-cement roofing, which offers many advantages for such structures as cowhouses' (vol 65, p 469).
94. Colam, R. 'Pighousing', *Agriculture*, vol 45, September 1938, p 553, assumed without comment that this type of roofing would be used. Dixey, R. N. 'The cost of erecting cowhouses', *The Farm Economist*, vol 1, 1935, pp 197–9, assumed buildings of concrete or brick with asbestos-cement or corrugated iron roofs. The order of the roofing materials is significant.
95. In Leicestershire in the 1950s two surviving cruck barns were measured and described. One was roofed with corrugated iron sheeting, one with asbestos cement sheeting (Webster, V. R. 'Cruck-framed buildings in Leicestershire', *Transactions of the Leicestershire Archaeological Society*, vol 30, 1954, p 55).
96. Jenkins, H. M. 'Report on the practice of ensilage', *Journal of the Royal Agricultural Society of England*, 2nd ser, vol 20, 1884, p 207; Scott, J. *Farmbuildings*, 1884, p 43.

97. Many Dutch barns were built from the 1880s onwards by landowners to encourage the change from corn production to mixed farming and 'to combat the depression that they found on smaller farms' (Peters, J. E. C. *The Development of Farm Buildings in Western Lowland Staffordshire up to 1880*, 1969, p 95; Mingay, G. E. ed, *The Victorian Countryside*, 1981, vol 2, p 434). There are numerous references to Dutch barns in the reports of the farm prize competition in the *Journal of the Royal Agricultural Society* in the earlier years of this period, for example, 2nd ser, vol 21, 1885, pp 555, 561–3, 568; 3rd ser, vol 1, 1890, p 781; 3rd ser, vol 2, 1891, pp 554, 574. 'Mr Little's report on the western and southern counties', *Journal of the Bath and West of England Society*, 3rd ser, vol 14, 1882, p 84, recommended greater use of Dutch barns, and Clarke, A. D. *Farm Buildings*, 1899, p 125, described them as 'increasing in popularity'. Some of these late Victorian Dutch barns were farm-made, but others were purchased prefabricated. 'Haybarns constructed entirely of iron are now very plentiful' (Stephens, H. *The Book of the Farm*, 1889, p 442). See also Wiliam, E. *Traditional Farm Buildings in North-East Wales, 1550–1900*, 1982, pp 154–5.

98. Winder, T. *Handbook of Farm Buildings*, 1908, p 131; Lawrence, C. P. *Economic Farm Buildings*, 1919, p vi; McHardy, D. N. *Modern Farm Buildings*, 1932, p 161.

99. McHardy, D. N. *Modern Farm Buildings*, 1932, p 161.

100. In 1893 a textbook followed tradition by stating that, in the choice of a site for farm buildings, 'the first thing to be done . . . is to ascertain where water is most conveniently obtainable', but added that a hydraulic ram or 'other mechanical method' could be used to obtain it (Youatt, W. *The Complete Grazier*, Fream, W. ed, 1893, p 659). The first textbook reference to the water mains which enabled farm buildings to be sited independently of springs or streams appeared in 1908 (Winder, T. *Handbook of Farm Buildings*, p 5), but the general value of local water supplies continued. When the Hendersons in 1924 surveyed the Oxfordshire farm they were later to make famous, they noted among its assets 'a fine spring of water which supplied every field' (Henderson, G. *The Farming Ladder*, 1956, p 15). Shortly after the end of this period, a survey found that only just over a third of the farmsteads in England and Wales had a piped water supply and a quarter depended on wells. The remainder relied on roof water, streams, etc and, in some cases, on neighbours (*National Farm Survey of England and Wales, 1941–3*, HMSO, 1946, p 61).

101. Peters, J. E. C. *The Development of Farm Buildings in Western Lowland Staffordshire up to 1880*, 1969, pp 69, 98; Peters, J. E. C. at the Vernacular Architecture Group meeting December 1977 referred to a barn of this type built at Mendlesham, Suffolk, as late as 1894.

102. Brunskill, R. W. *The Vernacular Architecture of the Lake Counties*, 1974, p 86, for bank barn; Durham County Council Library Local History Publications, *Rural Durham*, 1977, pp 45–7, refers to byrehouses still in use in 1925.

103. In Nottinghamshire as late as the 1880s pigeons played 'a quite appreciable part in the economy of most farms' and manure from their cotes made 'quite an important addition to the general supply' (Cooke, T. S. 'Report on prize competition in Nottinghamshire and Lincolnshire', *Journal of the Royal Agricultural Society of England*, 2nd ser, vol 24, 1888, p 534). For the re-use of abandoned pigeoncotes for non-farm purposes see *Country Life*, 1 November 1956, p 57; Taylor, C. *The Cambridgeshire Landscape*, 1933, p 172, plate 12.

104. For farm butter and cheese see p 172. In the earlier years of this period, the traditional circular horse-driven cider mills were gradually replaced by power-driven mills (Radcliffe Cooke, C. W. *A Book about Cider and Perry*, 1898, pp 39–40; Barker, T. P. 'Cider and cider making fifty years ago', in *Science and Fruit*, Wallace T. and Marsh, R. W. ed, Bristol University, 1953, p 36–7). In the later years cider ceased to be made on farms. By the time of the Second World War about 1,000 farms were still making cider for sale, but they were the last of their line. 'Prior to the present century, most of the cider in this country was made on the farm from fruit grown in the farm orchard . . . A complete change has occurred within the last fifty years . . . Production has to a great extent been transferred from the farm to the factory' (Barker, B. T. P. 'Cider Apple Production', *Ministry of Agriculture and Fisheries Bulletin* 104, 1937, p 2). For methods and equipment in the last age of farm cider-making see Harper, J. 'Cidermaking', *Journal of the Bath and West and Southern Counties Society*, 4th ser, vol 4, 1893–4, pp 82–98.

105. A Welsh farmstead rebuilt in 1896 with a barn where feed-preparation machinery was driven by a portable steam engine may have been the last example of its type (Wiliam, E. *Traditional Farm Buildings in North-East Wales, 1550–1900*, 1982, p 153). For the last age of waterpower see Reynolds, J. *The Hampshire Barn*, unpublished thesis, Architectural Association, 1978, p 26, and personal communication, which refers to the replacement in 1888 of an old farm waterwheel by a new wheel which originally drove a threshing machine but was later converted to generate electricity and continued in use possibly up to the Second World War; Warren, D. W. 'Chedgey's Foundry, Watchet', *Journal of the Somerset Industrial Archaeology Society*, vol 3, 1981, pp 6–9; Pitkin, M. *The Farm Wheel and Machinery at Temple Balsall*, unpublished thesis, Birmingham School of Architecture, 1982,

describing a mid-Victorian waterwheel installation which drove a threshing machine and a range of other machinery and continued in service until 1945–6; Wiliam, E. *Traditional Farm Buildings in North-East Wales, 1550–1900*, 1982, pp 129, 149–51, which includes Pelton wheels. In 1981–2 the Southampton University Industrial Archaeology Group excavated a farm waterwheel site at Brownwich Farm, near Titchfield, Hampshire. This installation was built about 1880 and continued in service until shortly before the Second World War. It was powered from a pond which had once been a monastic fishpond (personal communication, Dr Edwin Course, Southampton University, 1983). See also p 155 and Scott, J. *The Complete Textbook of Farm Engineering*, 2nd ed, 191–, pt 5, p 12.

106. There is no systematic evidence of changes in the number and function of estate yards in this period. This statement, therefore, is mainly based on general probability and casual observation. Woodforde, J. *Bricks to Build a House*, 1976, pp 164, 168, notes that 'several landed proprietors had their own brickyards until well into the twentieth century', and that Ashburnham Estate brickyard in Sussex would have closed in the 1920s but for the interest of the owner in commercial brickmaking for the general market. One of the Holkham estate brickyards was closed in the 1870s, the other in the 1930s (Wade-Martins, S. *A Great Estate at Work*, 1980, pp 83–4). The remains of an estate brickyard which apparently closed about 1930 can be seen at Angle in Pembrokeshire.

107. Wiliam, E. *Traditional Farm Buildings in North-East Wales, 1550–1900*, 1982, p 176.

108. Malden, W. J. *Farm Buildings*, 1896, p 16; Henderson, R. *The Modern Farmstead*, 1902, p 227; Walton, J. 'South Pennine barn buildings', *Architectural Review*, vol 90, October 1941, p 124; Hartley, M. and Ingilby, J. *Life in the Moorlands of North-East Yorkshire*, 1972, p 65, plate 113; Devon County Council, *Devon's Traditional Buildings*, 1978, p 22–3; Wiliam, E. *Traditional Farm Buildings in North-East Wales, 1550–1900*, 1982, p 104, which includes the astonishing survival into the 1880s on a smallholding of threshing by beating corn against a wall or a stone.

109. Textbooks (Henderson, R. *The Modern Homestead*, 1902, p 226; McDonald, J. ed, *Stephens' Book of the Farm*, 5th ed, 1908, vol 1, plates 1 and 2; vol 2, pp 221–2; Scott, J. *The Complete Textbook of Farm Engineering*, 2nd ed, 191–, pt 5, p 63, continued to include sections of horsegear, partly for the sake of completeness, but also because it was still in use For survivals of such installations in this period see Laycock, C. H. 'The old Devon farmstead', *Report and Transactions of the Devonshire Association*, vol 52, 1920, p 165; Laycock, C. H. 'The roundhouse or machine house', *Devon and Cornwall Notes and Queries*, vol 11, 1920, p 287; Peters, J. E. C. *The Development of Farm Buildings in Western Lowland Staffordshire up to 1880*, 1969, p 103; *Country Life*, 12 March 1970, p 640; *Country Life*, 7 May 1970, p 1085; Hellen, A. 'Some provisional notes on wheelhouses and their distribution in Northumberland', *Journal of the Geographical Society of the University of Newcastle upon Tyne*, vol 18, 1970, p 21; Hellen, A. 'Agrarian history unobserved', *Country Life*, 11 November 1971, p 1325; Hartley, M. and Ingilby, J. *Life in the Moorlands of North-East Yorkshire*, 1972, p 70, plate 117; Devon County Council, *Devon's Traditional Buildings*, 1978, pp 22–3; Cook, O. and Smith, E. *English Cottages and Farmhouses*, 1982, p 180; Wiliam, E. *Traditional Farm Buildings in North-East Wales, 1550–1900*, 1982, p 153. In certain northern areas such outfits survived till the 1930s when some were converted to tractor power or electric drive without passing through the steampower stage (Pawson, H. C. *A Survey of the Agriculture of Northumberland*, 1961, p 37; Brunskill, R. W. *Design and Layout of Farmsteads in parts of Cumberland and Westmorland*, Royal Institute of British Architects, Neale Bursary 1963, Manchester 1965, sec. 8). In 1967 it was still possible to meet a Northumberland farmer who, as a young man, had trained horses for driving threshing machines. He remembered particularly the ease with which they learned to step over the revolving shaft on the floor that carried the power to the machine in the barn (personal experience). A reference in financial accounts of 1899 to 'making and fixing horse gear on Washford Farm' (Warren, D. W. 'Chedgey's Foundry, Watchet', *Journal of the Somerset Industrial Archaeological Society*, vol 3, 1981, p 9) probably refers to repair work, but could conceivably refer to a very late example of a new installation.

110. For the memories of a farm worker who worked the pump of a liquid manure installation between 1915 and 1926, see *Farmers Weekly*, 28 August 1981, p 98. See also *Journal of the Land Agents Society*, vol 42, 1943, pp 156–8, 178.

111. See pp 202–3.

112. In 1896 the report of a Royal Commission on rural conditions in Wales included descriptions of various longhouses still in use. But their number was falling rapidly, largely because of the requirements of sanitary legislation (Peate, I. C. *The Welsh House*, 1944, pp 60, 66, 73). The tradition, however, died hard and longhouses inhabited by cattle and families survived well into the twentieth century (see p 256).

113. Scott, J. *Farm Buildings*, 1884, pp 116–17; Malden, W. J. *Farm Buildings*, 1896, p 36. The first reference to a fertiliser store dates from 1850 (see p 144), but this was

exceptional. It was not until the later nineteenth century that the use of fertiliser became common practice.

114. Clarke, A. D. *Modern Farm Buildings*, 1889, pp 45–6; Lawrence, C. P. *Economic Farm Buildings*, 1919, p 53; Gunn, E. *Farm Buildings*, 1935, pp 11, 40–1.

115. McHardy, D. N. *Modern Farm Buildings*, 1932, pp 172–3.

116. Throughout this period most farmers continued to do such office work as was necessary at a desk in the living room or on the kitchen table, using the clock on the mantelpiece as a convenient filing place. But the amount of office work judged necessary was increasing. Early in the period, textbooks recommended farm offices for accounts. These, however, were no more than desks in a small general-purpose storeroom (Malden, W. J. *Farm Buildings*, 1896, p 39; Clarke, A. D. *Modern Farm Buildings*, 1899, p 17). A generation later, the control of the purchase and issue of concentrate feed on a large and advanced Cotswold farm required its own system of invoices and disposal sheets (Skilbeck, D. 'Notable farming enterprises, Mr Webster Cory's farms', *Journal of the Royal Agricultural Society of England*, vol 93, 1932, p 149).

117. Curtis, C. E. *Farm Buildings*, 1912, pp 25–6.

118. In *Practical Farming*, 1906, which was intended as a manual for trainee land agents, E. T. Shepherd condemned 'the practice of erecting buildings only for use for a single purpose . . . as the stability of any section (of present day agriculture) is extremely doubtful . . . Every building should, as far as possible, be so constructed as to be easily convertible to some other use than that for which it was originally intended' (pp 125, 138). 'It used to be said that the mark of a good landlord was the erection of enduring rather than "jerry" buildings, but an intelligent writer like Miss Jebb has seriously contended that the permanent character of buildings is a drawback because it offers obstacles to speedy change dictated by an alteration in the methods of farming, and that buildings should be such that they could be readily "scrapped" ' (personal communication from L. L. Price quoted in Orr, J. *Agriculture in Oxfordshire*, 1916, p 149). A generation later a reference to the importance of 'free adaptability to possible future uses' as a factor in farm building design in Gunn, E. *Farm Buildings*, 1935, p 59, suggests that by this time this was accepted doctrine.

# 9 REVIVAL AND DEVELOPMENT: 1939–60

## The Farming Revolution

In the first decade of this period, the pressure of overseas competition was abruptly replaced by desperate domestic need. War restored and peace continued the ancient challenge of hunger which two generations of Englishmen had all but forgotten. In response, farming revived, expanded, developed, repaying drastically increased investment by drastically increased production. In the second, the old competitive order gradually re-established itself in modified form and the recreated farming system adapted itself to the changing economic times. But there was no return to pre-war conditions. Farming remained a prosperous, progressive and intensive industry.

Indeed, intensification was the dominant theme of these years. The total agricultural acreage changed little, for the reclamation of such minor areas of the waste as survived was counterbalanced by the loss of farmland to the builder and engineer. But production increased steadily and by the end of the period it was some 60 per cent above the pre-war level.

One reason for this striking achievement was the conversion to ploughland of huge areas of less demanding, less productive permanent pasture. Another was the increase in all types of livestock and the adoption of more specialised systems of management. Throughout the post-war years, the number of farms carrying dairy cattle, pigs and poultry fell and the average size of herd or flock rose. But behind them was another reason on which in large measure their success depended. This was a rapid and pervading technical revolution, using new knowledge, new methods and new equipment. The farmer employed fewer men and ceased to use the horse as a source of power; but he spent a growing proportion of his resources on technical aids from the factory, from the laboratory and from the warehouse. The rise in production per acre, per beast and per man testified to their efficiency.

Nevertheless, none of this changed the basic character of the farming system. In the years after the war, as in the years before it, the farmer earned three-quarters of his income from his cattle, pigs, sheep, and poultry, only a quarter from the sale of his arable crops.

207

Most of what was grown on the farm continued to reach the consumer as milk or meat. British agriculture remained essentially a livestock industry.

## New Needs, Old Farmsteads

Once more, therefore, old farmsteads faced new needs. The farmer wanted to store and process more crops, house more stock and protect more machinery and materials from the weather. Moreover, he wanted to do many of those things in new ways and with new equipment. But the buildings he had inherited from the past could not cope with the demands he now made on them. There were not enough of them, there were too many bad ones, and there were too many of the wrong kind.

The extent of this deficiency was only partly shown by an official survey undertaken during the war. This found that the buildings of no more than 39 per cent of English and Welsh holdings which were equipped with buildings could be classed as satisfactory. Of the remainder, 49 per cent were classed as fair and 12 per cent as bad.[1] These figures, however, referred only to the structural condition of the buildings, not to their agricultural value, and some which needed little repair were obsolete or otherwise unsuitable for the needs of the farm. Furthermore, of course, the survey was only concerned with the buildings that were there. It was not concerned with the buildings that should have been there, and therefore took no account of the inadequacy of existing steadings for contemporary needs. On this evidence, well below a third of British farms were at the time satisfactorily equipped with buildings.

So the nation faced in wartime the problem which Henry Williamson had faced in peacetime when he prepared his inventory of the buildings on the semi-derelict arable farm in Norfolk he planned to restore. 'Most of the walls were undermined by rat-runs . . . The corn barn needed a buttress, the wall was cracked and leaning outwards . . . Many of the rafters of the cartshed were rotten . . . The roof of the granary . . . was broken in one place and three or four yards of the floor were sodden . . . There were no drains to the yards, stable or cowhouses . . .'[2] This was a fairly extreme case, for in the slump the corn areas had suffered worse than the livestock areas, but the difference was merely one of degree. Over all the country the same generality held. The occasional survival of longhouses inhabited by cattle as well as families,[3] of horse-driven or water-driven barn machinery and even flail threshing[4] provided picturesque support for the more sombre and extensive evidence which Hanoverian barns and Victorian stables provided on the extent to which obsolete equipment

Plate 29   A relic of the old order; a Devonshire ash house. The local stone of which it is built contrasts with the factory-made concrete blocks of the wall that joins it (see page 77) (*Nigel Harvey*)

Plate 30   A relic of the new order; a silo built by a pioneering Herefordshire farmer in 1885 (see page 200) (*The Hereford Times*)

Plate 31 'Down corn, Up horn.' This barn was built, probably in the later eighteenth century, to serve the needs of the corn-harvest. When milk was more profitable than corn in the years between the wars, it was converted to a cowhouse. Note the contrast between the original local timber, and the concrete and factory-made steel fittings of the twentieth century (*Farmers Weekly*)

Plate 32 Post-war mechanisation. A graindrier stands in a barn where flailers once worked, a tractor fuel store stands outside it (*Farmers Weekly*)

continued in commercial use. The effects of such survivals were obvious. By depriving the farmer's central workshop of maintenance and modernisation, the depression had limited the efficiency and intensity of agricultural development and left a bitter and restricting legacy to the next age.

### Improvement, not Reconstruction

Yet it was some time before the farming industry could even consider any general modernisation. In the 1940s, immediate needs were too pressing, available resources too few, to allow more than first-aid and the most urgent of minor improvements to the farmstead. In any case, expenditure of money and materials was rigidly controlled by the government. In the immediate post-war period, therefore, the general condition of farm buildings was little better than in pre-war years. For example, grain, feedstuffs and fertilisers are peculiary liable to damage by damp. Yet in 1948 a survey of Exmoor, one of the most exposed areas in southern England, found that only half of the farms studied had enough dry storage space to accommodate them.[5] Again, cleanliness and convenience are the two chief needs of the cowhouse. Yet in 1951 a survey of 2,500 representative dairy steadings showed that only two-thirds of them had piped water and only half had electric light.[6] Then, too, a survey in the late 1940s of buildings in four milk-producing areas in England and Wales classified over 45 per cent of cowhouses as 'old', 40 per cent as 'modernised' and less than 15 per cent as 'modern', while nearly 15 per cent of farms had no dairies.[7] In 1947 Robertson Scott specifically excluded farm buildings from his list of rural improvements in the previous quarter of a century. 'It stares every motorist, cyclist and walker in the face,' he wrote, that 'most of the farm buildings of Great Britain are unequal to playing their part in an up-to-date agriculture.'[8]

In the happier 1950s, conditions were more favourable. Building restrictions ended, farming was prosperous and agricultural development had made obvious the cost to the industry of inefficient buildings. Indeed, on many farms the inadequacy of the farmsteads had become the main limiting factor to increased production or profits. Throughout this decade, therefore, investment in farm buildings increased and a steady flow of advisory publications reflected the growing need for technical guidance.[9] Few new farmsteads were built, for the days of substantial reclamation were past and it was seldom practicable to demolish even the most dilapidated of farmsteads and start all over again. But there was a general modernisation of existing farmsteads. At first this commonly took the form of minor or particular improvements, such as the erection of a Dutch barn, the gutting and re-equipment of a cowhouse and the addition of a dairy to serve it, the conversion of a stable to a milking parlour and bullock yards to dairy yards, or the installation of a grain-drying and storage plant in an old barn.[10] Towards the end of the period, however, when building restrictions were a mere memory and the speed and pressures of technological change were increasing, remodelling became more thorough and systematic. There was more demolition, more new buildings, less piecemeal adaptation. Even so, these years saw little comprehensive reconstruction and the familiar juxtaposition of new and old, good and bad, contemporary, traditional and frankly historical buildings continued. But the increasing proportion of new work was obvious to the most casual visitor to the countryside.

It was equally obvious in the statistics. A survey at the end of the period showed that the average farmstead, that characterless but informative abstraction, contained 2.5 buildings built since 1945, 2.4 built between 1918 and 1945 and 6.0 built before 1914.[11] In only fifteen years, half of them years of scarcity and restriction, the national stock of farm buildings was increased by over a quarter. The resultant improvement in efficiency cannot be measured but was probably at least as great. It was a remarkable achievement.

## New Knowledge

Physically, of course, this achievement was based on the traditional resources of the farming industry. But technically it owed much to the industry's use of new information from new sources, above all information from the expanding research services.

Traditionally, farm buildings had been designed by practical men for practical men on the basis of practical experience. Experimental evidence played little part in their decision, and deviations from this sternly empirical approach were few and inconspicuous. But in these years, for the first time, the conclusions of the research worker became an accepted factor in the design of most types of farm building. The farmer and his technical allies began to depend increasingly for knowledge and ideas on the growing mass of reports from a growing number of research centres on the needs of stock, on the properties of materials, on types of equipment, on methods of organising and housing the varied activities of the farmstead.

Some of these reports came from the industrial research services. In particular, the farm shared in the benefits of general research into building methods and materials. But the majority came from specifically agricultural centres. A number were directly concerned with the performance of selected types of farm building. But most of them were concerned with the processes around which farm buildings were designed, providing in increasing volume and with increasing precision data on the agricultural problems for which the designer sought structural solutions. He still needed his old skills, his old practical understanding. But he added a new and valuable type of evidence to his stock-in-trade. Once again, the technical literature illustrates the change. In 1945 it was still possible to compile a textbook by collating the views and experience of practical men. But the official committee which produced it lamented the lack of knowledge on such subjects as the health and comfort of livestock and urged research into farm buildings problems. The plea was heard. The next major textbook, published twenty years later, was largely based on the research findings of the intervening period.[12]

This was in itself a considerable revolution, but it was also part of a larger revolution which ended the insularity of farm buildings development in this country. For until this time the influence of foreign research and experience had been minimal. Now, however, many of the research reports which offered the British farmer directly or indirectly relevant information and advice came from the Continent, from Australia and New Zealand, above all from the USA. And with them came a mass of less academic accounts of the practices and ideas of farmers elsewhere, frequently collected and made available to the home farmer by the wandering agricultural scholars who in this period began to earn themselves a place in agricultural history.[13] The British farmer was now a beneficiary of an unco-ordinated but effective international information service. The appearance in this country of the loose-housing system incorporating American experience, of the herring-bone parlour originally developed in New Zealand, of slatted-floor yards based on Norwegian practice and broiler houses designed with the aid of data from American experimentation illustrated the use he made of this new resource. So did the introduction of industrial-type work study, largely as a result of American experience, as an aid to the planning of farmstead operations and therefore of farm buildings.[14]

The British farmer and his commercial allies, however, were no mere passive recipients of other people's ideas. The landlord of rented acres, necessarily concerned with the possible needs of future tenants, tended to prefer proven systems and types of building that would be efficient for present purposes but adaptable to future uses. The owner-occupier, however, who in this period increased his share of the national farmland from a third to a half,[15] could afford to try more specialised systems and indulge his own particular views and hopes. With the aid of the builder and the engineer, he experimented with the new ideas, adapted them to his particular needs and produced others of his own. He also pioneered untried systems and evolved variations of methods developed for different circumstances in different countries. The full technical history of this highly active period, which added a dozen new processes and a score of new types of buildings to the farmstead, has yet to be written. But the available evidence suggests the emergence in these years of a general pattern of innovation and development.

A new idea appeared, derived perhaps from research, perhaps from overseas practice, perhaps from the brain of some thoughtful farmer; research workers studied it, enterprising farmers and manufacturers applied it with various modifications; and, finally, with the aid of continuing research, it established itself in common practice. So the final process and the buildings which housed it came as the result of a number of efforts by a number of individuals and groups.[16]

In theory, it was possible to picture the creation of a new type of farm building in terms of an assembly-line along which scientists provided the basic data on the process to be housed, engineers and builders designed equipment to serve it and structures to house it, and field investigators surveyed its performance under farm conditions, each group making their particular contribution while the farmer waited patiently for the finished product. In practice, farmer and manufacturer between them simplified the process considerably. They welcomed research, but did not wait for it. They applied what they knew when they could and the field investigator was commonly studying buildings erected long before final or perhaps even interim research findings had been published. The farmer, particularly the 'mad farmer' so rightly admired by Stapledon, and the manufacturer were necessary partners of the research worker in the business of farm buildings development.

## Official Support

Another partner in the process was less obvious, less personal. This was the government, which financed most of the relevant research work undertaken in Great Britain. But it also aided the revival of farm buildings in more direct fashion. At first, official assistance was confined to technical information and advice. The issue in 1945 of a monumental textbook on farm buildings prepared by the Ministry of Agriculture and Fisheries[17] was followed a year later by the inclusion in the new official extension services of a number of general and specialist officials whose job was the provision of technical information on farm buildings problems and advice on its application under particular circumstances.[18] Later, the government turned financier as well as adviser, notably by providing grants towards the capital cost of most types of farm building under the Farm

214

Improvement Scheme which came into operation in 1957. By the end of this period, the official leaflet behind the clock on the farmhouse mantelpiece, the cars parked beside the village hall where the local advisory official was holding a meeting on the design of piggeries or the choice of building materials, and the new grant-aided building in the farmstead were rural commonplace. 'The man from the Ministry' had taken his place among the farmer's allies.

## The Problem of Communication

The growing mass of information on farm building design and construction helped to solve many problems. But it also created a new one. Those who advised the farmer on his buildings, which included as the years passed a growing number of private and commercial advisers as well as Ministry officials, found increasing difficulty in keeping themselves adequately informed on current developments.

For gradually the increasing volume of publications surpassed the individual's reading capacity and the task became too great for even the specialist adviser. There was too much to read and it was too scattered in too many journals. In the early post-war period the number of research publications affecting farm building design and construction was small. But the rate of increase was rapid. By 1955, they were appearing at the rate of 180 a year, by 1960 at the rate of over 400 a year.[19] No figures are available for general or advisory publications or for trade literature, but the increase here was probably at least proportional. Of course, only a fraction of this mass of documentation was immediately relevant, but the amount which a properly informed adviser could reasonably be expected to scan for points of interest was considerable. The gap between existing knowledge and general practice was, of course, an old one. But hitherto it had been the landowner or farmer who for various reasons failed to make the best use of available information. Now it was the adviser who could not keep fully abreast of publications and possibilities.

This difficulty was increased by professional fragmentation. Before the war, the land agent and his estate staff or the local builder had met most of the farmer's building needs. But in the post-war years, as the volume and complexity of farm building work increased, they were joined by architects, surveyors, engineers, manufacturers of components and equipment, general agriculturists, anybody with the necessary interest and experience, some working as full-time specialists, most spending only part of their time on farm-building problems. Such men shared a common trade, but they did not share a common profession or a common information service.[20] Various efforts were made to meet the demand thus created. In 1949 the oldest continuing agricultural textbook, *Fream's Elements of Agriculture*, included for the first time a section on farm buildings; in 1956 the first association of those concerned with farm buildings was formed; and throughout this period a growing number of conferences, demonstrations and publications strove to popularise the information developed by research and practice.[21] Success was considerable but inadequate. The problem of communication was one of the legacies left by this generation to the next.[22]

## Mechanisation

Research and advisory services were new factors in farm buildings design. So was mechanisation in the forms it now took. In this period, the mechanisation of field work was complete. This meant larger and more complex equipment and therefore bigger and better implement sheds, sometimes including an enclosed bay for housing the tractor. It also meant more farm workshops, ranging from a workbench and a few pieces of equipment in the tractor shed on small farms to a separate building complete with inspection pit and overhead joist for lifting tackle on large ones.[23] These needs could often be met by the adaptation of existing buildings, notably and appropriately disused stables, but the new need for storage for tractor fuel required a more obtrusive type of installation. By the end of this period British farms were using over a million tons of liquid fuel annually, most of it in tractors, and the greasy black tanks on piers which commonly stood by the side of the roadway on large farms reminded visitors that they were entering the premises of an increasingly industrialised enterprise.[24]

The mechanisation of work in the buildings was less comprehensive but its effects on the farmstead were considerably greater. Of course, mechanical power was no stranger there. But in these years it increased so dramatically in scale and scope that it began to dominate the buildings it had once served. Economically, this reflected the growing pressures of familiar trends, rising wages, a declining labour force, and the increasing importance of farmstead processes, particularly livestock processes, in the farming system. Technically, however, it reflected a new development, the coming of cheap and convenient electric power which first reinforced and then in part replaced the internal-combustion engine.

The scope of this change is shown in the figures. Between 1939 and 1960 the proportion of farms served by public electricity grew from 11 per cent to 80 per cent and the average consumption of electricity per farm increased fourfold.[25] In the same period the number of static internal combustion engines in farmsteads rose from 120,000 to a maximum of 200,000 in 1952 and then declined to 171,000, but the number of electric motors rose steadily from 11,000 to 253,000. The farmer's appreciation of mechanical power was obvious. So was his preference for electricity.[26]

The most obvious achievement of the new equipment was the final mechanisation of the static chores in the farmstead begun by the steam engine in Hanoverian times. By the end of this period nearly all cows were milked, nearly all home-grown feed ground and mixed, and nearly all water pumped by machinery. The new technical resource also brought less precedented benefits. It brought light and with it a general increase in efficiency and cleanliness. It brought localised heating of a type suitable for rearing piglets and chicks. Above all, it brought the means of controlling the micro-climate in livestock houses. Few innovations in this period were more important than the electric fan and the thermostat on which the predetermined, man-made environments in the new piggeries and poultry houses depended.

Yet this revolution had its limitations. Its effect, of course, varied greatly from area to area, from farm to farm. It took, for instance, sixty hill farms in Wales to muster the total of thirty-four motors which an advanced farmer in Oxfordshire installed in the buildings of his 85 acre holding.[27] More fundamentally, it mechanised stationary work, but failed to replace man as the prime-mover in the transport and handling of materials which form so large a part of farmstead routines.

Sometimes, it is true, whole processes could be comprehensively mechanised and neatly housed in such special-purpose installations as the milking parlour and the grainstore or in the more dramatic silo-to-trough cattle-feeding systems which appeared on the farm in the last years of this period. But this was exceptional. More commonly, permutations and combinations of fixed and mobile equipment, of conveyors, pumps and pipelines, of tractor-mounted scrapers and foreloaders, self-unloading trailers and portable augers, could do no more than increase the efficiency of existing systems of movement. They secured substantial reductions of the labour required, but the design of existing buildings and the scale of existing enterprises prevented the general adoption of industrial-type circulations. For example, the increasing volume of fertilisers, now one of the basic raw materials of the farmer's trade, was manhandled in sacks from lorry to farmstore for later and equally laborious loading on to the trailer for distribution to the fields. Similarly, in the 1950s the amount of feedstuffs bought by the British farmer rose from 4 to 8 million tons, all of it consumed in or around the farmstead. Yet the sack remained the unit in which this mass of material was handled. Only at the very end of the period was any of it delivered in bulk to the farm ready for distribution in bulk in the farmstead.[28]

At the end of this period a speaker at a conference expressed amazement at the number of ways in which farm materials could be mechanically carried, scraped, dragged, blown, sucked or floated from one place to another. He might well have expressed equal amazement at the amount which was still moved by manual effort. The point was made more generally in the statistics. Between 1945 and 1958, it was calculated, production per agricultural man-hour rose on average 6.4 per cent annually, but the increase in production per man-hour spent on livestock, nearly all of it on work in buildings, rose only 3.6 per cent annually.[29] In the fields, horsepower was by this time almost totally mechanised. In the buildings, manpower was still an important prime-mover.

## Grain Storage

The revival of farming included an increase in corn production and throughout these years the cereal acreage remained well above its pre-war level. The most important change, however, was technical, not statistical. In this period, the combine-harvester fulfilled the promise it had shown in the fields of its pioneers a generation earlier. In so doing it raised on a national scale the problems once confined to their farmsteads.

As the number of combines in the country rose from 3,200 in 1946 to 10,000 in 1950, 31,000 in 1956 and nearly 50,000 in 1960, the proportion of the harvest which waited for the threshing machine as sheaves neatly stacked in thatched rick or Dutch barn shrank, the proportion delivered as grain requiring storage, and therefore drying to make it ready for storage, rose rapidly. So the grain-drying and storage installations which had first appeared in British farms in the 1930s increased in number and developed types of design suitable for a wider range of farms. At first dryer and bins were separate. Then smaller and cheaper systems, notably, the 'ventilated bin' which dried grain in the structure in which it was stored and the self-explanatory 'on-floor system', were evolved. The on-floor system was designed to make use of existing buildings, and a number of other types of plant, particularly those serving large arable farms, found convenient homes in old barns. But many were housed in appropriately factory-type buildings of appropriately factory-made materials.[30]

In 1946 there were about 1,000 such plants in the country. By 1960 there were over 16,000, and in many areas the once familiar cornstack had become as obsolete as the windmill or the flail, and the starkly

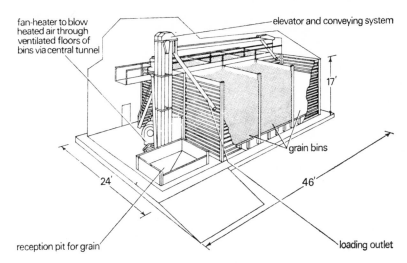

fan-heater to blow heated air through ventilated floors of bins via central tunnel

elevator and conveying system

17'

grain bins

24'

46'

reception pit for grain

loading outlet

24 A modern grain drying and storage plant. In this example of a 'housed mechanical process' grain is conveyed mechanically to bins in which it is dried by heated air. Such plants are usually protected by simple structures of steel or reinforced concrete roofed with asbestos-cement sheeting (*Crittal-Hope Ltd*)

industrial outlines of the farm grainstore had replaced the barn as the dominant feature of the farmstead (see Fig 24). Behind this general change lay a mass of detailed technical achievements in research and development centres at home and overseas. A similar combination was now preparing to bring further change to the corn grower's farmstead.

In the 1950s research in this country made possible the introduction of a system, originally developed in France, of storing undried grain in airtight silos.[31] The method was limited to farms where grain was fed to livestock, for grain thus stored is unsuitable for milling or for seed. Nevertheless, its economic advantages were obvious, particularly to the grower and feeder of barley, for an airtight silo did not cost much more than a conventional one but it ended the expensive necessity of drying equipment. Yet the first silos of the new type which appeared on British farms at the very end of this period illustrated more than a change in local methods. They were imported from the USA, and so symbolised the increasing integration of the British farmer into a technological order which paid little attention to frontiers.[32]

The point of course, was not new. In 1954, for example, Pierce Worlidge of Biggins Farm, Dagenton, had reflected on the variety of resources which made possible the new grain dryer and bins that safeguarded his corn crop. 'The water that had threatened and often destroyed the grain harvests here for a thousand years and more was now no longer a danger . . . but only a nuisance to be thrust aside at some expense but nearly no trouble. The rubber plantations of

Malaya, the softwood forests of Scandinavia, the aluminium ore of Canada and the oil fields of Kuwait would in future each play their part . . . in keeping wheat and barley from Dagenton fields dry and clean and sweet until it became a biscuit for a small boy or beer for an old man.'[33] He spoke in fiction but expressed fact, though not exhaustively, for he omitted from his list the contribution made by the research stations of a half a dozen countries. The tall towers of American steel which exploited to the farmer's advantage biological processes whose predictability had been established in English and French laboratories merely continued his argument. Agriculturally, they proclaimed the coming of a new technique. Historically, they were just another example of a familiar process. In the nineteenth century, the British farmstead had become part of the national steam age economy. In the twentieth, it began to form part of the international scientific order which succeeded it.

## Potato Storage

The same general tendencies were illustrated on a smaller scale by the development of indoor potato storage. At the beginning of this period, nearly all potatoes not sold off the farm at harvest wintered in the fields in clamps of straw and earth. By the end, nearly half were stored indoors. This change was made necessary by a combination of economic and technical pressures. Labour was becoming too expensive to use for building such temporary stores as clamps or for working in rain, cold and mud when it could be employed more efficiently under a roof; the supply of long, firm straw suitable for clamps was shrinking as the growing fleet of combines delivered only short, broken straw; and the new system allowed greater possibilities of mechanisation. But it was made possibly by comprehensive research into the properties of potatoes in storage and the insulation, ventilation and structural strength required in buildings to house them, which began in 1946 and produced the first new-model potato store two years later.[34] The new stores, sometimes special-purpose buildings, sometimes existing buildings adapted to new purposes, provided potatoes with improved conditions for conservation, and the men who loaded and graded them with improved working conditions. In so doing, they illustrated the growing ability of the research worker to specify the needs of farm materials and of the engineer and builder to meet them.[35]

## Hop Buildings

So did the buildings which served the hop grower. In the hop areas, some farmers still used the traditional cowled oasts, but they no longer built them. For the pre-war innovations of oil-firing, electric fans and roof louvres had made possible an improved but less picturesque design of kiln which was now accepted practice. An equally conspicuous physical change was the appearance of large industrial-type sheds to house the hop-picking machines which came into general use after the war and by the end of this period picked three-quarters of the crop. As it was on the general farm, so it was, in microcosm, on the specialised hop farm. Major changes in the farmstead reflected major changes in methods of harvesting and handling crops.[36] The sentiments of the farmer who continued to maintain his obsolete oasts because they were local landmarks, 'like the guardtowers of a mediaeval city', and he did not want his farmstead to look like 'a blasted factory site', did him credit. But he lived and worked in fiction.[37] Few farmers who lived and worked in the world of commercial reality could afford such costly and unprofitable investment.

## Dairy Buildings

The dairy farmer of this period inherited the specialised trade of liquid milk production, farmhouse butter-making being now all but forgotten and farmhouse cheese-making surviving only on a decreasing handful of farms.[38] He also inherited an expanding market and an agreeable lack of competition, for the importation of fresh milk was not a practical proposition and urban milk production was now nearing its end.[39] Nevertheless, throughout these years his systems of production were exposed to a variety of particular economic and technical pressures as well as to the general demands of the Milk and Dairies Regulations, administered since 1944 by the Ministry of Agriculture and Fisheries, which compelled a steady sequence of changes in his methods and his buildings.

The starting point of these changes was the traditional cowhouse in which cows were tied in individual stalls while men milked them and carried their milk to the dairy all through the year and brought them food and litter and removed their manure during the months of winter housing. The system had many advantages, but it was developed in the days when labour was cheap and farmers were prepared to pay men to spend most of their time on purely mechanical haulage chores. Consequently it continued unchallenged only as long as wages were low and men plentiful. From the outbreak of war onwards, however, wages rose continuously and farmers sought increasingly to reduce the labour costs of their cowhouses. In particular, they followed the example of the pre-war pioneers and introduced milking machines, so that by the end of this period the hand-milked herd was a curiosity. Many, too, introduced mechanical equipment or trolleys for handling milk, fodder or manure, but there were limits to the economies such methods could secure. Over the years, more and more farmers abandoned their cowhouses for some form of the 'loose-housing' system in which cows and machines did more work and men did less.

Essentially, this system provided two separate and specialised areas, one where the cows lay and one where they were milked, and relied on the cows' legs to solve the transport problems thus created. Men no longer brought the job to the cows; the cows went to the job. And since the jobs involved the whole herd instead of individual cows in individual stalls, machinery could deal wholesale with work formerly done retail by hand or barrow. The principles of the new order in dairy housing were simple, but its practice was varied and complicated.

Consider first the cow's lying area. The original break with the individual stall of the cowhouse tradition came at the end of the war, when farmers began to house their cows communally in yards.[40] One of the main causes of this change was the desire to reduce labour by replacing the daily manual chore of mucking-out by a mechanical annual clearance. This was achieved and other benefits followed in its train. Loose-housed cows were commonly cleaner than cows in cowhouses and suffered fewer injuries, while yards could be adapted to expanding herds more cheaply and conveniently than cowhouses. But, as the years passed, new difficulties appeared. A fall in the corn acreage, the combine-harvester which left more straw in the fields than the reaper-and-binder, and the increased use of short-strawed varieties of corn steadily reduced the supply of litter on which the efficiency of the system depended, while inexorably rising wages increased the cost of hauling it into the yards as bedding and out again as trodden manure. Once more the farmer sought means of adapting his methods to changing circumstances.

One possibility was the forgotten slatted floor system, which dealt drastically with the litter problem. It required no litter at all, for the cattle trod their manure through the floor into a cellar from which it was removed in solid or liquid form. Slatted floors aroused considerable interest when reintroduced to Britain from Norway in 1955,[41] but evidence of their performance on dairy farms was inconclusive and, while the technical debate on their virtues and weaknesses continued, a new and startlingly simple alternative appeared. This was the cubicle system, which provides one of the most remarkable success stories of modern agriculture.

Cubicle housing combines the best features of the cowhouse and the yard and adds certain advantages of its own. It provides the cows with individual stalls where they can lie and ruminate in peace, yet allows them freedom of movement and access to a common feeding area. Admittedly, the cubicles require bedding, but little litter or labour is needed since their design compels the cows to drop their dung in the

passage behind them and not in their beds. The system pleases cows
and cowmen alike, and within a few years of its appearance in 1960 it
housed a significant and increasing proportion of the national dairy
herd. Seldom has a new type of farm building been adopted so rapidly,
so widely and so painlessly.[42]

Changes in the milking parlour were as drastic as those in the
housing system. The early 'abreast' parlours, as the name implies,
continued the tradition of the cowhouse in which the cows were
milked side-by-side on a level floor. Consequently the cowman spent
much of his time and more of his energy on continuous stooping as he
attached and detached the teat cups. So the first major change in
parlour design was the appearance shortly after the war of the
'tandem' parlour, in which cows stood at a higher level than the
cowman who thus worked with the cow at convenient elbow-height. It
was typical of the times that this difference in heights, once decided
empirically, was later precisely determined by the first application of
ergonomic research to farmstead problems.[43] It was equally typical
that the improvement was no more than a temporary stage in parlour
development.

For this original form of two-level parlour decreased the effort of
milking but increased the amount of walking required, since the cows
stood head-to-tail in the parlour with their udders a cow's length
instead of a cow's breadth apart. But a New Zealand system, first
introduced into this country in 1956, neatly economised both time and
energy. It continued the two-level system but reduced the distance
between udders by 'angle-parking' the cows at some 30° to the milker's
pit with their heads pointing away from it, thus forming on plan the
cow-pattern which earned it the now internationally famous name of
the 'herring-bone' parlour. It was a highly sophisticated installation,
at first glance rather resembling the interior of a submarine. It was
also highly efficient and enabled each man to operate more milking
units and therefore milk more cows per hour than any other system so
far devised (see Fig 25).

The herring-bone parlour, like the cubicle, was the successful
product of a lengthy process of evolution. Yet their origins were
radically different. The new housing systems were all introduced by
farmers and many of the later improvements in them came from trial
and error on commercial farms. But the development of the milking
parlour was necessarily a more complicated matter. In particular, it
depended on the availability of the necessary special-purpose
equipment. From the first, therefore, its future lay in the hands of 'the
Trade'. Hosier, it is true, continued to improve the parlour he had
originated, but he did so as engineer, not as farmer. Similarly, the
herring-bone parlour was invented by a New Zealand farmer named

abreast

tandem

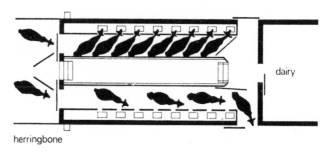

dairy

herringbone

25    The development of the milking-parlour

Sharp, but his system was adapted to British conditions mainly by commercial firms which devised, *inter alia*, the feeding and milk-recording equipment required in this country.[44] Technical development decreased the ability of the farmer to apply his own ideas but increased the efficiency with which others could do so.

Technological change and the manufacturing presence were equally obvious in the dairy. First came electricity, which gradually replaced coal as the means of raising steam for sterilising equipment, then chemicals which began to replace steam as a means of sterilisation, then refrigeration equipment which began to replace water from pipe or well for cooling the milk, and finally the refrigerated tank which enabled the advanced and substantial milk producer to cool and store his milk in bulk instead of cooling it by the pailful and storing it in churns. There were, however, more parties to this last change than farmer and engineer. The bulk system certainly reduced labour and milk loss on the farm, but its capital cost was heavy and the savings with the smaller herds were seldom sufficient to make the investment profitable. The main beneficiaries were the hauliers and processors of the milk and it was largely their attitudes which determined the rate of spread of this innovation.[45]

The effects of external developments on the buildings of the farmstead were illustrated in neater and more abrupt form by the story of the bullpen in these years. In the later 1930s efforts to raise the standard of breeding stock included the introduction of progeny-testing schemes which made it profitable to keep potentially valuable bulls on the farm until the milk yields of their daughters were known. By this time their strength and weight were considerable and, more important, their natural tendency to bad temper had increased with age. Clearly, some form of housing better for the bull and safer for the farmer and his men than the traditional stall in a cowhouse or box in a corner of the yard was required. The war allowed only homemade improvements. But the following years saw the general adoption of a fairly standardised form of pen and run which provided the bull with shelter, the opportunity for exercise in the open air, and a service box for his essential function, and also incorporated various safety devices that made it unnecessary for the stockman to enter the building while the bull was loose. The most important single animal on the farm was at last honoured with a house specially planned for his particular needs. But he seldom enjoyed it for long, for the post-war development of artificial insemination made his general presence on the farm unnecessary. Between 1950 and 1960 the number of bulls on farms was nearly halved and many of the new bullpens were abandoned or used, not very conveniently, for some other purpose. The artificial insemination centre, not the farm, was the true beneficiary of the new improved bullpen.[46]

All these changes affected the design of dairy buildings, but the growing intensification of agriculture also began to influence the duration of their use, for in the middle 1950s modernised forms of the forgotten practice of soilage were introduced to the country from America under the name of 'zero-grazing'. These systems were made possible by new field equipment, notably the forage-harvester and the self-unloading trailer which cut and carried the grass to the permanently yarded cattle. But they served the old principle of making better use of pasture by taking grass to the cows instead of cows to the grass. In so doing, they also made better use of the buildings which were occupied all the year round instead of lying empty during the grazing season. The managerial difficulties of zero-grazing, however, were considerable and the technique did not spread far or fast. But its appearance reflected the trends of the time. Under economic pressure, the farmer was seeking ways of making more intensive use of both land and buildings.[47]

## Housing for Beef Cattle

Methods of housing dairy cattle changed radically, methods of housing the less profitable beef cattle changed hardly at all. Economics ensured that fattening cattle were run in the fields or in such yards as were available, where they continued their traditional functions of turning bulky fodders into meat and straw into manure. In the 1950s the development by research workers of systems of fattening cattle entirely on barley and supplements enabled farms which did not produce bulk feeds to carry beef enterprises but did not inspire any general development in types of building. More intensive methods of housing were sometimes discussed but seldom practised. Characteristically, the only major structural innovation in these years was the limited but successful use of the slatted-floor system which required less labour and litter than the conventional yard; and this, as we have seen, was originally reintroduced from Norway as a system for housing the dairy herd.

## Grass Conservation

The necessity of feeding more cattle from fewer acres of pasture helped to produce the general revolution in grassland management, predicted and inspired by Stapledon, which was one of the most substantial achievements of this period. This revolution began with improvements in the production of grass but continued inevitably with improvements in its conservation. Equally inevitably, it brought further changes to the farmstead where the produce of the fields was stored and eaten. It was a sign of the international times that many of these changes reflected American developments or, more pointedly, incorporated American equipment.

In 1939, nearly all grass was conserved as hay. A little was made into silage, a little was dried, but silo and dryer were alike exceptional. In 1960, most grass was still made into hay, though not all of it was now cured in the field. 'Barn hay drying', the practice of drying hay in buildings by a forced draught of cold or warmed air, which was

Plate 33   The corrugated iron roof of this farm building is modern; the brickwork is probably nineteenth century; the squared stones are Roman, looted from nearby Wroxeter (*Nigel Harvey*)

Plate 34   Part of an early courtyard steading in Shropshire. Probably built in the seventeenth century, it includes later buildings which illustrate changes in constructional methods and materials. It is still in use (*Nigel Harvey*)

Plate 35    The development of a Berkshire farmstead. The barn and flanking ranges of livestock buildings round three sides of an open yard illustrate the basic design of the Hanoverian and early Victorian farmstead. The buildings with corrugated iron roofing were probably added early this century, the buildings with asbestos-cement roofing after World War II (*Aerofilms Ltd*)

Plate 36    This massive mid-Victorian farmstead was designed for a corn-and-beef system. Now dairy cows are milked in a parlour which stands in one of the yards where fattening bullocks once trod straw into manure. Concrete blocks and asbestos-cement sheeting contrast with bricks and slate, and steampower has been replaced by electricity (*Nigel Harvey*)

introduced from America at the end of the war, had established itself in some of the wetter areas where a better quality end product more than compensated for the higher cost of production.[48] Nevertheless, hay had acquired a rival. Grass drying, it is true, was now hardly a competitor. In the decade after the war, when concentrate feeds were scarce, the number of grass-drying plants in their new sheds of reinforced concrete members and asbestos-cement sheeting rose to over 1,200. But expansion ceased in the early 1950s, when concentrates were again imported freely. Many plants went out of production and those which continued in operation became part of specialised enterprises which supplied the manufacturers of pig and poultry feed with high-grade meal.[49] On the other hand, the making of silage had now become common practice.

The twentieth century had overcome many of the weaknesses which had prevented the development of silage in Victorian times. The scientist had provided greater understanding of the biological processes involved, the adviser had made such knowledge generally available, and in 1946 an enterprising farmer had invented the buckrake which, in conjunction with the tractor and its hydraulic lift, made possible the complete mechanisation of the peculiarly exacting chore of silage-making.[50] Nevertheless, it was some time before the farmstead showed any very obvious signs of the establishment of this revived technique.

In the 1940s, a number of farmers built small and often temporary versions of the tall pre-war tower silos, sometimes of prefabricated concrete panels, sometimes of timber or wire mesh and sisal paper. But the majority came to prefer pits or, more commonly, above-ground clamps walled with sleepers or concrete slabs which fitted conveniently into the loose-housing system developed by the diary farmer. These were cheap to build and simple to operate.[51] They also allowed cattle to feed themselves from the silage face through light, movable barriers, thus ending the laborious necessity of cutting and carting a heavy and unpleasant material from silo to trough. This self-feeding technique, which originated in the USA and first appeared in Great Britain in the early 1950s,[52] was soon followed by a more tangible and conspicuous type of import. The tall towers began to return, and some of them came from America. Farmers on both sides of the Atlantic faced similar problems. But economic pressures and therefore technical responses developed earlier in the USA, and British farmers frequently found it convenient to begin this process of adjustment by adopting ready-made American systems.

Economically, wages were rising and with them the incentive to invest in labour-saving equipment, while the growing size of enterprise made possible capital expenditure on a scale hitherto unprofitable.

Technically, the Americans had developed new types of tower silo, and a variety of mechanical equipment to load, unload and distribute their contents, thus achieving a degree of 'press button farming' never before seen in the cattleyard. The forgotten prediction made by Dr George Thurber a lifetime earlier was finally and literally fulfilled. The whole matter of silage had now been Americanised; and the British farmer was among those to take advantage of it.[53]

The first installations of this type appeared in Great Britain in the later 1950s. Most of them used imported equipment, including the expensive but efficient airtight silos made of glass-lined steel which, by preventing the entry of oxygen, eliminated one of the main causes of wastage.[54] These huge new towers dominated not only the farmstead but the landscape around it and provided the travelling townsman with sudden and spectacular evidence of agricultural change. Nevertheless, they were the results, not the causes, of such change. They were no more than the most conspicuous parts of a new and pervading system of farmstead mechanisation. Machines now handled grass in the buildings, just as they cultivated and harvested it in the fields. The connection between the development of machinery and the progress of silage-making which contemporaries noted illustrated one of the prerequisites of many changes in the farmstead of this period.[55]

## Pig Housing

War and scarcity made necessary a dramatic increase in agricultural production. They also, however, made necessary an equally dramatic decrease in pig production, for the war prevented importation of the concentrated feedstuffs on which the pig industry had previously depended. In 1939 there were $3\frac{1}{2}$ million pigs in England and Wales; in 1947 less than $1\frac{1}{4}$ million. Once supplies became available again, however, recovery was rapid. In 1951 the pig population reached nearly 3 million, in 1952 nearly 4 million, and for the rest of the decade it never fell below $4\frac{1}{2}$ million.

The need for more piggeries was obvious. So was the need for bigger and better piggeries. For the return of imported feedstuffs was accompanied by the return of imported pig products. The home farmer met this competition by specialisation and intensification. As the years passed, a growing proportion of the national herd was concentrated on a shrinking number of farms and the piggery became an increasingly important means of ensuring productive efficiency. In the depression, the farmer had exploited the pig's ability to adapt itself to a wide variety of conditions. Now he exploited its ability to respond to the right kind of environment created by the right kind of housing.

He was also able to exploit the findings of the research workers who, in the years after the war, patiently produced a growing mass of evidence on the environmental needs of pigs. Their findings left plenty of scope for individual decision and managerial skills, but the new knowledge ended the old dependence on tradition and informed guesswork. From now onwards the farmer could specify in reasonable detail the micro-climate his pigs required and judge the work of the builder and the engineer by the efficiency with which their designs provided it. Thus was fulfilled the prophecy inherent in the recommendation of an official committee in 1945 that research should be undertaken into 'the influence of design and structure on housing environment and the effect of environment on pig health and comfort'.[56] Such research was undertaken and within a few years it revolutionised pig housing.

The change can be followed in the technical literature on fattening houses. The textbook which the committee sponsored could only quote those familiar pre-war types of piggery, the cottager's pigsty and the Danish house.[57] The first edition of its official successor in 1953 repeated the description of these two systems and added a variety of new designs produced by enterprising farmers and frequently called after them. Clearly, tradition and empiricism still ruled. But its second edition, published in 1962, illustrated the coming of the new scientific order. It began with definitions of such terms as thermal conductivity, saturation deficit and sensible heat, and filled a third of its length with graph-illustrated sections on temperature, relative humidity, insulation and ventilation before it described its first piggery.[58] Finally, in the following year, another manual bore precise documentary witness to the realisation of the committee's hopes. It supported its chapter on the environmental needs of the pig by references to twenty-five scientific papers, all of which had been published in the previous fifteen years.[59]

Nevertheless, the committee's order of priorities required reversal, for it was the effect of environment on the pig that determined the design and construction of its housing. In particular, research showed that pigs required higher and more constant temperatures than was previously believed. For farrowing sows and their litters this meant greater use of artificial heating, generally by infrared lamps. For fatteners it meant the development of housing which conserved the pigs' natural heat, which in turn meant carefully planned combinations of insulation and ventilation to maintain proper conditions in the building. It meant, in short, increased environmental control and therefore increasingly enclosed buildings. Piggeries which relied on deep straw to keep the pigs warm were replaced first by piggeries which relied on insulation and natural ventilation, and then by piggeries which relied on insulation and artificial ventilation. Once more the textbooks tell the story. In 1953 the first edition of the official bulletin on pig housing previously quoted described artificial ventilation by fans as experimental. Its second edition, only nine years later, took artificial ventilation for granted and unenthusiastically informed such farmers as were compelled by circumstances to use natural ventilation that they could expect 'fair results' if proper care was taken.[60]

It was typical of the changed times that the pig farmer who had once devised his own buildings turned to the research worker and the engineer for improvements to ease the working of his new houses. The slatted-floor system which he began to adopt at the end of this period to reduce the labour of manure-handling came to him not from other farmers but from research centres in Norway and the USA. It was equally typical that within ten years of its first appearance in a piggery this technique had produced a research literature of over fifty papers.[61]

The general consequences of these changes were obvious to the most casual visitor to the countryside. He would still see sows and their litters housed in arks in the fields and occasional groups of pigs in yards in the farmstead. But he would no longer see pig fattening in sties or in Danish piggeries a few bays long on the mixed farms he passed. From time to time, however, he would pass long, vaguely industrial-type buildings in which the more specialised pig producer was raising and fattening pigs in environments specified by the scientist and created by the builder and the engineer (see Fig 26, Plate 40).

## Poultry Housing

The general development of the poultry enterprise and therefore of poultry housing paralleled that of the pig enterprise and pig housing. There was a considerable, though less drastic decrease in numbers in the war years and a similar rapid recovery when feedstuffs became freely available, the same specialisation and increase in size of unit, and the same replacement of traditional types of housing by new and more intensive systems based on the new knowledge gained from research. There was also the same independence of the productive capacity of the land, for the poultry farmer, like the pig farmer, fed his stock on the processed products of other people's farms.

Yet there was one important difference. The pig farmer continued his familiar lines of production. The poultry farmer added to his business a major new line of production dependent upon the most intensive system of management yet seen on the farm. The achievement of the traditional poultry farmer, the egg producer, was considerable. In the 1930s, Great Britain imported a third of its eggs;

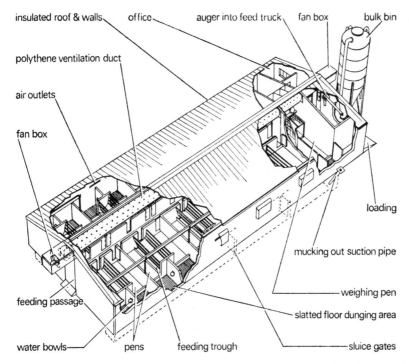

insulated roof & walls    office    auger into feed truck    fan box    bulk bin

polythene ventilation duct

air outlets

fan box

loading

mucking out suction pipe

weighing pen

feeding passage

slatted floor dunging area

water bowls    pens    feeding trough    sluice gates

26  A fattening house for 200 pigs built in the 1960s. Note the degree of environmental control and the mechanisation of feeding (Based on *Power Farming*, vol 35, no 4, October 1965, enclosure pp3–4) (*Mr W. Marshall*)

in the later 1950s it was virtually self-supporting in eggs. But it was surpassed by that of a new type of poultryman, the broiler producer, who started business in 1953 and seven years later was marketing 100 million birds a year. So one of the themes of this period is the intensification of an inherited system, another the rise of a system intensive from its beginnings.

The background to these changes was the extensive 'range' system of light, fixed houses or movable folds standing in pasture fields which, in the later 1940s, housed nearly all the hens in the country. Such a system required little capital outlay and improved the fertility of the soil which the birds scratched and manured. But its labour costs were high and it suffered from the inherent weakness of low winter egg yields, for egg production is stimulated by light and the range birds were necessarily dependent on such light as nature thought fit to provide. When post-war economics emphasised the rewards of winter egg production and research made clear the importance of duration and periods as well as the extent of lighting, it became obvious that some system which allowed greater control of the factors affecting production was required.

One answer was the intensive cage battery system which allowed a substantial control over environment in general and complete control over lighting in particular, with consequent increase of egg yields at a cost of greater capital investment. This method had established itself in Great Britain before the war but had barely survived the restrictions on feedstuffs in the years of scarcity. Once supplies of concentrates returned, however, its expansion was rapid and by the end of the period it housed over a third of all the hens in the country.[62] Meanwhile, however, an alternative method of housing had appeared. This was the deep-litter system which concentrated the birds in an enclosed building, thus enabling the farmer to exploit artificial lighting to maintain winter egg production, but allowing the hens free movement on a floor of straw bedding. Introduced from the USA in 1948, it spread rapidly and by 1960 housed another third of the national flock. With the aid of new buildings, therefore, the egg producer had intensified in little more than a decade two-thirds of a once extensive enterprise.[63]

So egg production achieved intensification and with it the mechanisation of henhouse operations which allowed a steady increase in the number of birds for which one man could be effectively responsible. But broiler production was born intensive. It depended for its success on securing the most efficient rate of growth from birds at their most efficient period of growth, which is the first three months of life, and it pressed into service nutritional, genetic and veterinary science, the skills of the builder and the engineer, and a standard of managerial ability seldom previously applied to the business of food production. All these resources were concentrated in the new broiler houses which so suddenly appeared in the farmlands to house the increasing multitude of young chickens which fattened with factory-type precision on a factory-type schedule for preplanned delivery to the packing station.

Indeed, the whole development was to some extent preplanned, for the broiler industry originated in the USA in the war years and its quick and profitable expansion was watched by enterprising Englishmen for some years before the end of feedstuffs rationing in 1953 enabled them to introduce it to Great Britain, where the first broiler house was built in 1953.[64] The advantages of such vicarious experience was reflected in the phenomenal rate of expansion of the new trade which far exceeded that of any other line of farm production. Changes in the structure of the industry were equally rapid, for here as elsewhere economics favoured the big battalions. A number of the early broiler producers raised flocks of under 1,000 birds but a few years later some of the groups that were formed to run co-operative packing stations demanded a minimum delivery of

10,000 per batch from prospective members. Broiler houses grew larger. They also grew more standardised and more efficient.

Essentially, these houses were a means of providing a closely specified environment, notably a temperature of 65–70°F (18–21°C), subdued lighting for predetermined periods, and clean air free from excessive moisture. This implied careful design, artificial heating, heavy insulation and the precise control of ventilation. At first, attempts were made to adapt existing buildings for the new purposes. It was soon clear, however, that specially designed buildings were preferable, and specialist firms began to produce prefabricated houses.[65] There were, of course, numerous differences in detail, but the basic design became increasingly standardised. For example, growing appreciation of the effects of light regimes on growth caused a steady increase in the proportion of windowless houses. In general, similar needs produced similar installations – parallel lines of long, low, widespread buildings, each housing mechanically fed and mechanically watered flocks whose average size increased inexorably as the years passed. Typically, the most conspicuous objects in the broilerised farmstead were the tall hoppers with which houses were commonly equipped to receive the bulk deliveries of feedstuffs which the size of these enterprises made economic. A new, intensive and large-scale trade had produced a new and appropriate type of building.[66]

Yet the broiler house was not as revolutionary as it appeared to many men of the time. It certainly formed part of a new system of production, for successful broiler farming implied the development of an economic chain linking the hatchery, the broiler house and the packing station with the retailer. It is no accident that one of the pioneers of the broiler industry was also the author of one of the first books published in Great Britain on vertical integration in agriculture.[67] But technically it did no more than present old and general trends in a new and particular form. The broiler-house system was not dependent on its own farmland, for the producer bought the materials of his trade, chicks, litter and feed, as well as his buildings; but neither was the battery system for layers nor the urban cowhouses and fattening houses of an earlier age. It provided livestock with a man-made environment; but in this it differed only in degree from any other type of building which sought to influence micro-climate. Indeed, it hardly differed even in degree from some contemporary piggeries. Nevertheless, the historical importance of the broiler house is considerable. For it made manifest with spectacular efficiency the capabilities of the advanced agricultural building and the part it could play in the enterprise it served.[68]

## Sheep Housing

An interesting byproduct of the general intensification of agriculture was the beginning of a revival of sheep housing. Traditionally, the hill farmer had wintered his ewe lambs on lowland farms. By the 1950s, however, many of the lowland farmers who had once received these lambs had turned milk producer and were unwilling to lease to other people's sheep the winter grazings from which they expected the valuable 'early bite' of spring grass for their own cows. So upland farmers began to devise shelters, sometimes floored with wooden slats, which would enable their lambs to winter on the hills. By the end of this period this new form of housing was barely out of the experimental stage. But its success was one of the factors which encouraged the development of all types of sheep housing which was so striking a feature of farm buildings development in the next decade.[69]

## The Farm Office

Clearly, the demands of the farm on the farmstead were growing. So were its demands on the farmer who, year by year, needed more technical knowledge, more records and more figures to assist him in his increasingly crucial managerial decisions, including decisions on investment in farm buildings.[70] By the later 1950s, therefore, farm management had established itself among the major agricultural disciplines and the description of the farm office as 'the most important building on the farm' had found a place among familiar rural proverbs. Most farmers, it is true, continued to use the traditional desk in the front room, but on the larger and more intensive holdings neat new buildings or refurbished sections of old ones, through whose windows wall-graphs could be seen and a typewriter heard, became increasingly common. The formal acceptance by the farming community of contemporary business techniques and apparatus was symbolised shortly after the end of this period by the first appearance in a textbook on farm buildings of a section, complete with plans, on the farm office and its equipment.[71]

## Prefabrication and Adaptability

In this period the industrial system took final control of the construction of farm buildings. The most obvious sign of this was a comprehensive change in the materials of which they were built. Nearly all those used in new work now came from the factory: cement to make concrete for floors where earth would not suffice,[72] steel and reinforced concrete, including prestressed concrete, for framing, concrete blocks for walls, asbestos-cement sheeting for cladding and, almost universally, for roofing instead of the corrugated iron which required maintenance, or the tiles and slates which required more complicated and expensive forms of roof construction.[73] Less familiar products, too, were now beginning to make their appearance in the farmstead, aluminium sheeting, plastic rainwater goods and roof-lights, and a variety of plastic or mineral insulating materials on which the efficiency of so many new livestock buildings depended. It was typical of the new order that the only old materials to retain a place in it were those which did so on its industrial terms.

Thus, bricks were no longer made in local brickyards. They were bought through the general trade from the big brickworks. Timber adapted itself more subtly to the new demands with the aid of industrial resources. Timber connectors decreased the weight and increased the scope of wooden members, waterproof glues made possible new forms of plywood and laminated components, and new preservatives prolonged its life and lowered its ultimate cost by ending the need for maintenance. It became, in fact, a sort of industrial product. But stone and thatch could not so transform themselves and, typically, the most memorable reference to thatch in this period was a frankly elegiac description of 'the strange intermingled crop' of ragwort and willowherb that grew on the roof of an abandoned stable.[74]

With these changes in the materials of building, went less immediately obvious but more basic changes in the methods of building. Traditionally, farm buildings had been built with substantial walls that carried the weight of the roof. But new buildings were increasingly formed of a frame of reinforced concrete, steel or timber to which roofs and walls or side-cladding were added. The principle, of course, was not new. It was as old as the timber-framed barn and had been successfully exploited by the industrial age which made the framed Dutch barn the most common and conspicuous of all agricultural buildings. But its practice in this form and on this scale was revolutionary. So were its implications.

By this time the farmer had, of course, ceased to grow, dig or fell his own materials. Nevertheless, as long as he bought such small components as blocks, sheets and minor members he remained master of the size and shape of the buildings he erected. But the dimensions of prefabricated frames were determined by the sizes of the columns and trusses on which they depended and these were determined by the commercial and technical decisions of the firms which made them. Furthermore, the type of framework the farmer chose frequently influenced his choice of the materials with which he clad it. In many cases, therefore, it was manifestly more convenient to buy whole buildings, frames, roofs and walls together, from the firms which supplied them, particularly if, as was usual, they were prepared to erect them as well. Again, there was nothing totally unfamiliar in all this. It was the scope and scale that were new. The work of the local builder continued. So did the familiar tradition of improvisation, self-help and the re-use of old materials.[75] But an increasing proportion of the new buildings erected in these years came to the farm as sets of factory-made components.

The development and acceptance of prefabrication were rapid. In the post-war years, mass production techniques were increasingly and successfully applied to the manufacture of sets of structural parts, generally based on some form of the frame system, from which the farmer could choose those which provided the particular building he required. This revolution was not, of course, either painless or complete. The design, transport and erection of factory-made buildings presented a variety of technical and physical problems, while no range of prefabricated buildings could hope to meet more than a majority of needs on a majority of farms. In particular, such standardised products could not always be conveniently fitted into the limited spaces available when farmsteads were remodelled. Nevertheless, by the end of this period the prefabricated framed building was widely accepted as 'a means of providing 90 per cent of our agricultural building needs'.[76] The farmer had long been accustomed to choose his building materials from catalogues. Now he was becoming accustomed to choosing the buildings themselves from the same source.

This change reflected the general advantage inherent in any system of mass production and the standardised assembly of standardised components. But the increased use of the framed building also reflected a particular agricultural advantage. Such a building was inherently easier to adapt to other purposes than the traditional type of structure. The insertion of new doors or new windows, the conversion of a four-sided house into a three-sided shelter, the addition or removal of a bay, all were simpler and cheaper in a building where the weight of the roof was supported on vertical members spaced some fifteen feet apart instead of on necessarily substantial walls.

The question of adaptable designs had been raised academically thirty years earlier,[77] but this was the first age in which it assumed general importance. For the farmers of the post-war years had lived through a series of technical revolutions which showed no signs of ending and many signs of accelerating. They were, indeed, the first agricultural generation to take rapid, drastic and continuing change as a normal and natural condition. They had spent much of their working lives fitting new technologies into old farmsteads and they strove to plan their new buildings in accordance with the lessons they had learnt.

The importance of this point was appreciated early in this period, and the first post-war textbook on farm buildings listed adaptability high among design considerations.[78] In the following years many others said the same thing at greater length. Indeed, no discussion of farm buildings was complete without some reference to the problem.[79] Certain types of building were inherently specialised. How could the less committed designs be planned to allow for future change?

In principle, there were three possible answers. At one extreme, the most obvious form of temporary building was one with a limited life which could be scrapped when its purpose ended and a new one built in its place. This implied, of course, a cheap building. Yet there was no generally acceptable type of construction between the architectural equivalent of stick-and-string suitable for only a few agricultural purposes and the conventional buildings of indefinite life which were too costly to abandon after only a few years' use. At the other extreme stood the multi-purpose building designed *ab initio* to be readily and cheaply convertible to a variety of possible uses. But the difficulties of combining in one structure immediate efficiency for known purposes with possible future efficiency for hypothetical purposes were considerable. Between these, however, stood the framed building which served present needs as efficiently as its heavy-walled predecessors yet offered considerably greater possibilities for conversion. In the 1950s, therefore, it was generally agreed that a framed building of wide enough span to allow relatively easy adaptation to a number of different purposes was the most practicable answer on most farms; and the components of such buildings came from the factory. Once again, the resources of the industrial age helped the farmer to control a problem which its pressures had created.

## NOTES

1. *National Farm Survey of England and Wales, 1941–3*, HMSO, 1946, p 41.
2. Williamson, H. *The Story of a Norfolk Farm*, 1941, pp 86–7.
3. Some Welsh longhouses were still inhabited in the later 1950s (Jope, E. M. and Threlfall, R. I. 'Excavation of a mediaeval settlement at Beere, North Tawton, Devon', *Mediaeval Archaeology*, vol 2, 1958, p 122). In Devon the use of the cowhouse section of surviving longhouses was 'not uncommon' well into the twentieth century (Hulland, C. 'Devonshire farmhouses', *Report and Transactions of the Devonshire Association*, vol 112, 1980, pp 154–9). On Dartmoor, the cowhouse of one longhouse was in regular use till 1945 (Alcock, N. W. 'Houses in an East Devon parish', *Report and Transactions of the Devonshire Association*, vol 94, 1962, p 228) and another till at least 1960 (Hoskins, W. G. 'Farmhouses and history', *History Today*, vol 10, 1960, p 339). See also p 256.
4. Scourfield, E. *The Welsh Farming Scene*, published by the Welsh Folk Museum, 1974,

p 31, for horsegear; Hartley, M. and Ingilby, J. *Life in the Moorlands of North-East Yorkshire*, 1972, p 69, for waterpower, and p 113, for flailing; Pitkin, M. *The Farm Wheel and Machinery at Temple Balsall*, unpublished thesis, Birmingham School of Architecture, 1982, for a waterpowered installation which continued in use till 1945–6. For a Victorian turbine survival see p 155.

5. Baker, V. 'Exmoor, an economic survey', *Bristol University, Selected Papers in Agricultural Economics*, vol 2, 1949, p 69.

6. 'Equipment and facilities on dairy farms', *Home Farmer*, vol 18, no 9, September 1951, pp 15–16; vol 18, no 10, October 1951, pp 14–16.

7. Leech, F. B., Egdell, T., Hoskin, P. and Thomas, S. 'Methods of milk production; some results of a survey in four areas of England and Wales', *Journal of Agricultural Science*, vol 56, part 1, 1955, pp 78–89.

8. Robertson Scott, J. W. *England's Green and Pleasant Land*, 1947 ed, p 170. For case studies of the working of such obsolete farmsteads see National Institute of Agricultural Engineering, *Farm Mechanisation Enquiry, Farm Case Study no 4*, 1946, pp 3, 4, 12, 13; Sykes, F. *The Farming Business*, 1946, p 151. Both farmers were competent and successful. Both paid a heavy toll in wastage of resources to their antiquated and inefficient buildings.

9. The 1950s saw the publication of two new textbooks on farm buildings (see p 268), of the first Ministry of Agriculture and Fisheries bulletins on piggeries (*The Housing of Pigs*, 1953) and on grain storage (*Farm Grain Drying and Storage*, 1954) and of a series of Ministry leaflets on the Fixed Equipment of the Farm, most of which concerned farm buildings. This series began in 1951. See also p 214.

10. This process of change is admirably typified in a novel of the period. 'At the Worlidges' new farm a revolution was being wrought; a quiet and gradual change, indeed, for capital was too short to allow everything to be done at once, but a revolution none the less. For a quarter of a century the buildings had been the rotting framework into whose corners the undemanding agriculture of old Amos Jackman had been thrust. It was a farming frame which had descended to him from his predecessors here and which he had been content not only to leave unchanged but also to leave to moulder and rot and fall away . . . The superficial signs of the new order were a clean, concrete yard; new field gates well hung; unblocked drains; patched and weatherproof walls and roofs; and the disembowelling of the cowsheds and stables to make freer, more spacious covered quarters for calves and yearlings and in-calvers' (Trow-Smith, R. *Clay Village*, 1954, p 174). For a Berkshire case study see Sanders, H. G. and Eley, G. *Farms of Britain*, 1946, pp 22–23. For a Devon case study see Wood, N. B. 'Farm buildings', *Agriculture*, vol 59, July 1952, pp 154–6. For a general description of such changes in an arable area in these years see Sayce, R. B. 'The farm buildings of Norfolk', *Agriculture*, vol 64, July 1957, p 169. Sections on the adaptation of old buildings to new purposes are included in the textbooks of the period as a matter of course. One of these books, subtitled 'Conversions and improvements', was essentially a collection of case studies of farmstead remodelling (Benoy, W. G. *Farm Buildings*, 1956).

11. Charlick, R. H. *Farm Buildings Survey of Wales*, 1965, p 6; *Farm Buildings Survey of England*, 1967, p 6, published by the Agricultural Research Council (figures kindly collated for England and Wales by the author).

12. *Post-war Building Studies, No 17, Farm Buildings*, HMSO, 1945, pp 7, 30; Weller, J. B. *Farm Buildings*, 1965. The former quoted no research findings and listed only one research body among the thirteen organisations from which it received written evidence (p 202); the latter cited a mass of research findings and included a list under eight headings of 'The organisations that promote research' in a chapter entitled 'The need for research' (pp 25–8). A minor but striking instance of the same change was the discussion in another textbook of the 1960s of the ancient need of farmsteads for shelter with the aid of advice from an 'Index of exposure to driving rain' published by the Building Research Station (Pasfield, D. H. *Farm Building Design and Construction*, 1965, pp 7–9).

13. A series of official missions immediately after the war to study agricultural developments on the Continent and in North America was followed by an increasing flow of individual and group visits by farmers and agriculturists to universities and interesting farming areas overseas, particularly those in the USA. Many of these visitors were concerned in one way or another with farm buildings and their reports added substantially to the literature of the subject. The influence of particular individuals or reports can seldom be assessed but the total effect of the publications and lectures of these agricultural travellers must have been considerable. The contribution to the development of British farm buildings of visitors sponsored by such bodies as the Kellogg and the Nuffield Foundations would make an interesting study in technical communications and their consequences.

14. For examples of the application of this technique to operations in and around farm buildings see Branston, B. *Time and Motion on the Farm*, 1953; Harvey, N. *Farm Work Study*, 1958; Fraser, A. K. and Lugg, G. W. *Work Study in Agriculture*, 1962. See also Reid, I. G. and Dominy, J. *An Enquiry into the Layout of Farm Buildings*, Reading University,

1954; Clough, P. A. and Dodd, F. H. 'The measurement of performance in machine milking', *NAAS Quarterly Review*, no 43, Spring 1959, pp 103–11; Harvey, N. 'Work study and the pigfarmer', *Pigbreeders Gazette*, October 1959, pp 55–8; Lugg, G. W. 'Farm management and work study', *Journal of the Farm Buildings Association*, vol 3, 1959, pp 11–19 (farmstead case study); Roberts, F. *An Investigation into the Efficiency of Farm Buildings by the Application of Work Study*, unpublished MSc thesis, University of Wales, 1961.

15. One sign of the decline of the traditional landlord and tenant system was the decrease in the importance of the estate yard which had formerly been responsible for the construction and maintenance of so many farm buildings. See the figures on labour used in the construction of farm buildings in 1965 and 1967 surveys in note 75. It is significant that the illustration in the relevant section of Houldsworth, J. W. *The Repair and Maintenance of Agricultural Property*, 1967, pp 67–70, shows an estate yard built in the 1950s for a new type of landowner, the British Steel Corporation.

16. The introduction of most of the major innovations in this period came within this general pattern. For a case study of a minor but typical instance see Harvey, N. 'The Ruakura farrowing pen', *Agriculture*, vol 67, no 10, January 1961, pp 550–3.

17. *Post-war Building Studies, No 17, Farm Buildings*, HMSO, 1945.

18. In 1946 the Ministry of Agriculture and Fisheries established the National Agricultural Advisory Service which included advice on farm buildings among its responsibilities. In 1948 this responsibility was transferred to a new organisation, the Agricultural Land Service, created in the previous year. This service issued a journal, the *ALS Quarterly Notes*, later the *Land Service Journal*, from 1949 to 1956. See also *Report of the Committee Appointed to Review the Provincial and Local Organisation and Procedures of the Ministry of Agriculture, Fisheries and Food*, Cmnd 9732, 1956, pp 24–8; De la Warr, Lord, 'The Wilson report', *Journal of the Farmers' Club*, pt 6, 1956, p 75; Agricultural Advisory Council, *Second Progress Report*, 1967, p 13; Clayton, J. *Farm Buildings in a Planned Environment*, unpublished PhD thesis, University of London, 1970, which includes a study of Agricultural Land Service advice to planning authorities. In 1971 the Agricultural Land Service became part of a new organisation, the Agricultural Development and Advisory Service.

19. Figures from the issues for this period of the *Bibliography of Farm Buildings Research* published by the Agricultural Research Council.

20. The hopes expressed in the early days of post-war reconstruction that the architectural profession would, in general, play a large part in the design of farm buildings and, in particular, develop a specialised class of farm architect were not fulfilled (*Post-war Building Studies, No 17, Farm Buildings*, HMSO, 1945, pp 32–3). The only systematic study in these years of those responsible for the design of farm buildings found that about a third of the buildings in the survey were designed by professionally qualified men, two-thirds of whom were land agents, one-third architects. In addition one building in six was planned with the help of an official adviser, who probably had qualifications in land agency or architecture. The remainder, about half, were designed by landowners, farmers and builders (Ingersent, K. A. and Manning, P. *New Housing for Dairy Cows in the East Midlands*, 1960, p 20). At the end of this period an architect noted sadly that none of the winning designs in a milking parlour competition were by members of his profession (Voelcker, J. 'Farm buildings competition', *Architect's Journal*, vol 133, 22 June 1961, p 917).

21. The Farm Buildings Association, which by 1960 numbered some 500 members. For examples of publications see note 9.

22. A curious illustration of the extent of this was the frequency of demands for research into particular problems without regard to existing research literature on the subject which was in many cases substantial. Significantly, these first became obvious in the middle 1950s, when the volume of published work was beginning to outstrip the individual adviser's ability to master its contents. Equally significantly, one of the first tasks of the Farm Buildings Unit established by the Agricultural Research Council in 1957 was the compilation of a *Bibliography of Farm Buildings Research* of material from 1945 onwards. The first volume appeared in 1959, the last in 1970 (Agricultural Research Council, *Agricultural Research, 1931–1981*, 1981, p 55).

23. The first book on farm workshops appeared in 1953 (Hine, H. J. *The Farmworkshop*). The increase of implement sheds was noted as a recent development in Oxfordshire in 1949 (Huthnance, S. L. 'Farming in Oxfordshire and Berkshire', *Journal of the Royal Agricultural Society of England*, vol 110, 1949, p 5). The first formal study of implement housing was undertaken in 1952, the first official leaflet on the subject issued in 1955 (Denman, D. and Roberts, H. *The Provision of Implement Accommodation*, 1959, p ii; *The Implement Shed and Farm Workshop*, HMSO, 1955).

24. The first official advisory leaflet on this subject was issued in 1956 (*The Tractor Fuel Store*, HMSO).

25. In 1953 the British Electricity Authority launched a rural electrification programme

which planned to increase the number of farms connected to a public supply to 85 per cent by 1963. This figure was reached eighteen months ahead of schedule (Abell, R. H. and Meadows, F. P. 'Rural electricity supply', *Proceedings of the Rural Electrification Conference*, 1962, pt 1, p 61).

26. For the uses of electricity on the farm in the latter years of this period see Rowland, F. E. *Electricity in Modern Farming*, 1963. See also Weller, J. *History of the Farmstead*, 1982, pp 170–8.

27. Slater, J. and Jones, J. 'A survey of Welsh hill farm mechanisation', *Journal of Agricultural Engineering Research*, vol 2, no 3, 1957, pp 222–34; Henderson, G. *Farmer's Progress*, 1950, p 95.

28. 'Developments in handling grain and feed', *Agricultural Merchant*, vol 38, no 11, November 1958, p 54; 'Delivery of feed in bulk', *Agricultural Merchant*, vol 41, no 2, February 1961, p 59.

29. Calverley, D. J. B. 'Mechanisation in livestock husbandry', *Journal of the Royal Agricultural Society of England*, vol 128, 1967, p 69.

30. For the development of these types of plant see Mountfield, J., Oxley, T., Cashmore, W. and Williamson, W. *Storage and Drying of Grain in Bulk. Bin Ventilation*, 1946; *Grain Storage, Drying and Marketing in the USA*, HMSO, 1952, which summarised the lessons of American experiences; *Grain Drying and Storage in Great Britain*, HMSO, 1952; Theophilus, T. *Economics of Grain Drying and Storage*, 1955; Gammon, F. 'Grain drying survey', *Journal of the Institution of British Agricultural Engineers*, vol 13, no 13, 1957, pp 28–32; Mathieson, M. *The Mechanisation of the Grain Harvest*, 1961; and also the various advisory bulletins and leaflets of the Ministry of Agriculture, Fisheries and Food and the publications of the National Institute of Agricultural Engineering, where much of the research was undertaken. For a detailed account of the development of one system of grain drying by an inventive farmer see Ensor, T. *Floor-drying of Cereals*, 1967.

31. The main causes of deterioration in stored grain are moulds, fungi and insects. This method turns these enemies of grain against themselves. The respiration of these organisms in sealed grain, aided by the respiration of the grain itself, replaces the oxygen in the atmosphere of the container by carbon dioxide which represses or kills them before they can do much damage.

32. British manufacturers first produced silos for the storage of damp grain in 1962 (Messer, H. J. M., Hill, H., Whittenbury, R. and Lacey, J. *The Use of Concrete Stave Silos for Storing High Moisture Grain*, 1967, p 7). See also Hyde, M. and Oxley, T. 'Experiments on the airtight storage of damp grain', *Annals of Applied Biology*, vol 48, no 4, 1960, pp 687–9; the publications of the Pest Infestation Laboratory where much of the research was undertaken; and p 179.

33. Trow-Smith, R. *Clay Village*, 1954, pp 172–3.

34. Twiss, P. T. G. 'Electricity and potato storage', *Agriculture*, vol 68, no 5, August 1961, p 264).

35. 'The first important growth in indoor storage came . . . about 1947. This pre-dated the publication of British research findings, but is perhaps less surprising when one considers that farmers were active from the start as innovators. The three-man mission to North America may be said to have begun the scientific study of the subject . . . [This mission] to America found a bewildering range of stores, mostly of rather complicated construction . . . It was a significant achievement on the part of the research teams to have shown that under British conditions the basic requirements were few and simple' (Dawson, E. *Potato Production in Yorkshire*, 1967, pp 24, 26). See also Burton, W. G. and Mann, G. 'Late storage of potatoes in England and Wales', *Agriculture*, vol 60, no 10, January 1954, pp 466–72; Bisset, G. B., Dawson, E. and Jones, R. B. *The Economics of Potato Storage*, 1959; and the various advisory bulletins and leaflets of the Ministry of Agriculture, Fisheries and Food and the publications of Ditton Laboratory where much of the research was undertaken.

36. Locke, P. E. 'Landscape with oasts', *House of Whitbread*, vol 19, no 1, pp 17–20, which includes a reference to a 1956 survey by the Kent Council of Social Services Committee for the Preservation of Rural Kent showing that less than half of the 650 oasts recorded were still used for drying; Darling, H. S. 'Hop growing in England', *Journal of the Royal Agricultural Society of England*, vol 122, 1961, p 91; Burgess, A. H. *Hops*, 1964, pp 17, 193; Cox, A. and Gallagher, P. 'A small oast house', *Traditional Kent Buildings*, no 3, 1983, pp 24–25, published by Kent County Council. This oast house became redundant in the 1930s.

37. John Moore, *September Moon*, Companion Book Club edition, 1958, p 103.

38. At the outbreak of the Second World War there were over a thousand farmhouse cheese-makers, in 1960 only one hundred (Cheke, V. *The Story of Cheesemaking in Great Britain*, 1959, p 272; personal communication from P. D. Anderson, Milk Marketing Board). These were small industrial enterprises rather than continuations of the older agricultural tradition.

39. The last cow was milked in the last cowhouse in the City of London in 1954, when

# Revival and Development: 1939–60

David Carson of Swedenborg Square, Stepney, abandoned production (Stout, A. 'London's cowkeepers', *Farmers Weekly*, 18 August 1978, p xiii). R. J. Jones and Sons of Black Lion Yard, Whitechapel, ran him close, though it is not certain when this firm closed ('London's last cowkeeper', *Home Farmer*, June 1951, pp 11–13); personal communication, Mr J. L. Vosper, Express Dairy Group Services Ltd, London). For a totally enclosed herd in Ilford see Speakman, G. 'The Town Farmer', *Farmer and Stockbreeder*, 16 February 1954, p 129. J. Jorden of Lugard Road, SE 15, probably the last cowkeeper in a fully built-up area of London, ceased production in 1967 (Williams, M. 'Milk and beef five miles from Trafalgar Square', *Farmers Weekly*, 16 April 1965, p 50; Stout, A. 'London's cowkeepers', *Farmers Weekly*, 18 August 1978, p xiii). Such other herds as survived in London had access to pasture and were therefore different types of enterprise from these totally enclosed herds. See also Stout, A. 'London's cowkeepers', *Farmers Weekly*, 18 August, 1978, pp v–xiii. In Liverpool between 1936–40 and 1956–60 the number of licensed cowhouses fell from 210 to 35 (Grundy, J. E. *The origins of the Liverpool Cowkeepers*, unpublished MA thesis, Lancaster University, 1982, p 36).

40. The origins of the yarding system are obscure. It apparently began in East Anglia, where farmers increasing their dairy herds beyond the capacity of their cowhouses naturally considered the possibilities of their large and frequently understocked or empty bullock yards. Its origin was certainly spontaneous. Abbot's pre-war innovation (see p 179) was forgotten and little was known for some years of the parallel but unconnected developments in the USA. Indeed, the negligible use made at the time of American experience of this system was one of the earliest instances of the growing failure of the farm building designer to keep abreast of current literature.

41. Buckler, P. 'Slatted floors and other forms of bedding', *Journal of the Farmers' Club*, 1961, pt 4, p 51. The first slatted floor yard in this country since Victorian times was built by a Devon farmer ('Slatted floors', *Farmers Weekly*, 1 July 1960, pp 112–13). See pp 154–5 for earlier examples of this system.

42. The cubicle system was originated in Great Britain by a Cheshire farmer. Various forms of cubicle appeared independently about the same time in Germany and the USA but had no immediate influence on British developments. Howell Evans, the inventor of the cubicle, was awarded the MBE for this service to agriculture and so became the first man officially honoured for developing a new type of farm building (Atkinson, R. 'A private bedroom for every cow', *Farmers Weekly*, vol 59, no 11, 16 March 1962, p vii; Livingston, H. R. *Cow Cubicles*, 1965, p 7; Evans, H. *Cow Cubicles*, 1964).

43. Morris, W. L. and Boyd, L. 'Time and effort to milk cows', *Agricultural Engineering*, vol 36, no 8, August 1955, pp 532–5.

44. Easton, P. H. and Harvey, C. N. *The Development and Performance of the Herringbone Parlour*, published by the Agricultural Research Council, 1964, pp 7–9.

45. The first pilot scheme for the bulk collection of milk began in 1955. By 1962 there were some thirty schemes in operation (*Bulk Milk Collection, The Producer's Guide to Bulk Collection*, Milk Marketing Board, 1962, p 3).

46. Macintosh, J. 'Dairy farming and dairy work', *Journal of the Royal Agricultural Society of England*, vol 99, 1938, p 259; Brighten, C. W. 'How to keep a bull till proven', *Agriculture*, vol 51, no 7, October 1944, pp 301–3. The first official pamphlet on the housing of the bull was published in 1951 (*The Bull Pen*, HMSO).

47. Wellesley, R. 'Labour-aiding in practice', *Journal of the Farmers' Club*, 1958, pt 6, pp 82–3; Jones, J. L. 'The case for zero-grazing', *Country Life*, vol 130, no 3376, 16 November 1961, pp 1188–9.

48. *Barn Hay Drying*, National Agricultural Advisory Service Technical Report 10, Ministry of Agriculture, 1957, pp 1–2; *Greencrop Drying*, Electricity Council (EDA Division), 1967, pp 11–12.

49. Raymond, W. F. 'Grassdrying', *Agriculture*, vol 75, no 4, April 1968, p 156.

50. Hebblethwaite, P., Phillipson, A. and Hepherd, R. Q., 'Forage harvester performance in field tests', *Journal of the British Grassland Society*, vol 14, no 2, 1959, p 140.

51. Dixey, R. N. 'Some costs of silos', *The Farm Economist*, July–September 1942, pp 32–3.

52. Turner, C. 'Self-feeding of silage', *Agriculture*, vol 60, no 8, November 1953, pp 358–9; Beynon, V. H. and Langley, J. A. *Self-feeding of Silage in Devon*, 1958, pp 1–2; Powell, R. 'The self-feeding of silage', *Agricultural Merchant*, vol 38, no 4, April 1958, p 53; Milk Marketing Board, *The Self-feeding of Silage in Dairy Herds*, 1962, which includes a review of the effects of this technique on farmstead planning. A variation of this system, called 'bed and breakfast' because cows were bedded on the silage pack which they later ate, was introduced to this country from Northern Ireland in 1956 (Long, D. 'Bed and breakfast', *Farmers Weekly*, vol 54, no 14, 7 April 1961, p 91).

53. See p 200.

54. Farmer, P. 'Haylage', *Agriculture*, vol 69, no 9, December 1962, pp 435–6. For a

243

detailed account of the development and production of these silos in the USA see Suter, R. C. *The Courage to Change*, Interstate Printers and Publishers Inc, 1964.

55. Hebblethwaite, P., Phillipson, A. and Hepherd, R. Q. 'Forage harvester performance in field tests', *Journal of the British Grassland Society*, vol 14, no 2, 1959, p 140.

56. *Post-war Building Studies, No 17, Farm Buildings*, HMSO, 1945, p 123.

57. *Post-war Building Studies, No 17, Farm Buildings*, HMSO, 1945, pp 113–23.

58. Ministry of Agriculture and Fisheries Bulletin 160, *The Housing of Pigs*, 1953 and 1962 editions.

59. Sainsbury, D. W. B. *Pig Housing*, 1963, pp 39–40.

60. Ministry of Agriculture and Fisheries Bulletin 160, *The Housing of Pigs*, 1953 edition, p 32; 1962 edition, p 20.

61. Easton, P. H. and Harvey, C. N. *Slatted Floor Systems for Pigs*, 1965, pp 7, 22–4, published by the Agricultural Research Council.

62. This expansion was encouraged by the development of small, hybrid birds which needed less floor space per head than the old breeds. Further, the older system required one bird per cage so that the farmer could identify and cull poor yielders, but the evenness of performance of the new hybrids rendered such culling unnecessary. Consequently more than one bird could be housed per cage with a further reduction in floor space. All these factors reduced the capital cost per head of the cage system, and also provided a classic illustration of the effects of technical change on housing systems.

63. Coles, R. 'Current developments in the poultry industry', *Journal of the Royal Agricultural Society of England*, vol 122, 1961, pp 40, 43. The favourable report on the deep litter system by an official mission to North America was the main cause of its adoption in Great Britain (*Development of the Poultry Industry in North America*, HMSO, 1947, pp 7, 13, 26). Two of the farmers on this mission had, however, already pioneered it in Great Britain (Coles, R. *Development of the Poultry Industry of England and Wales,1945–1959*, 1960, p 24). The continuing influence of its country of origin was illustrated by the production in England of a wide span house on American lines and the inclusion of American designed equipment in a prefabricated house (Soutar, D. 'Deep litter poultry houses', *Agricultural Review*, vol 3, no 4, September 1957, pp 36–7). A Wiltshire farmer developed an indigenous system, the less intensive, less efficient but also less expensive henyard (Sykes, J. *The Henyard System*, 1952, p 30). But this failed to survive the competition of the more intensive systems and fell into disuse.

64. Sykes, G. *Agricultural History Review*, vol 18, pt 1, 1970, p 51. See also Edgar, C. D. 'Sir John Eastwood', *Journal of the Royal Agricultural Society of England*, vol 142, 1981, p 100.

65. Benoy, W. G. 'Recent developments in farm buildings', *Journal of the Farmers' Club*, pt 6, 1959, p 73, regarded poultry housing as a matter for specialist firms.

66. It also created as a byproduct a new and more intensive form of egg-production house. The first deep litter house with thermostatically controlled ventilation as well as automatic feeding, watering and cleaning equipment was built about 1956 to produce hatching eggs from specially selected stock for the broiler industry (Rogers, R. E. 'Some aspects of West Country farming', *Journal of the Royal Agricultural Society of England*, vol 118, 1956, p 21).

67. Sykes, G. *Poultry. A Modern Agribusiness*, 1963.

68. Golden, E. F. *Broilers*, 1955, pp 22–3; Feltwell, R. *Broiler Farming*, 1960, pp 13–40; James, B. J. F. *Economics of Broiler Production*, 1960, pp 8–10; Law, E. M. *Broiler Production in Berkshire*, 1960, pp 7–9. Incidentally, the new system brought new fuels to the farm: propane and butane gas for heating broiler houses.

69. Williams, L. J. 'Lambwintering sheds', *Agriculture*, vol 66, no 2, May 1959, pp 65–70. Young breeding stock had been housed in certain Pennine areas 'for generations', but this practice was highly exceptional (Clifton, E. 'Wintering housing of ewes', *Agriculture*, vol 71, no 1, January 1964, p 13). General interest in the inwintering of in-lamb ewes dates from about 1960 (Roberts, L. 'Inwintering ewes in-lamb', *Farmbuildings*, no 7, Summer 1965, p 37).

70. For studies of the considerations on investment in grain storage installations see Nottingham University, publication FR 131, *The Economics of Graindrying and Storage*, 1951; Cambridge University, Farm Economics Branch, School of Agriculture, Report 41, *Drying and Storing Grain on the Farm*, 1956. For a study of the factors affecting the development of a particular type of building in a particular area see Hoare, J. 'The milking parlour system in Cheshire', *Chartered Surveyor*, vol 90, November 1957, pp 233–5.

71. Weller, J. B. *Farm Buildings*, 1965, pp 89–93.

72. One new form of structure which appeared on the farm in this period was entirely composed of concrete. This was the apron on which sugarbeet was stacked for the lorries which took it to the factory. The first recorded example of this was built in 1952 (Trist, P. J. O. *A Survey of the Agriculture of Suffolk*, 1971, p 66).

Plate 37   The end of a long tradition. This longhouse in a Dorset village housed the farmer's family and his livestock under the same roof in the 1970s. The modern age has, however, made necessary the addition of a dairy, the small leanto building of concrete blocks with the churn outside (see page 259) (*Royal Commission on Historical Monuments, England*)

Plate 38   Changes in an East Anglian farmstead. The old buildings near the farmhouse were designed to serve a mixed farming system dependent on the power of men and animals. The new buildings beyond them were designed to serve a substantial, specialised and highly mechanised arable system. The large new building on the left, nearest the camera, houses field machinery and a workshop. The other new buildings provide accommodation for the storage and processing of grain, potatoes and onions (*Crown Copyright, Ministry of Agriculture, Fisheries and Food, Aerial Photography Unit*)

Plate 39 A rotary parlour in which the cows are slowly moved to the milker. The first parlour of this type was built in this country in 1969 (Fullwood and Bland Ltd, *Why go round in circles?* Brochure, 1971, page 1) (*Mr Colin Turner*)

Plate 40 The housing of pigs has become steadily more intensive; from woodlands to the yard (see Plate 7); from the yard to the cottager's pigsty (see Plate 27); from the pigsty to this modern, environmentally controlled fattening house, with mechanical feeding (*Vencel Resil Ltd*)

73. 'Regrettably, tiles and slates must be considered things of the past' (Dominy, J. N. 'Progress towards economic farm buildings', *Agricultural Review*, vol 3, no 7, December 1957, p 37).

74. Grigson, G. *An English Farmhouse*, 1948, p 64.

75. The encouragement of do-it-yourself habits by the long years of the depression, the sudden and acute scarcities of wartime and the increase of owner-occupation which gave farmers full control of their buildings, ensured the continuation of the old tradition of improvisation and the reuse of old materials, especially on smaller farms. In England, about a quarter of the labour used on farm buildings erected between 1945 and 1961 was provided by farm staff, a third by contractors, including estate labour on tenanted farms, and the remainder by a combination of farm and contractor's staff. In Wales, the land of small farms, the figures were half, a quarter and a quarter respectively (Charlick, R. H. *Farm Buildings Survey of England*, 1967, p 10; *Farm Buildings Survey of Wales*, 1965, p 10, published by the National Institute of Agricultural Engineering). Imperial Chemical Industries, *Agriculture in the British Economy*, 1957, p 233, estimated that 50 per cent of the cost of farm buildings went on materials, 25 per cent on building trade workers' wages and 25 per cent on agricultural workers' wages. No systematic information on the use of secondhand buildings or building materials is available, but the farming press and the farming landscape alike bore witness to the strength of the farmer's continuing interest in cheap improvisation. A pleasing example was the use of an abandoned windmill as a silo) 'Notes from a land agent's diary', *Journal of the Land Agents Society*, vol 42, 1943, p 92), while in the 1970s officials of the RAF Museum at Hendon, seeking parts of First and Second World War aircraft, found farmsteads a useful source of material (*Times RAF Museum Supplement*, 18 November 1972, p 11). One of the most successful farmers of this period mentioned with pride his grain store built 'mainly by farm labour with scrap steel' (Paterson, R. *Milk from Grass*, 1965, p 19). A textbook of the 1950s, written by a farmer for farmers, typified this tradition. It was entitled *Build Your Own Farm Buildings* and contained advice on the use of strawbales, Nissen huts and materials salvaged from demolished buildings (Henderson, F. *Build Your Own Farm Buildings*, 1955, pp 15, 40, 70, 174–7, 202). Ten years later, another textbook which sought to 'show the farmer what is available by way of new methods of construction . . . and to present the architect, surveyor, or engineer or contractor with the farmer's problems', described ways of using railway sleepers for the walls of yards and horizontal silos (Pasfield, D. H. *Farm Building Design and Construction*, 1965, p 131). Less precedently in this period the Ministry of Agriculture made an unexpected contribution to the ancient tradition of reusing old building materials. In the years immediately after the war, when all materials were scarce and most were rationed, it made available to farmers through trade channels components manufactured from steel salvaged from air raid shelters from which the frameworks of a variety of farm buildings using a range of standardised dimensions could be constructed (*Journal of the Land Agents Society*, vol 47, 1948, pp 72, 89).

76. Benoy, W. G. 'Recent developments in farm buildings', *Journal of the Farmers' Club*, pt 6, 1959, p 74.

77. See p 196.

78. 'It is essential that new farm buildings should be capable of adaptation to other uses without unreasonable difficulty or expense' (*Post-war Building Studies, No 17, Farm Buildings*, HMSO, 1945, pp 6, 8, 10).

79. For example, Culverwell, J. D. 'Adaptability in farm buildings', *Journal of the Land Agents Society*, vol 52, 1953, pp 335–7; Harvey, N. 'Farm buildings, present trends and future possibilities', *Journal of the Land Agents Society*, vol 61, 1962, pp 28–30; Clayton, J. R. *Versatility in Farm Buildings*, unpublished MSc thesis, University of London, 1964.

# 10 POST-WAR
# FARMSTEADS:
# SOME EXAMPLES

## New Wine in Old Bottles

The Hanoverians were primarily concerned with planning new farmsteads for new farms, the Victorians with planning new farmsteads for old farms. But their successors in the mid-twentieth century were preoccupied with the improvement of old farmsteads on old farms. So the main theme of case studies in this period was the remodelling of particular sets of buildings for particular needs, and such plans of new farmsteads as were prepared illustrated the desirable rather than the immediately practical.

## Principle and Practice in Oxfordshire

The discrepancy between technical possibilities and economic realities was strikingly shown by the work of the Henderson Brothers. In the 1920s this remarkable pair bought a rundown farm of 85 acres in Oxfordshire and by the sustained application of the traditional agricultural virtues gradually made it one of the most successful and famous farms in the country. As the farm improved, so did the farm buildings, and by the outbreak of war a series of adaptations and additions had converted the original farmstead, which probably dated from enclosure-time and consisted of a barn, a range of livestock buildings and a yard, into a set of buildings capable of meeting the needs of an intensive farm carrying pigs, poultry and a milking herd.[1]

The farmstead thus developed (see Fig 27) was markedly above average. But the Hendersons were well aware of the weakness inherent in such piecemeal improvement. So the design of a steading for a farm of 100 acres with which Frank Henderson won first prize in a national competition in 1947 illustrated by contrast the consequences of a more radical and less restricted application of contemporary resources to contemporary problems.[2]

The proposed farmstead is shown in Fig 28. Its advantages over the real one were numerous. It was more compact and therefore wasted no space and minimised travelling and haulage distances; it provided easier access to the road from which came the lorries to collect milk and livestock and deliver feedstuffs, fertilisers and tractor fuel; and it

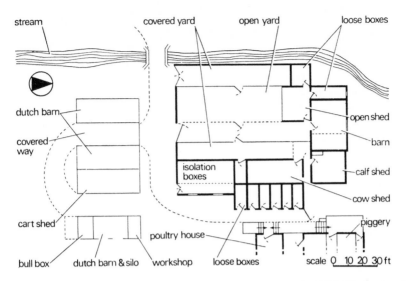

27   Plan of steading on an Oxfordshire farm of 85 acres in the early 1950s. The barn and some of the livestock buildings forming the yard probably date from the late eighteenth century when the parish was enclosed (*Faber & Faber, Mr G. Henderson*)

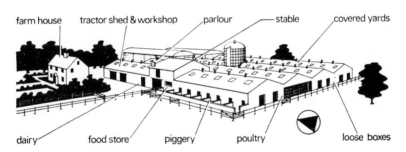

28   Model farmstead for a farm of 100 acres designed by the farming brothers who developed the steading shown in Fig 27 (*Farmer and Stockbreeder*)

gave better protection to men, animals and manure as roofing covered everything except the pigsty runs. Many of these benefits were secured simply by better planning and better design, but there was one significant change of method: the abandonment of the cowhouse system for the loose-housing system. For the combination of milking parlour and yards, the former allowing more thorough mechanisation of the milking process, the latter the removal of manure by tractor, illustrated the growing use of machinery in the farmstead which was so conspicuous a feature of this period. Nevertheless, the days of general mechanisation in field or buildings were still in the future. The plan included stables as well as a tractor shed and assumed human prime-movers for most of the farmstead chores.

249

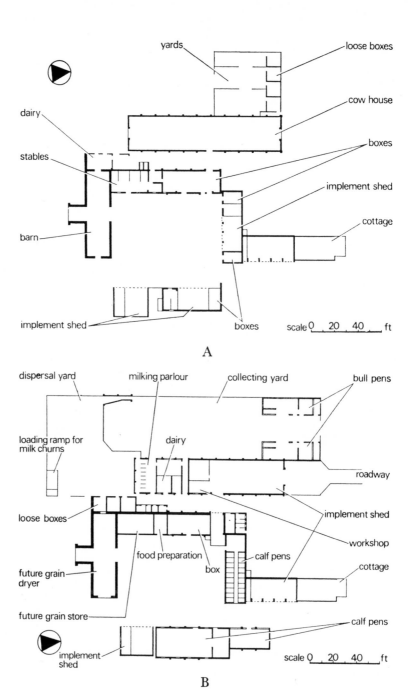

yards

loose boxes

cow house

dairy

boxes

stables

implement shed

cottage

barn

implement shed

boxes

scale 0 20 40 ft

A

dispersal yard

milking parlour

collecting yard

bull pens

loading ramp for
milk churns

dairy

roadway

loose boxes

implement shed

workshop

future grain
dryer

food preparation

box

calf pens

cottage

future grain store

calf pens

implement
shed

scale 0 20 40 ft

B

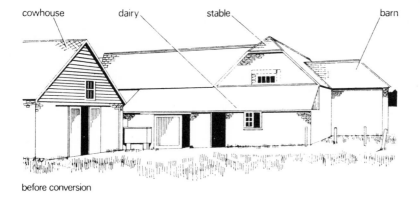

cowhouse dairy stable barn

before conversion

C

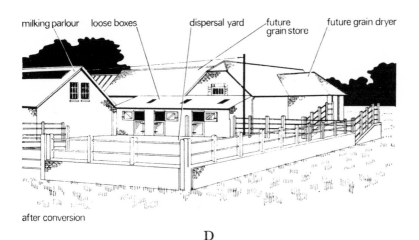

milking parlour loose boxes dispersal yard future grain store future grain dryer

after conversion

D

29 A Dorset farmstead before and after modernisation in the 1950s:
(A) plan before modernisation; (B) plan after modernisation; (C) view from the south-west before modernisation; (D) view from the south-west after modernisation (*Crosby Lockwood & Son Ltd, Mr G. Benoy*)

## Modernisation of a Dorset Farmstead

Fig 29 shows a typical example of remodelling which was undertaken in the early 1950s on a large Dorset farm, whose buildings had already seen considerable adaptation to changing needs. The original steading, built in traditional fashion around a yard, dated from the early nineteenth century and implied a corn-and-meat system of farming in which yarded bullocks trod straw from the barn into

251

manure for the light and hungry fields of the area. A lifetime later, when this system was overthrown by imports from overseas and the British farmer turned increasingly to the production of milk which faced no such competition, a dairy unit of cowhouse, yards and looseboxes was added. But the present modernisation was less drastic. It sought not to introduce a substantial new enterprise but to improve the efficiency of existing ones.[3]

The main change was the replacement of milking in the cowhouse by milking in the parlour. This necessitated new yards to control the cows as they entered and left the parlour but, since local soil and climate allowed the herd to lie out in the fields all the year round, released the cowhouse for other uses. Part of it was converted, appropriately, to the milking parlour, the remainder to an implement shed and workshop. At the same time, the barn was made ready for a grain dryer to condition the corn received from the new combine-harvester, the stable for the silos in which this grain would be stored. Minor improvements included the adaptation of two existing ranges of buildings to calfsheds for the increased head of young stock and the housing of the farm's two bulls in special-purpose pens which were safer and healthier than the dark, constricted looseboxes of the old order.

Externally, the modernisation showed itself in a series of comparatively minor structural improvements and additions whose factory-produced concrete, tubular steel, asbestos-cement sheeting and plastic glazing contrasted technically as well as physically with the older materials from brickyard, quarry and woodland. But the refurbished buildings of the pre-mechanical age now housed the new mechanised processes of parlour milking and bulk-grain handling and the routines of the farmstead were rearranged around them.

### New Work on a Devon Farm

As the years passed, it became increasingly difficult to fit the growing mass of new techniques and equipment into the old farmstead framework. This last example, therefore, illustrates the tendency to house new systems in new ranges of buildings instead of adapting existing ones to them (see Fig 30). The particular unit shown was completed in 1964 and represents advanced practice as known at the very end of our period.[4]

The general problem of this 177 acre Devon farm, the modernisation of an old farmstead to meet new needs – in this case the housing of a sixty-head dairy herd – was familiar. But its solution used a combination of new techniques, notably cubicles for housing the cows, a herring-bone parlour system for milking them and mechanical

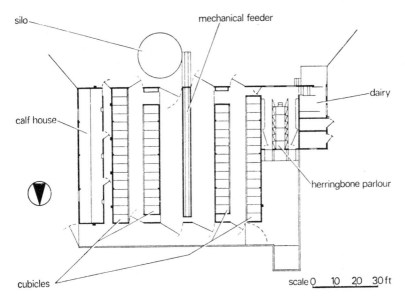

silo

mechanical feeder

dairy

calf house

herringbone parlour

cubicles

scale 0 10 20 30 ft

30   Plan of dairy unit built in 1964 (*Farmers Weekly, Mr A. L. Flower*)

conveying equipment for feeding them with bulk fodder from the silo, at once too large and too complex to be incorporated into the existing buildings. So a new dairy unit, designed around a series of industrially equipped mechanical processes and constructed of industrially produced or industrially treated components and materials, was built on the opposite side of the road and the old farmstead relegated to such subsidiary jobs as housing dry cows.

The physical change on this farm was greater than in either of the previous examples. Indeed, it came near to fulfilling the dream of Henderson when he had planned his model farmstead over fifteen years earlier. But it fulfilled it with substantial technical differences. Henderson assumed the mechanisation of the milking and mucking-out. This new design included a more comprehensive mechanical milking system, a simplified because strawless form of mechanised muck-removal which pumped the liquid wastes on to the fields, mechanical refrigeration in the dairy and the even more recent innovation of machinery for transporting silage from store to trough. But this comparison offers more than technical lessons. It also illustrates the speed of change in the modern agricultural economy. By 1964 the prize-winning proposal of 1947 was already part of history.

## NOTES

1. Henderson, G. *The Farming Ladder*, 1956, pp 18, 168–71.
2. *New Ideas for Farm Buildings*, published by Farmer and Stockbreeder, 1947, pp 3–6.
3. Benoy, W. G. *Farm Buildings*, 1956, pp 74–5.
4. 'All-new dairy unit', *Farmbuildings*, no 8, Autumn 1965, p 104.

# 11 EPILOGUE: OUR OWN TIMES

### Changing Economics

By the early 1960s the major innovations of the previous period had successfully and substantially established themselves in general practice. Loose-housing systems and milking parlours, grain drying and storage plants, silage installations, environmentally controlled piggeries and poultry houses, mechanical materials-handling, and concrete and asbestos-cement construction had between them gone far to transform the farmstead in a generation.

Indeed, the growing proportion of new buildings and remodelled farmsteads, white and stark in the green landscape, provided conspicuous evidence of the revival of the farming system in which they played so important a part. But the next period brought to this system economic stresses and strains of an intensity forgotten for nearly a quarter of a century. The scarcities and demands of the previous period had passed, and more traditional types of economic incentive and constraint returned, continuing in varying form with varying force. The general background to this period was summarised in a review published in 1969. 'Food supplies were running to surplus throughout the western world, production had caught up with rising prosperity, and the crisis facing agriculture was no longer one of shortages but of overproduction in almost all commodities.'[1] The terms of trade had turned against the farmer.

In general, the farming industry responded to the new conditions by specialisation and intensification, running fewer but bigger enterprises on fewer but bigger farms and making steadily greater use of the aids and knowledge provided by research and development to lower costs and increase output. Such drastic changes in systems meant equally drastic changes in buildings. In many ways, however, the farmer of these decades was better equipped than his father to develop or adapt his farmstead to changing needs.

### New Resources

He could obtain official grants towards the cost of new buildings, he was served by a substantial and experienced trade, he could seek advice from a growing number of private and corporate consultants

254

who now supplemented the official advisory services and receive recommendations based on a growing volume of research findings. It was typical of the times that in 1964 the Farm Buildings Centre, later renamed the Farm Buildings Information Centre, was founded by private enterprise; in 1966 the Farm Buildings Unit of the Agricultural Research Council completed its experimental period and became a permanent department of the National Institute of Agricultural Engineering; in 1974 the Royal Institute of British Architects established a 'special interest group' called Architects in Agriculture; and between 1978 and 1981 the British Standards Institute issued in sections the first comprehensive code of practice for the design and construction of farm buildings.[2]

The effects of such developments on the farmstead were considerable and pervading. Improvements were more comprehensive and more systematic. There was much less adaptation of old farm buildings to new farm purposes, much more demolition and new construction. Planning was more sophisticated and more informed. The evolution of efficient milking routines for different sizes of herd and types of parlour, for example, produced a substantial technical literature, while even the growing revival of the ancient practice of inwintering sheep, which only require relatively simple structures, owed much to the findings of research centres on the environmental needs of the flock and ways and means of meeting them.

## Technical Development

By this time, however, the technical revolution of the immediate post-war years had run its course and the increasing efforts to improve efficiency and reduce costs relied on the development of existing technologies and their more widespread use rather than on radical changes in methods and structures. For example, new types of milking parlour fitted with such new types of equipment as automatic cluster removers increased the number of cows that could be milked per man-hour. Potato stores acquired more sophisticated ventilation systems and heavier insulation to enable growers to meet the increasingly exacting specifications of retailers. New forms of mechanical handling simplified work routines and necessitated the planning of farmsteads to allow the linear runs which such equipment required for efficient operation. There was also continuing interest in the possibilities of reducing capital costs and easing any future demolitions or adaptations by such cheap or limited-life methods of construction as monopitch roofs, polebarns, frameworks with plastic cladding and, inevitably, do-it-yourself improvisations.

Little of this was new in principle. But there were, in addition, various novelties. Some, such as tanks for the storage of liquid fertilisers and special-purpose stores for pesticides, met new needs created by new technologies. Others, such as computers in the farm office and electronic monitoring and control systems in livestock buildings and cropstores, were more prophetic, foreshadowing possible new types of process and eventually new types of structure.[3]

## The Lingering Past

The future was taking shape. But the astonishing variations in speed of technical change, and consequently between new and old in farming practice, which are such remarkable features of our farming economy, continued. The years which saw the first electronic presence in the farmstead also saw some lingering survivals from the past make their final departure into history. In the 1960s a Victorian waterwheel still turned on a Shropshire farm, though it generated electricity instead of grinding corn.[4] In the 1970s it was still possible to find a couple of longhouses occupied by the farmer and his family at one end and by cattle at the other;[5] the last of the Liverpool cowkeepers, who incidentally fed his herd in summertime on grass cut from Everton Football Club's training ground, went out of business in 1975;[6] and corn was threshed by flail in a Yorkshire barn in 1976.[7]

## New Types of Problem

Meanwhile, the implications of the present and the appreciation of the past were bringing unfamiliar problems to the farm. In these years for the first time the general public began to react to developments in the farmstead and demand changes in its design and management.

## Livestock Welfare and Livestock Wastes

Thus, the growing intensification of livestock systems raised questions of animal welfare which led to the appointment of an official committee of enquiry and the formulation of official codes for the guidance of designers and stockmen.[8] Intensification also raised problems of pollution. In general, it meant the concentration of increasing numbers of livestock and therefore of manure on limited areas of land. In particular, it included the spread of labour-saving cubicles for dairy cows and slatted-floor systems for beef cattle and pigs which did not require litter. The wastes these produced took the form not of the traditional semi-solid manure but of a slurry requiring systems of storage and spreading which were liable to cause local nuisances of smell and more serious hazards to human and animal

256

health. There was no single answer to the problems thus created. Nevertheless, by the 1970s research, development and field experience had evolved systems of treatment and management which provided satisfactory solutions on most farms.[9]

Meanwhile, less objective pressures were beginning to affect farmer and builder. These raised different questions in different areas at different times. But they all originated in the growing public concern for the conservation of the environment, particularly for the protection of the countryside and the valued legacies from the past which it contained.

## The Appearance of Farm Buildings

The first issue raised was aesthetic. The new types of building and building materials were chosen to satisfy the criteria of those whose first priority was the efficient production of food. They did not always satisfy the criteria of those who sought recreation and visual pleasure in the countryside. So visitors from the towns joined with the increasing number of former townsmen who had settled in the country in their resentment of the cruder forms of structural reminder that the farms they saw around them were merely the rural equivalent of the factories they had left behind them in the cities.

The lengthy controversy thus created was confused by the traditional unconcern with visual quality of most of those who built and used commercial farm buildings and by the conservationists' difficulties in formulating consistent and systematic advisory doctrines. It was worse confounded by farmers' general fears of undue influence by protesters who had no necessary connection with farm or countryside and no necessary understanding of the effects of their demands, and by their more particular fears of increased planning controls and increased building costs without economic return. But the considerable literature this issue produced suggests that over the years most of the problems it produced were adequately controlled by local argument, by local examples, which were sometimes encouraged by award schemes, by local compromises and by mutual education.[10]

## Conservation and Conversion

Soon, however, public concern extended from the appearance of the new to the preservation of the old. The contribution of traditional farm buildings to the landscape had, of course, long been appreciated by visitors as well as by painters. Their historical importance was now increasingly recognised. But their numbers were shrinking. Every year, individual farm buildings and sometimes, following farm

257

amalgamations, whole farmsteads, were demolished or abandoned and allowed to collapse because they no longer served contemporary farming needs; and the rate of loss increased with the increasing speed of farming change. Agriculturally, such changes were inevitable and desirable, for the farmer can no more work efficiently with obsolete buildings than the manufacturer can work efficiently with obsolete plant. Nevertheless, the countryside was steadily and irrevocably losing a source of pleasure and understanding.[11]

In principle, the problem was familiar. The legacies of the past in this country are manifestly too numerous for automatic preservation and the proportion which can be preserved or even properly recorded is controlled by the amount of limited resources available. All this implies some system of priorities. Farm buildings, however, were a recent arrival in the long queue of threatened types of building applying for preservation or recording, while the formulation of general priorities or criteria for individual selection presented unfamiliar problems. For such decisions require research into the history of the farm and the agricultural history of the area if the historical importance of particular farm buildings or farmsteads is to be properly assessed. Yet few conservationists were familiar with agrarian history or with the industry which for its own particular purposes first built and then abandoned these buildings.[12]

Furthermore, every farm building was the property of some individual entrepreneur whose livelihood was directly affected by the efficiency of his farmstead. He might not object to his buildings being recorded, though even this could raise fears of official restrictions on adaptation or demolition. But he was seldom able or willing to pay indefinitely for the preservation of a building from which he derived little or no material advantage and frequently appreciable material disadvantage; and few others were prepared to provide the necessary funds. The point was made sadly clear by the failure of private interest and public authority to save from partial collapse through neglect that artistic, agricultural and structural treasure, the twelfth-century monastic barn at Coggeshall which is probably, outside Japan, the oldest timber building in the world and certainly one of the most impressive.[13]

Nevertheless, the importance of preserving or recording a shrinking asset has been increasingly realised, and much has been achieved by official and private organisations. In particular, a number of individual farm buildings or steadings have been conserved in varying degrees by conversion to housing, riding stables, workshops for light industries or crafts, or village social centres[14] (see Plate 43). Some, too, have been re-erected in open-air museums or used to house agricultural exhibitions.[15] Only a small proportion, however, are capable of such conversion or are likely to attract the funds necessary for indefinite survival. On present probabilities, structural recording and the collection of such information on the building's agricultural background and history as can be found without excessive effort seem the best investment for much of the limited time and skill available.[16]

## The Continuity of Tradition

It is appropriate to end a history of farm buildings with a plea for the conservation or recording of the surviving but threatened raw material on which the development of the subject depends. It is equally appropriate to recall the continuity of the story from the first to the last chapter. For all the changes of recent years in farmsteads have caused no break with tradition. On the contrary, the landowners and farmers of today are continuing the oldest and wisest of all the traditions that guide those who equip farmland with buildings. The men who build silos, parlours, grainstores and intensive livestock houses of steel, concrete and asbestos-cement and fit them with mechanical and electronic equipment are in a direct line of descent from the forgotten peasantry who built longhouses and cruck barns from local timber, stone, clay and straw. Like their professional ancestors down the centuries, they are using the resources of their time to meet the needs of their time.

## NOTES

1. Donaldson, J. G. S., Donaldson, F. and Barber, D. *Farming in Britain Today*, 1969, p 3.
2. British Standards Institution, BS 5502, *Design of Buildings and Structures for Agriculture*, Section 1, 1978; Section 2, 1980; Section 3, 1981. See also Farm Buildings Association *Guide to BS 5502*, 1980.
3. The technical developments of this period can be followed in the periodical *Farmbuildings*, published from 1963 to 1967; the perodical *Farm Buildings Digest* and the other publications of the Farm Buildings Information Centre; the *Journal of the Farm Buildings Association*; and the relevant publications of the Ministry of Agriculture, Fisheries and Food, including from 1977 the *Annual Report* of the Agricultural Advisory and Development Service. See also the textbooks of this period listed on p 268. For examples of the continuing tradition of do-it-yourself improvisation and the reuse of old materials, which do not normally find a place in the specialised technical journals, see *Farmers Weekly*, 3 April 1970, p 35; 10 March 1972, p 47; 25 August 1978, p vii.
4. This waterwheel survives at the Hem Farm, Shifnal, Shropshire. (Institute of Industrial Archaeology, 'Recording farm buildings' course, October 1983.)
5. In Cornwall some longhouses survived in full use into the 1960s (*Mediaeval Archaeology*, vol 6–7, 1962–3, pp 281–2). For two survivals of longhouses for family and for cattle into the 1970s see Mercer, E. *English Vernacular Houses*, 1975, p 44 (Charity Farm, Osmington, Dorset, which is shown on plate 37) and *Mediaeval Archaeology*, vol 22, 1978, p 182 (North Devon).
6. For the last of the Liverpool cowkeepers see *Better Breeding*, published by the Milk Marketing Board, Spring 1975, p 6. This herd ceased production in the same year (personal communication, Miss V. Alexander, Milk Marketing Board). See also Grundy, J. E. *The Origins of Liverpool Cowkeepers*, unpublished MA thesis, Lancaster University, 1982, which covers the whole history of this trade.
7. Hartley, M. and Ingilby, J. *Life in the Moorlands of North-East Yorkshire*, 1976, p 113.
8. *Report of the Technical Committee to Enquire into the Welfare of Animals Kept Under*

*Intensive Livestock Husbandry Systems*, HMSO, 1965, commonly called the 'Brambell report' after its chairman. The Minister of Agriculture was empowered by the Agriculture (Miscellaneous Provisions) Act 1968 to issue 'codes of recommendation for the guidance of persons connected with livestock, and the first code was published in 1969. The Act also established the Farm Animals Welfare Standing Committee to keep the problem under review. This Committee was developed in 1979 into the Farm Animal Welfare Council and given wider powers.

9. Agricultural Research Council, *Studies on Farm Livestock Wastes*, 1976, pp 1–8, which gives an account of the origins and development of this problem; Harvey, N. *Farm Livestock Wastes and Silage Effluent*, annotated bibliography 148H, 1977, in Departments of the Environment and Transport Headquarters Library bibliography series, 1977; Royal Commission on Environmental Pollution, Seventh report, *Agriculture and Pollution*, 1979, pp 126–59, 196–205; National Agricultural Centre, report of conference on *Farm Odours – New Answers to Old Problems*, 1982. For an advisory summary of this problem and its control, including public health aspects and relevant legislation, see Ministry of Agriculture, Fisheries and Food Booklet 2077, *General Information; Farm Waste Management*, revised 1983.

10. Harvey, N. *Farm Buildings, Planning and Appearance*, annotated bibliography 198 in Departments of the Environment and Transport Headquarters Library bibliography series, 1979, which includes references to the costs of meeting the amenity requirements of planning authorities and to awards for good design by Cheshire County Council, the Country Landowners Association and the *Financial Times*. For a recent summary of advisory recommendations see Noton, N. H. *Farm Buildings*, 1982, pp 170–9.

11. No general, up-to-date figures are available on the national stock of old farm buildings or on the rate of loss. For figures on existing old farm buildings see Peters, J. E. C. *The Development of Farm Buildings in Western Lowland Staffordshire up to 1880*, 1969; Wiliam, E. *Traditional Farm Buildings in North-East Wales, 1550–1900*, 1982; and the surveys listed under Other Modern Publications on p 269 and under Unpublished Thesis on p 270. The only type of building for which estimated numbers are available is the barn. The Society for the Protection of Ancient Buildings estimated in 1979 that there were in England and Wales between 15,000 and 20,000 barns built before the eighteenth century (*Report of the Committee of the Society*, 1978–9, p 8). Brunskill, R. W. *Traditional Farm Buildings of Britain*, 1982, p 143, estimated from various evidence, including studies in Westmorland and in Essex (Essex County Council, *The Essex Countryside, Historic Barns*, 1980, pp 44–5), that the number of barns in England and Wales was between 60,000 and 70,000. Few figures on losses have been published. Sweetland, P. *Barns of Bredon Hill*, unpublished thesis, Birmingham School of Architecture, 1979, p 46, identified sixty-one barns existing or known to have existed in the area. Of these, six had been converted to other uses and twenty-three had been demolished. Seventeen of the twenty-three which had been demolished were lost between 1930 and 1972. Essex County Council, *The Essex Countryside, Historic Barns*, 1980, p 45, estimated that half or a third of the original number of barns in the county survive. Caffyn, L. *A Study of Farm Buildings in Selected Parishes in East Sussex*, unpublished MA thesis, Manchester University, 1981, p 94, found that three barns, the oldest dating from the sixteenth century, and one farmstead had disappeared in a small area around East Chittington church in the past few years.

12. In 1980 The Montagu Report, (see note 14) noted that 'agricultural buildings . . . have only recently become a preservation issue' and that 'the vast majority of architecturally or historically interesting farm buildings remain unidentified and unprotected' (pp 24–5). An organisation provisionally called the Historic Farm Land and Buildings Group, formed in 1984, seeks to serve as a forum for the various disciplines and interests concerned with this subject.

13. For the barn see Hewett, C. A. *English Historic Carpentry*, 1980, p 47; Rackham, O. *Ancient Woodland*, 1980, p 147. For its recent history see 'A chronicle of collapse', *Architect's Journal*, vol 168, 22 November 1978, pp 992–3. In 1982 Braintree District Council obtained grants from the Historic Buildings Council of England and the National Heritage Memorial Fund for its purchase and restoration. So the story has a happy ending. But its ending is happier than its implications.

14. The first general review of the possibilities of converting redundant farm buildings to non-agricultural uses appeared in 1980 (*Britain's Historic Buildings; a Policy for their Future Use*, published by the British Tourist Authority, pp 24–9, 45, 81. This is commonly called 'the Montagu report' after Lord Montagu, the chairman of the Working Party which compiled it). The considerable literature on this subject includes Davies, N. W. I. *Barns and Barn Conversion in Cumbria*, unpublished BSc thesis, Brunel University, 1979; Sweetland, P. *Barns of Bredon Hill*, unpublished thesis, Birmingham School of Architecture, 1979, pp 49–55; Countryside Commission, *Bunkhouse Barns*, 1980; Essex County Council, *The Essex Countryside, Historic Barns*, 1980; Hampshire County Council Planning Department, *New*

*Uses for Redundant Farm Buildings*, 1980; Architects in Agriculture, *Coleshill Model Farm, Oxfordshire*, 1981; Council for Small Industries in Rural Areas, *Profit From Those Redundant Farm Buildings*, 1981; Darley, G. *The National Trust Book of the Farm*, 1981, pp 240–5; Brunskill, R. W. *Traditional Farm Buildings of Britain*, 1982, pp 140–8; Council for Small Industries in Rural Areas, *Old Buildings, New Opportunities*, 1982; Hampshire County Council Planning Department, *Saving Old Farm Buildings*, 1982; Ministry of Agriculture, Fisheries and Food, *Converting Old Farm Buildings*, Booklet 2407, 1982, and *New Uses for Surplus Farm Buildings*, Leaflet 805, 1982; Pitkin, M. *The Farm Wheel and Machinery at Temple Balsall*, unpublished thesis, Birmingham School of Architecture, 1982; Society for the Protection of Ancient Buildings, *The SPAB Barns Book*, 1982; Ministry of Agriculture, Fisheries and Food, 'Historic farm buildings; conservation can pay', *Current Topics*, no 29, 31 October 1983, pp 1–3. The development of interest in this  subject is illustrated by the Henley Scheme, instituted by the Country Landowners Association in 1981, which offers awards for the best conversions of redundant farm buildings to other purposes, and by the booklets listing such farm buildings available for sale and possible conversion to residential or commercial purposes issued in 1981 and 1982 by a firm of Chartered Surveyors, Chartered Auctioneers and Estate Agents, G. W. Finn and Sons of Canterbury. For case studies of the conversion of redundant farm buildings to non-agricultural purposes see, for example, McIntosh, G. ' A new home for Knebworth's barns', *Country Life*, 17 August 1972, pp 386–7; Venn, D. 'Converting Old Farm Buildings', *Country Landowner*, December 1975, pp 33–4; Harvey, G. 'Small firms inject new life into old buildings', *Farmers Weekly*, 27 June 1980, pp xxxiii–xxxv; Rhodes, J. 'Welcome to the granary', *Farmers Weekly*, 30 January 1981, pp xi–xiii; Smith, S. 'A barn with a view' and 'Kath's bungalow once housed a milking herd', *Farmers Weekly*, 11 June 1982, pp 99–101; 'The Fingringhoe Centre', leaflet issued by the Essex Naturalists Trust, Fingringhoe Wick Nature Reserve, Colchester, Essex, (n.d.). Sometimes, however, 'rural conservation' assists in the destruction of old farm buildings by providing incentives for their demolition and the quarrying of their traditional materials for the repair of other vernacular buildings or the embellishment of less traditional buildings (Sweetland, P. *The Barns of Bredon Hill*, unpublished thesis Birmingham School of Architecture, 1979, p 49; *Britain's Historic Buildings; a Policy for their Future Use*, the British Tourist Authority, 1980, p 26; review of Harrison, J. A. C. *Old Stone Buildings; Buying, Extending, Renovation*, 1982, in *SPAB News*, vol 4, January 1983, p 10).

15. Toulson, S. *Discovering Farm Museums and Farm Parks*, 1977; Armstrong, J. R. *Traditional Farm Buildings Open to the Public*, 1979 (see pp 271–2, Plates 5, 8, 9, 12, 16, 21).

16. For systems of classification and recording see Chapman, V. 'Recording farmsteads', *Bulletin* 3, Industrial Archaeology Society for the North-East, 1967 (also in *History Field Studies in the Durham Area*, Durham University Institute of Education, 1966); Brunskill, R. W. 'Recording the buildings of the farmstead', *Transactions of the Ancient Monuments Society*, vol 21, 1976, pp 114–50; Peters, J. E. C. *Discovering Traditional Farm Buildings*, 1981, pp 76–77. For systems of classification and recording in operation see Peters, J. E. C. *The Development of Farm Buildings in Western Lowland Staffordshire up to 1880*, 1969; Wiliam, E. *Traditional Farm Buildings in North-East Wales, 1550–1900*, 1982; and the area surveys listed under 'Unpublished Theses' on p 270. The first course on recording farm buildings was held by the School of Continuing Education, University of Kent, in May 1983. No 'standard form', however, has been published for obtaining any readily available information on the farm on which the recorded building stands, the historical function of the building in relation to the other buildings of the farmstead, the farming system for which it was built or adapted, and on relevant local history. For case studies of the historical development of particular farmsteads, for the most part with information on the agricultural context, see under Other Modern Publications p 269. A series of such detailed studies of farm buildings as part of farming history would make a valuable contribution to our understanding of the agrarian past. It would also provide useful guidance on research procedures and on conservation priorities.          .

# APPENDIX

# DATING PRE-INDUSTRIAL FARM BUILDINGS

The dating of pre-industrial buildings for which documentary evidence is not available presents considerable difficulties. The general problem is illustrated in extreme form by a 'much altered' barn in Gloucestershire. A pointed window and buttresses suggest a medieval origin. The stonework, however, includes a Roman sculpture reused as masonry; one inscription in the barn records that it was built in 1300 and another that it was burnt down in 1728 and rebuilt in 1729. 'Even when "obvious" evidence is plentiful, dating a barn can be quite difficult' (Fowler, P. *Farms in England*, 1983, plates 51–3).

This appendix gives a selected list of references on the methods used to date pre-industrial farm buildings. See also Index entries under 'Dating'. Nearly all the references concern barns.

### Dating by Design and Construction

Dating by design and construction is frequently difficult and unreliable because traditional types of building and building materials and methods often continued with little change over long periods; many buildings have been altered, patched or reconstructed during their long lives; and a number incorporate reused materials.

References to the continuity of design and construction include Cottrill, F. 'Old farm buildings in Hampshire', *Country Landowner*, vol 17, August 1966, p 218; Pryor, K. A. 'Excavations at "The Park", Carshalton', *Surrey Archaeological Collections*, vol 20, 1975, p 8; Brown, F. E. 'Aisled timber barns in Kent', *Vernacular Architecture*, vol 7, 1976, pp 36–40; Reynolds, J. *The Hampshire Barn*, unpublished thesis, Architectural Association, 1979, pp 9, 12, 14–15; Sweetland, P. *Barns of Bredon Hill*, unpublished thesis, Birmingham School of Architecture, 1979, pp 19–20; Brown, F. E. 'Aisled timber barns in East Kent', *Traditional Kent Buildings*, published by Kent County Council, no 1, 1980, pp 26–8; Roberts, H. M. 'Cruckframed roofs in the City of Durham', *Transactions of the Architectural and Archaeological Society of Durham and Northumberland*, NS vol 5, 1980, p. 95; Tyson, B. 'Rydal Hall Farm. The development of a Westmorland farmstead before 1700', *Transactions of the Cumberland and Westmorland Antiquarian and Archaeological Society*, vol 80, 1980, p 126; Cook, O. *English Cottages and Farmhouses*, 1982, p 140.

Plate 41  An example of the mechanisation of materials handling. Forage is blown
from the tower through telescopic pipework to the waiting cattle (*Mr R. Warner*)

Plate 42  The re-use of old buildings for agricultural purposes is an ancient tradition. This barn was once a church (*Nigel Harvey*)

Plate 43  Nowadays the process is reversed. This redundant winter yarding unit has recently been converted into a workshop for a firm which restores antiques (*Council for Small Industries in Rural Areas*)

References to alteration, patching and partial reconstruction include Alcock, N. W. 'Devonshire farmhouses. Some Dartmoor houses', *Report and Transactions of the Devonshire Association*, vol 101, 1969, p 92; Devon County Council, *Devon's Traditional Buildings*, 1978, p 18; Reynolds, J. *The Hampshire Barn*, unpublished thesis, Architectural Association, 1978, p 6; Sweetland, P. *Barns of Bredon Hill*, unpublished thesis, Birmingham School of Architecture, 1979, p 21; *SPAB News*, vol 3, October 1982, p 53 (Buglawton Hall Barn, Cheshire).

For the reuse of old materials see Index entries under 'Reuse of old building, building materials', including case study of the dating difficulties caused by this practice on p98. A farm buildings survey in progress in Shropshire has found a considerable reuse of old timbers. (Personal communication, Mrs Carol Ryan, Planning Department, Shropshire County Council, 1983.) Hewett, C. A. *English Historic Carpentry*, 1980, describes, and illustrates with examples that include barns, a system of dating medieval, sixteenth- and seventeenth-century timber buildings by changing techniques of structural carpentry. References to the use of this system include Castle, S. A. 'The mediaeval aisled barns at Kingsbury Manor Farm, St Albans, and Croxley Hall Farm', *Hertfordshire Archaeology*, vol 3, 1973, pp 134–8; Gibson, A. V. B. 'The mediaeval aisled barn at Parkbury Farm, Radlett', *Hertfordshire Archaeology*, vol 4, 1974–6, pp 158–63; Brown, F. E. 'Aisled barns in Kent', *Vernacular Architecture*, vol 7, 1976, p. 36; Reynolds, J. *The Hampshire Barn*, unpublished thesis, Architectural Association, 1978, p 13; Roberts, J. H. 'Five mediaeval barns', *Hertfordshire Archaeology*, vol 7, 1979, pp 159, 164; Brown, F. E. 'Aisled timber barns in East Kent', *Traditional Kent Buildings*, published by Kent County Council, no 1, 1980, pp 22–8; Essex County Council, *The Essex Countryside, Historic Barns*, 1980, pp 14–16, 18–21; Snow, T. and Wong, T. Y. 'Upper Hardacres barn', *Traditional Kent Buildings*, published by Kent County Council, no 2, 1981, pp 11–14.

## Datestones and Period Ornamentations

Datestones are not always as informative as they appear. Wiliam, E. *Traditional Farm Buildings in North-East Wales, 1550–1900*, 1982, pp 23–4, notes that such stones, as the single most ornamental feature in a building, are likely to be reused when the building is replaced, while some may mark an addition to a building and others may refer to some event, such as the granting of a three-year life to the tenant, which has nothing to do with the building. Consequently, his lists of dated buildings only use dates from stones which appear from the evidence of the building to record its construction. The need for caution is illustrated by a Cheshire barn which bears a 1704 datestone commemorating not its construction but its reconstruction (Hoey, D. J. 'Bird's Barn, Wallasey', *Transactions of the Historical Society of Lancashire and Cheshire*, vol 117, 1965, pp 53–7).

References to datestones include Sheldon, L. 'Devon barns', *Report and Transactions of the Devonshire Association*, vol 64, 1932, p 393, (1604); Ward, J. D. U. 'Tithe barns of the south-west', *Agriculture*, vol 65, 1958, p

197 (various); Wood Jones, R. B. *Traditional Domestic Buildings of the Banbury Region*, 1963, p 15, (1382); Society for the Protection of Ancient Buildings, *SPAB Barns Book*, 1982, p 31, (1581) and to a formal timber datemark Hewett, C. A. *The Development of Carpentry 1200–1700*, 1969, p 161 (1650).

Occasionally, major manorial barns carry ornamentation which indicates the period in which they were built. References include Walton, J. 'The timberwork of English barns', *Country Life*, 19 June 1942, p 1181, (Tudor emblems) and Scarfe, N. *The Suffolk Landscape*, 1972, p 172, (Mowbray and Bigod emblems).

## Graffiti Dates

Graffiti dates, of course, only establish the minimum age of the buildings they ornament, though they also create an agreeable rapport between the modern visitor and the forgotten men who whiled away a rainy hour by carving initials and dates on beam or truss. References to graffiti include Mackie, J. 'A plea for adaptable buildings', *Farm Buildings Association Journal*, vol 3, 1959, p 10, (1704); Nicholson, P. 'Wiltshire farm buildings, III', *Wiltshire Folklife*, vol 2, Spring 1978, pp 23–6, (1737, 1745, 1747); Reynolds, J. *The Hampshire Barn*, unpublished thesis, Architectural Association, 1978, p 13, plate 18, (various, 1771 to 1846); Beck, S., Doyle G., Edwards, A. and Wittich, A. 'Hode Farm, Patrixbourne', *Traditional Kent Buildings*, published by Kent County Council, no 2, 1981, p 5, (1735); Caffyn, L. A. *A study of Farm Buildings in Selected Parishes of East Sussex*, unpublished MA thesis, Manchester University, 1981, p 96, (1564). There is some 1786 graffiti on the main beam of a truss of a barn at Arkley on the north-western outskirts of London. A ridge-tile on which W. Spears scratched his name and the date 1805 was found on a barn at Salisbury Hall, near St Albans, during repairs in the 1970s.

## Carbon Dating

References to the use of this technique include Horn, W. and Charles, F. W. B. 'The cruckbuilt barn of Little Middleton in Worcestershire, England', *Journal of the Society of Architectural Historians*, vol 25, 1966, p 238; Essex County Council, *The Essex Countryside, Historic Barns*, 1980, pp 3, 10; Hewett, C. A. *English Historic Carpentry*, 1980, pp 23–4, 37, 43.

## Dendrochronology

References to the use of this technique include 'Tree-ring dates for buildings', *Vernacular Architecture*, vol 11, 1980, p 22; Hillam, J. and Ryder, P. 'Tree-ring dating of vernacular buildings in Yorkshire', *Vernacular Architecture*, vol 11, 1980, pp 23–31; Fletcher, J. 'A list of tree-ring dates for building timbers in southern England and Wales', *Vernacular Architecture*, vol 11, 1980, pp 32–8; Fletcher, J. 'Tree-ring dates for building with oak timber', *Vernacular Architecture*, vol 12, 1981, pp 38–40.

# A NOTE ON SOURCES

As is clear from the references quoted in the preceding chapters, most of the material on the history of farm buildings comes from more general agricultural, historical and architectural sources which deal only incidentally with farm buildings. This note, therefore, lists only the more specialised sources concerned with the subject. For sources on developments since 1960 see p 268.

### Bibliographical Sources

Adams, I. H. *Agrarian Landscape Terms*, 1976 ('Settlement' section).
Hall, R. de Z. *A Bibliography of Vernacular Architecture*, 1972.
Michelmore, D. J. H. *A Current Bibliography of Vernacular Architecture*, 1979.
*The Agricultural History Review*, published by the British Agricultural History Society, includes an annual list of books and articles on agrarian history.
*British Archaeological Abstracts*, published by the Council for British Archaeology, include relevant material.

### General Sources

The agricultural landscape is very varied physically and historically. So local information is essential for the understanding of local farming systems and the buildings which formed part of them. One standard source of local information is the *Victoria County History* series of volumes published by the Institute of Historical Research, University of London. Another is the series of county inventories of historical monuments published by the Royal Commission on Historical Monuments for England, which also maintains the National Monuments Record for England and the Royal Commission on Ancient and Historical Monuments for Wales, which also maintains the National Monuments Record for Wales. These inventories list and describe surviving monuments, including a number of farm buildings.

*The Agrarian History of England and Wales*, now in course of publication by the Cambridge University Press, will, when the series of volumes is complete, give a detailed and comprehensive history of farming from Roman times to the present century. Falconer, K. *A Guide to England's Industrial Heritage*, 1980, includes examples of farm buildings and farm waterpower installations.

# A Note on Sources

## Journals

There is no specialised journal on the history of farm buildings. Journals which contain relevant material include:
*Agricultural History Review*
*Industrial Archaeology*
*Journal of the Society of Architectural Historians*
*Landscape History*
*Mediaeval Archaeology*
*Postmediaeval Archaeology*
*Vernacular Architecture*

## Modern Books

These include in date order of first publication:
Peate, I. C. *The Welsh House*, 1944.
Grigson, G. *An English Farmhouse*, 1948.
Briggs, M. S. *The English Farmhouse*, 1953.
Harvey, N. *The Story of Farm Buildings*, 1953.
Cook, O. and Smith, E. *English Cottages and Farmhouses*, 1954.
Barley, M. W. *The English Farmhouse and Cottage*, 1961.
Horn, W. and Born, E. *The Barns of the Abbey of Beaulieu and its Granges of Great Coxwell and Beaulieu St Leonards*, 1965.
Peters, J. E. C. *The Development of Farm Buildings in Western Lowland Staffordshire up to 1880*, 1969.
Harvey, N. *A History of Farm Buildings in England and Wales*, 1970.
Royal Commission on Historical Monuments, *Shielings and Bastles*, 1970.
Brunskill, R. W. *The Vernacular Architecture of the Lake Counties*, 1974.
Allen, E. *Buildings as History. Farms*, 1977.
Ebbage, S. *Barns and Granaries*, 1977 (Norfolk).
Harvey, N. *Old Farm Buildings*, 1977.
Arts Council, *Traditional Farm Buildings*, 1978.
Brunskill, R. W. *Illustrated Handbook of Vernacular Architecture*, 1978.
Devon County Council, *Devon's Traditional Buildings*, 1978.
Essex County Council, *The Essex Countryside, Historic Barns*, 1980.
Harvey, N. *The Industrial Archaeology of Farming in England and Wales*, 1980.
Hewett, C. A. *English Historic Carpentry*, 1980.
Wade-Martins, S. *A Great Estate at Work*, 1980 (Holkham).
Architects in Agriculture, *Coleshill Model Farm, Oxfordshire*, 1981
Darley, G. *The National Trust Book of the Farm*, 1981.
Peters, J. E. C. *Discovering Traditional Farm Buildings*, 1981.
Brunskill, R. W. *Traditional Farm Buildings of Britain*, 1982.
Cook, O. *English Cottages and Farmhouses*, 1982.
Society for the Protection of Ancient Buildings, *The SPAB Barn Book*, 1982.
Weller, J. *History of the Farmstead*, 1982.
Wiliam, E. *Traditional Farm Buildings in North-East Wales, 1550–1900*, 1982.

Fowler, P. *Farms in England*, 1983.
The following have been published since this book went to press:
Martin, D. and Martin, B. *Historic Farm Buildings in Eastern Sussex, 1450–1750*, 1982.
Robinson, J. M. *Model Farms – a Study of Decorative and Model Farm Buildings in the Age of Improvement, 1700–1846*, 1983.
Taylor, C. *Village and Farmstead*, 1983.
Woodforde, J. *Farm Buildings in England and Wales*, 1983.

## Other Modern Publications

The following surveys in date order include information of historical value:
*National Farm Survey of England and Wales, 1941–3*, HMSO, 1946, pp 39–41, 59–69.
Charlick, R. H. *Farm Buildings Survey of Wales*, 1965, and *Farm Buildings Survey of England*, 1967, published by the National Institute of Agricultural Engineering.
Hill, B. *Farm Buildings Capital, An Empirical Study*, 1972, published by Wye College (Berkshire).
Hill, B. and Kempson, R. E. *Farm Buildings Capital in England and Wales*, 1977, published by Wye College.
Case studies of the historical development of particular farmsteads, for the most part with information on their agricultural context, include in date order:
Bonham-Carter, V. *Farming the Land*, 1959, pp 49–57 (unnamed West-country farm).
Alcock, N. W. 'A Devonshire farm; Bury Barton, Lapford', *Report and Transactions of the Devonshire Association*, vol 98, 1966, pp 122–9.
Alcock, N. W., Child, P. and Laithwaite, M. 'Sanders, Lettaford. A Devon longhouse.' *Devon Archaeological Society Proceedings*, vol 30, 1972, pp 227–33.
Popham, J. H. *Farm Buildings, Functions and Form*, unpublished thesis for Diploma in Conservation Studies, Institute of Advanced Architectural Studies, York University, 1973, pp 26–7, Drawing A4.3 in Appendix 4. (Aldro Farm, Birdsall Estate, Yorkshire. Also in Allison, K. J. *The East Riding of Yorkshire Landscape*, 1976, pp 166–7.)
Woodhams, N. (Ministry of Agriculture, Fisheries and Food, Wolverhampton) *The Story of an Agricultural Building*, pp 3–4, mimeo, issued at Architects in Agriculture meeting March 1976 (Home Farm, Abberly, Worcestershire).
Chapman, V. 'North country farms of the moorland fringe', *Beamish One, First Report of the North of England Open Air Museum Joint Committee*, 1978, pp 41–60. (Three North Country farms, notably Cordilleras Farm, near Marske, Yorkshire, pp 45–51.)
Wade-Martins, S. 'Cannister Hall Farm', *Journal of the Norfolk Industrial Archaeology Society*, vol 2, no 3, 1978, pp 22–4.
Steane, J. ed, *Cogges, a Museum of Farming in the Oxfordshire Countryside*, published by Oxfordshire County Council, Department of Museum Services, 1980.

Beck, S., Doyle, G., Edwards, A., and Wittich, A. 'Hode Farm, Patrixbourne', *Traditional Kent Buildings*, no 2, 1981, pp 5–10, published by Kent County Council Education Committee.

Tyson, B. 'Skirwith Hall and Wilton Tenement (Kirkland Hall). The rebuilding of two Cumbrian farmsteads in the eighteenth century', *Transactions of the Cumberland and Westmorland Antiquarian and Archaeological Society*, vol 81, 1981, pp 94–113 (Skirwith Hall Farm).

Snoxell, T. 'Brenley Farm', *Traditional Kent Buildings*, no 3, 1983, pp 27–34, published by Kent County Council.

## Unpublished Theses

In date order:

Davies, D. C. G. *Historic Farmstead and Farmhouse Types of the Shropshire Region*, MA thesis, Manchester University, 1952.

West, G. T. *Farm Buildings in South-East Surrey Before 1837*, Royal Institute of British Architects Bannister Fletcher Silver Medal Essay, 1952.

Roberts, F. *An Investigation into the Efficiency of Farm Buildings by the Application of Work Study*, MSc thesis, University of Wales, 1961.

Pilkington, R. *Sussex Downland Farms*, Architectural Association School of Architecture thesis, 1962.

Roberts, W. P. *Study of the Use, Design and Layout of Buildings on the Small Dairy Farm*, PhD thesis, University of Reading, 1963.

Clayton, J. *Versatility in Farm Buildings*, MSc thesis, University of London, 1964.

Brunskill, R. W. *Design and Layout of Farmsteads in Parts of Cumberland and Westmorland*, Royal Institute of British Architects Neale Bursary 1963, Manchester 1965.

Clayton, J. R. *Farmbuilding in a Planned Environment*, PhD thesis, University of London, 1970.

Popham, J. H. *Farm Buildings, Function and Form*, (Aldro Farm, Birdsall Estate, Yorkshire). Thesis for Diploma in Conservation Studies, Institute of Advanced Architectural Studies, York University, 1973.

Wade-Martins, S. *The Holkham Estate in the Nineteenth Century; with Special Reference to Farm Building and Agricultural Improvement*, PhD thesis, University of East Anglia, 1975.

Reynolds, J. *The Hampshire Barn*, postgraduate thesis, Architectural Association, 1978.

Davies, N. W. I. *Barns and Barn Conversion in Cumbria*, BSc thesis, Brunel University, 1979.

Sweetland, P. *Barns of Bredon Hill*, Birmingham School of Architecture, fifth year thesis, 1979.

Caffyn, L. A. *A Study of Farm Buildings in Selected Parishes of East Sussex*, MA thesis, Manchester University, 1981.

Grundy, J. E. *The Origins of Liverpool Cowkeepers*, MA thesis, Lancaster University, 1982.

Pitkin, M. *The Farm Wheel and Machinery at Temple Balsall*, Birmingham School of Architecture, 1982.

## A Note on Sources

### Textbooks and Reference Books

These provide information on contemporary principles and practice and on the assumptions and context of the period. They include in date order of first publication:

Garret, D. *Designs and Estimates of Farmhouses etc for the County of York, Northumberland, Cumberland, Westmorland and the Bishopric of Durham*, 1747.

Board of Agriculture, *Communications to the Board of Agriculture on Farm Buildings*, vol 1, part 1, 1797.

Loudon, J. C. *Designs for Laying Out Farms and Farm Buildings in the Scotch Style Adapted to England*, 1811.

Waistell, C. *Designs for Agricultural Buildings*, 1827.

Loudon, J. C. *An Encyclopaedia of Cottage, Farm and Village Architecture*, 1833.

Ewart, J. *A Treatise on the Arrangement and Construction of Agricultural buildings*, 1851.

Andrews, G. H. *A Rudimentary Treatise on Agricultural Engineering*; vol 1, *Buildings*, vol 2, *Motive Power and Machinery of the Steading*, 1852.

Starforth, J. *The Architecture of the Farm*, 1853.

Stephens, H. and Burn, R. S. *The Book of Farm Buildings*, 1861.

Denton, J. B. *Farm Homesteads of England*, 1863.

Scott, J. *Farm Buildings*, 1884.

Clarke, A. D. *Modern Farm Buildings*, 1891.

Malden, W. J. *Farm Buildings*, 1896.

Henderson, R. *The Modern Farmstead*, 1902.

Taylor, S. *Modern Homesteads*, 1905.

Winder, T. *Handbook of Farm Buildings*, 1908.

Curtis, C. E. *Farm Buildings*, 1912.

Lawrence, C. P. *Economic Farm Buildings*, 1919.

McHardy, D. N. *Modern Farm Buildings*, 1932.

Gunn, E. *Farm Buildings*, 1935.

*Post-war Buildings Studies, No 17, Farm Buildings*, HMSO, 1945.

*Farmer and Stockbreeder, New Ideas for Farm Buildings*, 1947.

Henderson, F. *Build Your Own Buildings*, 1955.

Benoy, W. G. *Farm Buildings, Conversions and Improvements*, 1956.

Pasfield, D. H. *Farm Building Design and Construction*, 1965.

Weller, J. B. *Farm Buildings*, vol 1, 1965; vol 2, 1972.

Sayce, R. B. *Farm Buildings*, 1966.

Farm Buildings Information Centre, *Planning Farm Buildings*, 1977.

Weller, J. B. *Agricultural Buildings. Planning and Allied Controls*, 1981.

Architects in Agriculture, *Information Sources for the Farm Buildings designer*, 1982.

Noton, N. H. *Farm Buildings*, 1982.

### Museums

The national centres for agricultural history are the Museum of English Rural Life at Reading and the Welsh Folk Museum at St Fagans, near

271

Cardiff. The Science Museum in London and many local museums include agricultural departments and there are a large number of farm museums and collections. Some of the farm museums are housed in converted farm buildings or include farm buildings and barn machinery among their exhibits. See Toulson, S. *Discovering Farm Museums and Farm Parks*, 1977; Armstrong, J. R. *Traditional Buildings Open to the Public*, 1979.

## Films

Central Office of Information and the Ministry of Agriculture, Fisheries and Food.

*Farmstead in the Landscape.*
Colour. 20 minutes. 16 mm. 1974
Available through the Central Film Library of the Central Office of Information, their reference UK 3222.

Shell UK Ltd
*The Farmstead*
Colour. 21 minutes. 16 mm. 1982
Available on free loan from the Shell Film Library, 25 The Burroughs, Hendon, London NW4, to educational, commercial, industrial associations, clubs etc but not to private individuals. Teacher's notes provided.

# ACKNOWLEDGEMENTS

The writer wishes to thank all those who have given him permission to use their illustrations, as formally acknowledged elsewhere, and also all those who have so generously helped in other ways, namely: Mr P. Anderson of the Milk Marketing Board; Mrs G. Armstrong; Mr G. A. Barley of the Milk Marketing Board; Mr M. M. Barnes of the Cement and Concrete Association; Professor Maurice Beresford; Mr R. H. Charlick; Dr John Clayton; Dr R. Coles; Miss Jenny Costigan of the Avoncroft Museum of Buildings; Dr Edwin Course of Southampton University; Mr John Creasey of the Museum of English Rural Life; Mrs Janet Davison of the Beamish North of England Open Air Museum; Mr Philip Easton; Mr G. G. English of Messrs Gabriel Wade and English; the Librarian of the Forestry Commission; the Librarian of the Forest Products Research Laboratory; the late Mr Peter Girdlestone; Mr J. R. Gray; Mr T. F. Hall of the Beamish North of England Open Air Museum; Mrs M. Hallam of the Weald and Downland Museum; the Controller of Her Majesty's Stationery Office; Mr J. W. Houldsworth; the Librarian of the Institute of Civil Engineers; Miss Jill Jones of Keele University; Commander H. R. Kidston, RN; Mr David Lee of Turners Asbestos Cement Co; Mrs N. R. Lloyd; Mr David Long; Mr I. J. Loynes of the Farm Buildings Information Centre; the late Mr W. Marshall, editor of the *Farm Buildings Association Journal*; Mr C. L. Matthews; Mr John Moffitt, CBE; the Librarian of the National Monuments Record (England); the Librarian of the National Institute of Agricultural Engineering; the Librarian of the National Maritime Museum; Mr R. P. de B. Nicholson; Mr L. M. Parsons; Mr K. O. Pawley of Unigate Ltd; Mr A. D. M. Phillips of Keele University; Mr Peter Pilkington; Mr S. E. Rigold; the Librarian of the Royal Institute of British Architects; the Librarian of the Royal Institution of Chartered Surveyors; the Librarian of the Royal Society of Arts; the late Mr A. R. Sarsons, editor of the *Journal of the Chartered Land Agents Society*; Mr T. R. F. Skemp; the Librarian of the Society of Antiquaries; Mr J. M. Steane of the Manor Farm Museum, Cogges; Mr J. D. Sykes of Wye College; Mr H. Thomas of the Avoncroft Museum of Buildings; the Librarian of the Timber Research and Development Association; Mr

I. Turnbull; Mr H. J. Vaughan; Mr Alan Vickery; Mr J. L. Vosper of Express Dairy Group Services Ltd; Dr Sadie Ward of the Museum of English Rural Life; Mr J. B. Weller; and Mr L. S. Whicher.

He also wishes to thank the following who have kindly given him permission to quote from their unpublished theses, namely: Miss Lucy Caffyn; Mr N. W. I. Davies; Mrs Joan Grundy; Mr M. A. Pitkin and the Birmingham School of Architecture; Mr John Popham; Mr John Reynolds; Mr Peter Sweetland and the Birmingham School of Architecture; and Mrs Susanna Wade-Martins.

It is with particular pleasure that he thanks Professor Duckham for interrupting his retirement to write a foreword; Mr Keith Huggett for the care and skill with which he has prepared simplified and standardised drawings from such a variety of originals; the Librarian of the Ministry of Agriculture, Fisheries and Food and his staff for their unfailing helpfulness over a long period of steady demands on their time and knowledge; and his wife, Barbara, for so patiently and cheerfully checking text, proofs and index.

# INDEX

*Figures in italic denote illustrations*